Memoirs of a Dutiful Daughter

SIMONE DE BEAUVOIR

Memoirs of a Dutiful Daughter

*

Translated from the French by
James Kirkup

HARPER**PERENNIAL** ● MODERN**CLASSICS**

HARPER**PERENNIAL** ◑ MODERN**CLASSICS**

This book was originally published under the title MÉMOIRES D'UNE JEUNE FILLE RANGÉE. It is reprinted here by arrangement.

MEMOIRS OF A DUTIFUL DAUGHTER. Copyright © 1958 by Gallimard, Paris. Translation © 1959 by The World Publishing Company. Foreword © 2005 by Hazel Rowley. All rights reserved. Printed in the United States of America. No part of this book may be used or reproduced in any manner whatsoever without written permission except in the case of brief quotations embodied in critical articles and reviews. For information, address HarperCollins Publishers, 195 Broadway, New York, NY 10007.

HarperCollins books may be purchased for educational, business, or sales promotional use. For information, please e-mail the Special Markets Department at SPsales@harpercollins.com.

First Harper Perennial Modern Classics edition published 2005.

Library of Congress Cataloging-in-Publication data has been applied for.

ISBN-10: 0-06-082519-7 (pbk.)
ISBN-13: 978-0-06-082519-5 (pbk.)

HB 08.02.2023

FOREWORD

Simone de Beauvoir was a prolific writer, in a remarkable range of genres. She will always be associated with that twentieth-century landmark *The Second Sex*, and for her novel *The Mandarins*, depicting the political squabbles and love affairs of a group of French intellectuals in the postwar world. But without any doubt Simone de Beauvoir is most warmly remembered for her memoirs. In them she tells her best and most stirring story, the story of her own life.

Few writers have recorded their own experiences so compulsively. This first volume, *Memoirs of a Dutiful Daughter* (1958), would be followed by three more: *The Prime of Life* (1960), *Force of Circumstance* (1963), and *All Said and Done* (1972). But Beauvoir's autobiographical writings did not end there. Two of her novels, *She Came to Stay* and *The Mandarins*, were closely based on dramatic episodes in her own life. In *America Day by Day* she wrote about her four-month sojourn in the United States. *A Very Easy Death* is a tender memoir about the death of her mother; *Adieux: A Farewell to Sartre* is a wrenching account of her companion's last years.

We all know the photographs of Beauvoir and Sartre writing in Left Bank cafés—places that are now full of tourists who, while they sip their drinks, invariably make mention of the famous pair. Beauvoir, just like Sartre, was happiest writing with the hubbub of the world around her—in cafés, train stations, wherever she could get out her notebook and fountain pen, and fill pages with the scrawling, scarcely decipherable handwriting her friends all complained about. Since her death, in 1986, her war journal and several volumes of love letters (to Sartre, Nelson Algren, and Jacques-Laurent Bost) have seen the light of day. With each new publication, readers find themselves freshly astounded. There seems to have been no limits to this woman's energy, her passion for life, her sparkling intelligence, her sheer *vitality*. How did she fit so much into one lifetime?

Jean-Paul Sartre was a guiding force and moral support for Beauvoir, just as she was for him. He encouraged her, in the true sense of the word; he brought out her courage. During their long years of literary apprenticeship—years in which they both produced draft after draft that would end up, like their other manuscripts, relegated to a drawer—Sartre saw that Beauvoir was at her best when she portrayed her own experience. "Look," he told her one day, as they sat in a noisy, smoke-filled Paris café discussing their work, "why don't you put *yourself* into your writing?" Beauvoir writes that she felt the blood rush to her cheeks. "I'd never dare to do that," she said. "Screw up your courage," Sartre said.*

That conversation resulted in *She Came to Stay* (1943). Inspired by the amorous trio Beauvoir and Sartre had formed with a young woman, the novel skated so close to real life that it shocked even their friends—not to speak of the French Catholic bourgeoisie. Beauvoir's very first book caused a frenzy of gossip, and seeded the Sartre-Beauvoir legend. From the beginning, and this would never change, the name Simone de Beauvoir carried a strong whiff of scandal.

No sooner had the war ended than Sartre and Beauvoir found themselves in the glare of fame. It happened almost overnight. Existentialism became a craze, the new intellectual

---

* *Prime of Life*, p. 380.

fashion. Sartre's philosophy struck a chord, particularly with young people who, having experienced the Holocaust and the atomic bomb, no longer believed in the old myth of eternal progress and were tired of feeling powerless. Existentialism acknowledged the absurdity of the human condition, while at the same time insisting on individual freedom and choice.

Sartre and Beauvoir often discussed the extent to which their friends were free, or not free, to choose their lives. What interested them was to understand a person's *situation*—one's social class, family dynamics, physical constitution, self-image, and so on—while scrutinizing, as if under a microscope, any signs of rebellion or moments of compliance. They saw these as defining moments, which reflected fundamental choices. Since, according to these two existentialists, choices were demonstrated by *actions* (it is not interesting to *want* to write a book; you have to actually write one), people's actions cast light on their "original project."

It was 1946 when Beauvoir first thought of writing her childhood memoirs. She was keen to consider her own childhood and adolescence through an existential framework. What had made her decide to be a writer? Which were the turning points in her life, when she had chosen the person she had become? Sartre made the comment that she would need to think carefully about what it had meant to be a woman, how it had affected her upbringing, her aspirations and choices. Beauvoir said—probably with a touch of impatience—that she didn't think it had affected her much at all. She had never felt inferior because she was a woman, and her education placed her among the privileged few. She and Sartre had not married, they did not have children, they did not live under the same roof, they each had other lovers; she felt freer than most of the men she knew. "All the same," Sartre insisted, "you weren't brought up in the same way as a boy would have been; you should look into it further."

Convinced she could dispense with the subject quickly, Beauvoir went to the Bibliothèque Nationale and looked up everything she could find about women and the myths of femininity. After some weeks, she felt as if her head had been turned inside out. "It was a revelation," she would write. "This world was a masculine world, my childhood had been nourished by myths forged by men, and I hadn't reacted to them in at all the same way I should have done if I had been a boy."*

She temporarily put aside her memoir project, and wrote *The Second Sex*. The book would cause an outcry when it appeared in France in 1949. Beauvoir had broached so many taboo subjects: women's sexuality, lesbianism, abortion, and the horror of aging. Not for the first time—nor would it be the last—she was accused of exhibitionism, impropriety, vulgarity, godlessness, and even ridiculing the French male.

Beauvoir did not return to her childhood memoirs for ten years. In the meantime her life had changed dramatically. *The Second Sex* had been highly acclaimed in the United States, with none of the sour resentment that had greeted the book in France. She had written about her travels in the United States and in China. In 1954 *The Mandarins* won the most prestigious literary prize in France, proving that Beauvoir was far more than a brilliant polemicist; she was also a first-rate fiction writer. The novel was dedicated to the Chicago writer, Nelson Algren, and Beauvoir made no secret of the fact that the "American love story" was closely based on their affair. By the time Beauvoir sat down to write her memoirs, she was regarded throughout the world as an outstanding example of that rather dubious phenomenon: the independent woman. She would now look back upon her past through a rather different prism.

---

* *Force of Circumstance*, p. 103.

Memoirs of a Dutiful Daughter would take Beauvoir eighteen months to write. Never had she enjoyed researching a book more. It was an excuse to peruse old journals and letters, to go back to the library and look at newspapers from her childhood, to reread the books that had influenced her as a girl, to swap memories with her sister, and her childhood friends. She worried that memoirs were a self-indulgent art form, but Sartre reminded her that the most deeply personal writing was also the most universal.

Memoirs of a Dutiful Daughter is a fascinating picture of a Victorian girlhood. Born into the French bourgeoisie in 1908, Simone de Beauvoir grew up at a time in which women did not vote. France's most elite educational institutions were for men only and in order to aspire to a socially desirable marriage, a young woman, however beautiful and cultivated, had to come with a substantial dowry. In Catholic circles, nobody minded if men went to church or not (Simone's father was an atheist), but women who did not believe in God were thought of as monsters. (When Simone stopped believing in God at the age of fifteen, she felt obliged, for several years, to keep her dark secret to herself.) Respectable women did not drink or smoke in public, and did not set foot in cafés, let alone in bars. Whereas bourgeois young men were encouraged to "sow their wild oats" in brothels or with servant girls, their female counterparts remained virgins until they were married. Woe betide those who remained "on the shelf," an unmarried woman was an object of pity.

With her memoirs, Simone de Beauvoir found herself once again pushing against boundaries. As a "committed intellectual," she considered that she had a responsibility to tell the truth, to debunk myths, to expose the ideologies that deprived people of their freedom. But how could she write openly about her parents, their extended family and friends, and the nuns who had taught her at school? Her father had died during the war, but her mother was still alive, and she would be hurt and mortified by a book in which Simone exposed family secrets and conflicts. Beauvoir discussed these problems with Sartre. Did she dare write about her friend Zaza's family, and show how Zaza's parents had destroyed Zaza's life? What about the young men Simone had been in love with, before deciding that they did not measure up to Sartre? Even if she protected certain people by using pseudonyms, they would recognize themselves instantly, and so would anyone who knew them. In the weeks before the book came out, Beauvoir made nervous entries in her journal: "I do feel uneasy—almost remorseful—when I think of all the people I've brought into it and who'll be furious."*

Beauvoir looks back at her past with the precision of a historian, the detachment of a sociologist, the insight of a psychologist, and the dramatic flair of a novelist. As always, she is questioning, probing, and fiercely intelligent. The narrative is suffused with gentle humor (a quality that sadly becomes rare in her later memoirs), and she is often self-mocking. Those passages in which she describes her childhood summers in the countryside of Limousin are among her most lyrical writing ever.

We see young Simone in a stifling, repressive environment, painfully alone and often quite desperate. How was the future existentialist in any way free? At eighteen, she was still completely dependent on her parents, and did not dare disobey them or lie to them, but her mother often forbade her to do things that would have stretched her horizons. "I was choking with fury," Beauvoir writes. "Not only had I been condemned to exile, but I was not even allowed the freedom to fight

---

* *Force of Circumstance*, p. 459.

against my barren lot; my actions, my gestures, my words were all rigidly controlled."* What would save her from this wasteland of boredom and passivity?

In the opening pages of *All Said and Done*, Beauvoir muses more overtly and analytically about the factors that shape our destinies. "How is a life formed? How much of it is made up by circumstances, how much by necessity, how much by chance, and how much by the subject's own options and his personal initiatives?" She declares it a piece of good luck that her father lost his fortune at the end of World War I. It meant that she and her sister would not have a dowry, and could no longer aspire to what was considered a good marriage. As a consequence, her father encouraged Simone to become a secondary school teacher. In what way did Simone de Beauvoir herself choose her path? As she sees it, her "original project," which she constantly pursued and strengthened, was "*savoir et exprimer*," to know and to communicate. As a child, she already had a powerful curiosity, which she would never lose. Her reading broadened her horizons; her desire to learn opened doors. The decision to take the high-flying *agrégation* led to what she terms "the most important event in my life," her meeting with Jean-Paul Sartre.†

Memoirs of a Dutiful Daughter carries a strong message: Have the courage to go toward freedom, however difficult this might be. If the book ends on a highly dramatic note, it's because Zaza, Simone de Beauvoir's closest childhood friend, felt unable to take this path. She remained a dutiful Catholic daughter, stifled and repressed, at the expense of her talent and desires. Beauvoir believes it was this inner conflict that killed Zaza, at the tender age of twenty-one. "For a long time," Beauvoir writes, "I believed that I had paid for my own freedom with her death."

---

* *Memoirs of a Dutiful Daughter*, p. 211.
† *All Said and Done*, p. 19.

When *Memoirs of a Dutiful Daughter* was published in 1958, readers loved it. The reception was so encouraging that Beauvoir decided to embark on a sequel, and then another. Her memoirs appeared during the sixties and seventies, those years of heady social upheaval, and countless young people took Sartre and Beauvoir's open relationship as their model.

With the advent of the women's movement in the late sixties, Beauvoir's star glittered more brightly than ever, while Sartre's faded somewhat. Some of the hotheaded young feminists had little time for Sartre, and for the deferential way in which Beauvoir, in her memoirs, insisted on seeing him as her superior. Beauvoir became defensive. She who had spent a lifetime railing against stultifying "roles," now tended to project herself as the model independent woman in a model independent relationship. But life is never quite that simple. There were things Beauvoir could not say, things she did not want to say. Her memoirs paint a somewhat idealized picture of her relationship with Sartre.

Beauvoir plunged into life with indefatigable energy and curiosity, determined to live every moment to the fullest. For her, writing about it made the experience of living sharper. With this second tasting, she could reflect on her life, give it form and shape, and turn it into an adventure. Already as an adolescent, she had dreamed of making her life into a grand story that would inspire others. Writing would guarantee her an immortality that would make up for the loss of a heaven. "There was no longer any God to love me, but I should have the undying love of millions of hearts. By writing a work based on my own experience I would re-create myself and justify my existence. At the same time I would be serving humanity: What more beautiful gift could I make it than the books I would write?"*

---

* *Memoirs of a Dutiful Daughter*, p. 142.

This is the fifty-year-old author smiling at her youthful dreams, but in fact she never lost them, and she was right not to. It's impossible to read about Simone de Beauvoir's life without thinking about your own. You find yourself wanting to live more courageously, with more commitment and passion. She makes you want to read more books, travel across the world, fall in love again, take stronger political stands, write more, work harder, play more intensely, and look more tenderly at the beauty of the natural world. That is a beautiful gift.

—Hazel Rowley

Memoirs of a Dutiful Daughter

BOOK ONE

I was born at four o'clock in the morning on the 9th of January 1908 in a room fitted with white-enamelled furniture and overlooking the boulevard Raspail. In the family photographs taken the following summer can be seen ladies in long dresses and ostrich-feather hats and gentlemen wearing boaters and panamas, all smiling at a baby: they are my parents, my grandfather, uncles, aunts; and the baby is me. My father was thirty, my mother twenty-one, and I was their first child. I turn the page: here is a photograph of Mama holding in her arms a baby who isn't me; I am wearing a pleated skirt and a tam-o'-shanter; I am two and a half, and my sister has just been born. I was, it appears, very jealous, but not for long. As far back as I can remember, I was always proud of being the elder: of being first. Disguised as Little Red Riding Hood and carrying a basket full of goodies, I felt myself to be much more interesting than an infant bundled up in a cradle. I had a little sister: that doll-like creature didn't have me.

I retain only one confused impression from my earliest years: it is all red, and black, and warm. Our apartment was red: the upholstery was of red moquette, the Renaissance dining-room was red, the figured silk hangings over the stained-glass doors were red, and the velvet curtains in Papa's study were red too. The furniture in this awful sanctum was made of black pear wood; I used to creep into the knee-hole under the desk and envelop myself in its dusty glooms; it was dark and warm, and the red of the carpet rejoiced my eyes. That is how I seem to have passed the early days of infancy. Safely ensconced, I watched, I touched, I took stock of the world.

My feeling of unalterable security came from the presence of Louise. She used to dress me in the mornings and undress me at night; she slept in the same room as myself. Young, without beauty, without mystery – because she existed, as I thought, only in order to watch over my sister and myself – she never raised her

[5]

voice, and never scolded me without good reason. Her calm gaze protected me when I made sand-pies in the Luxembourg Gardens and when I nursed my doll Blondine who had descended from heaven one Christmas Eve with a trunk containing all her clothes. As dusk began to fall she used to sit beside me and show me pictures and tell me stories. Her presence was as necessary to me, and seemed to me just as natural, as the ground beneath my feet.

My mother, more distant and more capricious, inspired the tenderest feelings in me; I would sit upon her knees, enclosed by the perfumed softness of her arms, and cover with kisses her fresh, youthful skin. Sometimes, beautiful as a picture, she would appear at night beside my bed in her dress of green tulle decorated with a single mauve flower, or in her scintillating dress of black velvet covered with jet. When she was angry with me, she gave me a 'black look'; I used to dread that stormy look which disfigured her charming face: I needed her smile.

As for my father, I saw very little of him. He used to leave every morning for the Law Courts, carrying a briefcase stuffed with untouchable things called dossiers under his arm. He sported neither a moustache nor a beard, and his eyes were blue and gay. When he came back in the evening, he used to bring my mother a bunch of Parma violets, and they would laugh and kiss. Papa often laughed with me, too: he would get me to sing *C'est une auto grise* or *Elle avait une jambe de bois*; he would astonish me by pulling francs out of the tip of my nose. I found him amusing, and I was pleased whenever he made a fuss of me; but he didn't play any very well-defined role in my life.

The principal function of Louise and Mama was to feed me; their task was not always an easy one. The world became more intimately part of me when it entered through my mouth than through my eyes and my sense of touch. I would not accept it entirely. The insipidity of milk puddings, porridge, and mashes of bread and butter made me burst into tears; the oiliness of fat meat and the clammy mysteries of shellfish revolted me; tears, screams, vomitings: my repugnance was so deeply rooted that in the end they gave up trying to force me to eat those disgusting things. On the other hand, I eagerly took advantage of that privilege of childhood which allows beauty, luxury, and happiness to be things that can be eaten: in the rue Vavin I would stand transfixed before the windows of confectioners' shops, fascinated by the luminous sparkle of candied fruits, the cloudy lustre of jellies, the kaleido-scopic inflorescence of acidulated fruit-drops – green, red, orange, violet: I coveted the colours themselves as much as the pleasures they promised me. Mama used to pound sugared almonds for me in a mortar and mix the crunchy powder with a yellow cream; the pink of the sweets used to shade off into exquisite nuances of colour, and I would dip an eager spoon into their brilliant sunset. On the evenings when my parents held parties, the drawing-room mirrors multiplied to infinity the scintillations of a crystal chan-delier. Mama would take her seat at the grand piano to accompany a lady dressed in a cloud of tulle who played the violin and a cousin who performed on the cello. I would crack between my teeth the candied shell of an artificial fruit, and a burst of light would illuminate my palate with a taste of black-currant or pine-apple: all the colours, all the lights were mine, the gauzy scarves, the diamonds, the laces; I held the whole party in my mouth. I was never attracted to paradises flowing with milk and honey, but I envied Hansel and Gretel their gingerbread house: if only the universe we inhabit were completely edible, I used to think, what power we would have over it! When I was grown-up I wanted to crunch flowering almond trees, and take bites out of the rainbow nougat of the sunset. Against the night sky of New York, the neon signs appeared to me like giant sweetmeats and made me feel frustrated.

Eating was not only an exploration and an act of conquest – an acquired taste in the real sense of the phrase – but also my most solemn duty: 'A spoonful for Mama, and another for grandmama. . . . If you don't eat anything, you won't grow up into a big girl.' I would be stood up against the door-frame in the hall and a pencilled line would be drawn level with the top of my head; the new line would then be compared with an earlier one: I had grown two or three centimetres; they would congratulate me, and I would swell with pride. But sometimes I felt frightened. The sunlight would be playing on the polished floor and the white-enamelled furniture. I would look at Mama's armchair and think: 'I won't be able to sit on her knee any more if I go on growing up.' Suddenly the future existed; it would turn me into another being, someone who would still be, and yet no longer seem, myself. I had forebodings of all the separations, the refusals, the desertions to come, and of the long succession of my various deaths. 'A spoonful for grandpapa. ....' I went on eating, all the same, and I was proud that I was growing; I had no wish to remain a baby all my life. I must have been intensely aware of this conflict to be able to remember in such minute detail a certain book from which Louise used to read me the story of Charlotte. One morning Charlotte found on her bedside chair a huge egg, almost as big as herself, made of pink sugar. This egg fascinated me, too. It was both stomach and cradle, and yet you could eat it. Refusing all other food, Charlotte grew smaller day by day; she became minute: she was nearly drowned in a saucepan, the cook accidentally threw her away into the dustbin, and she was carried off by a rat. She was rescued; Charlotte, now chastened and scared, stuffed herself so greedily she began to swell and swell until she was like a gigantic bladder of lard: her mama took this monstrous balloon-child to the doctor's. I gloated, but with a new restraint, over the pictures illustrating the diet the doctor had prescribed: a cup of chocolate, a nicely coddled new-laid egg, and a lightly grilled chop. Charlotte returned to normal size and I came out of the adventure safe and sound after having been reduced to a foetus and then blown up to matronly dimensions.

I kept on growing and I realized that my fate was sealed: I was condemned to be an outcast from childhood. I sought refuge in my own reflection. Every morning Louise would curl my hair and I would gaze with satisfaction at my face framed with ringlets: dark hair and blue eyes did not often, so they had told me, go together, and I had already learned to appreciate the value of the unusual. I was pleased with myself, and I sought to please. My parents' friends encouraged my vanity: they politely flattered me and spoiled me, I would stroke the ladies' furs and their satin-sheathed bosoms; I admired even more the gentlemen with their moustaches, their smell of tobacco, their deep voices, their strong arms that could lift me nearly up to the ceiling. I was particularly anxious to arouse the interests of the men: I tried to attract their attention by fidgeting and playing the ingénue, seizing any look or word that would snatch me out of my childhood limbo and give me some permanent status in their grown-up world. One evening, in the presence of one of my father's friends, I rudely shoved away a plate of Russian salad: on a postcard sent to us during the summer holidays this friend asked, with rather laboured wit: 'Does Simone still like Russian salad?' The written had even more prestige than the spoken word: I was exultant. I had been taken notice of! The next time we met M. Dardelle, in front of the church of Notre-Dame-des-Champs, I was counting on a renewal of his delicious teasing; I attempted to provoke him to another display of brilliant badinage, but found no response. I tried again, even harder. I was told to keep quiet. I had discovered, to my sharp vexation, the ephemeral nature of fame.

I was generally spared this sort of disappointment. At home, the slightest incident became the subject of vast discussions; my stories were listened to with lavish attention, and my witticisms were widely circulated. Grandparents, uncles, aunts, cousins, and a host of other relatives guaranteed my continuing importance. In addition, a whole race of supernatural beings were for ever bent over me, I was given to understand, in attitudes of divine solicitude. As soon as I could walk, Mama had taken me to church: she had shown me, in wax, in plaster, and painted on the walls, portraits of the Child Jesus, of God the Father, of the Virgin, and of the angels, one of which, like Louise, was assigned exclusively to my service. My heaven was constellated with a myriad benevolent eyes.

Here below, Mama's sister and mother tended to my physical needs. Grandmama had rosy cheeks, white hair, and trembly diamond ear-rings; she sucked wine-gum pastilles, hard and round as boot buttons, whose translucent colours enchanted me; I loved her because she was old; and I loved Aunt Lili because she was young: she lived with her parents, like a little girl, and I felt she was closer to me than the other adults. Red-faced, bald-headed, his chin daubed with a prickly, frothy grey scum, grandpa used to dance me dutifully up and down on his foot, but his voice was so gruff one never knew whether he was speaking in fun or in anger. I lunched with them every Thursday: rissoles, blanquette, 'shape' – known in our family as 'floating island' – grandmama always had a treat for me. After the meal grandpapa would doze in a tapestry armchair, and I, underneath the table, played the sort of games that make no noise. Then he would go out, and grandmama would bring out of the cupboard the metal humming-top into which we slipped, while it was spinning, circles of multi-coloured cardboard: in the backside of a lead figure she called 'Mister Skitters', she would light a white capsule out of which poured long coils of twisting brown matter. She played dominoes with me, and beggar-my-neighbour and spillikins. I felt stifled in that dining-room, which was as overcrowded as an antique dealer's back shop; not an inch of wall was left bare: there were tapestries, porcelain plates, dingy oil paintings; a stuffed turkey hen displayed on a heap of very green cabbages; the side tables were covered with velvet and plush and lace; the aspidistras imprisoned in burnished copper flower-pot bowls filled me with sadness.

Sometimes Aunt Lili took me out; I don't know how it happened, but on several occasions she took me to a horse show. One afternoon, sitting beside her in the stands at Issy-les-Moulineaux, I saw biplanes and monoplanes see-sawing through the sky. We got on well together. One of my earliest and most pleasant memories is of the time we stayed at Châteauvillain in the Haute-Marne, with one of grandmama's sisters. Old Aunt Alice, having lost long ago her husband and daughter, was mouldering slowly away, in a deaf and lonely old age, inside a great house surrounded by a huge garden. The little town, with its narrow streets, its low houses, looked as if it had come straight out of one of my fairy-story books; the shutters, in which trefoil and heart shapes had been cut, were held back against the walls by hooks representing little figures; the door knockers were hands; a monumental gate opened on a park in which there were fallow deer; wild honeysuckle wreathed itself round a ruined stone tower. The old ladies of the town made a great fuss of me. Mademoiselle Élise gave me ginger-bread hearts; Mademoiselle Marthe had a magic mouse in a glass box: you wrote a question on a card and pushed it through a slot: the mouse spun round and round, then pointed its nose at a certain compartment in the box, in which was the answer to the question, printed on a slip of paper. The thing that amazed me most of all was the eggs with designs drawn on them in charcoal which were laid by Doctor Masse's hens; I picked them up with my own hands, which allowed me to reply, rather smartly, to a sceptical little friend: 'But I picked them up with my own two hands!' I liked the neatly trimmed yews in Aunt Alice's garden, the sacramental odour of box, and, in a thatched arbour, an object as delightfully equivocal as a watch made of raw meat—a rock which was also a table, a stone table. One morning there was a thunderstorm; I was playing with Aunt Lili in the dining-room when the house was struck by lightning; it was a serious accident, which filled me with pride: every time something happened to me, I had the feeling that I was at last *someone*. I enjoyed an even more subtle satisfaction. On the wall of the outside water closets clematis was growing; one morning, Aunt Alice called me to her in her dry, squeaky voice; a flower was lying on the ground; she accused me of having picked it. Picking flowers in the garden was a crime whose gravity I was well aware of; but I hadn't done it, and I denied the accusation. Aunt Alice didn't believe me. Aunt Lili defended me with vigour. She was the representative of my parents, and my only judge. Aunt Alice, with her speckled old face, belonged to the race of wicked fairies who persecute little children; I witnessed with great complacency the struggle waged for my benefit by the forces of good against the forces of error and injustice. In Paris my parents and grandparents indignantly took up arms in my defence, and I was able to savour the triumph of virtue.

Sheltered, petted, and constantly entertained by the endless novelty of life, I was a madly gay little girl. Nevertheless, there must have been something wrong somewhere: I had fits of rage during which my face turned purple and I would fall to the ground in convulsions. I am three and a half years old, and we are lunching on the sunny terrace of a big hotel at Divonne-les-Bains; I am given a red plum and I begin to peel it. 'No,' says Mama; and I throw myself howling on the ground. I go howling all along the boulevard Raspail because Louise has dragged me away from the square Bourcicaut where I was making sand-pies. At such moments, neither Mama's black looks nor Louise's stern voice, nor even Papa's special interventions could make any impression upon me. I used to howl so loudly, and so long, that in the Luxembourg Gardens I was sometimes looked upon as a child martyr by benevolent and misinformed nursemaids and mothers. 'Poor little thing!' cried one lady, offering me a sweet. All the thanks she got from me was a kick in the shins. This episode caused a sensation; an obese and bewhiskered aunt who wielded a pious pen recorded it in *La Poupée Modèle*. I shared with my parents an almost religious respect for print: as Louise read me the improving tale, I became aware of myself as a person of some standing; but gradually doubts began to creep in. 'Poor Louise often wept bitterly as she thought of her lost sheep,' my aunt had written. Louise never wept; she had no sheep; she loved me: and how could a little girl be a sheep? From that day forward I suspected that literature had only very dubious connexions with the truth.

I have often wondered what were the causes of these outbursts, and what significance they had. I believe they can be partly explained by an impetuous vitality and by a lack of all moderation which I have never grown out of completely. I carried my disgusts to the point of vomiting, and when I coveted anything I did so with maniacal obsession; an unbridgeable chasm separated the things I loved and those I hated. I could not remain indifferent to the precipitous drop from plenty to poverty, from bliss to horror; I accepted it only if I felt it was inevitable; I have never unleashed my rage against a mere object. But I refused to submit to that intangible force: words. What I resented was that some casual phrase beginning 'You must . . .' or 'You mustn't . . .' could ruin all my plans and poison all my happiness. The arbitrary nature of the orders and prohibitions against which I beat unavailing fists was to my mind proof of their inconsistency; yesterday I peeled a peach: then why shouldn't I peel a plum? Why must I stop playing just at that particular moment? I seemed to be confronted everywhere by force, never by necessity. At the root of these implacable laws that lay as heavily as lead upon my spirit I glimpsed a sickening void: this was the pit I used to plunge into, my whole being racked with screams of rage. All flailing arms and legs, I would cast myself upon the ground, resisting with all the weight of my flesh and bones the tyranny of that insubstantial power; I forced it to take on material form: I would be seized and shut away in a dark cupboard among the brooms and feather dusters; there I could kick my feet and beat my hands against real walls instead of battling helplessly against the abstractions of another's will. I knew the struggle was in vain; from the instant that Mama had snatched the dripping plum out of my hands and Louise had packed my spade and pail away in her basket, I knew myself beaten; but I wouldn't give in. I fought my losing battle to the bitter end. My convulsions and the tears that blinded me served to shatter the restraints of time and space, destroying at once the object of my desire and the obstacles separating me from it. I was engulfed in the rising dark of my own helplessness; nothing was left but my naked self that exploded in prolonged howls and screams.

I felt I was not only the prey of grown-up wills, but also of their consciences, which sometimes played the role of a kindly mirror in which I was unwillingly and unrecognizably reflected. They had also the power to cast spells over me; they could turn me into an animal, into a thing. 'What beautiful legs this little girl has!' enthused a lady who bent down to feel my calves. If I'd been able to say: 'Silly old woman! She thinks I'm a boiling fowl,' I'd have been all right. But at three years of age I had no means of redress against that fatuous voice, that gloating smile: all I could do was yell, and throw myself screaming to the pavement. Later I learnt to defend myself in other ways; but I became even more unreasonable: to provoke my wrath someone only had to treat me as a baby; though I was limited in my knowledge and my capabilities, that did not prevent me from considering myself to be a grown-up person. One day in the place Saint-Sulpice, walking along hand-in-hand with my Aunt Marguerite who hadn't the remotest idea how to talk to me, I suddenly wondered: 'How does she see me?' and felt a sharp sense of superiority: for I knew what I was like inside; she didn't. Deceived by outward appearances, she never suspected that inside my immature body nothing was lacking; and I made up my mind that when I was older I would never forget that a five-year-old is a complete individual, a character in his own right. But this was precisely what adults refused to admit, and whenever they treated me with condescension I at once took offence. I was as cantankerous as any bed-ridden old woman. If grandmama cheated at cards in order to let me win, or if Aunt Lili asked me riddles that were too easy, I threw a fit. I often suspected the grown-ups of acting a part; I thought too highly of their intelligence to imagine that they believed in the parts they played for my benefit; I thought that they were in league with each other to make a fool of me. At the end of a birthday dinner, grandpapa wanted me to drink his health, and I flew into paroxysms of rage. One day when I had been running Louise took out a handkerchief to mop my brow but I flung myself angrily out of her arms: I had felt her gesture of concern to be false. As soon as ever I suspected, rightly or wrongly, that people were taking advantage of my ingenuousness in order to get me to do something, my gorge rose and I began to kick out in all directions.

My violence made people nervous, I was scolded, I was even punished a little; only very rarely did I get a slap. As Mama said: 'If you raise as much as a finger to Simone, she turns purple in the face.' One of my uncles, exasperated beyond endurance, took the law into his own hands: I was so flabbergasted at being struck that my convulsions suddenly stopped. It would probably have been very easy for my parents to knock the nonsense out of me: but they didn't take my tempers very seriously. Papa parodying some actor or other, took great delight in repeating: 'This child is unsociable.' They would also say about me, not without a touch of pride: 'Simone is as stubborn as a mule.' I took advantage of all this. I allowed myself every caprice; I used to disobey for the sheer pleasure of being disobedient. I would put my tongue out at family photographs, and turn my back on them: everyone laughed. These minor victories encouraged me in the belief that rules and regulations and routine conformity are not insurmountable; they are at the root of a certain optimism which persisted in me despite all corrections.

As for my defeats, they bred in me neither humiliation nor resentment; when, having exhausted my tears and screams, I finally capitulated, I was too worn-out to regret my losses; often I even forgot what all the fuss had been about. Ashamed then of excesses for which I could now find no justification, I used to feel only remorse; but this soon disappeared because my pardon was always readily granted. On the whole, my rages were adequate compensation for the arbitrary nature of the laws that bound me; they prevented me from brooding over rancorous grudges. And I never seriously called authority in question. The conduct of adults only seemed to me to be suspect in so far as it took advantage of my youthful condition: this is what I was really revolting against. But I accepted without question the values and the tenets of those around me.

The two major categories into which my universe was divided were Good and Evil. I inhabited the region of the good, where happiness and virtue reigned in indissoluble unity. I experienced certain forms of pain, it is true, that seemed to me unmerited: I sometimes bumped my head or grazed my elbow; an outbreak of eczema disfigured my face: a doctor cauterized my pimples with silver nitrate and I yelled. But these accidents were quickly forgotten, and they did not upset my belief that man experiences joy or pain according to his merits.

Living in such intimate contact with virtue, I knew that there were degrees and shades of goodness. I was a good little girl, and I had my faults; my Aunt Alice was always praying; she would surely go to heaven, and yet she had been very unjust to me. Among the people to whom I owed love and respect, there were some whom my parents censured for some reason or other. Even grandpapa and grandmama did not escape their criticism: they had fallen out with some cousins whom Mama often visited and whom I found very nice. I disliked the very word 'quarrel': why *did* people quarrel? and how? The word 'wrangle', too, unpleasantly reminded me of tangled hanks of wool. Wrangling and quarrelling seemed to me most regrettable activities. I always took my mother's side. 'Whom did you go to see yesterday?' my Aunt Lili would ask me. 'I shan't tell you: Mama told me not to.' She would then exchange a significant look with her mother. They sometimes made disagreeable remarks like: 'Your Mama's always going somewhere, isn't she?' Their spiteful tone discredited them in my eyes, and in no way lowered Mama in my own estimation. But these remarks did not alter my affection for them. I found it natural, and in a sense satisfactory that these secondary characters should be less irreproachable than those supreme divinities – Louise and my parents – who alone could be infallible.

A sword of fire separated good from evil: I had never seen them face to face. Sometimes my parents' voices took on a rancorous note: judging by their indignation and anger, I realized that even in their own most intimate circle there were some really black sheep: I didn't know who these were, or what their crimes might be. Evil kept a respectful distance. I could imagine its agents only as mythical figures like the Devil, the wicked fairy Carabosse and the Ugly Sisters: not having encountered them in the flesh, I reduced them to pure essences; Evil did wrong, just as fire burns, inexcusably and inevitably; hell was its natural habitat, and endless torment its proper fate; it would have seemed sacrilegious to feel pity for its pain. Indeed, the red-hot iron boots which the Seven Dwarfs made Snow-White's stepmother wear and the flames burning Lucifer in hell never evoked in my mind the image of physical suffering. Ogres, witches, demons, stepmothers, and torturers – all these inhuman creatures symbolized an abstract power and their well-deserved defeat was illustrated by sufferings that were only abstractions.

When I left for Lyon with Louise and my sister, I cherished the fond hope that I should meet the Evil One face to face. We had been invited to stay by distant cousins who lived in a house set in a large park on the outskirts of the town. Mama had warned me that the Sirmione children had lost their mother, that they were not always very well-behaved, and that they didn't always say their prayers: I was not to be put out if they laughed at me when I said mine. I was given to understand that their father, an elderly professor of medicine, didn't believe in God. I saw myself draped in the white robes of Saint Blandine before she was thrown to the lions: I was sadly disappointed, for no one tried to martyr me. Whenever Uncle Sirmione left the house, he would mumble in his beard: '*Au revoir*. God bless you,' so he couldn't be a heathen. My cousins – aged from ten to twenty – certainly behaved in a strange way: they used to throw pebbles through the railings of the park at the boys and girls in the street outside; they were always fighting; they used to torment a poor little feeble-minded orphan girl who lived in the house; at night, to frighten her, they would drag out of their father's study a skeleton draped in a sheet. Though I found them disconcerting, I saw no real harm in these anomalies; I couldn't discover in them the pitchy depths of real evil. I played quietly by myself among the clumps of hydrangeas and the seamy side of life still remained beyond my ken.

But one evening I thought the end of the world had come. My parents had come to join us. One afternoon Louise took me with my sister to a fair where we enjoyed ourselves immensely. When we left for home dusk was falling. We were chattering and laughing and I was chewing one of those imitation objects I liked so much – a liquorice braid – when Mama suddenly appeared at a turning in the road. She was wearing on her head a green muslin scarf and her upper lip was swollen: what sort of time was this to be coming home? she wanted to know. She was the oldest, and she was 'Madame', so she had the right to scold Louise; but I didn't like the look of her mouth or the tone of her voice; I didn't like to see something that wasn't friendliness in Louise's patient eyes. That evening – or it might have been some other evening, but in my memory the two incidents are intimately connected – I was in the garden with Louise and another person I can't remember; it was dark; in the black façade of the house, a window was open on a lighted room; we could see two moving figures and hear raised voices: 'There's Monsieur and Madame fighting again,' said Louise. That was when my universe began to totter. It was impossible that papa and mama should be enemies, that Louise should be their enemy; when the impossible happened, heaven was confused with hell, darkness was conjoined with light. I began to drown in the chaos which preceded creation.

[16]

This nightmare didn't last for ever: the next morning, my parents were talking and smiling as they always did. Louise's snicker still lay heavy on my heart, but I put that behind me as soon as possible: there were many small things which I was able to banish thus into the limbo of forgetfulness.

This ability to pass over in silence events which I felt so keenly is one of the things which strike me most when I remember my childhood. The world around me was harmoniously based on fixed coordinates and divided into clear-cut compartments. No neutral tints were allowed: everything was in black and white; there was no intermediate position between the traitor and the hero, the renegade and the martyr: all inedible fruits were poisonous; I was told that I 'loved' every member of my family, including my most ill-favoured great-aunts. All my experience belied this essentialism. White was only rarely totally white, and the blackness of evil was relieved by lighter touches; I saw greys and half-tones everywhere. Only as soon as I tried to define their muted shades, I had to use words, and I found myself in a world of bony-structured concepts. Whatever I beheld with my own eyes and every real experience had to be fitted somehow or other into a rigid category. the myths and the stereotyped ideas prevailed over the truth: unable to pin it down, I allowed truth to dwindle into insignificance.

As I had failed in my efforts to think without recourse to language, I assumed that this was an exact equivalent of reality; I was encouraged in this misconception by the grown-ups, whom I took to be the sole depositaries of absolute truth: when they defined a thing, they expressed its substance, in the sense in which one expresses the juice from a fruit. So that I could conceive of no gap into which error might fall between the word and its object; that is why I submitted myself uncritically to the Word, without examining its meaning, even when circumstances inclined me to doubt its truth. Two of my Sirmione cousins were sucking sticks of candy-sugar: 'It's a purgative', they told me in a bantering tone: their sniggers warned me that they were making fun of me; nevertheless the word they had used incorporated itself in my mind with the sticks of candy-sugar; I no longer liked them because they now seemed to me a dubious compromise between sweets and medicine.

Yet I can remember one case in which words did not override my reason. During our holidays in the country I was often taken

[17]

to play with a little cousin; he lived in a beautiful house in vast grounds and I rather enjoyed playing with him. 'The boy's half-witted,' my father remarked one evening. Cendri, who was much older than myself, seemed to me to be quite normal, because he was someone I knew well. I don't know if I had ever been shown what a half-wit was, or had an idiot described to me: I imagined idiots as having a slobbery mouth, a vacant smile, and a blank stare. The next time I saw Cendri, I tried in vain to apply this image to his own face, but the mask wouldn't stick; perhaps without showing it on the outside his essential nature resembled that of an idiot, but I couldn't bring myself to believe it. Driven by a desire to clear the matter up, and also by an obscure resentment against my father for having insulted my playmate, I asked Cendri's grandmother: 'Is it true that Cendri is a half-wit?' 'Of course not!' she retorted with some indignation. She knew her grandson well enough. Could it be that Papa had made a mistake? It was very puzzling.

I wasn't terribly attached to Cendri, and the incident, though it astonished me, didn't particularly upset me. I could perceive the sinister effect of words only when their black magic clutched at my heart.

Mama had just been wearing for the first time an orange-yellow dress – tango-coloured, we called it. Louise said to the housemaid from over the road: 'Did you see the way Madame was got up today? Proper eccentric she looked!' Another day, Louise was gossiping in the hall with the caretaker's daughter: two storeys up Mama was accompanying herself at the piano: 'Oh!' said Louise. 'There's Madame at it again, screaming like a macaw!' Eccentric. Macaw. These words sounded awful to me: what had they to do with Mama, who was beautiful, elegant, and sang and played so well? And yet it was Louise who had used them: how could I counter their sinister power? I knew how to defend myself against other people: but Louise! She was justice in person; she was truth itself, and my respect for her forbade me to pass judgement on anything she said. It would not have been sufficient to question her good taste; in order to neutralize her malevolence, I should have had to put it down to bad temper, and therefore to admit that she did not get on well with Mama; in which case, one of them must be in the wrong about something! No. I wanted to have them both perfect. I endeavoured to drain Louise's words of their meaning: certain strange sounds had issued from her mouth, for reasons which were beyond my ken. I was not altogether successful. From then on, whenever Mama wore a new dress or sang at the top of her voice, I always felt a certain uneasiness. Moreover, knowing now that it wouldn't do to attach too much importance to what Louise had to say, I no longer listened to her with quite the same docility as before.

I was always quick to turn a blind eye on anything that seemed to threaten my security, and so I preferred to dwell on 'safe' questions. The problem of birth did not bother me very much. At first I was told that parents bought their children in a shop; well, the world was so vast and so full of unknown wonders that there might well be stores selling babies somewhere. Gradually this idea was forgotten, and I contented myself with a vaguer solution: 'It is God who makes children.' He had created the earth out of chaos, and shaped Adam out of clay: so there was nothing unusual in the idea that He could produce a baby from an empty cradle. Submission to the divine will satisfied my curiosity: in the end, it could explain everything. As for the details of this divine operation, I was sure that I should gradually get to know them. What did intrigue me very much was the great care my parents sometimes took to prevent my overhearing certain conversations: as I drew near, they would lower their voices or stop talking altogether. So there were things that I could understand but that I was not intended to hear! Whatever could they be? Why were they kept from me? Mama forbade Louise to read me one of Madame de Ségur's fairy-tales: she said it would give me nightmares. What eventually became of that boy clothed in the skins of wild animals – for that was how the pictures showed him? My inquiries were fruitless. *Ourson* – the bear-cub – appeared to me to be the very incarnation of secrecy.

The great mysteries of religion were much too remote and too difficult to cause me any surprise. But the familiar miracle of Christmas often set me wondering. I thought it was quite incongruous that the all-powerful Christ-child should prefer to come down the chimney like a common sweep. I pondered this problem for a long time and finally appealed to my parents for enlightenment; they confessed their deception. I was stupefied to think that I could have believed so firmly in something that wasn't true, to realize that what one had accepted as the truth could be untrue. I didn't learn from experience, either. I didn't tell myself that my parents had deceived me, and that they might deceive me in other ways. Probably I could not have forgiven them for telling me a lie which was intended to frustrate my own desires or which pained me deeply; I should have revolted, and become suspicious. But in fact I was no more put out than someone to whom a conjurer explains how his tricks are performed. Indeed I was so delighted to find my doll Blondine sitting on her little trunk beside my Christmas stocking that I was rather grateful to my parents for such an amiable deception. Perhaps too I would have held it against them if I hadn't learnt the truth from their own lips: by admitting that they had been playing a trick on me, they convinced me of their sincerity. They were treating me now, I thought, as a grown-up; proud of my new dignity, I happily accepted the fact that they had had to indulge their baby, because I was a baby no longer: it seemed to me perfectly natural that we should continue to hoax my little sister. I was now on the side of the adults, and I presumed that henceforward I should always be told the truth.

My parents were very willing to answer my questions; my ignorance was dissipated as soon as I gave voice to it. But there was, I realized, a gap which couldn't be bridged: to the eyes of an adult, the black marks in books were words; I would look at them: I could see them too, but I couldn't make them out at all. I had been taught to play with letters from an early age. When I was three I knew that 'o' is called 'o', and that 's' is 's', just as a table is a table; I knew the alphabet fairly well, but the printed page remained a closed book to me. One day, it all seemed to click into place. Mama had opened on the dining-room table the Regimbeau reading-book for infants; I was looking at the picture of a cow, and the letters c and h which are pronounced ch in the word vache. I suddenly understood that they didn't have names, as objects do, but that they represented sounds: I understood now that they were symbols. After that, I soon learnt to read. Even afterwards, however, some blocks remained in my brain. I felt that the printed letter *was* the sound it corresponded to; they both proceeded from the thing they expressed, and were so closely linked that no arbitrary constants were possible in their fixed equation. The understanding of the symbol did not necessarily pre-suppose an understanding of its conventional application. This is why I put up such a strong resistance when grandmama wanted to teach me the notes of the scale. Using a knitting needle, she pointed to the notes on the stave; this line, she tried to explain, corresponded to that note on the pianoforte. But why? How could it possibly do that? I could see nothing in common between the ruled manuscript paper and the keys of the instrument. Whenever people tried to impose on me such unjustified compulsions and assumptions, I rebelled; in the same way, I refused to accept truths which did not have an absolute basis. I would yield only to necessity; I felt that human decisions were dictated more or less by caprice, and they did not carry enough weight to justify my compliance. For days I persisted in my refusal to accept such arbitrary regulations. But I finally gave in: I could finally play the scale; but I felt I was learning the rules of a game, not acquiring knowledge. On the other hand I felt no compunction about embracing the rules of arithmetic, because I believed in the absolute reality of numbers.

In October 1913 – I was five and a half years old – it was decided to send me to school, a private institution with the alluring name of Le Cours Désir. The head of the elementary classes, Mademoiselle Fayet, received me in an awe-inspiring study with padded doors. All the time she was talking to my mother, she kept stroking my hair. 'We are not governesses,' she explained, 'but educators.' She wore a high-necked dress with a long skirt and I found her manner revoltingly suave; I preferred something more severe. Nevertheless on the eve of my first day under her tutelage, I jumped for joy in the hall: 'I'm going to school tomorrow!' 'You won't always feel so happy about it,' Louise assured me. I was quite sure that for once she was mistaken. The idea of entering upon a life of my own intoxicated me. Until now I had been growing up as it were on the fringe of adult life; from now on I should have my satchel, my books, my exercise books, and my homework: my days and weeks would be arranged according to my own timetable; I had glimpses of a future which, instead of keeping me away from myself would leave its cumulative deposits in my memory: every year I would become more and more myself, and at the same time remain faithful to the schoolgirl whose birth I was celebrating at this very moment.

I was not disappointed. Every Wednesday and Saturday I participated in an hour-long ceremony whose almost religious pomp transfigured the whole week. The pupils took their places round a large oval table; the gathering was presided over by Mademoiselle Fayet, enthroned in a sort of professorial chair; from the rarefied heights of her gilded frame, Adeline Désir, our foundress, a stony-faced lady with slightly hunched shoulders who was in the process of beatification, gazed down upon us. Our mothers, installed on black imitation leather settees, did their embroidery or their knitting. According to whether we had been more or less well-behaved they bestowed good-conduct notes upon us which we had to give out at the end of the lesson. Mademoiselle entered them in her register. Mama always gave me ten out of ten: to give me only nine would have brought, we felt, disgrace upon us both. Then Mademoiselle would distribute 'Excellent' or 'Satisfactory' tokens to the righteous; at the end of each term we exchanged these for gilt-edged prize books. Then Mademoiselle took up her position at the door: she placed a kiss upon our foreheads, and whispered a word or two of good advice. I could read and write already, and count a little: I was the star turn of the 'O' class. Towards Christmas, I was garbed in a white robe bordered with gold braid and represented the Infant Jesus: all the other little girls had to come and bend the knee before me.

Mama helped me with my homework, and heard my lessons with the utmost care. I loved learning. The gospel story seemed to me much more amusing than Perrault's fairy-tales because the miracles it related had really happened. The maps in my atlas enchanted me. I was moved by the solitude of islands, by the boldness of promontories, by the fragility of those tenuous strips of land that connect peninsulas to continents. I was to experience that ecstasy again when I was grown-up and saw from an aeroplane the islands of Corsica and Sardinia etched on the blue of the Mediterranean, and when, at Kolkhis, illumined by a real sun, I saw an ideal isthmus choked between two seas. The world of severe and unimaginable shapes, of stories firmly carved in the marble of the centuries, was an album of brilliantly coloured pictures that I looked at with rapturous delight.

If I took so much pleasure in study, it was perhaps because my daily life no longer satisfied me. I lived in Paris, in man-made surroundings in which everything had been completely domesticated; streets, houses, tramways, street lamps, kitchen utensils: things, as flat as pure concepts, were reduced to their material functions. The Luxembourg Gardens with its clumps of untouch-

[22]

able shrubs and acres of forbidden lawns was to me no more than a common playground. Sometimes a rent in the canvas gave a glimpse, beyond the surface paint, of confused, gloomy depths. The tunnels of the underground railway stretched infinitely away towards the earth's secret core. In the boulevard Montparnasse, on the site where the Coupole now stands, was the Juglar coal depot out of which came black-faced men with coal sacks on their heads; among the piles of coke and anthracite, like wisps of charred paper in the sooty limbo of a chimney, those creatures whom God had cast out of the kingdom of light could be seen creeping about their daily tasks. But I had no hold on them. In the police state in which I was imprisoned, few things surprised me, because I did not know where the power of man began and ended. The aeroplanes and dirigibles that from time to time moved across the skies of Paris were a source of much greater wonder to adults than they were to me. Distractions were few. My parents took me to see the king and queen of England on their processional route along the Champs-Élysées; I attended some of the Lenten processions, and later the funeral of Gallieni. I followed in the wake of processions and visited the resting-places of great men. I hardly ever went to the circus, and very rarely to a Punch and Judy show. I had a few toys that amused me, but only one or two that I really loved. I enjoyed very much squinting through the lenses of a stereoscopic toy which transformed two photographic plates into a single, three-dimensional scene. I loved to rotate the strip of pictures in my kineoscope and watch the motionless horse begin to gallop. I was given tiny books which could be turned into moving pictures by flicking their pages: the little girl began to jump, the boxer to box. Shadow theatres, magic lanterns: what interested me in all these optical illusions was that they were the product of my own eyes, like the mirages which haunt the traveller in the desert. Altogether, the scanty resources of my city childhood could not compete with the riches to be found in books.

Everything was different when I left the city and was transported among animals and plants and faced with the infinite variety of nature.

We used to spend the summers in the ancient province of Limousin, with my Papa's family. My grandfather had retired to an estate that had been bought by his father in the neighbourhood of Uzerche. He sported white side-whiskers, a black-peaked cap, and the ribbon of the Légion d'Honneur. He used to hum to himself all day long. He told me the names of the trees, the flowers, and the birds. Peacocks displayed their tails in front of the house, which was covered with wistaria and begonia; in the aviary, I admired the scarlet-headed cardinal tanagers and the golden pheasants. The stream – we called it 'the English river' – was barred by artificial waterfalls and starred with drifting water lilies among which goldfish swam. Its waters surrounded a tiny island linked to the mainland by two sets of stepping-stones. There were cedars, wellingtonias, purple beeches, Japanese dwarf trees, weeping willows, magnolias, monkey-puzzles, deciduous and evergreen varieties, shrubberies, thickets, and coverts: the park, surrounded by a white fence, was not very big, but its diversity was such that I felt I could never explore it completely. We used to leave there in the middle of the holidays and go to stay with Papa's sister who had married one of the local gentry; they had two children. They would come to fetch us in the brake, which was drawn by four horses. After a family lunch, we would arrange ourselves on the blue leather-covered seats that smelt of dust and sun and straw. My uncle would lead the way on horseback. After a ride of about twenty kilometres, we would arrive at La Grillière. The park, vaster and wilder than my grandfather's at Meyrignac, but less diverting, surrounded a sinister château flanked with turrets and roofed with slate. Aunt Hélène treated me with complete indifference. Uncle Maurice, moustached, leather-booted, a hunting crop always in his hands, frightened me a little with his sudden alternations of temper and sulky silence. But I liked to play with Robert and Madeleine, who were five and three years older than myself. At my aunt's, as at my grandfather's, I was allowed to run freely over the lawns and touch everything. Scratching at the earth, playing with lumps of clay, stroking leaves and flowers, polishing horse-chestnuts, popping seed pods, I was learning things that are never taught by books or official syllabuses. I learnt to recognize the buttercup and the clover, the phlox, the fluorescent blue of the morning glory, the butterfly, the ladybird, the glow-worm, the dew, the spiders' webs and the strands of gossamer; I learnt that the red of the holly is redder than the cherry laurel or the mountain ash, that autumn blooms the peach and bronzes the leaves, that the sun rises and sets in the sky although you cannot see it moving. The wealth of colours and scents excited me.

Everywhere, in the green water of the ponds, in the waving grasses of the fields, under the thorny hedgerows and in the heart of the woods were hidden treasures that I longed to discover.

*

Since I had started going to school, my father had become interested in my progress and my successes, and he was beginning to mean much more in my life. He seemed to me to belong to a rarer species than most men. In that era of beards and moustaches, his clean-shaven face, with its powers of mimicry, was astonishing: his friends said he resembled Rigadin the actor. No one in my circle of acquaintances was nearly as funny, as interesting and as brilliant as he; no one else had read so many books, or knew so much poetry by heart, or could argue with such passion. Standing with his back to the fireplace, he would talk volubly, with lots of gestures; and people listened to him. He was the life and soul of the party at all family reunions: he could recite monologues, or *The Monkey*, by Zamacoïs, and everybody applauded him. The most unusual thing about him was that during his leisure hours he was an amateur actor: whenever I saw photographs of him in the costume of Pierrot, or disguised as a waiter or a soldier or even as Sarah Bernhardt, I took him to be a kind of magician: wearing a dress and a white apron and with a cap perched on his head, he would open wide his great blue eyes and make me cry with laughter in the role of a simple-minded cook named Rosalie.

Every year my parents spent three weeks at Divonne-les-Bains with a troupe of amateur actors who put on plays at the Casino; they amused the summer visitors and the director of the Grand Hotel gave them free accommodation. In 1914 Louise, my sister and I went to await their arrival at Meyrignac. There we found my Uncle Gaston, who was Papa's elder brother, my Aunt Marguerite, whose pallor and thinness alarmed me, and my cousin Jeanne, who was a year younger than myself. They lived in Paris, and we often saw one another there. My sister and Jeanne used to submit to my tyranny with good grace. At Meyrignac I would harness them to a little cart and make them trot with me all over the park. I gave them lessons, and drew them into escapades which I prudently never allowed to go very far. One morning we were playing in the woodshed among the fresh sawdust when the alarm bell sounded: war had been declared. I had heard the word for the first time at Lyon the year before. In wartime, I had been told, people kill each other, and I had wondered: where shall I go and hide? In the course of the year, Papa had explained to me that war means the invasion of one's country by foreigners, and I began to look askance at the numerous Japanese who in those days used to sell fans and paper lanterns at the street corners. No. Our enemies apparently were the Germans with their pointed helmets who had already robbed us of Alsace and Lorraine and whose grotesque ugliness I discovered in the books of Hansi.

I now knew that in wartime it is only soldiers who kill one another, and I knew enough geography to know that the frontier was a long way from the Limousin. Nobody in our neighbourhood seemed to be alarmed, and so I was not unduly frightened. Papa and Mama arrived out of the blue after having spent forty-eight hours on the train. Orders for the requisitioning of horses and vehicles were nailed to the door of the coach-house, and grandpapa's horses were taken off to Uzerche. The general agitation, the huge headlines in the *Courrier du Centre* all excited me; I was always glad when something was going on. I invented games appropriate to the circumstances: I was Poincaré, Jeanne was George V and my sister was the Tsar. We held our conferences under the cedars and cut the Prussians to ribbons with our sabres.

In September, at La Grillière, I learnt how to perform my duty as a loyal daughter of France. I helped Mama to make lint and knitted a balaclava helmet. My Aunt Hélène harnessed the dog-cart and we went to the nearby railway station to distribute apples to tall, beturbaned Indians who gave us handfuls of buckwheat; we took cheese and paste sandwiches to the wounded. The local women, loaded with foodstuffs, made their way along the convoys on the roads. 'Souvenir! Souvenir!' they cried; and the soldiers would give them buttons from their greatcoats or empty cartridge cases. One day a woman offered a German prisoner a glass of wine. There were murmurs of disapproval from the other women. 'Well!' she said. 'They're men, too, like the others.' The sounds of disapproval grew stronger. Aunt Hélène's eyes were filled with holy rage. The Boche was a born criminal; he aroused hatred, not indignation: you can't feel just indignant about the Devil in person. Traitors, spies, and unpatriotic Frenchmen and women sent

[26]

deliciously scandalized shivers through our virtuous breasts. I stared with studied horror at the woman who was known from then on as the 'Frau'. In her I beheld at last Evil incarnate.

I embraced with passionate devotion the cause of the righteous. My father, who had been discharged from the Reserve because of heart trouble not long before, found himself called up for active service with the Zouaves. Mama and I went to visit him at Ville-taneuse where he was in training; he had let his moustache grow, and under his tarboosh his face had a gravity which made a great impression on me. I should have to show myself worthy of such a brave father. I had already given proof of exemplary patriotism by stamping on a celluloid doll, 'made in Germany', which belonged, by the way, to my sister. It was only with great difficulty that I was restrained from throwing out of the window our silver knife-rests, which were branded with the same infamous device. I went round sticking the flags of the Allies in all the flower vases. In my games I was always a valiant Zouave, a heroic daughter of the regiment. I wrote everywhere in coloured chalks: *Vive la France!* The grown-ups admired my devotion to the cause. 'Simone is an ardent patriot,' they would say, with proud smiles. I stored the smiles away in my memory and developed a taste for unstinted praise. I don't know who it was presented my mother with a length of the 'sky blue' cloth from which officers' uniforms are made; a tailor made it up into coats for my sister and myself that were exact copies of military greatcoats. 'You see: there's even a bayonet frog!' my mother exclaimed to her admiring or astonished friends. No other child wore a garment as original and as patriotic as mine: I felt I was a dedicated person.

It doesn't take much for a child to become the sedulous ape; I had always been willing to show off: but I refused to play the parts expected of me in false situations concocted by adults for their own amusement. Now that I was too old to lend myself to their caresses, their fondlings, and their cajoleries, I began to feel ever more keenly in need of their approbation. They suggested a part that was easy to play and in which I felt I should be very well cast: I seized the opportunity with both hands. In my sky-blue greatcoat, I rattled a collecting box outside the door of a Franco-Belgian institution on the grand boulevard which was run by a friend of my mother. 'Remember the poor little Belgian refugees!' I piped. Coins rained into my flower-trimmed basket and the smiles of the passers-by assured me that I was an adorable little patriot. But one woman all in black eyed me from head to foot and said: 'And what about the poor little French refugees?' I was quite disconcerted. Brave little Belgians were our heroic allies; but if one was to be a real patriot one should put the French first: I felt I had been beaten on my own ground. When, at the end of the day, I went back to the Franco-Belgian institution, I was fulsomely congratulated. 'Now I'll be able to pay for coal!' carolled the lady in charge. 'But the money is for the poor little Belgian refugees!' I howled. I had difficulty in admitting that their interests might overlap; I had imagined much more spectacular charities. To add insult to injury, Mademoiselle Fevrier, having kept for herself half of what I had collected, pretended to hand over the full amount to a nurse who dutifully cried: 'Twelve francs! That's simply wonderful!' I fell into a terrible rage. I wasn't being taken at my true value; I had thought I was the star of the proceedings, and I'd only been an accessory: I'd been cheated.

Nevertheless I retained a rather glorious memory of that afternoon, and I persevered in my good deeds. I walked in procession with other little girls in the basilica of the Sacré-Cœur, singing and waving the sacred banner of St Denis. I offered up litanies and endlessly told my beads as special intentions for our dear, brave lads at the front. I repeated all the slogans and observed all the rules. I used to read in the Métro and in the trams: 'Careless talk costs lives! Walls have ears!' People talked about spies who stuck needles into women's behinds and about others who distributed poisoned sweets among the children. I played for safety all the way. One day, as I was coming out of school, the mother of one of my schoolmates offered me a bag of jujubes; I refused them; she smelt heavily of scent, her lips were made-up, she wore huge rings, and worst of all she was called Madame Malin – the Evil One! I didn't really believe that her sweets would poison me, but I thought it was a good thing to practise being suspicious.

One part of my school had been fitted out as a hospital. In the corridor, an edifying pharmaceutical odour mingled with the smell of floor polish. Under their white head-dresses, neatly spotted with blood, our teachers looked like saints and I was deeply moved when they kissed my forehead. A little refugee girl from the north was put in our class; the evacuation had seriously deranged her mind; she stammered and had nervous tics. I was always being told about the little refugees and I wanted to find some way of relieving their sufferings. I hit on the idea of putting in a box all the nice things I was given to eat: when it was full of stale cake and slightly mouldy chocolate and dry prunes, Mama helped me to wrap it up nicely and I took it to the ladies of mercy. They took care not to congratulate me too effusively, but I couldn't help overhearing some very flattering whispers.

My feet were well set now upon the path of virtue; no more capricious rages; it had been explained to me that if I were good and pious God would save France. When the chaplain at the Cours Désir took me in hand I became an exemplary little girl. He was young, pale, infinitely suave. He taught me my catechism, and introduced me to the sweet delights of confession. I knelt down before him in a little chapel and replied to his questions and promptings with dramatic fervour. I can't think what I could have told him, but, in the presence of my sister, who told me about it later, he congratulated Mama upon the radiant beauty of my soul. I fell in love with this soul which I imagined to be white and shining like the host itself, exposed in a silver monstrance. I piled up good deeds. Abbé Martin distributed to us at the beginning of Advent pictures representing the Infant Jesus: whenever we did a good deed, we had to prick with a pin the outline of the figure, which was drawn in violet ink. On Christmas Day, we had to go and place our pictures round the crib at the end of the church, where the light played through the pin-prick holes. I invented every kind of mortification, sacrifice, and edifying behaviour in order that my picture might be richly bedight with pinpricks. These goings-on irritated Louise. But Mama and my teachers encouraged me along the straight and narrow path. I joined a children's confraternity known as 'The Angels of the Passion'. This gave me the right to wear a scapular, and it was my duty to meditate upon the seven sorrows of Our Lady. In accordance with the recent instruction of Pius X, I prepared my communion in private; I went into retreat. I didn't quite understand why the Pharisees (*pharisiens*), whose name was so disturbingly like that of the inhabitants of Paris, had been so much against Jesus, but I went all the way with Him in His sufferings. Dressed in white tulle with my head covered with a veil of Irish lace, I swallowed my first consecrated wafer. From then on, Mama took me three times a week to communion at Notre-Dame-des-Champs. In the grey light of early morning,

I liked to hear the sound of our feet on the flagged floor of the church. Sniffing the fragrance of incense, my eyes watering with the reek of candles, I found it sweet to kneel at the foot of the cross and dream vaguely of the cup of hot chocolate awaiting me when we got back home.

This pious collusion bound me even more closely to my mother: she definitely took the first place in my life. Her brothers had been mobilized; Louise had returned to her parents to help them on the land. For Raymonde, the new maid, frizzy-haired, affected and pretentious, I had nothing but disdain. Mama hardly ever went out now, and had few visitors; she devoted nearly all her time to my sister and me; she made more of me than she did of my sister; she, too, was an elder sister, and everyone said how much I resembled her: I had the feeling that she belonged to me in a peculiarly privileged way.

Papa left for the front in October; I can see again the corridors of the Métro, and Mama walking beside me, her eyes brimming . . . she had beautiful brown eyes and two tears were slowly rolling down her cheeks. I was very touched by the sight. But I never realized that my father was in danger. I had seen wounded men; I knew there was a connexion between war and death. But I could not conceive that this great collective adventure could possibly concern *me*. And besides I was convinced that God would protect my father very specially for me: I was incapable of imagining any misfortune happening to him.

Events confirmed my optimism; after suffering a heart attack, my father was evacuated to the military hospital at Coulommiers, then transferred to the Ministry of War. He put on a different uniform and shaved off his moustache. About the same time, Louise returned to us. Life got back to normal.

I had made a definite metamorphosis into a good little girl. Right from the start, I had composed the personality I wished to present to the world; it had brought me so much praise and so many great satisfactions that I had finished by identifying myself with the character I had built up: it was my one reality. I was not quite so lively as before: I was growing rapidly, and an attack of measles had made my face look pale and interesting; I took sulphur baths and nourishing patent foods; I no longer upset the grown-ups with turbulent outbursts of rage; besides, my tastes fitted in well with the sort of life we were leading, so that there was not much occasion to reprimand or thwart me. If there was disagreement, I was now able to ask why, and to discuss the matter. Often all they had to say to me was: 'It's not done. When I say no I *mean* no!' Even when that happened, I no longer thought of myself as a down-trodden child. I was sure that my parents were only trying to do their best for me. And besides, it was the will of God their lips gave utterance to: He had created me; He had died for me; He was entitled to my total submission. I felt I bore upon my shoulders the reassuring yoke of necessity.

And so I said good-bye to the independence which I had tried so hard to preserve in my earliest years. For some time, I was to be the docile reflection of my parents' will. Now it is time to put down what I know about them.

*

I know very little about my father's childhood. My great-grand-father, who was Inspector of Taxes at Argenton, must have left his sons a fairly substantial fortune, because even the youngest was able to live on his private income; the eldest son, my grandfather, inherited among other properties an estate of about five hundred acres: he married a middle-class girl from a large, rich family in the north. However, either from inclination or because he had three children, he took up a post in Paris, in the Town Hall; he had a long career; when he retired he was head of a department and had been decorated. His mode of life was more brilliant than his situation. My father spent his childhood in a fine apartment on the boulevard Saint-Germain, and was brought up, if not in opulent then at least in moderately luxurious surroundings. He had an elder sister and an elder brother, a complete duffer, noisy and often violent, who used to bully him. Papa, who was not very strong, detested violence of any kind. He found means of compensating for his physical weakness: he sought to please: he was his mother's favourite, and his teachers' star pupil. His tastes were completely opposite to those of his elder brother; disliking sports and gymnastics, he loved reading and studying. My grandmother encouraged him: he lived in her shadow and his only wish was to please her in every way. She came from an austere bourgeois family of unshakeable Catholic faith in God, in work, in duty, and in strict personal values; she insisted that he should be a model pupil as well as a model son. Every year Georges won the first prize at the Collège Stanislas. During the holidays, he would round up the farmers' children and give them lessons: an old photograph shows him in the courtyard at Meyrignac, surrounded by about a dozen pupils, boys and girls. A maidservant, in a white cap and apron, is holding a tray full of glasses of orangeade. His mother died when he was thirteen years old; not only did he feel violent grief at her death, he was suddenly left to his own devices. To him my grandmother had been the incarnation of law and order; my grandfather was quite unable to take her place. He meant well, of course, and had all the right ideas: he hated the *communards* and spouted Déroulède. But he was more conscious of his rights than he was aware of his duties. Half-way between the aristocracy and the bourgeoisie, between the landed gentry and the office worker, respecting but not practising the Catholic religion, he felt himself neither completely integrated with society nor burdened with any serious responsibilities: he represented an epicurean good taste. He took up a sport only less distinguished than fencing – singlesticks – and attained the rank of assistant master in the art, a rank of which he was very proud. He didn't like arguments or worries and let his children have a free rein. My father continued to distinguish himself in the subjects that interested him – in Latin and literature: but he no longer won first prizes. He had stopped trying.

After certain monetary compensations had been paid to my father and his sister, Meyrignac was to revert to my Uncle Gaston, and he, with his future assured, devoted himself to complete inactivity. His situation as younger brother, his attachment to his mother and his scholastic successes had led my father – whose future was not at all assured – to renounce his individuality: but he saw that he had certain gifts, and determined to make the best of them. The legal profession attracted him on account of its dramatic possibilities, because he was already a fine public speaker. He enrolled in the Faculty of Law. But he often told me that if the attitude of the family had not made it impossible, he would have entered the Conservatoire and trained as an actor. This was no idle whim: nothing was more genuine than his love for the theatre. While he was studying law, he discovered, to his great delight, the works of the best authors of his time; he spent his nights reading Alphonse Daudet, Maupassant, Bourget, Marcel Prévost, and Jules Lemaître.

But he found even greater enjoyment in the pit at the Comédie Française or the music hall. He went to all the new plays; he was in love with all the actresses and idolized the great actors of his time: he shaved his face so that he might look like an actor. In those days, there was much amateur play-acting in private houses: he took elocution lessons, studied the art of make-up and joined a group of amateurs.

My father's unusual vocation can be explained, I think, by his social standing. His name, certain family connexions, childhood friends, and those he associated with as a young man convinced him that he belonged to the aristocracy, so he adopted their manner of living. He appreciated elegant gestures, charming compliments, social graces, style, frivolity, irony, all the free-and-easy self-assurance of the rich and well-born. The more serious virtues esteemed by the bourgeoisie he found frankly boring. Thanks to a very good memory, he passed his examinations, but his student years were devoted mainly to pleasure: theatres, races, cafés, and parties. He cared so little for the common run of success that once he had passed his qualifying examinations he didn't bother to present a thesis but registered himself in the Court of Appeal and took a post as secretary to a well-established lawyer. He was contemptuous of successes which are obtained at the expense of hard work and effort: according to him, if you were 'born' to be some-one, you automatically possessed all the essential qualities – wit, talent, charm, and good breeding. The trouble was that in the ranks of that high society to which he laid claim for admittance, he found he was a nobody; the 'de' in de Beauvoir showed he had a handle to his name, but the name was an obscure one, and did not auto-matically open for him the doors of the best clubs and the most aristocratic salons; and he hadn't the means to live like a lord. He attached little importance to the positions that were open to him in the bourgeois world – the distinguished lawyer, the father of a family, the respected citizen. He set out in life with empty hands, and despised the advantages he acquired. There was only one solution left to him: to become an actor.

But an actor needs an audience: my father did not care for country life or solitude; he was only happy when he was in society. He found his profession amusing only in so far as it gave him opportunities as an actor. When he was a young man he took great care with his appearance and became quite a dandy. Having practised since childhood the art of pleasing others, he soon gained a reputation for being a brilliant talker and a great charmer. But these successes did not satisfy him; they raised him only to the lower ranks in those fashionable drawing-rooms where wealth and noble ancestry counted above all else. In order to challenge the fixed hierarchies of aristocratic society, he would have to make himself a place that was outside the accepted categories. Literature takes its revenge on reality by making it the slave of fiction; but though my father was an avid reader he knew that writing requires those tedious virtues, patience and application, that it is a solitary occupation with a public that exists only in the writer's imagination. On the other hand the theatre brought a ready-made solution to his problems. The actor is spared the horrors of creation: he is offered on a plate an imaginary universe in which a special place has been created for him; he occupies that place in the flesh, before an audience of flesh and blood. Reduced to the role of a mirror, the audience faithfully reflects his image; on the stage he is king and he really exists, he really feels himself to be a king. My father took a special delight in making-up; he could escape from himself by putting on a wig and a false moustache. In this way he could avoid identification; he was neither a nobleman nor a commoner: this indeterminacy lent itself to every kind of impersonation; having fundamentally ceased to be himself, he could become anyone he liked, and could outshine them all.

He never dreamed of flouting the conventions of his social group and becoming a professional actor. He devoted himself to the stage because he could not resign himself to an inferior position in society; he never contemplated the possibility of losing caste. He was doubly successful. Seeking a means of admittance to a society which was very reticent in opening its arms to him, he decided to force his way in through the front door. Thanks to his talents as an amateur, he did in fact gain access to more elegant and less austere circles than the ones he had been brought up in; witty men, pretty women, and every kind of pleasure were the things they appreciated there. As an actor and man of the world, my father had found his true vocation. He devoted all his leisure to comedy and mime. On the very eve of his marriage, he acted in a play. As soon as he had returned from the honeymoon he put Mama on the stage, where her beauty made up for her lack of experience. I have already mentioned that every year, at Divonne-les-Bains, they took part in theatrical performances given by a company of amateurs. They often went to the theatre. My father subscribed to *Comédia*, the theatrical magazine, and kept up to date with all the back-stage gossip. Among his intimate friends was an actor from the Odéon. During his convalescence in the hospital at Coulommiers, he wrote and played in a revue in collaboration with another patient, the young singer Gabriello, who was often invited to our house. Later on, when he no longer had the means to keep up a gay social life, he still found opportunities to tread the boards, even if it was only an affair in a church hall.

His singular individuality came out to the full in this insatiable passion for the theatre. In other respects, my father was a true representative of his period and his class. He considered the re-establishment of the monarchy a Utopian dream; but the Republic only filled him with disgust. Without actually subscribing to *L'Action Française*, he had many friends among the Camelots du Roi* and he admired Maurras and Léon Daudet. He would not hear any criticism of the nationalist movement in politics; if some-one were sufficiently ill-advised to discuss it, he would laugh up-roariously and refuse to take part; his love for his native land was above and beyond all arguments and all words: 'It's my only religion,' he used to say. He detested foreigners, and was indignant that Jews should be allowed to take part in the government of the country; he was as convinced of Dreyfus' guilt as my mother was of the existence of God. He read *Le Matin* and flew into a temper one day because one of our Sirmione cousins had brought a copy of *L'Œuvre* into the house: 'That rag!' he called it. He considered Renan to be a great thinker, but he respected the Church and was horrified by the bills passed by Émile Combes. His private morality was based upon the cult of the family; woman, in her role as mother, was sacred to him; he demanded the utmost fidelity from married women and all young girls had to be innocent virgins, but he was prepared to allow great liberties to men, which led him to cast an indulgent eye upon women known as 'fast'. As is nearly always the case with idealists, he was sceptical almost to the point of cynicism. He responded to *Cyrano* with quiver-ing emotion, enjoyed Clément Vautel, delighted in Capus, Donnay, Sacha Guitry, Flers, and Callavet. Both nationalist

* Young royalists grouped round the royalist paper *L'Action Française* (Translator's note).

and man about town, he knew the value both of grandeur and of frivolity.

While I was still very small, he had won me over by his gaiety and gift of the gab; as I grew older, I came to admire him for more serious reasons: I was amazed at his culture, his intelligence, and his infallible good sense. At home, his pre-eminence was undisputed, and my mother, younger than he by eight years, willingly took second place. It was he who had introduced her to life and the world of books. 'The wife is what the husband makes of her: it's up to him to make her someone,' he often said. He used to read aloud to her Taine's *Les Origines de la France contemporaine* and Gobineau's *L'Essai sur l'inégalité des races humaines*. He had no overweening pretensions: on the contrary, he prided himself on knowing his limitations. He brought back from the front subjects for short stories which my mother found delightful but which he didn't develop any further for fear of writing something banal. This modesty gave proof of a lucidity of mind which authorized him to pass final judgements on any case in question.

As I grew up, he paid more and more attention to my education and my appearance. In particular he took great pains with my handwriting and spelling: whenever I wrote him a letter, he would send it back to me, with corrections. During the holidays he used to dictate tricky passages to me, chosen usually from Victor Hugo. As I was a great reader, I made few mistakes, and he told me with great satisfaction that I was a natural speller. In order to help form my taste in literature, he had assembled a little anthology for me in an exercise book covered with shiny black imitation leather: *Un Évangile*, by Coppée, *Le Pantin de la petite Jeanne* by Banville, *Hélas! si j'avais su!* by Hégésippe Moreau, and several other poems. He taught me to read them aloud, 'putting in the expression'. He read the classics aloud to me: *Ruy-Blas, Hernani*, the plays of Rostand, Lanson's *Histoire de la littérature française*, and Labiche's comedies. I asked him many questions, which he answered willingly. He never intimidated me, in the sense that I never felt the slightest uneasiness in his presence; but I did not attempt to bridge the distance that lay between us; there were many subjects that I could not imagine myself discussing with him; to him I was neither body nor soul, but simply a mind. Our relationship was situated in a pure and limpid atmosphere where unpleasantness could not exist. He did not condescend to me, but raised me up to his level, and then I was proud to feel myself a grown-up person. When I fell back to my ordinary level, I was dependent upon Mama; Papa had allowed her to take complete charge of my bodily and moral welfare.

My mother had been born at Verdun, in a rich and devout bourgeois family; her father, a banker, had studied with the Jesuits; her mother had been brought up in a convent. Françoise had a brother and sister younger than herself. Grandmama, entirely devoted to her husband, showed her children only a distant affection, and it was Lili, the youngest, who was her father's favourite. Mama suffered from their coldness towards her. A day-boarder at the Couvent des Oiseaux, she found some consolation in the warm regard of her teachers; under the guidance of the nuns, she eagerly threw herself into her school work and her religious duties, and, after she had passed her lower certificate of education, the Mother Superior supervised her studies. She suffered many sad disappointments in her adolescence. Her childhood and youth filled her heart with a resentment which she never completely forgot. At the age of twenty, her neck squeezed into whalebone collars, accustomed to suppressing all her natural spontaneity, resorting to silence and brooding over bitter secrets, she felt herself alone and misunderstood; despite her great beauty, she lacked assurance and gaiety. She went without enthusiasm to meet a strange young man at Houlgate. They liked one another. Won over by my father's exuberant vitality, and made confident by the proofs of tenderness he gave her, my mother began to blossom. My earliest memories of her are of a laughing, lively young woman. She also had about her something wilful and imperious which was given a free rein after her marriage. My father enjoyed the greatest prestige in her eyes, and she believed that the wife should obey the husband in everything. But with Louise, my sister, and myself she showed herself to be dictatorial and overbearing, sometimes passionately so. If one of her intimate friends or relations happened to cross her or offend her, she often reacted with anger and outbursts of violent frankness. But in society she was always timid. Brusquely transported into a social group that was very different from her provincial circle, she found difficulty in adapting herself. Her youth, her inexperience, her love for my father all made her vulnerable: she dreaded criticism, and, in order to avoid it, took pains to be 'like everybody else'. In her new environment, her convent morality was only half-respected. She didn't want to be taken for a prude, and so she renounced her own standards of judgement: instead she decided that she would take the rules of etiquette as her guide. Papa's best friend was living with a woman, and that meant he was living in sin; that didn't prevent him from paying frequent visits to our house; but his mistress could not be received. My mother never dreamed of protesting in any way against an illogicality sanctioned by social conventions. She consented to many other compromises; they did not do violence to her principles; it was even perhaps in order to compensate for these concessions that she preserved, in her heart of hearts, a rigorously inflexible personal morality. Although she had been without doubt happy in her marriage, she was apt to confuse sexuality with vice: she always associated fleshly desires with sin. Convention obliged her to excuse certain indiscretions in men; she concentrated her disapproval on women; she divided women into those who were 'respectable' and those who were 'loose'. There could be no intermediate grades. 'Physical' questions sickened her so much that she never attempted to discuss them with me; she did not even warn me about the surprises awaiting me on the threshold of puberty. In all other matters, she accepted my father's ideas without ever appearing to find any difficulty in reconciling them with her religion. My father was constantly astonished by the paradoxes of the human heart, by the playful tricks of heredity, and by the strangeness of dreams; I never saw my mother astonished by anything.

In complete contrast to my father's negligence, she was profoundly conscious of her responsibilities, and took to heart the duties of mother and counsellor. She sought guidance from the Union of Christian Mothers, and often attended their meetings. She took me to school, attended my classes and kept a strict eye on my homework and my lessons; she learnt English and began to study Latin in order to be able to follow my progress. She supervised my reading, and accompanied me to Mass and compline; my mother, my sister, and I performed our devotions together, morning and evening. At every instant of the day she was present, even in the most secret recesses of my soul, and I made no distinction between her all-seeing wisdom and the eye of God Himself. None of my aunts – not even Aunt Marguerite who had been brought up in the Sacré-Cœur – practised their religion with as much zeal as she. She regularly received Holy Communion, prayed long and fervently and read numberless works of piety. Her personal conduct was an outward expression of her deep faith: with ready unselfishness, she devoted her entire being to the welfare of those near and dear to her. I did not look upon her as a saint, because I knew her too well and because she lost her temper far too easily; but her example seemed to me all the more unassailable because of that: I, too, was able to, and therefore ought to emulate her in piety and virtue. The warmth of her affection made up for her unpredictable temper. If she had been more impeccable in her conduct, she would also have been more remote, and would not have had such a profound effect upon me.

Her hold over me stemmed indeed a great deal from the very intimacy of our relationship. My father treated me like a fully developed person; my mother watched over me as a mother watches over a child; and a child I still was. She was more indulgent towards me than he: she found it quite natural that I should be a silly little girl, whereas my stupidity only exasperated my father; she was amused by my childish sayings and scribblings; he found them quite unfunny. I wanted to be taken notice of; but fundamentally I needed to be accepted for what I was, with all the deficiencies of my age; my mother's tenderness assured me that this wish was a justifiable one. I was flattered most by praise from my father; but if he complained because I had made a mess in his study, or if he cried: 'How stupid these children are!' I took such censure lightly, because he obviously attached little importance to the way it was expressed. On the other hand, any reproach made by my mother, and even her slightest frown was a threat to my security: without her approval, I no longer felt I had any right to live.

If her disapproval touched me so deeply, it was because I set so much store by her good opinion. When I was seven or eight years old, I kept no secrets from her, and spoke to her with complete freedom. I have one very vivid memory which illustrates this lack of sophistication. My attack of measles had left me with a slight lateral curvature of the spine; a doctor drew a line down my vertebral column, as if my back had been a blackboard, and he prescribed Swedish exercises. I took some lessons with a tall, blond gymnastic instructor. As I was waiting for him one afternoon I did a little practice on the horizontal bar; when I sat astride the bar, I felt a curious itching sensation between my thighs; it was agreeable and yet somehow disappointing; I tried again; the phenomenon was repeated. 'It's funny,' I told Mama, and then described my sensations to her. With a look of complete indifference on her face she began talking of something else, and I realized that I had asked one of those tiresome questions to which I never received any answer.

After that, my attitude seemed to change. Whenever I wondered about the 'ties of blood' which are often mentioned in books, or about the 'fruit of thy womb' in the Hail, Mary, I did not turn to my mother for confirmation of my suspicions. It may be that in the meanwhile she had countered some of my questions with evasions I have now forgotten. But my silence on these subjects arose from a more general inhibition: I was keeping a watch on my tongue and on my behaviour as a whole. My mother rarely punished me, and if ever she was free with her hands her slaps did not hurt very much. However, without loving her any less than before, I had begun to fight shy of her. There was one word which she was fond of using and which used to paralyse my sister and me: 'It's *ridiculous*!' she would cry. We often heard her making use of this word whenever she was discussing with Papa the conduct of a third person; when it was applied to us, it used to dash us from the cosy heights of our family empyrean into the lowest depths where the scum of humanity lay grovelling. Unable to foresee what gesture or remark might unleash this terrible word upon us, we learnt to look upon any kind of initiative as dangerous; prudence counselled us to hold our tongues and stay our hands. I recall the surprise we felt when, after asking Mama if we might take our dolls on holiday with us, she answered simply: 'Why not?' We had repressed this wish for years. Certainly the main reason for my timidity was a desire to avoid her derision. But at the same time, whenever her eyes had that stormy look or even when she just compressed her lips, I believe that I feared the disturbance I was causing in her heart more than my own discomfiture. If she had found me out telling a lie, I should have felt the scandal it created even more keenly than any personal shame: but the idea was so unbearable, I always told the truth. I obviously did not realize that my mother's promptness to condemn anything peculiar or new was a forestalling of the confusion that any dispute aroused in her: but I sensed that careless words and sudden changes of plan easily troubled her serenity. My responsibility towards her made my dependence even greater.

And that is how we lived, the two of us, in a kind of symbiosis. Without striving to imitate her, I was conditioned by her. She inculcated in me a sense of duty as well as teaching me unselfishness and austerity. My father was not averse to the limelight, but I learnt from Mama to keep in the background, to control my tongue, to moderate my desires, to say and do exactly what ought to be said and done. I made no demands on life, and I was afraid to do anything on my own initiative.

The harmony that bound my parents to one another strengthened the respect I felt for both of them. It allowed me to skirt one difficulty which might have embarrassed me considerably: Papa didn't go to Mass, he smiled when Aunt Marguerite enthused over the miracles at Lourdes: he was an unbeliever. This scepticism did not effect me, so deeply did I feel myself penetrated by the presence of God; yet Papa was always right: how could he be mistaken about the most obvious of all truths? Nevertheless, since my mother, who was so pious, seemed to find Papa's attitude quite natural, I accepted it calmly. The consequence was that I grew accustomed to the idea that my intellectual life – embodied by my father – and my spiritual life – expressed by my mother – were two radically heterogeneous fields of experience which had absolutely nothing in common. Sanctity and intelligence belonged to two quite different spheres; and human things – culture, politics, business, manners, and customs – had nothing to do with religion. So I set God apart from life and the world, and this attitude was to have a profound influence on my future development.

My situation in the family resembled that of my father in his childhood and youth: he had found himself suspended between the airy scepticism of my grandfather and the bourgeois earnestness of my grandmother. In my own case, too, my father's individualism and pagan ethical standards were in complete contrast to the rigidly moral conventionalism of my mother's teaching. This imbalance, which made my life a kind of endless disputation, is the main reason why I became an intellectual.

For the time being, I felt I was being protected and guided both in matters of this life and of the life beyond. I was glad, too, that I was not entirely at the mercy of grown-ups; I was not alone in my children's world; I had an equal: my sister, who began to play a considerable role in my life about my sixth birthday.

We called her Poupette; she was two and a half years younger than me. People said she took after Papa. She was fair-haired, and in the photographs taken during our childhood her blue eyes always appear to be filled with tears. Her birth had been a disappointment, because the whole family had been hoping for a boy; certainly no one ever held it against her for being a girl, but it is perhaps not altogether without significance that her cradle was the centre of regretful comment. Great pains were taken to treat us both with scrupulous fairness; we wore identical clothes, we nearly always went out together; we shared a single existence, though as the elder sister I did in fact enjoy certain advantages. I had my own room, which I shared with Louise, and I slept in a big bed, an imitation antique in carved wood over which hung a reproduction of Murillo's *Assumption of the Blessed Virgin*. A cot was set up for my sister in a narrow corridor. While Papa was undergoing his army training, it was I who accompanied Mama when she went to see him. Relegated to a secondary position, the 'little one' felt almost superfluous. I had been a new experience for my parents: my sister found it much more difficult to surprise and astonish them; I had never been compared with anyone: she was always being compared with me. At the Cours Désir the ladies in charge made a habit of holding up the older children as examples to the younger ones; whatever Poupette might do, and however well she might do it, the passing of time and the sublimation of a legend all contributed to the idea that I had done everything much better. No amount of effort and success was sufficient to break through that impenetrable barrier. The victim of some obscure malediction, she was hurt and perplexed by her situation, and often in the evening she would sit crying on her little chair. She was accused of having a sulky disposition; one more inferiority she had to put up with. She might have taken a thorough dislike to me, but paradoxically she only felt sure of herself when she was with me. Comfortably settled in my part of elder sister, I plumed myself only on the superiority accorded to my greater age; I thought Poupette was remarkably bright for her years; I accepted her for what she was – someone like myself, only a little younger; she was grateful for my approval, and responded to it with an absolute devotion. She was my liegeman, my *alter ego*, my double; we could not do without one another.

I was sorry for children who had no brother or sister; solitary amusements seemed insipid to me; no better than a means of killing time. But when there were two, hopscotch or a ball game were adventurous undertakings, and bowling hoops an exciting competition. Even when I was just doing transfers or daubing a catalogue with water-colours I felt the need of an associate. Collaborating and vying with one another, we each found a purpose in our work that saved it from all gratuitousness. The games I was fondest of were those in which I assumed another character; and in these I had to have an accomplice. We hadn't many toys; our parents used to lock away the nicest ones – the leaping tiger and the elephant that could stand on his hind legs; they would occasionally bring them out to show to admiring guests. I didn't mind. I was flattered to possess objects which could amuse grown-ups; and I loved them because they were precious: familiarity would have bred contempt. In any case the rest of our playthings – grocer's shop, kitchen utensils, nurse's outfit – gave very little encouragement to the imagination. A partner was absolutely essential to me if I was to bring my imaginary stories to life.

A great number of the anecdotes and situations which we dramatized were, we realized, rather banal; the presence of the grown-ups did not disturb us when we were selling hats or defying the Boche's artillery fire. But other scenarios, the ones we liked best, required to be performed in secret. They were, on the surface, perfectly innocent, but, in sublimating the adventure of our childhood, or anticipating the future, they drew upon something secret and intimate within us which would not bear the searching light of adult gazes. I shall speak later of those games which, from my point of view, were the most significant. In fact, I was always the one who expressed myself through them; I imposed them upon my sister, assigning her the minor roles which she accepted with complete docility. At that evening hour when the stillness, the dark weight, and the tedium of our middle-class domesticity began to invade the hall, I would unleash my fantasms; we would make them materialize with great gestures and copious speeches, and sometimes, spellbound by our play, we succeeded in taking off from the earth and leaving it far behind until an imperious voice suddenly brought us back to reality. Next day we would start all over again. 'We'll play *you know what*,' we would whisper to each other as we prepared for bed. The day would come when a certain theme, worked over too long, would no longer have the power to inspire us; then we would choose another, to which we would remain faithful for a few hours or even for weeks.

I owe a great debt to my sister for helping me to externalize many of my dreams in play: she also helped me to save my daily life from silence; through her I got into the habit of wanting to communicate with people. When she was not there I hovered between two extremes: words were either insignificant noises which I made with my mouth, or, whenever I addressed my parents, they became deeds of the utmost gravity; but when Poupette and I talked together, words had a meaning yet did not weigh too heavily upon us. I never knew with her the pleasure of sharing or exchanging things, because we always held everything in common; but as we recounted to one another the day's incidents and emotions, they took on added interest and importance. There was nothing wrong in what we told one another; nevertheless, because of the importance we both attached to our conversations, they created a bond between us which isolated us from the grown-ups; when we were together, we had our own secret garden.

We found this arrangement very useful. The traditions of our family compelled us to take part in a large number of duty visits, especially around the New Year; we had to attend interminable family dinners with aunts and first cousins removed to the hundredth degree, and pay visits to decrepit old ladies. We often found release from boredom by running into the hall and playing at 'you know what'. In summer, Papa was very keen on organizing expeditions to the woods at Chaville or Meudon; the only means we had of enlivening the boredom of these long walks was our private chatter; we would make plans and recall all the things that had happened to us in the past; Poupette would ask me questions; I would relate episodes from French or Roman history, or stories which I made up myself.

What I appreciated most in our relationship was that I had a real hold over her. The grown-ups had me at their mercy. If I demanded praise from them, it was still up to them to decide whether to praise me or not. Certain aspects of my behaviour seemed to have an immediate effect upon my mother, an effect which had not the slightest connexion with what I had intended. But between my sister and myself things happened naturally. We would disagree, she would cry, I would become cross, and we would hurl the supreme insult at one another: 'You *fool*!' and then we'd make it up. Her tears were real, and if she laughed at one of my jokes, I knew she wasn't trying to humour me. She alone endowed me with authority; adults sometimes gave in to me: she obeyed me.

One of the most durable bonds that bound us together was that which exists between master and pupil. I loved studying so much that I found teaching enthralling. Playing at school with my dolls did not satisfy me at all: I didn't just want to go through the motions of teaching: I really wanted to pass on the knowledge I had acquired.

Teaching my sister to read, write, and count gave me, from the age of six onwards, a sense of pride in my own efficiency. I liked scrawling phrases or pictures over sheets of paper: but in doing so I was only creating imitation objects. When I started to change ignorance into knowledge, when I started to impress truths upon a virgin mind, I felt I was at last creating something real. I was not just imitating grown-ups: I was on their level, and my success had nothing to do with their good pleasure. It satisfied in me an aspiration that was more than mere vanity. Until then, I had contented myself with responding dutifully to the care that was lavished upon me: but now, for the first time, I, too, was being of service to someone. I was breaking away from the passivity of childhood and entering the great human circle in which everyone is useful to everyone else. Since I had started working seriously time no longer fled away, but left its mark on me: by sharing my knowledge with another, I was fixing time on another's memory, and so making it doubly secure.

*

Thanks to my sister I was asserting my right to personal freedom; she was my accomplice, my subject, my creature. It is plain that I only thought of her as being 'the same, but different', which is one way of claiming one's pre-eminence. Without ever formulating it in so many words, I assumed that my parents accepted this hierarchy, and that I was their favourite. My room gave on to the corridor where my sister slept and at the end of which was my father's study; from my bed I could hear my father talking to my mother in the evenings, and this peaceful murmur often lulled me to sleep. But one evening my heart almost stopped beating; in a calm voice which held barely a trace of curiosity, Mama asked: 'Which of the two do you like best?' I waited for Papa to say my name, but he hesitated for a moment which seemed to me like an eternity: 'Simone is more serious-minded, but Poupette is so affectionate. . . .' They went on weighing the pros and the cons of our case, speaking their inmost thoughts quite freely; finally they agreed that they loved us both equally well: it was just like what you read in books about wise parents whose love is the same for all their children. Nevertheless I felt a certain resentment. I could not have borne it if one of them had preferred my sister to myself; if I was resigned to enjoying an equal share of their affection, it was because I felt that it was to my advantage to do so. But I was older, wiser, and more experienced than my sister: if my parents felt an equal affection for us both, then at least I was entitled to more consideration from them; they ought to feel how much closer I was to their maturity than my sister.

I thought it was a remarkable coincidence that heaven should have given me just these parents, this sister, this life. Without any doubt, I had every reason to be pleased with what fate had brought me. Besides, I was endowed with what is known as a happy disposition; I have always found reality more rewarding than the mirages of the imagination; now the things whose existence was most real to me were the things I owned myself: the value I attached to them protected me from all disappointments, nostalgias, and regrets; my affection for them overcame all baser longings. Blondine, my doll, was old-fashioned, dilapidated, and badly dressed; but I wouldn't have exchanged her for the most gorgeous doll queening it in a smart shop window: the love I had for her made her unique and irreplaceable. I wouldn't have changed the park at Meyrignac for any earthly paradise, or our apartment for any palace. The idea that Louise, my sister, and my parents might be any different from what they were never entered my head. And as for myself, I couldn't imagine myself with any other face, or with any other body: I felt quite satisfied with the way I was.

It is not a very big step from contentment to complacency. Highly satisfied with the position I occupied in the world, I regarded it as a specially privileged one. My parents were exceptional human beings, and I considered our home to be exemplary in every way. Papa liked making fun of people, and Mama had a shrewd critical bent; few were the persons who found favour in their eyes, but I never heard anyone run *them* down: hence their way of life could be taken to represent the absolute norm of behaviour. Their superiority was reflected on myself. In the Luxembourg Gardens, we were forbidden to play with strange little girls: this was obviously because we were made of finer stuff. Unlike the vulgar race of boys and girls, we did not have the right to drink from the metal goblets that were chained to the public fountains; grandmama had made me a present of an opalescent shell, a mother-of-pearl chalice from which I alone might drink: like my horizon blue greatcoat, it was an exclusive model. I remember a Mardi-Gras at which our bags were filled, not with common confetti, but with rose petals. My mother bought her cakes only from specially designated pastrycooks: the éclairs made by the family baker might as well have been constructed of plaster, so inedible did we consider them: the delicacy of our stomachs, too, distinguished us from baser mortals. While the majority of the children in my circle took a popular children's magazine called *La Semaine de Suzette*, I was presented with a subscription to *L'Étoile Noëliste*, which Mama considered to be of a higher moral tone. I did not go to a state school, but attended a private establishment which manifested its originality in many ways; the classes, for example, were numbered in a curious way: zero, first, second, first-third, third-second, first-fourth, and so on. I studied my catechism in the school's private chapel, without having to mix with a whole herd of other children from the parish. I belonged to an élite.

However, in this very select circle, certain of my parents' friends enjoyed one great advantage over us: they were rich; as a mere corporal, my father earned about five cents a day, and we were obliged to practise a genteel economy. We were often invited, my sister and I, to children's parties on a staggeringly lavish scale: in vast suites of rooms draped with satins and velvets and dripping with chandeliers a host of children would gorge themselves on ices, cakes, and *marrons glacés*; there would be Punch and Judy shows and performances by ventriloquists and conjurers, and we would all dance round a huge, gift-laden Christmas tree. The other little girls would be arrayed in gorgeous silks and laces; but we wore woollen frocks the colour of mould or mud. I used to feel a little uncomfortable in such surroundings; at the end of the day, exhausted, sticky, and feeling decidedly ill, I would be nauseated by the rich carpets, the crystal chandeliers, the silks and taffetas; I was always glad when I got back home. My entire upbringing continually re-affirmed that virtue and culture were more desirable than material wealth, and my own tastes encouraged me to believe it; I therefore accepted with equanimity our more modest state. True to my calculated optimism, I even convinced myself that our condition was an enviable one; I saw in our mediocrity the golden mean. I considered the poor and the people of the streets as rank outsiders; but princes and millionaires, too, were outside the real world: their peculiar situation excluded them from normal society. As for myself, I believed I had access to the very highest, as well as to the very lowest ranks of the social scale; actually the former were closed to me, and I was radically cut off from the latter.

Few things could disturb my equanimity. I looked upon life as a happy adventure; my faith protected me from the terrors of death: I would close my eyes when my time came, and in a flash the snowy hands of angels would transport me to the celestial regions. In a gilt-edged prize volume, I read a moral fable which set the final seal on my convictions; a little larva which lived at the bottom of a pond began to feel worried; one after the other her companions disappeared into the night of the aquatic firmament: would she, too, one day disappear? Suddenly she found herself on the other side of the dark: she had wings, and she could fly, under the sun's caressing rays, among hosts of marvellous flowers. The analogy, it seemed to me, was irrefutable; a thin azure curtain separated me from paradises resplendent with the true light; time and again I would dispose my limbs upon the carpet, close my eyes and join my hands in prayer, and then command my soul to make her escape. It was only a game; if I had really believed my final hour had come, I should have shrieked with terror. But the idea of death at least did not frighten me. One evening, however, I was chilled to the marrow by the idea of personal extinction. I was reading about a mermaid who was dying by the sad sea waves; for the love of a handsome prince, she had renounced her immortal soul, and was being changed into sea-foam. That inner voice which had always told her 'Here I am' had been silenced for ever, and it seemed to me that the entire universe had foundered in the ensuing stillness. But – no, it couldn't be. God had given me the promise of eternity: I could not ever cease to see, to hear, to talk to myself. Always I should be able to say: 'Here I am.' There *could* be no end.

But there *had* been a beginning; that disturbed me sometimes. Children were born, I told myself, by divine decree; but, contrary to all orthodox thought, I set certain limits to the power of the Almighty. This presence within me which told me I was myself and no one else was dependent on nobody; nothing could touch it; it was impossible that anyone, were it God Himself, could have created it; God had merely provided, as it were, the outer wrapping. In the supernatural intervals of space there floated, I was convinced, myriads of invisible, impalpable souls awaiting incarnation. I had been one of them but had unfortunately forgotten everything about that state of bliss; they wandered between heaven and earth, but were never able to recall their wanderings. I realized, with dreadful anguish, that this absence of memory was the same as extinction, nothingness; everything conspired to suggest that, before making my first appearance in my cradle, I had not existed at all. I should have to correct this deficiency: I would capture in flight those will-o'-the-wisps whose delusive radiance illuminated nothing; I would lend them my eyes, I would dissipate their darkness, and the children who would be born the next day would remember. . . . I used to lose myself completely in these dizzy and otiose speculations, and vainly refuse to admit the scandalous divorce of consciousness and time.

I had at least emerged from the shades; but the things all round me remained lost in darkness. I enjoyed those tales in which needles were given ideas proper to needles, and the sideboard was provided with thoughts that were essentially those of a wooden sideboard: but they were, after all, just stories; objects had black, impenetrable hearts, and reposed upon the earth without being remotely aware that they were doing so, and without being able to murmur reassuringly: 'Here I am.' I have related elsewhere how, at Meyrignac, I stupidly gazed at an old jacket thrown over the back of a chair. I tried to put myself as it were inside the jacket, and say: 'I am a tired old jacket. It was quite impossible, and I was stricken with panic. In the darkness of the past, in the stillness of inanimate beings I had dire forebodings of my own extinction; I conjured up delusive fallacies, and turned them into omens of the truth, and of my own death.

It was through my own eyes that light was created; during the holidays particularly I revelled in visual discoveries; but from time to time I was beset by gnawing doubts: far from bringing me a revelation of the world around me, I felt my presence was a blot upon the face of the earth. I did not, of course, imagine that while I was asleep the flowers in the drawing-room went off to a ball, nor that behind shop windows the ornaments and trinkets played out insipid idylls. But I sometimes suspected the familiar country-side of imitating those enchanted forests that disguise themselves as something else when their secrets are about to be violated by an unwelcome intruder: mirages float before his eyes, he loses his way, and the clearings and coppices are able to preserve their mysteries. Hidden behind a tree, I would try in vain to surprise the solitary secret I imagined lay at the heart of every wood. An improving tale entitled *Valentine, or The Demon of Curiosity* made a great impression upon me. A wicked fairy godmother was taking Valentine for a ride in her carriage; she told him that they were passing through an enchanted kingdom, but the blinds had been lowered at the carriage windows, and he was not to lift them; driven on by his evil genius, Valentine disobeyed; but all he could see outside was utter darkness: his inquisitiveness had destroyed the very thing he wanted to see. I was not interested in the rest of the tale; while Valentine was at grips with his particular demon, I was busy waging an anxious war against blind ignorance.

Though they were sometimes agonizing, my fits of disquiet quickly passed away. The world was vouched for by the presence in it of grown-ups, and I only rarely attempted to penetrate its mysteries without their assistance. I preferred to follow them through the imaginary universes which they liked to create around me.

I used to squat in the hall, in front of the imitation-rustic corner cupboard on which stood a carved wood clock that concealed in its dusty interior two copper weights shaped like pine-cones and all the dark and backward abysms of time; beside it, in the wall, there was a hot air vent; through its gilded grating I could smell nauseating gusts of tepid air rising from the lower depths. This yawning chasm and the stillness measured by the solemn ticking of the clock used to fill me with awful apprehension. I found reassurance in books: they said what they had to say, and didn't pretend to say anything else; when I was not there, they were silent; if I opened one, it said exactly what it meant: if there was a word I didn't understand, Mama would explain it to me. Lying flat on the Turkey carpet, I used to read Madame de Ségur, Zénaïde Fleuriot, Perrault's fairy-tales, Grimm, Madame d'Aulnoy, the Bavarian author of children's tales, Canon Schmid, the books of Töpffer and Bécassine, the adventures of the Fenouillard family and those of Sapper Camember, *Sans famille*, Jules Verne, Paul d'Ivoi, André Laurie, and the series of little pink books, the 'Livres Roses' published by Larousse, which contained legends and folk tales from every country in the world, and which during the war included stories of the great heroes.

I was given only children's books, and they were chosen for me with the greatest care; they were based on the same moral standards as those observed by my parents and teachers; the good were rewarded, and the wicked punished; misadventures befell only those who were vain, ridiculous, and stupid. I accepted the fact that these essential principles were safeguarded for my benefit; usually I did not try to find any relationship between reality and the fantasies I read in books; they amused me, but as it were at a distance, as I would be amused by a Punch and Judy show; that is why, despite the strange ulterior significance that adults ingeniously discover in them, the novels of Madame de Ségur never caused me the slightest astonishment. Madame Bonbec, General Dourakine, together with Monsieur Cryptogame, the Baron de Crac and Bécassine were only animated puppets. A story was something nice in itself, like a marionette show or a pretty picture; I was aware of the necessity informing these constructions which have a beginning, a development, and an end, and in which words and phrases shine with their own peculiar radiance, like colours in a picture. But occasionally a book would speak to me more or less vaguely about the world around me or about myself: then it would make me wonder, or dream, and sometimes it would shake my convictions. Andersen taught me what melancholy is; in his tales, objects suffer from neglect, are broken and pine away without deserving their unhappy fate; the little mermaid, before she passed into oblivion, was in agony at every step she took, as if she were walking on red-hot cinders, yet she had not done anything wrong: her tortures and her death made me sick at heart. A novel I read at Meyrignac, which was called *The Jungle Explorers*, gave me a nasty shock. The author related his extravagant adventures sufficiently well to make me feel I was actually taking part in them. The hero had a friend called Bob, who was rather stout, a good trencherman and absolutely devoted to his companion in danger;

he won my sympathies at once. They were imprisoned in an Indian jail: they discovered a subterranean passage just wide enough to let a man crawl along. Bob went first; suddenly he uttered a terrible scream: he had encountered a python. With loudly beating heart and clammy palms I witnessed the grim tragedy: the serpent devoured good old Bob! This story obsessed me for a long time. The mere idea of being swallowed alive was enough to make my blood run cold; but I should have been less shaken if I had disliked the victim. Bob's frightful death made nonsense of all the rules of life: it was obvious, now, that anything could happen.

Despite their conventionality, my books helped to broaden my horizons; besides, I was charmed to be an apprentice to the sorcery that transmutes printed symbols into stories; and it was natural that I should want to reverse the magical process. Seated at a little table, I would transfer to paper sentences that were winding about in my head: the white sheet would be covered with violet blotches which purported to tell a story. The silence all round me in the room took on an aura of solemnity: I felt I was officiating at a solemn rite. As I did not look to literature for a reflection of reality, I never had the idea that I might write down my own experiences or even my dreams; the thing that amused me was to manipulate an object through the use of words, as I once used to make constructions with building-blocks; only books, and not life in all its crudity, could provide me with models: I wrote pastiche. My first work was entitled *The Misfortunes of Marguerite*. The heroine, from Alsace, and an orphan to boot, was crossing the Rhine with a brood of sisters and brothers in order to escape to France. But then I was piqued to learn that the river doesn't run where it ought to have, and my novel was abandoned. So then I dished up in a slightly different form *La Famille Fenouillard* which we all admired very much in our house: Monsieur and Madame Fenouillard with their two little daughters were a sort of blue-print for our own family. One evening Mama read to Papa my new story, which I had entitled *La Famille Cornichon*. It made her laugh, and he had smiled his approval. Grandpapa presented me with a volume bound in a yellow cover whose pages were entirely blank; Aunt Lili copied my story into this little book in her neat convent script: I gazed with pride upon this almost real object which owed its existence to me. I composed two or three other works which did not have quite the same success. Sometimes I contented myself with inventing titles for my future works. When we went to the country, I would play at being a bookseller; I entitled the silvery leaf of the birch *The Azure Queen*, and the varnished leaf of the magnolia *Flower of the Snows*; I arranged some scholarly displays of my stock. I wasn't sure whether when I was grown-up I wanted to write books or sell them, but in my view they were the most precious things in the world. My mother subscribed to a circulating library in the rue Saint-Placide. Impassable barriers prohibited my entry into those book-lined corridors which seemed to extend to infinity like the tunnels in the Métro. I admired the old ladies in their whalebone collars who were able to spend the rest of their days handling the volumes in their black bindings with titles displayed on a red or orange rectangle on the spine. Buried away in the silence, and masked by the sombre monotony of their bindings, all the words in the world were there, waiting to be deciphered. I dreamed of shutting myself away in those dusty avenues, and never coming out again.

About once a year we went to the Châtelet theatre. Alphonse Deville, the city councillor to whom my father had been secretary in the days when they had both been lawyers, used to place at our disposal the box reserved for members of the city council. So I saw *La Course au bonheur* and *Le Tour du monde en quatre-vingts jours*, and other spectacular productions. I loved the red curtain, the lights, the scenery, and the flower ballet; but the adventures taking place on the stage were of only minor interest to me. The actors were too real, and at the same time not real enough. The most sumptuous finery had not an iota of the brilliance of a carbuncle in a fairy-tale. I used to clap my hands and gasp with wonder, but in my heart of hearts I preferred a quiet afternoon alone with my books.

As for the cinema, my parents looked upon it only as a vulgar entertainment. They thought Charlie Chaplin was very childish, even for children. However, a friend of my father's having procured for us an invitation to see a private showing of a film, we went one morning to see *L'Ami Fritz*: everyone agreed that the film was charming. A few weeks later we saw, under the same privileged conditions, *Le Roi de Camargue*. The hero, engaged to a sweet blonde heroine, a simple peasant girl, was riding along the edge of the sea; he met a naked gipsy with smouldering eyes who slapped his horse's neck; for a long while they stared at one another in amazement; later he went into a little house with her in the middle of the marshes. At this point I noticed my mother and grandmother exchanging looks of alarm; in the end I gathered from their distraught mien that this story was not suitable for my tender years: but I couldn't quite understand why. While the blonde heroine was running desperately over the marshes, to be swallowed up by them in the end, I did not realize that the most frightful of all sins was being committed between the hero and the lovely dark gipsy. But her proud self-abandon had made no impression on me at all. In *The Golden Legend* and in the tales of Canon Schmid I had come across even more voluptuously naked scenes. But from then on, we did not go to the cinema.

I didn't mind; I had my books, my games, and, all around me, subjects more worthy of my interest and contemplation than a lot of flat pictures: men and women, in flesh and blood. Contrary to inanimate objects, human beings, endowed with minds, did not worry me at all: they were just like myself. At that hour of the evening when the fronts of houses become transparent, I would watch the lighted windows. I never saw anything out of the ordinary; but if I caught sight of a child sitting reading at a table, I would be deeply moved to see my own life displayed as it were on a lighted stage. A woman would be setting the table, a couple would be talking: played at a distance, illuminated by chandeliers or hanging lamps, these familiar scenes, to my mind, rivalled the brilliance of the spectacles at the Châtelet. I didn't feel shut out; I had the feeling that a single theme was being interpreted by a great diversity of actors in a great diversity of settings. Repeated to infinity from building to building, from city to city, my existence had a part in all its innumerable representations; it comprised the entire universe.

In the afternoons I would sit out on the balcony outside the dining-room; there, level with the tops of the trees that shaded the boulevard Raspail, I would watch the passers-by. I knew too little of the habits of adults to be able to guess where they were going in such a hurry, or what the hopes and fears were that drove them along. But their faces, their appearance, and the sound of their voices captivated me; I find it hard now to explain what the particular pleasure was that they gave me; but when my parents decided to move to a fifth-floor flat in the rue de Rennes, I remember the despairing cry I gave: 'But I won't be able to see the people in the street any more!' I was being cut off from life, condemned to exile. When we were in the country, I didn't mind being relegated to a rustic hermitage: I was overwhelmed by the wonders of Nature. But in Paris I was hungry for human company; the essence of a city is in its inhabitants: cut off from any more intimate contact, I had to be able to see them at least. Already I was beginning to want to escape from the narrow circle in which I was confined. A way of walking, a gesture, a smile would suddenly touch me deeply; I should have liked to run after the stranger turning the corner and whom I might never see again. One afternoon in the Luxembourg Gardens a big girl in an apple-green coat and skirt was playing with some children; they were skipping; she had rosy cheeks and a gentle, radiant smile. That evening, I told my sister: 'I know what love is!' I had had a glimpse of something new. My father, my mother, my sister, and all those I loved were mine already. I sensed for the first time that one can be touched to the very heart of one's being by a radiance from *outside*.

These brief impulses didn't prevent me from feeling firmly rooted in my own environment. Curious about others, I never dreamt that my fate might be different from what it was. Above all, I felt no disappointment at being a girl. As I have already said, I did not lose myself in vain desires but happily accepted whatever was given. Besides, I could see no positive reason for considering that I'd been given a hard deal.

I had no brother; there were no comparisons to make which would have revealed to me that certain liberties were not permitted me on the grounds of my sex; I attributed the restraints that were put upon me to my age. Being a child filled me with passionate resentment; my feminine gender, never. The boys I knew were in no way remarkable. The brightest one was little René, who, as a special favour, had been allowed to start school among the girls at the Cours Désir, and I always got better marks than he did. In the sight of God, my soul was no less precious than that of His little boys: why, then, should I be envious of them?

With regard to the grown-ups, my experience was rather ambiguous. In certain respects Papa, grandpapa, and my uncles appeared to me to be superior to their wives. But in my everyday life, it was Louise, Mama, grandmama, and my aunts who played the leading roles. Madame de Ségur and Zénaïde Fleuriot took children as their heroes, with grown-ups in subordinate parts; mothers had quite a prominent place in their books, while the fathers didn't have a look-in. As for myself, I thought of grown-ups essentially in their relationship to childhood: from this point of view, my sex assured my pre-eminence. In all my games, my day-dreams, and my plans for the future I never changed myself into a man; all my imagination was devoted to the fulfilment of my destiny as a woman.

I made this destiny suit my own wishes. I don't know why, but organic phenomena very soon ceased to interest me. When we were in the country, I helped Madeleine to feed her rabbits and her hens, but these tasks soon bored me and I cared very little for the softness of fur or feather. I have never liked animals. I found red-faced, wrinkled, milky-eyed babies a great nuisance. Whenever I dressed up as a nurse, it was to go and bring in the wounded from a battlefield; but I never nursed them. One day at Meyrignac I administered, with a rubber bulb, a simulated rectal injection to my cousin Jeanne, whose smiling passivity was an incitement to sadism: but I cannot remember any other similar event. When we played games, I accepted the role of mother only if I were allowed to disregard its nursing aspects. Despising other girls who played with their dolls in what seemed to us 'a silly way, my sister and I had our own particular way of treating our dolls; they could speak and reason, they lived at the same rate, and in the same rhythm as ourselves, growing older by twenty-four hours every day: they were our doubles. In reality, I was more inquisitive than methodical, more impulsive than finicky; but I revelled in schizophrenic day-dreams of strictness and economy: I made use of Blondine to satisfy this mania. As the perfect mother of an exemplary little girl, providing her with an ideal education from which she drew the maximum of profit, I made good the shortcomings of my daily existence under the guise of necessity. I accepted the discreet collaboration of my sister whom I high-handedly assisted in the bringing-up of her own children. But I refused to allow a man to come between me and my maternal responsibilities: our husbands were always abroad. In real life, I knew, things were quite different: the mother of a family is always flanked by her mate; she is over-burdened with a thousand tiresome tasks. Whenever I thought of my own future, this servitude seemed to me so burdensome that I decided I wouldn't have any children; the important thing for me was to be able to form minds and mould characters: I shall be a teacher, I thought.

Nevertheless, teaching, at least as it was practised by my own teachers, did not seem to me to give the teacher a sufficiently exclusive hold over the pupil; my pupil would belong to me completely. I should plan his day down to the minutest detail, in order to eliminate all chance disturbances; with ingenious precision combining occupation and distraction, I should exploit every moment without wasting a single one. I could see only one way of implementing this plan successfully: I should have to become a governess in a family. My parents threw up their hands in horror. But I was unable to imagine that someone charged with the education of the young could be a menial. When I considered the progress made by my sister under my tutelage, I knew the supreme happiness of having changed nothing into something; I could not conceive of any more lofty purpose in my future life than to mould a human being. It mustn't be just anyone, of course. I realize now that it was my own image I was projecting on my future creation, just as I had done on my doll Blondine. This was the meaning behind my vocation: when I was grown-up, I would take my own childhood in hand again and make of it a faultless work of art. I saw myself as the basis of my own apotheosis.

And so, in the present as well as in the future, I proudly imagined myself reigning alone over my own life. However, religion, history, and mythology suggested other personages I might play. I often imagined that I was Mary Magdalene, and that I was drying Christ's feet with my long hair. The majority of real or legendary heroines – Saint Blandine, Joan of Arc, Griselda, Geneviève de Brabant – only attained to bliss and glory in this world or in the next after enduring painful sufferings inflicted on them by males. I willingly cast myself in the role of victim. Sometimes I laid stress upon her spiritual triumphs: the torturer was only an insignificant intermediary between the martyr and her crown. My sister and I set ourselves endurance tests: we would pinch each other with the sugar-tongs, or flay each other with the sticks of our little flags; you had to die rather than recant, but I always cheated shamelessly, for I always expired at the first taste of the rod but I considered that my sister was still alive until she had recanted. At times I was a nun confined in a cell, confounding my jailer by singing hymns and psalms. I converted the passivity to which my sex had condemned me into active defiance. But often I found myself revelling in the delights of misfortune and humiliation. My piety disposed me towards masochism; prostrate before a blond young god, or, in the dark of the confessional with suave young Abbé Martin, I would enjoy the most exquisite transports: the tears would pour down my cheeks and I would swoon away in the arms of angels. I would whip up these emotions to the point of paroxysm when, garbing myself in the blood-stained shift of Saint Blandine, I offered myself up to the lions' claws and to the eyes of the crowd. Or else, taking my cue from Griselda and Geneviève de Brabant, I was inspired to put myself inside the skin of a persecuted wife; my sister, always forced to be Bluebeard or some other tyrant, would cruelly banish me from his palace, and I would be lost in primeval forests until the day dawned when my innocence was established, shining forth like a good deed in a naughty world. Sometimes, changing my script, I would imagine that I was guilty of some mysterious crime, and I would cast myself down, thrillingly repentant, at the feet of a pure, terrible, and handsome man. Vanquished by my remorse, my abjection, and my love, my judge would lay a gentle hand upon my bended head, and I would feel myself swoon with emotion. Certain of my fantasies would not bear the light of day; I had to indulge them in secret. I was always extraordinarily moved by the fate of that captive king whom an oriental tyrant used as a mounting-block; from time to time, trembling, half-naked, I would substitute myself for the royal slave and feel the tyrant's sharp spurs riding down my spine.

The idea of nakedness came into these incantations more or less clearly. The torn tunic of Saint Blandine revealed the whiteness of her thighs; Saint Geneviève had nothing but her long hair to protect her modesty. I had never seen grown-ups other than hermetically clad from top to toe; during my bath-time, Louise scrubbed me with such vehemence that self-appraisal was impossible; besides, I had been taught never to look at my naked body, and I had to contrive to change my underwear without uncovering myself completely. In our universe, the flesh had no right to exist. And yet I had known the softness of my mother's arms; in the neck of certain ladies' dresses I could see the beginning of a darkening cleft which both embarrassed and attracted me. I was not ingenious enough to be able to re-create those pleasurable sensations I had accidentally discovered during my gymnastic lessons; but from time to time the soft touch of downy flesh against my own, or a hand gently stroking my neck, made me shiver with tender anticipation. Too innocent to invent a caress, I had to resort to a subterfuge. Taking the image of the man—mounting-block as my pattern, I would effect the metamorphosis of the human body into an inanimate object. I used to carry it out on myself whenever I cast myself down at the feet of a sovereign lord and master. In order to absolve me, he would lay upon my bended head his judge's hand: and when I begged for pardon, I experienced sensual delight. But whenever I abandoned myself to these delicious downfalls, I never for one moment forgot that it was just a game. In reality I refused to submit to anybody: I was, and I would always remain, my own master.

I even tended to look upon myself, at least from the childhood level, as the One and Only. Of a sociable disposition, I took pleasure in associating with certain little girls of my acquaintance. We used to have games of Pope Joan or Lotto, and we would exchange books. But in general I hadn't the slightest respect for any of my little friends, whether boys or girls. I demanded that our play should be in dead earnest, with precise observance of all the rules, and that victory should be bitterly fought for and hardly won; my sister was equal to these exigencies; but the usually ineffectual playfulness and fundamental lack of seriousness of my other partners always exasperated me. I suppose that on the other hand I must often have taxed them beyond all endurance. At one period I used to arrive at the Cours Désir half an hour before class started; I would join in the games of the boarders; one day, seeing me coming across the playground, a little girl flapped her right hand under her chin in an expressive gesture: 'Oh, it's *her* again! She gets my goat!' This little girl was ugly, stupid, and wore spectacles: I was rather surprised at her outburst but was unable to feel any great annoyance. Another day we went out to the suburbs to visit some friends of my parents whose children had a croquet set. At La Grillière, croquet was our favourite pastime; all through lunch and during the afternoon walk with my parents' friends and children I kept talking about croquet. I was itching to play. The other children complained to my sister: 'She gets on our nerves with all that talk about how good she is at croquet!' When my sister repeated this to me later that evening, I greeted the information with complete indifference. I could not possibly be hurt by stupid children who demonstrated their inferiority by not liking croquet as passionately as I did. Entrenched in our own preferences, our manias, our principles, and our own particular set of values, my sister and I conspired to condemn the silliness of other children. The condescension of grown-ups turns children into a general species whose individual members are all alike: nothing exasperated me more than this. Once at La Grillière, as I was eating some cobnuts, the elderly lady who was Madeleine's governess announced fatuously: 'All children adore nuts.' I made fun of her to Poupette. My personal tastes were not dictated by my age; I was not 'a child': I was me, myself.

My sister benefited, as a humble vassal, from the supreme sovereignty which I conferred upon myself: she never disputed my divine right. I used to think that if I had to share that regal authority, my life would lose all meaning. In my class there were twins who understood one another in a way that was almost miraculous. I used to wonder how one could resign oneself to living with a double; I should have been, it seemed to me, only half a person; and I even had the feeling that my experiences, repeated identically in another would have ceased to be my own. A twin would have deprived my existence of the very thing that gave it value: its glorious singularity.

During my first eight years, I knew only one child for whom I had any respect: luckily for me, he did not turn up his nose at me. My bewhiskered great-aunt often used her grandchildren as models for her heroes in *La Poupée Modèle*. Their names were Titite and Jacques; Titite was three years older than me, Jacques only six months. They had lost their father in a motoring accident; their mother, who had married again, lived at Châteauvillain. During my eighth summer, we paid a rather long visit to my Aunt Alice. The two houses were almost next to one another. I attended the lessons given to my cousins by a sweet, blonde-haired young lady; not as advanced as they were, I was dazzled by Jacques' brilliant compositions, by his knowledge, his assurance. With his rosy cheeks, his amber eyes, his curly hair bright as freshly fallen horse-chestnuts, he was a very good-looking little boy. On the first floor landing there was a bookcase from which he would select books for me; sitting on the stairs, we would read side by side, I *Gulliver's Travels* and he *Popular Astronomy*. When we went down into the garden, it was always he who invented our games. He had begun the construction of an aeroplane which he had already baptized *Old Charlie*, in honour of Guynemer; in order to keep him supplied with materials, I collected all the empty tins I could find in the streets.

The aeroplane had not even begun to take shape, but Jacques' prestige did not suffer. When in Paris, he did not live in an ordinary building, but in an old house on the boulevard Montparnasse where stained-glass windows were made; on the street level were the offices, and above them the flat; the workshops occupied the next floor and the display rooms were at the very top; it was his house, and he did the honours when I visited him with all the authority of a master of men. He would explain to me the processes in the making of stained glass, and point out the differences between stained glass and ordinary vulgar painted stuff; he used to talk to the workmen in a kindly, concerned tone of voice, and I would listen open-mouthed to this little boy who already seemed to have a whole team of grown-ups under his authority: he inspired me with awe. He treated grown-ups as if he were on an equal footing with them, and he even shocked me a little when he treated his grandmother rather roughly. He usually despised girls, and so I valued his friendship all the more. 'Simone is a precocious child,' he had declared. The word pleased me vastly. One day with his own hands he made a real stained-glass window whose blue, red, and white lozenges were framed in lead; on it, in black letters, he had inscribed a dedication: 'For Simone.' Never had I received such a flattering gift. We decided that we were 'married in the sight of God' and I called Jacques 'my fiancé'. We spent our honeymoon on the merry-go-round's painted horses in the Luxembourg Gardens. I took our engagement very seriously. Yet when he was away I hardly ever thought about him. I was glad to see him when he came back, but I never missed him at all.

And so the picture I have of myself round about the years of discretion is of a well-behaved little girl, happy and somewhat self-opinionated. I remember one or two things which do not fit into this portrait and lead me to suppose that it wouldn't have taken very much to upset my self-assurance. When I was eight, I was no longer as hale and hearty as I had been when younger, but had become sickly and timorous. During the classes in gymnastics which I have talked about, I was togged out in a horrid skimpy pair of tights, and I had overheard one of my aunts saying to Mama: 'She looks like a little monkey.' Towards the end of the course, the teacher made me join a large mixed class, a group of boys and girls accompanied by a governess. The girls wore pale blue jersey costumes, with short skirts, elegantly pleated; their shining hair, their voices, their manners, everything about them was impeccable. Yet they ran and jumped and laughed and somersaulted with the freedom and daring which I had always associated with street-urchins. I suddenly felt I was clumsy, ugly, a milksop: a little monkey; that was certainly how those children must have looked upon me; they despised me; even worse, they ignored me. I was the helpless witness of their triumph and of my own extinction.

A few months later, a friend of my parents, whose children I didn't care for very much, took me with them to Villers-sur-Mer. It was the first time I had been away from my sister and I felt mutilated. I found the sea boring; the baths filled me with horror: the water took my breath away; I was terrified. One morning I lay weeping in my bed. Madame Rollin, in some embarrassment, took me on her knees and asked me why I was crying; it seemed to me that we were both acting in a play, and I didn't know my lines: no, no one had been bullying me, everyone was very nice. The truth was that, separated from my family, deprived of those affections which assured me of my personal worth, cut off from the familiar routine which defined my place in the world, I no longer knew where I was, nor what my purpose was here on earth. I needed to be confined within a framework whose rigidity would justify my existence. I realized this, because I was afraid of changes. But I suffered neither bereavement nor removal from familiar surroundings, and that is one of the reasons why I persisted so long in my childish pretensions.

But my equanimity was sadly disturbed during the last year of the war.

It was bitterly cold that winter and coal was unobtainable; in our ill-heated apartment I would vainly press my chilblained fingers on the tepid radiator. The period of restrictions had begun. Bread was grey, or else suspiciously white. Instead of hot chocolate in the mornings we had insipid, watery soups. My mother used to knock up omelettes without eggs and cook up 'afters' with margarine and saccharine, as there was very little sugar; she dished up chilled beef, horse-meat steaks, and dreary vegetables: 'Chinese' and 'Jerusalem' artichokes, 'Swiss' chard and other obscure members of the beet, turnip, and parsnip families. To make the wine pan out, Aunt Lili fabricated an abominable fermented beverage from figs, which was known as 'figgy-wiggy'. Meals lost all their old gaiety. The sirens often started wailing during the night; street lamps would go out and windows would be blacked-out; we would hear people running and the irritable voice of the air-raid warden, Monsieur Dardelle, crying: 'Put that light out!' My mother made us go down to the cellar once or twice; but as my father obstinately refused to leave his bed, she, too, finally decided not to bother. A number of tenants from the upper storeys used to come and take shelter in our hall; we put out armchairs for them in which they fitfully dozed. Sometimes friends of our parents, held up by the raid, would prolong a bridge party into the small hours of the morning. I enjoyed all this disorder, with the silent city lying behind the blacked-out windows suddenly coming to life again after the 'all clear'. The annoying thing was that my grandparents, who had a fifth-floor flat near the Lion de Belfort, took the alerts seriously; they used to rush down to the cellar, and the next morning we had to go and make sure they were safe and sound. At the first boom from Big Bertha, grandpapa, convinced that the Germans were about to arrive at any moment, dispatched his wife and daughter to Charité-sur-Loire: when the fatal moment came, he himself was to fly on foot to Longjumeau. Grandmama, exhausted by her husband's panic-stricken activity, fell ill. She had to be brought back to Paris for medical attention: but as she would no longer have been able to leave her fifth-floor flat during a bombardment, she was installed in our apartment. When she arrived, accompanied by a nurse, her flushed cheeks and empty stare frightened me: she could not speak and did not recognize me. She was given my room, and Louise, my sister, and I camped out in the drawing-room. Aunt Lili and grandpapa took their meals with us. Grandpapa, in his booming voice, would prophesy disaster or else would announce that he'd had a sudden stroke of good fortune. His catastrophism was in fact paralleled by an extravagant optimism. He had large banking interests in Verdun, and his speculations had ended in bankruptcy in which his capital and that of a good number of his clients had been swallowed up. But he still continued to have the utmost confidence in his lucky star and in his financial acumen. At the moment, he was running a boot and shoe factory which, thanks to army orders, was going fairly well; but this modest enterprise did not satisfy his passion for making business deals, considering offers, and thinking up new ways of getting rich quick. Unfortunately for him, he could no longer play about with adequate sums of money without the consent of his wife and children: he used to try to enlist my father's support. One day grandpapa brought him a small gold bar which an alchemist had made from a lump of lead before his very eyes: the secret of this astounding process was to make millionaires of us all, if only we would guarantee an advance to the inventor. Papa gave a disbelieving smile, grandpapa went purple in the face, Mama and Aunt Lili took sides, and everybody started shouting. This sort of scene often happened. Overwrought, Louise and Mama quickly 'got on their high horse'; they would 'have words'; it even used to come to the point where Mama quarrelled with Papa; she would scold my sister and me and box our ears for the slightest thing. But I'd grown a little older: I was no longer five years old, and the days were past when a row between my parents seemed to be the end of the world; nor did I fail to distinguish between impatience and injustice. All the same, at night, when through the glass door separating the dining-room from the drawing-room I heard the cries of hatred and anger, I hid my head under the bedclothes, and my heart would grow heavy. I would think of the past as a long-lost paradise. Would we ever find it again? The world no longer seemed the safe place I had once thought it to be.

It was my gradually developing powers of imagination that made the world a darker place. Through books, communiqués, and the conversations I heard, the full horror of the war was becoming clear to me: the cold, the mud, the terror, the blood, the pain, the agonies of death. We had lost friends and cousins at the front. Despite the promises of heaven, I used to choke with dread whenever I thought of mortal death which separates for ever all those who love one another. People said sometimes in front of my sister and myself: 'They are lucky to be children! They don't realize. . . .' But deep inside I would be shouting: 'Grown-ups don't understand anything at all about us!' Sometimes I would feel overwhelmed by something so bitter and so very definite that no one, I was sure, could ever have known distress worse than mine. Why should there be so much suffering? I would ask myself. At La Grillière, German prisoners and a young Belgian refugee who had been excused army service on the grounds of obesity supped their broth in the kitchen side by side with French farm labourers: they all got on very well together. After all, the Germans were human beings; they, too, could be wounded and bleed to death. Why should things be like this? I began praying desperately for an end to our misfortunes. Peace was to me more important than victory. I was going upstairs with Mama one day, and talking to her: she was telling me that the war would probably be over soon. 'Oh, yes!' I cried, 'let it be over soon! No matter how it ends as long as it's over soon!' Mama stopped and gave me a startled look: 'Don't you say things like that! France must be victorious!' I felt ashamed, not just of having allowed such an enormity to escape my lips, but even of having thought of it. All the same, I found it hard to admit that an idea or an opinion could be 'wrong'. Underneath our flat, opposite the peaceful Dôme where Monsieur Dardelle played dominoes, a rowdy café had just opened, called La Rotonde. You could see short-cropped, heavily made-up women going in, and curiously dressed men. 'It's a joint for wogs and defeatists,' declared my father. I asked him what a defeatist was. 'A bad Frenchman who hopes for the defeat of France,' he replied. I couldn't understand: thoughts come and go in our heads after their own fashion; you don't believe what you do *on purpose*. But my father's outraged tones and my mother's scandalized face left me in no doubt that it doesn't always do to say aloud those disquieting words which you find yourself whispering below your breath.

My hesitant pacifism did not prevent me from being proud of my parents' patriotism. Alarmed by the bombs and by Big Bertha, the majority of the pupils in my school left Paris before the end of the academic year. I was left alone in my class with a great silly twelve-year-old girl; we would sit at the big table facing Mademoiselle Gontran; she paid special attention to me. I took particular pleasure in those classes, which were as solemn as public lectures and as intimate as private lessons. One day, when I arrived with my sister and Mama at the school, we found the building empty: everyone had dashed down into the cellars. We were highly amused. Our own courage and spirit in the face of danger showed plainly that we were beings apart.

Grandmama recovered her wits and went back to her own house. During the holidays and when we returned to school I heard a lot about two traitors who had tried to betray France to Germany: Malvy and Caillaux. They should have been shot but weren't; anyhow, their plans were foiled. On the 11th of November

I was practising the piano under Mama's supervision when the bells rang out for the Armistice. Papa put on his civilian clothes again. Mama's brother died, shortly after being demobilized, of Spanish influenza. But I had hardly known him, and when Mama had dried her tears, happiness returned – for me at any rate.

*

At home, nothing was ever wasted: not a crust, not a wafer of soap, not a twist of string; free tickets and opportunities for free meals were always seized with avidity. My sister and I wore our clothes until they were threadbare, and even after that. My mother never wasted a second; she would knit while she was reading; when she talked to my father or to friends she would be sewing, patching, or embroidering; when she travelled by tram or by the Métro she would crochet miles of 'tatting' with which she ornamented our petticoats. In the evenings, she did her accounts; for years, every penny that passed through her hands had been noted down in a big black ledger. I used to think that not only in my own family but everywhere time and money were so exactly measured that they had to be distributed with the greatest economy and strictness: this idea appealed to me, because I wanted to see a world free from all irregularities. Poupette and I often used to play at being explorers lost in a desert or castaways on a desert island; or, in a besieged town, we would be gallant defenders dying of starvation: we used to perform miracles of ingenuity in order to draw the maximum of profit from our most infinitesimal resources; it was one of our favourite themes in our play. Everything must be put to use: I felt I must carry out this command to the letter. In the little notebooks in which I used to write down each week a résumé of my lessons, I began to cover every page with minute script, taking care not to leave the smallest blank space anywhere. My teachers were puzzled: they asked my mother if I had a mean streak. I got over that mania fairly quickly: gratuitous economy is a contradiction in terms, and it isn't interesting or amusing. But I remained convinced that one must make use of everything, and of one's self, to the utmost. At La Grillière there were often unoccupied moments before and after meals or at the end of Mass; I would fret and fidget: 'Can't that child sit still for just one minute?' my Uncle Maurice would mutter impatiently. My parents and I used to laugh at him when he talked that way: my father and mother condemned idleness. I found it all the more reprehensible because it bored me so. Duty therefore was mixed with pleasure. That is why, at this period, my existence was such a happy one: I simply had to do just as I liked, and everyone was delighted with me.

The Cours Désir – or, to give it its full name, the Adeline Désir Institute – had boarders, day-boarders, special day-pupils, and others who, like myself, simply followed the lessons; twice a week there were the General Culture classes, which lasted for two hours; I took as extras English, the piano, and the catechism. My neophyte awe had not abated: the moment Mademoiselle entered the classroom, every second became holy. Our teachers didn't tell us anything wildly exciting; we would recite our lessons, and they would correct our exercises; but I asked for nothing more than that my existence should be publicly sanctioned by them. My merits were inscribed in a register which perpetuated their memory. I had to surpass myself all the time, or at least to equal my previous achievement. There was always a fresh start to be made; to have failed would have filled me with consternation, and victory exalted me. These glittering moments shone like beacons down the year: each day was leading me further on. I felt sorry for grown-ups whose uneventful weeks are feebly irradiated by the dullness of Sundays. To live without expecting anything seemed to me frightful.

I expected, and I was expected. I was responding ceaselessly to a necessity which spared me from asking: why am I here? Seated at Papa's desk, doing an English translation or copying out an essay, I was occupying my rightful place on earth and doing what I should be doing. The formidable array of ash-trays, ink-stands, paper-knives, pens, and pencils scattered round the pink blotting-pad played their own parts in that unalterable necessity, which informed my entire world, and the world itself. From my study armchair I listened to the harmony of the spheres.

But I did not carry out all my tasks with the same eagerness. My wish to conform had not entirely killed in me certain desires and repulsions. At La Grillière, whenever Aunt Hélène served pumpkin pie, I would rush from the table in tears rather than touch it; neither threats nor thumpings could persuade me to eat cheese. I was obstinate in other, more important matters. I couldn't tolerate being bored: my boredom soon turned to real distress of mind; that is why, as I have remarked, I detested idleness; but tasks which paralysed my body without occupying my mind left me with the same feeling of emptiness. Grandmama succeeded in interesting me in tapestry work and embroidery; it was a question of accommodating the wool or cotton to a printed pattern on canvas, and this task used to keep me fairly well occupied; I cobbled up a dozen antimacassars and covered one of the chairs in my room with hideous tapestry. But I always made a mess of hems, 'whipped' seams, darning and mending, scallops, buttonhole and cross-stitch, raised satin-stitch and knotted-bar work. In order to stimulate my interest, Mademoiselle Fayet told me a little story: an eligible young man was being regaled with the list of a certain young lady's talents; she was a musician, and well-read, and gifted with hundreds of attractive qualities. 'Can she sew?' he inquired. Saving the respect I owed to my teacher, I found it quite ridiculous that I should be expected to conform to the requirements of an unknown young man. My skill with the needle did not improve. In every aspect of learning and culture, the more eager I was to learn, the more tiresome did I find the mechanics of study. When I opened my English text books, I seemed to be setting out on a journey, and I studied them with passionate absorption; but I could never take the trouble to acquire a correct accent. I enjoyed sight-reading a sonatina: but I could never bring myself to learn one by heart; my scales and Czerny exercises were always a scramble, so that in the pianoforte examinations I was always near the bottom. In solfeggio and musical theory I was hopeless: I sang either sharp or flat, and was a wretched failure in musical dictation. My handwriting was so shapeless that I had to have private lessons, which did not make any great improvement. If I had to trace the course of a river or the outline of a country, I was so clumsy that I was absolved from all blame for the messes I made. This characteristic was to remain with me all my life. I bungled all practical jobs and I was never any good at work requiring finicky precision.

It was not without some vexation that I became aware of my deficiencies; I should have liked to excel in everything. But they were too deeply rooted in my nature to be amenable to ephemeral spurts of will-power. As soon as I was able to think for myself, I found myself possessed of infinite power, and yet circumscribed by absurd limitations. When I was asleep, the earth disappeared; it had need of me in order to be seen, discovered, and understood; I was, I felt, charged with a mission which I carried out with pride; but I did not assume that my imperfect body could have any part in it: on the contrary, as soon as my physical activities intervened, things tended to go wrong. Doubtless in order to express the full truth of any piece of music it was necessary to play it 'with expression', and not to massacre it: but in any case, it would never, under *my* stumbling fingers, attain the fullest pitch of perfection, so why should I wear myself out trying to master it? Why should I want to develop capabilities which would always remain fatally limited, and have only a relative importance in my life? The modest results of so much effort repelled me, for I had only to look, to read, and to think in order to reach the absolute. When I translated an English text, I discovered in it the one, complete, universal meaning, whereas the *th* sound was only one modulation among millions of others in my mouth: I really couldn't bother my head about *that*. The urgency of my self-appointed task debarred me from wasting time on such futilities: there were so many things to be learned! I had to call the past to life, and illuminate every corner of the five continents, descend to the centre of the earth and make the circuit of the moon and stars. When I was compelled to do tiresome exercises, my mind cried out at the barren waste of my gifts, and I used to think that I was losing precious time. I was frustrated and filled with guilt: I got through such impositions as quickly as possible, bashing them out on the rocks of my impatience.

I think I must also have considered the task of the executant to be a very minor one, because it seemed to me to be concerned only with appearances. Fundamentally I believed that the essential truth of a sonata could be discovered in the notes on the stave, as immutable and eternal as the truth of *Macbeth* in a printed book. The task of the creator was something quite superior. I thought it was wonderful that you could bring into the world something real, something new. There was only one region in which I could venture my creative talent: literature. Drawing was no more than copying, and I didn't care for art, all the more so because I was not very good at it: I reacted to the general appearance of an object without paying much attention to its details; I could never succeed in drawing even the simplest flower. In compensation, I knew how to use language, and as it expressed the essence of things, it illuminated them for me. I had a spontaneous urge to turn everything that happened to me into a story: I used to talk freely, and loved to write. If I was describing in words an episode in my life, I felt that it was being rescued from oblivion, that it would interest others, and so be saved from extinction. I loved to make up stories, too: when they were inspired by my own experience, they seemed to justify it; in one sense they were of no use at all, but they were unique and irreplaceable, they *existed*, and I was proud of having snatched them out of nothingness. So I took a great deal of trouble over my French compositions: I even copied some of them into my 'book of gold'.

When July came round, the prospect of the long holiday in the country enabled me to say good-bye to the Cours Désir without too much regret. But when we returned to Paris I would feverishly await the first day of school. I would sit in the leather armchair beside the black pear-wood bookcase, and make the spines of my new books crack gently as I opened them for the first time; I would sniff their special smell, look at the pictures and the maps, skim through a page of history: I used to wish that with the wave of a wand I could make all the characters and all the landscapes hidden in the shade of the black and white pages spring to life. The power I had over them intoxicated me as much as their silent presence.

Apart from my school work, reading was the great passion of my life. Mama now got her books from the Bibliothèque Cardinale, in the place Saint-Sulpice. A table loaded with reviews and magazines occupied the centre of a large room beyond which extended corridors lined with books: the clients had the right to wander where they pleased. I experienced one of the greatest joys I ever knew as a child the day when Mama announced that she was taking out a personal subscription for me. I stood with arms akimbo in front of the section marked 'Works suitable for Children', in which there were hundreds of volumes. 'All this belongs to me!' I said to myself, bewildered by such a profusion of riches. The reality surpassed my wildest dreams: before me lay the entry to a rich and unknown paradise. I took a catalogue home with me: assisted by my parents, I made a selection from the works marked 'J' for juvenile, and I drew up lists of the books I required; each week I hovered, with delicious hesitations, over a multiplicity of desirable choices. In addition, my mother sometimes took me to a little bookshop near the school, to buy English novels; they were a 'good buy', because it took me a long time to get through them.

I took great pleasure in lifting, with the aid of a dictionary, the dark veil of foreign words; descriptions and stories retained a certain mystery; I used to find them more charming and more profound than if I had merely read them in French.

That year my father made me a present of *L'Abbé Constantin* in a beautiful edition illustrated by Madeleine Lemaire. One Sunday he took me to the Comédie Française to see the play which had been adapted from the novel. For the very first time I was admitted to a real theatre, one that was frequented by grown-ups: quivering with excitement, I took my place on the red plush seat and listened to the actors with religious attention: I was rather disappointed in them; Cécile Sorel's dyed hair and affected manner of speaking did not correspond at all to the image I had in my mind of Madame Scott. Two or three years later, weeping at *Cyrano*, sobbing over *L'Aiglon*, vibrating to *Britannicus*, I was to give myself up body and soul to the magic of the stage. But on that first afternoon what delighted me was less the performance than being taken out by my father; to be attending, alone with him, the performance of a play he had chosen specially for me, created such a feeling of intimacy between us that for a few hours I had the intoxicating impression that he belonged to me alone.

About this period, my feelings for my father took a loftier turn. He was often worried. He said that Foch had let himself be talked into giving way to the Germans. He talked a lot about the Bolsheviks, whose name dangerously resembled that of the Boche and who had, he said, ruined him; he was so pessimistic about the future that he didn't dare set up in business as a lawyer again. He accepted the post of co-director in my grandfather's factory. He had already suffered many disappointments; as a consequence of my grandfather's bankruptcy, my mother's dowry had never been paid over to him. Now, his career finished, the Russian stocks which had brought in the larger part of his income having slumped disastrously, he regretfully placed himself in the category of the 'newly-poor'. He nevertheless managed to preserve a good-tempered equanimity, and would rather seek the reason for his misfortunes in the state of the world than waste his time in self-pity: I was moved by the spectacle of a man of such superior attainments adapting himself so simply to the shabbiness of his new position in the world. I saw him one day playing, in a charity show, the leading part in *La Paix chez soi* by Courteline. He played the role of a hard-up newspaper hack, beset by money troubles and by the extravagant caprices of a child-wife; the latter bore no resemblance to Mama; nevertheless, I identified my father with the character he played; he gave his interpretation a disillusioned irony which moved me almost to tears; there was melancholy in his resignation: the hidden wound I sensed in him added to his stature. I adored him, with a romantic fervour.

On fine summer evenings he would sometimes take us for a walk after dinner in the Luxembourg Gardens; we would have ices on the terrace of a café in the place Médicis, then we would stroll back through the gardens as the bugle call warned us that the gates were about to be closed. I envied the Senators their nocturnal reveries in the deserted avenues. My daily routine was as inalterable as the rhythm of the seasons: the slightest deviation transported me almost into the realms of fantasy. To be walking in the tranquil twilight, at a time when Mama was usually bolting the front door for the night, was as startling and as poetical as finding a hawthorn in flower in the middle of winter.

There was one quite extraordinary evening when we were drinking hot chocolate on the terrace of the Café Prévost, near the offices of *Le Matin*. An electric sign on the top of the building was giving the progress of the fight between Dempsey and Carpentier in New York. The street corners were black with people. When Carpentier was knocked out, men and women burst into tears; I went home filled with pride at having been the witness of such a great event. But I was no less happy when we spent the evening at home in Papa's cosy study while he read us *Le Voyage de Monsieur Perrichon*; or we would each read our own book. I would look at my parents and my sister, and feel my heart flood with affectionate warmth. 'Us four!' I would say to myself, in silent rapture. And I would think: 'How happy we are.'

There was only one thing that sometimes cast a shadow on this happy state: I knew that one day this period in my life would come to an end. It seemed unbelievable. When you have loved your parents for twenty years or so, how can you leave them to live with a stranger, without dying of unhappiness? And how, when you have done without him for twenty years, can you up and love a man who is nothing to you? I asked Papa about it. 'A husband is something different,' he replied, with a little smile that did nothing to enlighten me. I always looked upon marriage with disfavour.

I didn't look upon it as servitude, for my own mother had nothing of the slave about her; it was the promiscuity of marriage that repelled me. 'At night when you go to bed, you won't be able to have a good cry in peace!' I would tell myself in horror. I don't know if my happiness was broken by fits of sadness, or whether I used to weep in the night for the sheer pleasure of it; I rather think that my tears were a borderline case: if I had forced myself to restrain them, I should have been denying myself that minimum of personal liberty which I needed so badly. All day long, I felt that people's eyes were upon me; I liked and even loved the people around me, but when I went to bed at night I felt a sharp sense of relief at the idea of being able to live at least for a little while without being watched by others; then I could talk to myself, remember things, allow my emotions a free rein and hearken to those tender inner promptings which are stifled by the presence of grown-ups. I should have felt it quite unbearable to be deprived of this respite. I needed to escape at least for a few moments from all parental solicitude and talk quietly to myself without interruptions from anyone.

*

I was very pious; I made my confession twice a month to Abbé Martin, received Holy Communion three times a week and every morning read a chapter of *The Imitation of Christ*; between classes, I would slip into the school chapel and, with my head in my hands, I would offer up lengthy prayers; often in the course of the day I would lift up my soul to my Maker. I was no longer very interested in the Infant Jesus, but I adored Christ to distraction. As supplements to the Gospels, I had read disturbing novels of which He was the hero, and it was now with the eyes of a lover that I gazed upon His grave, tender, handsome face; I would follow, across hills covered with olive groves, the shining hem of His snow-white robe, bathe His naked feet with my tears; and He would smile down upon me as He had smiled upon the Magdalen. When I had had my fill of clasping His knees and sobbing on His blood-stained corpse, I would allow Him to ascend into heaven. There He became one with that more mysterious Being to whom I owed my existence on earth, and whose throne of glory would one day, and for ever, fill my eyes with a celestial radiance.

[73]

How comforting to know that He was there! I had been told that He cherished every single one of His creatures as if each were the one and only; His eye was upon me every instant, and all others were excluded from our divine conversations; I would forget them all, there would be only He and I in the world, and I felt I was a necessary part of His glory: my existence, through Him, was of infinite price. There was nothing He did not know: even more definitely than in my teachers' registers my acts, my thoughts, and my excellences were inscribed in Him for eternity; my faults and errors too, of course, but these were washed so clean in the waters of repentance that they shone just as brightly as my virtues. I never tired of admiring myself in that pure mirror that was without beginning or end. My reflection, all radiant with the joy I inspired in God's heart, consoled me for all my earthly shortcomings and failures; it saved me from the indifference, from the injustice and the misunderstandings of human nature. For God was always on *my* side; if I had done wrong in any way, at the very instant that I dropped upon my knees to ask His forgiveness He breathed upon my tarnished soul and restored to it all its lustre. But usually, bathed as I was in His eternal radiance, the faults I was accused of simply melted away; His judgement was my justification. He was the supreme arbiter who found that I was always right. I loved Him with all the passion I brought to life itself.

Each year I went into retreat for several days; all day long, I would listen to my priest's instructions, attend services, tell my beads and meditate; I would remain at school for a frugal repast, and during the meal someone would read to us from the life of a saint. In the evenings, at home, my mother would respect my silent meditations. I wrote down in a special notebook the outpourings of my immortal soul and my saintly resolutions. I ardently desired to grow closer to God, but I didn't know how to go about it. My conduct left so little to be desired that I could hardly be any better than I already was; besides, I wondered if God was really concerned about my general behaviour. The majority of faults that Mama reprimanded my sister and me for were just awkward blunders or careless mistakes. Poupette was severely scolded and punished for having lost a civet-fur collar. When, fishing for shrimps in 'the English river', I fell into the water, I was overcome with panic at the thought of the telling-off I felt was in store for me; fortunately I was let off that time. But these misdemeanours had nothing to do with Sin, and I didn't feel that by steering clear of them I was making myself any more perfect. The embarrassing thing was that God forbade so many things, but never asked for anything positive apart from a few prayers or religious practices which did not change my daily course in any way. I even found it most peculiar to see people who had just received Holy Communion plunging straight away into the ordinary routine of their lives again; I did the same, but it embarrassed me. Taken all in all, it seemed to me that believers and non-believers led just the same kind of life; I became more and more convinced that there was no room for the supernatural in everyday life. And yet it was that other-worldly life that really counted: it was the only kind that mattered. It suddenly became obvious to me one morning that a Christian who was convinced of his eternal salvation ought not to attach any importance to the ephemeral things of this world. How could the majority of people go on living in the world as it was? The more I thought about it, the more I wondered at it. I decided that I, at any rate, would not follow their example: my choice was made between the finite and the infinite. 'I shall become a nun,' I told myself. The activities of sisters of charity seemed to me quite useless; the only reasonable occupation was to contemplate the glory of God to the end of my days. I would become a Carmelite. But I did not make my decision public: it would not have been taken seriously. I contented myself with the announcement that I did not intend to marry. My father smiled: 'We'll have plenty of time to think about that when you're fifteen years old.' In my heart of hearts I resented his smile. I knew that an implacable logic led me to the convent: how could you prefer having nothing to having everything?

This imaginary future provided me with a convenient alibi. For many years it allowed me to enjoy without scruple all the good things of this world.

*

My happiness used to reach its height during the two and a half months which I spent every summer in the country. My mother was always more relaxed there than in Paris; my father devoted more time to me then; and I enjoyed a vast leisure for reading and playing with my sister. I did not miss the Cours Désir: that feeling of necessity which study gave my life spilled over into the holidays My time was no longer strictly measured by the exigencies of a timetable; but its absence was largely compensated for by the immensity of the horizons which opened themselves before my curious eyes. I explored them all unaided: the mediation of grown-ups no longer interposed a barrier between the world and myself. The solitude and freedom which were only rarely mine during the course of the year were now almost boundless, and I had my fill of them. In the country all my aspirations seemed to be brought together and realized; my fidelity to the past and my taste for novelty, my love for my parents and my growing desire for independence.

At first we usually spent a few weeks at La Grillière. The castle seemed to me to be vast and very old; it had been built barely fifty years ago, but none of the objects — furniture or ornaments — that had been brought there half a century ago were ever changed or taken away. No hand ventured to sweep away the relics of the past: you could smell the odour of vanished lives. A collection of hunting horns hanging in the tiled hall, all of them made of shining copper, evoked — erroneously, I believe — the magnificence of bygone stag-hunts. In what was called the 'billiard room', which was where we usually foregathered, stuffed foxes, buzzards, and kites perpetuated this bloodthirsty tradition. There was no billiard table in the room, but it contained a monumental chimney-piece, a bookcase, always carefully locked, and a large table strewn with copies of hunting magazines; there were pedestal tables laden with yellowing photographs, sheaves of peacock feathers, pebbles, terracotta ornaments, barometers, clocks that would never go and lamps that were never lit. Apart from the dining-room, the other rooms were rarely used: there was a drawing-room, embalmed in the stink of moth balls, a smaller drawing-room, a study and a kind of office whose shutters were always closed and that served as a kind of lumber room or glory-hole. In a small box-room filled with a pungent smell of old leather lay generations of riding boots and ladies' shoes. Two stair-cases led to the upper storeys where there were corridors leading to well over a dozen rooms, most of them disused and filled with dusty bric-à-brac. I shared one of them with my sister. We slept in fourposter beds. Pictures cut out of illustrated magazines and amateurishly framed decorated the walls.

The liveliest place in the house was the kitchen, which occupied half the basement. I had my breakfast there in the mornings: *café au lait* and wholemeal bread. Through the window high in the wall you could see hens parading; guinea-fowl, dogs, and sometimes human feet passed by. I liked the massive wood of the table, the benches and the chests and cupboards. The cast-iron cooking range threw out sparks and flames. The brasses shone: there were copper pots of all sizes, cauldrons, skimming ladles, preserving pans, and warming pans; I used to love the gaiety of the glazed dishes with their paint-box colours, the variety of bowls, cups, glasses, basins, porringers, hors d'œuvre dishes, pots, jugs, and pitchers. What quantities of cooking pots, frying pans, stock pots, stewpans, *bains-marie*, cassolettes, soup tureens, meat dishes, saucepans, enamel mugs, colanders, graters, choppers, mills, mincers, moulds, and mortars – in cast-iron, earthenware, stoneware, porcelain, aluminium, and tin! Across the corridor, where turtle doves used to moan, was the dairy. Here stood great vats and pans of varnished wood and glazed earthenware, barrel-churns made of polished elm, great blocks of pattern-patted butter, piles of smooth-skinned cheeses under sheets of white muslin: all that hygienic bareness and the aroma of breast-fed babies made me take to my heels. But I liked to visit the fruit loft, where apples and pears would be ripening on wicker trays, and the cellar, with its barrels, bottles, hams, huge sausages, ropes of onions, and swags of dried mushrooms. Whatever luxury there was at La Grillière was to be found down there in the nether regions. The grounds were as dull as the upper parts of the house: not a single bed of flowers, not one garden seat, not even a sunny corner to sit and read in. Opposite the great central flight of stone steps there was a fishing stream where servants often did the household wash with a great whacking of wooden beaters; a lawn fell steeply away to an edifice even older than the château itself: the 'back place', as it was called, full of old harness and thick with spiders' webs. Three or four horses could be heard whinnying in the adjacent stables.

My uncle, my aunt, and my cousins led an existence which fitted this setting very well. Starting at six o'clock in the morning, Aunt Hélène would make a thorough inspection of all the cupboards. With so many servants at her disposal, she didn't have to do any housework; she rarely did any cooking, never sewed, and never read a book, and yet she always complained of never having a minute to herself: she never stopped poking about, from the cellars to the attic. My uncle would come downstairs about nine o'clock; he would polish his leggings in the harness-room, and then go off to saddle his horse. Madeleine would look after her pets. Robert stayed in bed. Lunch was always late. Before sitting down to table, Uncle Maurice would season the salad with meticulous care and toss it with wooden spatulas. At the beginning of the meal there would be a passionate discussion about the quality of the cantaloups; at its end, the flavours of different kinds of pears would be thoroughly compared. In between, much would be eaten and but few words spoken. Then my aunt would go back to her cupboard inspection, and my uncle would stump off to the stables, laying about him with his hunting-crop. Madeleine would join Poupette and me in a game. Robert usually did nothing at all; sometimes he would go trout-fishing; in September he would hunt a little. A few elderly, cut-rate tutors had tried to din into him the rudiments of arithmetic and spelling. Then an oldish lady with yellowed skin devoted herself to Madeleine, who was less of a handful and the only one in the family ever to read a book. She used to gorge herself on novels, and had dreams of being very beautiful and having lots of loving admirers. In the evenings, everyone would gather in the billiard room; Papa would ask for the lamps to be lit. My aunt would cry out that it was still quite light, but in the end would give way and have a small oil lamp placed on the centre table. After dinner, we would still hear her trotting about in the dark corridors. Robert and my uncle, with glazed eyes, would sit rigidly in their armchairs waiting silently for bed-time. Very occasionally one of them would pick up a sporting magazine and flick desultorily through it for a few minutes. The next morning, the same kind of day would begin all over again, except on Sundays, when, after all the doors had been locked and barred, we would all climb into the dog-cart and go to hear Mass at Saint-Germain-les-Belles. My aunt never had visitors, and she never paid visits herself.

This way of life suited me very well. I used to spend the best part of my days on the croquet lawn with my sister and cousin, and the rest of the time I would read. Sometimes we would all three of us set off to look for mushrooms in the chestnut plantations. We ignored the insipid meadow varieties, the tawny *grisettes* and the tough, crinkled *chanterelles* as well as the clumps of wild chicory: we studiously avoided the lurid Devil's Boletus with its red-veined stem and the sham flap-mushroom which we recognized by their dull colour and their rigid look. We despised mature *ceps* whose flesh was beginning to go soft and produce greenish whiskers. We only gathered young ones with nicely curved stalks and caps covered with a fine nigger-brown or blueish nap. Rummaging in the moss and parting fans of bracken and ferns, we would kick to pieces the puff-balls, which when they burst gave off clouds of filthy dust. Sometimes we would go with Robert to fish for fresh-water crayfish; or in order to get food for Madeleine's peacocks we would dig up ant-hills and wheel away barrow-loads of whiteish eggs.

The big waggonette was no longer allowed to leave the coach-house. In order to get to Meyrignac we had to spend an hour sitting in a little train that stopped every ten minutes, pile our luggage on a donkey cart and then walk over the fields to the house: I couldn't imagine any more agreeable place on earth to live. In one sense, our life there was an austere one. Poupette and I had no croquet or any other kind of outdoor amusement; my mother had refused, I don't know why, to let my father buy us bicycles. We couldn't swim, and besides the River Vézère was some distance away. If occasionally we heard the sound of a motor-car coming up the drive, Mama and Aunt Marguerite would hurriedly leave the garden to go and tidy themselves up; there were never any children among the visitors. But I could do without frivolous distractions. Reading, walking, and the games I made up with my sister were all I wanted.

The chief of my pleasures was to rise early in the morning and observe the awakening of nature; with a book in my hand, I would steal out of the sleeping house and quietly unlatch the garden gate: it was impossible to sit down on the grass, which would be all white with hoar-frost; I would walk along the drive, beside the meadow planted with specially chosen trees that my grandpapa called 'the landscape garden'; I would read a little from time to time, enjoying the feeling of the sharp air softening against my cheeks; the thin crust of rime would be melting on the ground; the purple beech, the blue cedars, and the silvery poplars would be sparkling with the primal freshness of the first morning in Eden: and I was the only one awake to the beauty of the earth and the glory of God, which mingled agreeably deep inside me with a dream of a bowl of hot chocolate and warm buttered toast. When

[79]

the bees began to hum and the green shutters were opened on the sunny fragrance of wistaria, I felt I was already sharing a secret past with the day that for the others was only just beginning. After the round of family greetings and breakfast, I would sit at a metal table under the catalpa tree and get on with my 'holiday tasks'. I liked those moments when, pretending to be busied with some easy exercise, I let my ear be beguiled by the sounds of summer: the fizzing of wasps, the chattering of guinea-fowls, the peacocks' strangulated cry, the whisperings of leaves; the scent of phlox mingled with the aromas of caramel and coffee and chocolate that came wafting over to me from the kitchen; rings of sunlight would be dancing over my exercise book. I felt I was one with everything: we all had our place just here, now, and for ever.

Grandpapa would come down about noon, his chin freshly shaven between his white side-whiskers. He would read the *Écho de Paris* until lunch-time. He liked good solid food: partridge with crisply steamed cabbage, chicken vol-au-vent, duck stuffed with olives, saddle of hare, pâtés, flans, tarts, marzipans, shapes, and trifles. While the ancient horned gramophone played a selection from *Les Cloches de Corneville*, he would be joking with Papa. They would chaff each other all through the meal, laughing, declaiming, singing even; again and again they would trot out the memories, anecdotes, quotations, witticisms, and nonsense-talk of the family folk-lore. After that, I usually went walking with my sister; scratching our legs on gorse and our arms on brambles, we would explore for miles around the chestnut groves, the fields, the moors. We made great discoveries: ponds; a waterfall; at the centre of a lonely heath, blocks of grey granite which we climbed to get a glimpse of the blue line of the Monédières. As we rambled along, we would sample the hazelnuts and brambleberries in the hedges, arbutus berries, cornel berries, and the acid berries of the berberis; we had bites out of apples from every orchard; but we were careful not to suck the milk of the wild-spurge or to touch those handsome bright-red spikes which are the proud bearers of the enigmatic name 'Solomon's Seal'. Drowsy with the scent of freshly mown hay, with the fragrance of honeysuckle and the smell of buckwheat in flower, we would lie down on the warm moss or the grass and read. I also sometimes used to spend the afternoons on my own in the landscape garden, when I would read and read to my heart's content as I watched the trees' shadows lengthening and the butter-flies tumbling over and over one another.

On rainy days, we stayed in the house. But while I chafed at restraints imposed by other people's wills, I felt no resentment at those inflicted on me by things like the weather. I liked being in the drawing-room with its armchairs upholstered in green plush, its french windows draped with yellowed muslin; on the marble chimneypiece, on the occasional tables and sideboards, quantities of dead things were slowly mouldering away; the stuffed birds were moulting, the everlasting dried flowers were crumbling to dust and the sea-shells were turning a dull, lifeless grey. I would climb on a stool and ransack the library shelves; there I could always find some novel by Fennimore Cooper or some *Pictorial Magazine*, its pages badly foxed, which I had not seen before. There was a piano, several of whose notes did not play or were completely out of tune; Mama would prop up on the music-stand the vocal score of the *Grand Mogul* or the *Noces de Jeannette* and warble grandfather's favourite airs: he would join in all the choruses with us.

When the weather was fine, I would go for a walk in the gardens after dinner; with the Milky Way overhead, I would smell the heart-stirring fragrance of the magnolias and keep an eye open for shooting stars. Then, a lighted candle in my hand, I would go up to bed. I had a room to myself; it gave on to the yard, overlooking the wood-shed, the laundry, and the coach-house which sheltered a victoria and a berlin, as out-of-date to me as the carriages of olden times. I was charmed by the smallness of the room: there was a bed, a chest of drawers, and, standing on a sort of locker, the wash bowl and water jug. It was a cell, made to my own measure, like the little niche under Papa's desk where I once used to hide myself away. Although my sister's company did not weigh upon me in any way, solitude exalted me. When I was going through one of my saintly periods, a room to myself allowed me to enjoy the mortifying bliss of sleeping on the bare floor. But above all, before going to bed I would stand a long time at my casement, and often I would rise in the middle of the night to look out upon the night breathing softly in its sleep. I would lean out and plunge my hands in the fresh leaves of a clump of cherry laurels; the water from the spring would be gurgling over a mossy stone; from time to time a cow would kick her hoof against the door of the byre: I could almost smell the odour of straw and hay. Monotonous and dogged as the beat of the heart would sound the stridulations of a grasshopper; against the infinite silence and the sky's infinities I used to feel that the earth itself was echoing that voice within me which kept on whispering: 'Here I am.' My heart oscillated between its living warmth and the frigid blazing of the stars. There was God up there, and He was watching me; under the breeze's soft caress I was intoxicated by the heady perfumes of the night, by this celebration in my blood that brought eternity within my reach.

*

There was one phrase grown-ups were always using: 'It's not proper!' I was rather uncertain as to what the true significance of this expression could be. At first I had taken it to have a scatological connotation. In Madame de Ségur's *Les Vacances*, one of the characters told a story about a ghost, a nightmare ending in soiled sheets which shocked me as much as it did my parents. It was not proper. At that period of my life I associated indecency with the baser bodily functions; then I learnt that the body as a whole was vulgar and offensive: it must be concealed; to allow one's underclothes to be seen, or one's naked flesh – except in certain well-defined zones – was a gross impropriety. Certain vestimentary details and certain attitudes were as reprehensible as exhibitionist indiscretions. These prohibitions were aimed particularly at the female species; a real 'lady' ought not to show too much bosom, or wear short skirts, or dye her hair, or have it bobbed, or make up, or sprawl on a divan, or kiss her husband in the underground passages of the Métro: if she transgressed these rules, she was 'not a lady'. Impropriety was not altogether the same as sin, but it drew down upon the offender public obloquy that was infinitely worse than ridicule. My sister and I felt very strongly that something of importance was being concealed behind a blandly deceptive front, and in order to protect ourselves against this mysterious something, we would promptly ridicule it. In the Luxembourg Gardens, we would nudge each other if we passed a pair of lovers. Impropriety to my way of thinking was related, though only extremely vaguely, to another enigma: 'unsuitable' reading matter. Sometimes, before giving me a book to read, my mother would pin a few pages together; in Wells's *The War of the Worlds* I found a whole chapter had been placed under the ban. I never took the pins out, but I often wondered: what's it all about? It was strange. Grown-ups talked freely in front of me; I went about the world without encountering any insurmountable obstacles; and yet under this surface transparency something was hidden; what? where? In vain my troubled gaze would ransack my expanding horizons, trying to seek out the occulted zone that was not masked by any screen and that yet remained invisible.

One day as I was working at my father's desk, I noticed at my elbow a novel with a yellow paper cover: *Cosmopolis.* I was tired and quite unthinkingly, with a purely mechanical gesture, I opened it; I had no intention of reading it, but it seemed to me that even without having consciously to connect the words and make them into phrases I could, at a quick glance, discover the flavour of its secret contents. Mama was suddenly towering over me. 'What are you doing?' I stammered something. 'You *must not!*' she cried, 'you *must not touch* books that are not meant for you.' Her voice had a pleading note and in her face I could read an anxiety which convinced me more than any reprimand could have done: a terrible danger was lying in wait between the pages of *Cosmopolis*, ready to spring out at me. I promised fervently never to do such a thing again. My memory has linked this episode indissolubly with a much earlier incident: when I was very tiny, sitting in that very same armchair, I had shoved my finger in the black hole of the electric point; the shock had made me cry out with surprise and pain. While my mother was talking to me did I look at the black circle in the middle of the porcelain plug, or did I not make the connexion until later? In any case, I had the impression that any contact with the Zolas and the Bourgets in the library would subject me to an unforeseeable and thundering shock. Just like the 'live' rail in the Métro which used to fascinate me because the eye slid along its burnished surface without being able to detect the least sign of its murderous energy, old books with illegible spines filled me with trepidation because there was nothing to give me warning of their baleful influence.

During the retreat I made before making my First Communion, the man of God, in order to put us on our guard against the temptations of curiosity, told us a story which only succeeded in stimulating my own inquisitiveness. A little girl, remarkably precocious and intelligent, but brought up by parents who had not been sufficiently vigilant, had one day come to make her confession: she had read so many bad books that she had lost her faith and grown utterly weary of existence. He tried to give her hope again, but she was too seriously contaminated: a few days later, he heard that she had committed suicide. My first reaction was a wave of jealous admiration for this little girl, only a year older than myself, who had known so much more than I. Then I found myself bogged down by perplexities. Faith was my insurance against hell: I dreaded it too much ever to commit a mortal sin; but if you ceased to believe, then all the infernal regions lay gaping at your feet: could such a terrible misfortune happen to you if you had not deserved it? The little girl who had committed suicide had not even been guilty of the sin of disobedience; she had simply exposed herself very carelessly to obscure forces that had played havoc with her tender soul; why had God not come to her aid? And how was it that words manipulated by mortal men were able to destroy the manifestations of the supernatural? The thing I understood least of all was that knowledge led to despair and damnation. Our spiritual mentor had not said that those bad books had given a false picture of life: if that had been the case, he could easily have exposed their falsehood; the tragedy of the little girl whom he had failed to bring to salvation was that she had made a premature discovery of the true nature of reality. Well, anyhow, I thought, I shall discover it myself one day, and it isn't going to kill *me*: the idea that there was a certain age when knowledge of the truth could prove fatal I found offensive to common sense.

Apparently it wasn't age alone that counted: Aunt Lili could only read books written 'for young ladies'; Mama had snatched a copy of *Claudine at School* out of the hands of Louise, and that evening, commenting on the incident to Papa, she had said: 'Fortunately she hadn't the least idea what it was about!' Marriage was the antidote which allowed you to partake freely and without danger of the sometimes highly suspect fruit of the Tree of Knowledge: but I simply couldn't understand why. I never dreamed of discussing these problems with my friends. One girl had been expelled from the school because she had had 'evil conversations' with some of the other girls; I took a virtuous pride in the thought that if she had tried to draw me into one of her infamous *tête-à-têtes* I should have turned a deaf ear.

Yet my cousin Madeleine read whatever she liked. Papa had been highly indignant one day when he had caught her, at the age of twelve, deep in *The Three Musketeers*: Aunt Hélène had merely shrugged her shoulders helplessly. Gorged with novels that were considered 'too old' for her, Madeleine did not appear to be contemplating suicide. In 1919, my parents found in the rue de Rennes a less expensive apartment than the one in the boulevard Montparnasse, and left my sister and me at La Grillière during the first fortnight in October while they moved house. We were alone with Madeleine from morning to night, and one day, quite out of the blue, after a game of croquet, I asked her what the mystery of all these forbidden books could be; I didn't wish for a revelation of their contents; I simply wanted to know why they were forbidden us.

We had laid aside our mallets and the three of us were reclining in the grass at the edge of the croquet-lawn. Madeleine hesitated at first, then giggled, and began to enlighten us. She pointed out to us that her pet dog had two balls between his hind legs. 'Well,' she went on, '*men* have them, too!' In a collection of stories she had read a certain very melodramatic tale, in which a marchioness who was jealous of her husband had his 'balls' cut off while he was asleep. This caused his death. I found this anatomy lesson was quite beside the point, and without realizing that I was indulging in an 'evil conversation' I urged Madeleine to be more forthcoming: what else was there? She then explained the meanings of the words 'lover' and 'mistress': if Mama and Uncle Maurice loved one another, she would be his mistress, and he would be her lover. She did not make clear what was meant by 'love', and so her incongruous hypothesis, while disconcerting me, did not enlighten me in any way. I only began to take an interest in what she was saying when she tried to explain to me how children were born; the intervention of the divine will in this phenomenon had long ago ceased to satisfy me, because I knew that, miracles apart, God's influence could work only through natural causality: the things of this world required a worldly explanation. Madeleine confirmed all my suspicions: babies are formed in their mother's womb; a few days earlier, while she was skinning a rabbit, the cook had found six little rabbits inside it. When a woman is expecting a baby, she is said to be pregnant, and her stomach swells up. Madeleine did not give us any other details. She went on to announce, however, that within a year or two certain things would happen inside my body; I should have my 'whites' and then I would bleed every month and I should have to wear some kind of bandage between my thighs. I asked if these emissions would be called my 'reds', and my sister was worried about how she would manage with all those bandages: how would she make water? These questions exasperated Madeleine; she said we were a couple of ninnies, lifted her shoulders in an expressive despair, and went off to feed her chickens. Perhaps she sensed our childish unpreparedness and considered us unworthy of a more elaborate initiation. I was dumbfounded by it all; I had imagined that the secrets so carefully guarded by grown-ups must be of a much loftier significance. On the other hand, Madeleine's sniggeringly confidential manner was hardly in keeping with the curious triviality of her revelations; there was something not quite right, but I didn't know what. She had not attempted to explain the problem of conception upon which I meditated deeply during the next few days; having grasped that cause and effect are of necessity intimately bound up with one another, I could not accept that it was the ceremony of marriage which caused a creature of flesh and blood to grow in a woman's stomach; there must be some sort of organic function which took place between the husband and the wife. The behaviour of animals might have shed some light on the problem: I had seen a big Alsatian glued to the hind quarters of Madeleine's little fox-terrier Criquette, while Madeleine, in tears, attempted to separate them. 'Her puppies will be too big: Criquette will die!' she howled. But I did not associate these animal frolics – no more than I did those of fowls and flies – with human behaviour. The expressions 'ties of blood', 'children of the same blood', 'blood relationship', 'one's own flesh and blood', and 'blood is thicker than water' suggested to me that on the wedding-day, once and for all, a little of the husband's blood was transfused into his partner's veins; I imagined the married pair standing beside one another with the man's right wrist bound to the woman's left wrist: it would be a solemn operation presided over by the priest and a few chosen witnesses.

Although they had been rather confusing, Madeleine's bits of gossip must have disturbed us profoundly, because my sister and I then abandoned ourselves to wild verbal debaucheries. Aunt Hélène, so gentle and so little prone to moralizing, with her air of always being somewhere else, did not intimidate us at all. We started saying all sorts of things in front of her that were 'not nice' or 'not proper'. In the drawing-room with its dust-sheeted furniture she would sometimes seat herself at the piano and sing us the songs of 1900, of which she had a large collection; we always chose the most questionable ones and took great delight in carolling: '*The white breasts are lovelier by far – to my hungry mouth – than the wild strawberries of the woods – and their milk I suck . . .*' The beginning of this particular ballad intrigued us very much: was it to be interpreted literally? Do men sometimes drink the milk from women's breasts? Is it one of a 'lover's' secret rites? In any case, the lines were decidedly 'improper'. We wrote them with our fingers on steamy window panes and recited them at the tops of our voices in front of Aunt Hélène; we pestered her with 'unsuitable' questions, at the same time hinting that the grown-ups couldn't take us in any longer. I think that our disordered exuberance was in fact highly organized; we were not accustomed to clandestinity, and we wanted to warn the grown-ups that we had rumbled their secrets; but we lacked the courage and so we felt the need to let off steam in some other way: our frankness took the form of provocation. When we got back to Paris, my sister, less inhibited than myself, ventured to ask Mama if babies came out of one's navel. 'Why do you ask such silly questions?' my mother said, rather tartly. 'You know everything already.' Aunt Hélène had apparently tipped her off. Relieved at having negotiated this initial barrier we pressed Mama for more details; she gave us to understand that little babies came out of the anus, quite painlessly. She spoke in a detached tone of voice; but we were not encouraged to make further inquiries: I never again discussed these problems with her, and she never said another word to us about them.

I can't remember having pondered very long over the phenomena of pregnancy and child-birth: nor did I associate them at all with my own future; I was averse to marriage and maternity, and so I felt they did not concern me. But our so-called initiation disturbed me in another way. It had left many mysteries unexplained. What relationship was there between this serious affair, the birth of a child, and things that were 'not nice' or 'not proper'? If there were none, then why did Madeleine's tone of voice and Mama's own reticence force us to suppose there was one? It had been only at our instigation that Mama had spoken to us, and very summarily, about these things, and she had said nothing about marriage. Physiological facts are as much a part of common knowledge as the rotation of the earth: what was it prevented her from telling us about them as about everything else? On the other hand, if forbidden books contained, as my cousin had suggested, only rather comical indecencies, what great harm was there in them? I did not actually ask myself these questions, but they tormented me all the same. It must be that the body was by reason of its own nature a dangerous object when every allusion to its existence, whether serious or frivolous, seemed fraught with peril.

Assuming that something was being deliberately concealed behind the grown-ups' veil of silence, I did not charge them with making a fuss about nothing. But I had lost all my illusions as to the nature of their secret: they had no access to occult spheres where the white radiance of eternity shone brighter for them than it did for us, or where the horizon was vaster than that of my smaller world. My disillusionment served to reduce the universe and mankind to a trivial day-to-day level. I did not realize it immediately, but the prestige of grown-ups had suffered a considerable diminution in my esteem.

*

I had been taught the vanity of vanity and the futility of futility; I should have been ashamed to attach importance to dress and to preen myself in front of a looking-glass; all the same, when circumstances authorized it, I found myself looking upon my reflection not with disfavour. Despite my timidity, I aspired, as in my early infancy, to play the leading roles in life. On the day of my First Communion, I had a resounding success. I had long been familiar with the Lord's Table, and felt I could now enjoy without any pangs of conscience the profane delights of the festive occasion. My robe, lent by a cousin, was nothing extraordinary; but instead of the usual tulle head-dress, the pupils of the Cours Désir wore a wreath of roses; this detail indicated that I did not belong to the common herd of children in the parish. Abbé Martin administered the host to a very select company; moreover, I was chosen to be the one to renew in the name of all my companions the solemn vows by which we had renounced, on our christening day, the pomps and vanities and evil works of the Arch Fiend. My aunt Marguerite gave in my honour a magnificent lunch at which I, as guest of honour, importantly presided. In the afternoon there was a tea-party at home and I displayed upon the grand piano all the gifts I had received. I was fêted and congratulated, and I was very pleased with myself: I thought I was looking particularly lovely. That night it was with great regret that I laid my finery aside; I comforted myself a little by entertaining the idea of marriage for a moment or two: the day would come when, clad in white satin, in a blaze of candles and under great blasts of organ-music I would be changed once again into a queen.

The following year, I was delighted to take over the lesser role of bridesmaid. Aunt Lili was getting married. The ceremony was without ostentation; but my own get-up enchanted me. I loved the silky feel of my blue foulard dress; my hair was tied with a black velvet ribbon and I wore a sunbonnet of natural straw garlanded with poppies and corn-flowers. My escort was a good-looking boy of nineteen who talked to me as if I were a grown-up person: I was quite certain that he found me irresistible.

I began to take an interest in the sort of figure I thought I should cut in life. Besides the more serious works and adventure stories which I borrowed from the circulating library, I also read the novels in a popular series called 'La Bibliothèque de ma Fille', which had enlivened my mother's adolescence and now occupied a whole shelf in my bedroom cupboard. When I was at La Grillière, I was allowed to read *Les Veillées des chaumières* and the volumes in the 'Stella' collection which enthralled Madeleine so much: Delly, Guy Chantepleure, *La Neuvaine de Colette, Mon oncle et mon curé*: these virtuous idylls I did not find very amusing; I thought their heroines were silly, their lovers insipid; but there was one book in which I believed I had caught a glimpse of my future self: *Little Women*, by Louisa M. Alcott. The March girls were Protestants, their father was a pastor and their mother had given them as a bedside book not *The Imitation of Christ* but *The Pilgrim's Progress*: these slight differences only made the things we had in common with the March girls stand out all the more. I was moved when Meg and Jo had to put on their poor brown poplin frocks to go to a matinée at which all the other children were dressed in silk; they were taught, as I was, that a cultivated mind and moral righteousness were better than money; their modest home, like my

[89]

own, had about it – I don't know why – something quite exceptional. I identified myself passionately with Jo, the intellectual. Brusque and bony, Jo clambered up into trees when she wanted to read; she was much more tomboyish and daring than I was, but I shared her horror of sewing and housekeeping and her love of books. She wrote: in order to imitate her more completely, I composed two or three short stories. I don't know if I dreamed of reviving my old friendship with Jacques, or if, rather more vaguely, I was longing for the barrier between my own world and the world of boys to be broken down, but the relationship between Jo and Laurie touched me to the heart. Later, I had no doubt, they would marry one another; so it was possible for maturity to bring to fruition, instead of denying them, the promises made in childhood; this thought filled me with renewed hope. But the thing that delighted me most of all was the marked partiality which Louisa Alcott manifested for Jo. As I have said, I detested the sort of grown-up condescension which lumped all children under the same heading. The defects and qualities which authors gave their young heroes seemed usually to be inconsequential accidents: when they grew up they would all be good as gold: moreover it was only their personal morality that distinguished them one from the other, never their intelligence; it was almost as if from this point of view their age had made them all equal. But in *Little Women* Jo was superior to her sisters, who were either more virtuous or more beautiful than herself, because of her passion for knowledge and the vigour of her thought; her superiority was as outstanding as that of certain adults, and guaranteed that she would have an unusual life: she was marked by fate. I, too, felt I was entitled to consider my taste for reading and my scholastic successes as tokens of a personal superiority which would be borne out by the future. I became in my own eyes a character out of a novel. I invented all kinds of romantic intrigues that were full of obstacles and setbacks for the heroine. One afternoon I was playing croquet with Poupette, Jeanne, and Madeleine. We were wearing beige pinafores with red scallops and embroidered with cherries. The clumps of laurel were shining in the sun, and the earth smelt good. Suddenly I was struck motionless: I was living through the first chapter of a novel in which I was the heroine; she was still almost a child, but we, too, were growing up. I decided that my sister and my cousins, who were prettier, more graceful, and altogether nicer than myself would be more popular than I; they would find husbands, but not I. I should feel no bitterness about it; people would be right to prefer them to me; but something would happen which would exalt me beyond all personal preference; I did not know under what form, or by whom I should be recognized for what I was. I imagined that already there was someone watching the croquet lawn and the four little girls in their beige pinafores: the gaze rested on me and a voice murmured: '*She* is not as other girls.' It was utterly ridiculous to compare me with a sister and cousins so lacking in all pretensions. But I aspired, through them, to those higher modes of being where I should be with my equals. I was convinced that I would be, that I was already, one in a million.

But it was only rarely that I gave myself up to these proud re-vindications of my personality: the great esteem in which I was held made them unnecessary. And if sometimes I thought I was an exceptional young person, I no longer looked upon myself as unique. Henceforward my self-sufficiency was tempered by feelings inspired by someone else outside my family. I had had the good fortune to find a friend.

*

The day I entered the fourth-first form – I was then rising ten – the seat next to mine was occupied by a new girl: she was small, dark, thin-faced, with short hair. While we waited for Mademoiselle to come in, and when the class was over, we talked together. She was called Elizabeth Mabille, and she was the same age as myself. Her schooling, begun with a governess, had been interrupted by a serious accident: in the country, while roasting some potatoes out in the open, her dress had caught fire; third-degree burns on her thighs had made her scream with agony for night after night; she had had to remain lying down for a whole year; under her pleated skirt, her flesh was still puffed up. Nothing as important as that had ever happened to me; she at once seemed to me a very finished person. The manner in which she spoke to the teachers astounded me; her natural inflexions contrasted strongly with the stereotyped expressionless voices of the rest of the pupils. Her conquest of me was complete when, a few days later, she mimicked Mademoiselle Bodet to perfection; everything she had to say was either interesting or amusing.

[91]

Despite certain gaps in her knowledge due to enforced inactivity, Elizabeth soon became one of the foremost in the class; I only just managed to beat her at composition. Our friendly rivalry pleased our teachers: they encouraged our association. At the musical and dramatic performance which was given every year round about Christmas, we played in a sketch. I, in a pink dress, my hair all in ringlets, impersonated Madame de Sévigné as a little girl; Elizabeth took the part of a high-spirited boy cousin; her young man's costume suited her, and she enchanted the audience with her vivacity and ease. The rehearsals, our repeated conversations in the glow of the footlights drew us closer and closer together; from then on we were called 'the two inseparables'.

My father and mother had long discussions about the different branches of various families they had heard of called Mabille; they decided that there was some vague connexion between Elizabeth's parents and themselves. Her father was a railway engineer, and held a very high post; her mother, *née* Larivière, belonged to a dynasty of militant Catholics; she had nine children and was an active worker for charity. She sometimes put in an appearance at our school in the rue Jacob. She was a handsome woman of about forty, dark-haired, with flashing eyes and a studied smile, who wore a black velvet ribbon adorned with an old-fashioned piece of jewellery round her neck. She softened her regal bearing with a deliberate amiability of manner. She completely won Mama over by addressing her as '*petite madame*' (my dear lady) and by telling her that she could easily have mistaken her for my elder sister. Elizabeth and I were allowed to go and play in each other's homes.

On my first visit to her home in the rue de Varennes my sister went with me and we were both scared out of our wits. Elizabeth – who was known in the family circle as Zaza – had an elder sister, a grown-up brother, six brothers and sisters younger than herself, and a whole horde of cousins and friends. They would run and jump about, clamber on the tables, overturn the furniture and shout all the time at the tops of their voices. At the end of the afternoon, Madame Mabille entered the drawing-room, picked up a fallen chair and smilingly wiped perspiring brows; I was astonished at her indifference to bumps and bruises, stained carpets and chair covers and smashed plates; she never got cross. I didn't care much for those wild games, and often Zaza too grew tired of them. We would take refuge in Monsieur Mabille's study, and, far away from the tumult, we would talk. This was a novel pleasure for me. My parents used to talk to me, and I used to talk to them, but we never talked together; there was not sufficient distance between my sister and myself to encourage discussion. But with Zaza I had real conversations, like the ones Papa had in the evenings with Mama. We would talk about our school work, our reading, our common friends, our teachers, and about what we knew of the world: we never talked about ourselves. We never exchanged girlish confidences. We did not allow ourselves any kind of familiarity. We addressed each other formally as '*vous*' (never '*tu*') and, excepting at the ends of letters, we did not give each other kisses.

Zaza, like myself, liked books and studying; in addition, she was endowed with a host of talents to which I could lay no claim. Sometimes when I called at the rue de Varennes I would find her busy making shortbread or caramels; or she would spike on a knitting-needle quarters of orange, a few dates, and some prunes, and immerse the lot in a saucepan full of a syrupy concoction smelling of warm vinegar: her imitation fruits looked just as delicious as those made by a real confectioner. Then she used to hectograph a dozen or so copies of a *Family Chronicle* which she edited and produced herself each week for the benefit of grandmothers, uncles, and aunts who lived outside Paris. I admired, as much as the liveliness of her tales, her skill in making an object which resembled very closely a real newspaper. She took a few piano lessons with me, but very soon became much more proficient and moved up into a higher grade. Puny-armed and skinny-legged, she nevertheless was able to perform all sorts of contortions; when the first fine days of spring came along, Madame Mabille would take us out to a grassy, wildflower suburb – I believe it was Nanterre – and Zaza would run into a field and do the cartwheel, the splits, the crab, and all kinds of other tricks; she would climb trees and hang down from branches by her heels. In everything she did, she displayed an easy mastery which always amazed me. At the age of ten she would walk about the streets on her own; at the Cours Désir she showed no signs of my own awkwardness of manner; she would talk to the ladies of the establishment in a polite but nonchalant way, almost as if she were their equal. One year at a music recital she did something while she was playing the piano which was very nearly scandalous. The hall was packed. In the front rows were the pupils in their best frocks, curled and ringleted and beribboned, who were awaiting their turn to show off their talents. Behind them sat the teachers and tutors in stiff black silk bodices, wearing white gloves. At the back of the hall were seated the parents and their guests. Zaza, resplendent in blue taffeta, played a piece which her mother thought was too difficult for her; she always had to scramble through a few of the bars: but this time she played it perfectly, and, casting a triumphant glance at Madame Mabille, put out her *tongue* at her! All the little girls' ringlets trembled with apprehension and the teachers' faces froze into disapproving masks. But when Zaza came down from the platform her mother gave her such a light-hearted kiss that no one dare reprimand her. For me this exploit surrounded her with a halo of glory. Although I was subject to laws, to conventional behaviour, to prejudice, I nevertheless liked anything novel, sincere, and spontaneous. I was completely won over by Zaza's vivacity and independence of spirit.

I did not immediately consider what place this friendship had in my life; I was still not much cleverer than I was as a baby at realizing what was going on inside me. I had been brought up to equate appearances with reality; I had not learned to examine what was concealed behind conventions of speech and action. It went without saying that I had the tenderest affection for all the members of my family, including even my most distant cousins. For my parents and sister I felt love, a word that covered everything. Nuances and fluctuations of feeling had no claim to existence in my world. Zaza was my best friend: and that was all. In a well-regulated human heart friendship occupies an honourable position, but it has neither the mysterious splendour of love, nor the sacred dignity of filial devotion. And I never called this hierarchy of the emotions into question.

*

That year, as in all other years, the month of October brought with it the exciting prospect of the return to school. The new books cracked when I opened them, and smelt just as good; seated in the leather armchair, I gloated over what the future had in store for me.

None of my expectations were realized. In the Luxembourg Gardens there were the bonfire smells and the yellowing leaves of autumn: they failed to move me; the blue of heaven had been dimmed. The classes bored me; I learnt my lessons and did my homework joylessly, and pushed my way sullenly through the front door of the Cours Désir. It was my own past coming to life again, and yet I did not recognize it: it had lost all its radiant colours; my life was dull and monotonous. I had everything, yet my hands were empty. I was walking along the boulevard Raspail with Mama and I suddenly asked myself the agonizing question: 'What is happening to me? Is this what my life is to be? Nothing more? And will it always be like this, always?' The idea of living through an infinity of days, weeks, months, and years that were void of hope completely took my breath away: it was as if, without any warning, the whole world had died. But I was unable to give a name to this distress either.

For ten to fifteen days I dragged myself somehow, on legs that seemed as weak as water, from hour to hour, from day to day.

One afternoon I was taking my things off in the cloakroom at school when Zaza came up to me. We began to talk, to relate various things that had happened to us, and to comment on them; my tongue was suddenly loosened, and a thousand bright suns began blazing in my breast; radiant with happiness, I told myself: 'That's what was wrong; I needed Zaza!' So total had been my ignorance of the workings of the heart that I hadn't thought of telling myself: 'I miss her.' I needed her presence to realize how much I needed her. This was a blinding revelation. All at once, conventions, routines, and the careful categorizing of emotions were swept away and I was overwhelmed by a flood of feeling that had no place in any code. I allowed myself to be uplifted by that wave of joy which went on mounting inside me, as violent and fresh as a waterfalling cataract, as naked, beautiful, and bare as a granite cliff. A few days later, arriving at school in good time, I looked in stupefaction at Zaza's empty seat. 'What if she were never to sit there again, what if she were to die, then what would happen to me?' It was rather frightening: she came and went unconcernedly in my life, and all my happiness, my very existence, lay in her hands. I imagined Madame Gontran coming in, her long black skirts sweeping the floor, and saying: 'Children, let us pray; your little companion, Elizabeth Mabille, was called away to the arms of God last night.' Well, if that were to happen, I told myself, I should die on the spot. I would slide off my seat and fall lifeless to the ground. This rationalization gave me comfort. I didn't really believe that God in His divine wisdom would take my life; neither did I really believe that I was afraid of Zaza dying. I had gone as far as to admit the extent of the dependence which my attachment to her placed upon me: I did not dare envisage all its consequences.

I didn't require Zaza to have any such definite feelings about me: it was enough to be her best friend. The admiration I felt for her did not diminish me in my own eyes. Love is not envy. I could think of nothing better in the world than being myself, and loving Zaza.

BOOK TWO

WE had moved house. Our new home, arranged more or less like the old one and with exactly the same furniture, was smaller and less comfortable. There was no bathroom, only a wash-place without running water: every day my father had to empty the heavy slop pail that stood under the wash-stand. There was no central heating; in winter, the apartment was icy cold, with the exception of the study, where Mama used to light a slow-combustion 'salamander' stove; I always did my homework there, even in summer time. The room I shared with my sister – Louise slept in the attics – was too tiny to sit about in. Instead of the spacious hall where I used to play my secret games, there was now only a corridor. Outside my bed, there wasn't a single corner I could call my own; I didn't even have a desk to put my things in. My mother often received callers in the study, and she and Papa would talk there in the evenings. I learnt to do my homework and study my lessons in a constant hum of voices. But I found it painful never to be on my own. My sister and I were filled with passionate envy of little girls who had a room of their own; ours was only a dormitory.

Louise got engaged to a slater; I came upon her one day in the kitchen sitting awkwardly on the knees of a red-headed man; she had very pale skin and he had very ruddy cheeks. Without knowing why, I felt sad; yet it was felt she had made a good match; although he was a manual worker, her husband was 'steady'. She left us. Catherine, a fresh, gay young country girl with whom I had played at Meyrignac, came to take her place; she was almost like one of my friends; but in the evenings she used to go out with the firemen from the barracks across the road: she was always 'running after men'. My mother gave her a good talking to, then sent her back home and decided to do without domestic help, for my father's business was doing badly. The boot and shoe factory was on the rocks. Thanks to the influence of a distant cousin who held a high position, my father went into 'financial advertising'; at first he worked on the *Gaulois*, then on various other newspapers; the trade bored him and brought in very little money. To make up for that he now went out in the evenings much more than formerly, to play bridge with friends or in a café; in summer he spent his Sundays at the races. Mama was often left alone. She did not complain, but she hated housework and poverty was hard for her to bear; her nerves were always on edge now. My father gradually lost his even good-temper. They never really quarrelled, but they used to shout very loudly at one another over the merest trifles, and often vented their irritation upon my sister and myself.

*

We stood staunchly by one another whenever it was a question of facing grown-up music; if one of us upset a bottle of ink, we both took the blame and claimed a common responsibility for what had happened. All the same, since I had got to know Zaza, our relationship had changed a little: my new friend's every word was law. Zaza made fun of everybody; she didn't spare Poupette, and looked upon her as a 'baby'; I followed her example. My sister became so unhappy that she tried to break away from my domination. One afternoon, we were alone together in the study; we had just had a row, and she suddenly said to me in a dramatic tone of voice: 'I have something to confess to you!' I had opened an English text book on the blotting-pad and had started to read; I barely moved my head to listen to her outburst. 'Well,' my sister began, 'I don't think I love you as much as I used to! There!' In a quiet, steady voice she went on to explain the growing indifference in her heart; I listened in silence and the tears rolled down my cheeks. She flung her arms round my neck: 'It's not true!' she cried. 'It's not true!' We kissed and hugged one another and I dried my tears. 'I didn't really believe you, you know!' I told her. And yet there had been some truth in what she had said; she was beginning to revolt against her position as the younger sister, and as I seemed to be drifting away from her she included me in her rebellion. She was in the same class as our cousin Jeanne, whom she quite liked but whose tastes she did not share; yet she was obliged to associate with Jeanne's friends; they were all silly, pretentious little girls, she hated them and was furious that they should be considered worthy of her friendship; to no avail. At the Cours Désir Poupette continued to be regarded as a mere reflection, necessarily imperfect, of her elder sister: she often felt humiliated, so she was said to be proud, and the ladies of the establishment, in the name of education, humiliated her still further. I was more advanced, and so my father took more interest in my progress: though my sister did not share the devotion I felt for him, she was hurt by this partiality. One summer, at Meyrignac, to prove that she had just as good a memory as I had, she learnt by heart a list of all Napoleon's marshals, with their names and titles; she rattled it off perfectly, and my parents only smiled. In her exasperation, she began to look upon me with a different eye: she picked on all my faults. It vexed me that she should seek, even half-heartedly, to rival, criticize, and do without me. We had always had rows, because I was brutal and she cried very easily; now she did not cry so much, but our quarrels became more and more serious: it became a question of pride; each wanted to have the last word. Yet in the end we always made it up: we needed one another. We both held the same opinion of our friends, our teachers, and the members of our family; we didn't hide anything from each other; and we still took as much pleasure in playing together. When our parents went out in the evening, we would have a spread: we would concoct a soufflé omelette which we would eat in the kitchen, then turn the flat upside-down, shouting at the tops of our voices. Now that we had to sleep in the same room, our games and conversations used to go on long after we had gone to bed.

*

That year, when we moved to the rue de Rennes, I began to have bad dreams. Had I not properly digested the revelations made by Madeleine? Only a thin partition now divided my bed from the one in which my parents slept, and sometimes I would hear my father snoring: did this promiscuity upset me? I had nightmares. A man would jump on my bed and dig his knees into my stomach until I felt I was suffocating; in desperation, I would dream that I was waking up and once again I would be crushed beneath the awful weight of my aggressor. About the same time, getting up became such a painful ordeal that when I thought about it the night before, my throat would tighten and my palms would grow damp with sweat. When I used to hear my mother's voice in the mornings I longed to fall ill, I had such horror of dragging myself out of the toils of sleep and darkness. During the day, I had dizzy spells; I became anaemic. Mama and the doctor would say: 'It's her development.' I grew to detest that word and the silent upheaval that was going on in my body. I envied 'big girls' their freedom; but I was disgusted at the thought of my chest swelling out; I had sometimes heard grown-up women urinating with the noise of a cataract; when I thought of the bladders swollen with water in their bellies, I felt the same terror as Gulliver did when the young giantesses displayed their breasts to him.

Now that the mysterious secret was out, forbidden books frightened me less than they used to; I would often let my gaze wander idly over the bits of old newspaper hanging up in the lavatory. In this way I read a fragment of a novelette in which the hero applied his burning lips to the heroine's white breasts. This kiss burned right through me; I was both hero and heroine, and watcher too; I both gave and received the kiss, and feasted my eyes upon it also. If I felt such violent excitement it was surely because my body was already ripe for it; but my daydreams were crystallized around that image; I don't know how many times I lingered over it before I fell asleep. I invented other erotic fantasies: I wonder where I could have got them from. The fact that married couples, scantily dressed, share the same bed, had not been enough to make me realize that they might embrace or caress one another: I suppose that it was my own need that made me imagine them. Because I was a prey to agonizing desires, with parched mouth, I would toss and turn in my bed, calling for a man's body to be pressed against my own, for a man's hand to stroke my flesh. Desperately I would reckon: 'Girls aren't allowed to marry until they're *fifteen*!' And even that was exceptional: I should have to wait much longer than that before I was released from my torment. It would all begin so nicely; in the warmth of the sheets, my fantasies made my heart pound deliciously with racing blood; I almost felt they were going to come true; but no, they fled away; no hand, no mouth came to soothe my itching flesh; my madapollam nightdress became a shirt of nettles. Sleep alone could deliver me from my torment. I never associated these deliriums with the idea of sin: their violence was too much for me and I felt I was the victim rather than the guilty one. Nor did I wonder if other little girls endured such sufferings. I was not in the habit of comparing myself with others.

We were staying with friends during the stifling heat of mid-July; I awoke horror-stricken one morning: I had spoiled my night-dress. I washed it, and got dressed: again I soiled my underclothes. I had forgotten Madeleine's vague prophecies, and I wondered what shameful malady I was suffering from. Worried, and feeling somehow guilty, I had to take my mother into my confidence: she explained to me that I had now become 'a big girl', and bundled me up in a very inconvenient manner. I felt a strong sense of relief when I learnt that it had happened through no fault of my own; and as always when something important happened to me, I even felt my heart swell with a sort of pride. I didn't mind too much when I heard my mother whispering about it to her friends. But that evening when we joined my father in the rue de Rennes, he jokingly made reference to my condition: I was consumed with shame. I had imagined that the monstrous regiment of women kept its blemish a secret from the male fraternity. I thought of myself in relationship to my father as a purely spiritual being: I was horrified at the thought that he suddenly considered me to be a mere organism. I felt as if I could never hold up my head again.

I was going through a difficult patch: I looked awful; my nose was turning red; on my face and the back of my neck there were pimples which I kept picking at nervously. My mother, over-worked, took little trouble with my clothes: my ill-fitting dresses accentuated my awkwardness. Embarrassed by my body, I developed phobias: for example, I couldn't bear to drink from a glass I had already drunk from. I had nervous tics: I couldn't stop shrugging my shoulders and twitching my nose. 'Don't scratch your spots; don't twitch your nose,' my father kept telling me. Not ill-naturedly, but with complete absence of tact, he would pass remarks about my complexion, my acne, my clumsiness, which only made my misery worse and aggravated my bad habits.

The rich cousin to whom my father owed his position organized a party for his children and their friends. He composed a revue in verse. My sister was chosen to introduce the items. In a dress of blue tulle spangled with stars, and with her beautiful long hair hanging down her back, she played the Queen of the Night to per-fection. After a poetic dialogue with Pierrot Lunaire, she declaimed rhymed couplets to introduce the young guests who paraded on a

platform in their fancy costumes. Disguised as a Spanish lady, I
was to flaunt up and down plying a fan while Poupette sang, to the
tune of *Funiculi-funicula* (more or less!):

> Here comes a lovely señorita
> With her head held high (twice)
> The very latest thing from Barcelona
> With a Spanish eye (twice)
> Olé! when she dances with her castanets
> She stamps her pretty feet . . . etc., etc., etc. . . .

With everyone's eyes upon me, and feeling a hot blush stain my
cheeks, I was in agony. A little later I attended the wedding of a
cousin in the north. Whereas on the occasion of my Aunt Lili's
marriage I had been enchanted by the figure I cut, this time my
appearance appalled me. It was only on the morning of the ceremony, at Arras, that my mother realized my beige crêpe-de-chine
dress, fitting tightly over a bust which was no longer that of a child,
accentuated my breasts in an obscene fashion. They were then
swathed in bandages and firmly flattened, so that all day I had the
feeling I was concealing in my bodice some uncomfortable physical
disability. During the long, boring ceremony and an interminable
banquet I was sadly conscious of what the wedding-photographs
later confirmed: badly dressed, ungainly, I was hovering shame-
facedly between girlhood and womanhood.

My nights lost some of their terrors. But on the other hand, in a
way I cannot define, the everyday world took on a troubling aspect.
This change did not affect Zaza: she was a person, not an object.
But in the class above mine there was a pupil whom I looked upon
as a beautiful, blonde, pink, smiling idol; her name was Marguerite
de Théricourt and her father was one of the wealthiest men in
France; she was brought to school by a governess in a big black car
driven by a chauffeur; already, at ten years of age, with her impeccable ringlets, her elegant dresses, and her gloves which she only
took off on entering the classroom, she seemed to me like a little
princess. She grew up into a pretty young girl, with long, pale-
blonde shining hair, china-blue eyes, and a gracious smile; I was
very conscious of her ease of manner, her reserve, her grave, musical voice. She was a good pupil who treated our schoolmistresses
with extreme deference, and they, dazzled by her beauty and her
fortune, adored her. She always spoke very kindly to me. It was

said that her mother was a permanent invalid: this misfortune enveloped Marguerite in a romantic aura. I told myself sometimes that if she were to invite me to her house I would swoon with happiness, but I didn't even dare to hope for such a thing: she moved in spheres that to me were as unattainable as the drawing-rooms of the English royal family. Besides, I had no wish to be an intimate friend of hers; I simply wanted to be able to gaze upon her from a little nearer at hand.

When I reached the age of puberty, this feeling grew stronger. At the end of my year in the third form from the top – which was called the sixth-first class – I was present at the solemn oral examination which the pupils who were about to enter their final year took in the school hall in order to acquire an 'Adeline Désir Diploma'. Marguerite was wearing a very stylish gown of grey crêpe-de-chine; through its transparent sleeves could be seen her pretty, rounded arms and shoulders. This chaste nudity had a stunning effect on me. I was too ignorant and too respectful to allow myself even the slightest stirring of desire; I could not even imagine a human hand ever profaning those white shoulders; but all through the examination I couldn't take my eyes away from her and I felt a strange tightening of my throat.

My body was changing, and my life was changing too: my past was being left behind. We had moved house, and Louise had gone. I was looking at some old photographs with my sister when I realized suddenly that one of these days I would lose Meyrignac. Grandfather was very old; he would die. When the property belonged to my Uncle Gaston – who was already the virtual owner – I would no longer feel at home there; I would go there as a stranger, an outsider, and then I would never go back again. The thought filled me with consternation. My parents kept telling us – and their own example seemed to confirm what they said – that as life goes on, childhood friendships are forgotten: would I forget Zaza? Poupette and I would anxiously ask one another if our affection would last as we grew older. The grown-ups did not share our games or our pleasures. I didn't know a single grown-up who appeared to enjoy life on earth very much: life's no joke, life's not what you read about in novels, they all declared.

I had always been sorry for the grown-ups' monotonous existence: when I realized that, within a short space of time, it would be my fate too, I was filled with panic. One afternoon I was helping

Mama to wash up; she was washing the plates, and I was drying; through the window I could see the wall of the barracks, and other kitchens in which women were scrubbing out saucepans or peeling vegetables. Every day lunch and dinner; every day washing-up; all those hours, those endlessly recurring hours, all leading no-where: could I live like that? An image was formed in my mind, an image of such desolate clarity that I can still remember it today: a row of grey squares, diminishing according to the laws of perspec-tive, but all flat, all identical, extending away to the horizon; they were the days and weeks and years. Since the day I was born I had gone to bed richer in the evening than I had been the day before; I was steadily improving myself, step by step; but if, when I got up there, I found only a barren plateau, with no landmark to make for, what was the point in it all?

No, I told myself, arranging a pile of plates in the cupboard; *my* life is going to lead somewhere. Fortunately I was not dedicated to a life of toil at the kitchen sink. My father was no feminist; he ad-mired the wisdom of the novels of Colette Yver in which the woman lawyer, or the woman doctor in the end sacrifice their careers in order to provide their children and husband with a happy home. But after all, necessity knows no law: 'You girls will never marry,' he often declared, 'you have no dowries; you'll have to work for a living.' I infinitely preferred the prospect of working for a living to that of marriage: at least it offered some hope. There *had* been people who had done things: I, too, would do things. I didn't quite know what; astronomy, archaeology, and palaeonto-logy had in their turn appealed to me, and I was still toying vaguely with the idea of writing. But these projects were all in the air; I didn't believe enough in any of them to be able to face the future with confidence. Already I was in mourning for my past.

This refusal to make the final break with the past became very clear when I read Louisa M. Alcott's *Good Wives*, which is a sequel to *Little Women*. A year or more had passed since I had left Jo and Laurie together, smiling at the future. As soon as I picked up the little paper-backed Tauchnitz edition in which their story was con-tinued I opened it at random. I happened on a page which without warning broke the news of Laurie's marriage to Jo's young sister, Amy, who was blonde, vain, and stupid. I threw the book away from me as if it had burned my fingers. For several days I was abso-lutely crushed by a misfortune which had seemed to strike at the very roots of my being: the man I loved and by whom I had thought I was loved had betrayed me for a little goose of a girl. I hated Louisa M. Alcott for it. Later, I discovered that Jo herself had turned Laurie down. After remaining unmarried for a long time, and after many trials, many mistakes, she met a professor, much older than she was, and endowed with the highest qualities: he understood her, consoled her, advised her, and in the end married her. This superior individual, even better than Laurie, coming as it were from the outside and becoming part of Jo's life, was the incarnation of that supreme Judge by whom I hoped one day to be acknowledged: all the same his intrusion upset me. Earlier, when I had read Madame de Ségur's *Les Vacances*, I had deplored the fact that Sophie did not marry Paul, her childhood friend, but an 'unknown', a young squire. Friendship, love – to my way of thinking that was something definite, eternal, and not a precarious adventure. I did not want the future to bring upheavals and disruptions; I wanted it to embrace the whole of my past life too.

I had lost the sense of security childhood gives, and nothing had come to take its place. My parents' authority remained inflexible, but as my critical sense developed I began to rebel against it more and more. I couldn't see the point of visits, family dinners, and all those tiresome social duties which my parents considered obligatory. Their replies: 'It's your duty', or 'That just isn't done', didn't satisfy me either. My mother's eternal solicitude began to weigh upon me. She had her own 'ideas' which she did not attempt to justify, and her decisions often seemed to me quite arbitrary. We had a violent argument about a missal which I wanted to give my sister for her First Communion; I wanted to choose one bound in pale fawn leather, like those which the majority of my schoolfellows had; Mama thought that one with a blue cloth cover would do just as well; I protested that the money in my money-box was for me to do what I liked with; she replied that one should not pay out twenty francs for an object that could be bought for fourteen. While we were buying bread at the baker's and all the way up the stairs and in the house itself I held my own against her. But in the end I had to give in, with rage in my heart, vowing never to forgive her for what I considered to be an abuse of her power over me. If she had often stood in my way, I think she would have provoked me to open rebellion. But in the really important things – my studies, and the choice of my friends – she very rarely meddled; she respected my work and my leisure too, only asking me to do little odd jobs for her like grinding the coffee or carrying the refuse bin downstairs. I had the habit of obedience, and I believed that, on the whole, God expected me to be dutiful: the conflict that threatened to set me against my mother did not break out; but I was uneasily aware of its underlying presence. My mother's whole education and upbringing had convinced her that for a woman the greatest thing was to become the mother of a family; she couldn't play this part unless I played the dutiful daughter, but I refused to take part in grown-up pretence just as much as I did when I was five years old. At the Cours Désir, on the eve of our First Communion, we were exhorted to go and cast ourselves down at our mothers' feet and ask them to forgive our faults; not only had I not done this, but when my sister's turn came I persuaded her not to do so either. My mother was vexed about it. She was aware of a certain reticence in me which made her bad-tempered, and she often rebuked me. I held it against her for keeping me so dependent upon her and continuing to impose her will upon me. In addition, I was jealous of the place she held in my father's affections because my own passion for him had continued to grow.

The more difficult life became for him, the more I was dazzled by my father's superior character; it did not depend on money or success, and so I used to tell myself that he had deliberately ignored these; that did not prevent me from being sorry for him: I thought he was not appreciated at his true value, that he was misunderstood and the victim of obscure cataclysms. I was all the more grateful to him now for his outbursts of gaiety, which were still quite frequent. He told stories, made wild fun of everybody, and said the wittiest things. When he stayed at home he read us Victor Hugo and Rostand; he talked about the writers he liked, about the theatre, great events of the past, and a host of other improving subjects which transported me far away from the everyday drabness of life. I couldn't imagine a more intelligent man than my father. In all the discussions at which I was present he always had the last word, and when he attacked people who were not present, he annihilated them. He admired passionately certain great men; but these belonged to such remote spheres that they seemed to me to be almost mythical beings, and in any case they were never absolutely irreproachable; the very excess of their genius condemned them to mistakes: they were overcome by pride and their minds went. This was the case of Victor Hugo whose poems my father would enthusiastically declaim but whose overweening vanity had finally led him astray; it was the same with Zola, Anatole France, and many others. My father looked upon their aberrations with serene impartiality. Even the works of those he admired without reserve had their limits: but my father spoke with the voice of a living man, his thought was ungraspable and infinite. People and things were summoned before him: he was the sovereign judge.

As long as he approved of me, I could be sure of myself. For years he had done nothing but heap praises on my head. But when I entered the 'difficult' age, he was disappointed in me: he appreciated elegance and beauty in women. Not only did he fail to conceal his disillusionment from me, but he began showing more interest than before in my sister, who was still a pretty girl. He glowed with pride when she paraded up and down dressed as the Queen of the Night. He sometimes took part in productions which his friend Monsieur Jeannot – a great advocate of religious drama – organized in the local church clubs; Poupette often acted with him. Her face framed in her long fair hair, she played the part of the little girl in Max Maurey's *Le Pharmacien*. He taught her to recite fables, putting in actions and expression. Though I would not admit it to myself, I was hurt by the understanding between them, and felt a vague resentment against my sister.

But my real rival was my mother. I dreamed of having a more intimate relationship with my father; but even on the rare occasions when we found ourselves alone together we talked as if she was there with us. When there was an argument, if I had appealed to my father, he would have said: 'Do what your mother tells you!' I only once tried to get him on my side. He had taken us to the races at Auteuil; the course was black with people, it was hot, there was nothing happening, and I was bored; finally the horses were off: the people rushed towards the barriers, and their backs hid the track from my view. My father had hired folding chairs for us and I wanted to stand on mine to get a better view. 'No!' said my mother, who detested crowds and had been irritated by all the pushing and shoving. I insisted that I should be allowed to stand on my folding chair. 'When I say no, I *mean* no!' my mother declared. As she was looking after my sister, I turned to my father and cried furiously: 'Mama is being ridiculous! Why can't I stand on my folding chair?' He simply lifted his shoulders in an embarrassed silence, and refused to take part in the argument.

At least this ambiguous gesture allowed me to assume that as far as he was concerned my father sometimes found my mother too domineering; I persuaded myself that there was a silent conspiracy between us. But I soon lost this illusion. One lunch-time there was talk of a wild-living cousin who considered his mother to be an idiot: on my father's own admission she actually was one. Yet he declared vehemently: 'A child who sets up as a judge of his mother is an imbecile.' I went scarlet and left the table, pretending I was feeling sick. I was judging my mother, and my father had struck a double blow at me by affirming their solidarity and by referring to me indirectly as an imbecile. What upset me even more is that I couldn't help passing judgement on the very sentence my father had just uttered: since my aunt's stupidity was plain to everyone, why shouldn't her son acknowledge it? It is no sin to tell oneself the truth, and besides, quite often, one tells oneself the truth unintentionally; at that very moment, for example, I couldn't help thinking what I thought: was that wrong of me? In one sense it was not, and yet my father's words made such a deep impression on me that I felt at once irreproachable and yet a monster of imbecility. After that, and perhaps partly because of that incident, I no longer believed in my father's absolute infallibility. Yet my parents still had the power to make me feel guilty; I accepted their verdicts while at the same time I looked upon myself with other eyes than theirs. My essential self still belonged to them as much as to me: but paradoxically the self they knew could only be a decoy now; it could be false. There was only one way of preventing this strange confusion: I would have to cover up superficial appearances, which were deceptive. I was used to keeping a guard on my tongue; I redoubled my vigilance. I took a further step. As I was not now admitting everything I thought, why not venture unmentionable acts? I was learning how to be secretive.

*

My reading was supervised with the same strictness as hitherto; apart from literature specially designed for children or else suitably bowdlerized, only a very small number of selected works were allowed to pass through my hands; passages even in these were often censored by my parents; my father used to make cuts in *L'Aiglon* itself. Yet, convinced as they were that I would take no dishonest advantage of my freedom, they did not lock the bookcase; at La Grillière, they would allow me to carry off bound volumes of *La Petite Illustration* after having pointed out to me the 'suitable' items. On holiday I was always short of reading matter; when I had finished *Primerose* or *Les Bouffons*, I would cast a greedy eye upon the mass of printed paper which lay beside me on the grass, within easy reach of hand and eye. For some time now I had been indulging in various kinds of harmless disobedience; my mother forbade me to eat between meals; but when we were in the country I would carry off a dozen apples in my apron every afternoon: no physical discomfort had ever punished me for these excesses. Ever since my conversations with Madeleine, I had begun to doubt whether Sacha Guitry, Flers and Callavet, Capus and Tristan Bernard would really do me any harm. I ventured on forbidden territory. I was reckless enough to sample Bernstein and Bataille; they didn't seem to have any harmful effect upon me. At home in Paris, pretending to limit my reading of Musset to his *Nuits*, I would install myself behind the huge volume of his collected works and read all his plays, *Rolla* and *Les Confessions d'un enfant du siècle*. From then on, every time I found myself alone in the house, I dipped quite freely into all the books in the bookcase. I spent wonderful hours curled up in the leather armchair, devouring the collection of paper-backed novels which had enchanted my father's youth: Bourget, Alphonse Daudet, Marcel Prévost, Maupassant, and the Goncourts. They completed, in a very inconsequential way, my sexual education. The act of love, it seemed, sometimes lasted a whole night, sometimes only a few minutes; sometimes it appeared to be flat and dull, at other times extraordinarily voluptuous; it comprised refinements and variations which remained a complete mystery to me. The obviously shady relationships between Farrère's male characters and their boy friends, between Colette's Claudine and her woman friend Rézi complicated the problem still further. Either because of lack of talent or because I knew at once too much and too little, no author succeeded in moving me as deeply as Canon Schmid had once done in his children's tales. On the whole, I rarely saw these stories in relation to my own experience; I realized that they evoked a way of life that was for the most part out of date; except for Claudine and

Farrère's Mademoiselle Dax, the heroines – inane young girls or frivolous 'women of the world' – had very little interest for me; and I found the men a mediocre lot. Not one of these novels evoked an image of human love or of my own destiny which afforded me the slightest satisfaction; I did not look to them for a foretaste of my own future; but they gave me what I wanted: they took me out of myself. Thanks to them, I broke free from the bonds of childhood and entered a complicated, adventurous, and unpredictable world. When my parents went out in the evenings, I would prolong far into the night these surreptitious delights; while my sister slept, I, propped up on my pillow, would be reading; as soon as I heard the key turning in the front door, I would put out the light; in the morning, as I made my bed, I would slip the book under the mattress until I got the chance to put it back in its place on the bookshelf. It was impossible for Mama to catch me out; but at moments the mere thought that *Les Demi-vierges* or *La Femme et le pantin* was lying under my pillow made me shudder with fright. From my own point of view, there was nothing reprehensible in my conduct: I was being entertained and instructed; my parents were anxious about my well-being: I was not going against their wishes because my reading wasn't doing me any harm. But if my actions were once made public, they would automatically become criminal.

Paradoxically, it was through reading a 'permitted' book that I was launched upon the dread paths of deception. I had given an account of the story of *Silas Marner* at school. Before going on holiday, my mother had bought me a copy of *Adam Bede*. Sitting under the poplars in the 'landscape garden' I had been patiently plodding my way through a slow, rather dull story. Suddenly, after a walk through a wood, the heroine – who was not married – found herself with child. My heart began to pound: heaven forbid that Mama should read this book! Because then she would know that I *knew*: I couldn't bear the thought. I was not afraid of being reprimanded. I was not to blame. But I had a panic-stricken fear of what would go on in her mind. Perhaps she would consider it her duty to have a talk with me: this prospect filled me with horror because, judging by the silence she had always maintained on these subjects, I deduced that she would find it repugnant to mention them. To me, the existence of unmarried mothers was an objective fact which was no more disturbing to me than the fact of the Antipodes; but my knowledge of the fact would become, in my mother's mind, a scandal that would defile us both.

Despite my anxiety I did not invent the simple pretext of having lost my book in the woods. Losing something, if it were only a toothbrush, unleashed such storms at home that this remedy was almost as frightening as the fact it would attempt to conceal. In addition, though I was quite unscrupulous in my use of mental blinkers, I wouldn't have had the nerve to tell my mother a positive falsehood; my stammerings and my blushes would have given me away. I simply took great care that *Adam Bede* did not fall into her hands. Fortunately she didn't think of reading it herself and I was spared her distress.

So my relationships with my family had become much less simple than formerly. My sister no longer idolized me unreservedly, my father thought I was ugly and harboured a grievance against me because of it, and my mother was suspicious of the obscure change she sensed in me. If they had been able to read my thoughts, my parents would have condemned me; instead of protecting me as once it did, their gaze held all kinds of dangers for me. They themselves had come down from their empyrean; but I did not take advantage of this by challenging their judgement. On the contrary, I felt doubly insecure; I no longer occupied a privileged place, and my perfection had been impaired; I was uncertain of myself, and vulnerable. All this was to modify my relationships with others.

*

Zaza's talents were outstanding; she could play the piano fairly remarkably for her age and she was beginning to learn the violin. While my own handwriting was grossly childish, hers astonished me by its elegance. My father appreciated, as I did, the stylishness of her letters and the vivacity of her conversation; he found it amusing to treat her with ceremonious politeness, and she lent herself to this game with charm and grace. The 'difficult' age was not making her lose her good looks; she dressed and arranged her hair without any affectation, and behaved with all the ease of a well-bred young lady. Yet she had not lost her boyish daring; during the holidays, she would gallop bare-back through the pine forests of the Landes with a fine disregard for the branches that whipped her face. She went on a visit to Italy; on her return, she talked to me about the buildings, the statues, and the pictures she had liked; I envied her the pleasures she had known in a legendary land, and I gazed with even greater respect at that little dark head which contained so many beautiful images. I was dazzled by her originality. I was less concerned with criticizing than with gaining knowledge, and so I was interested in everything. But Zaza was more selective; Greece enchanted her, the Romans bored her; insensible to the misfortunes of the royal family, she was enthusiastic about Napoleon. She admired Racine, but Corneille exasperated her; she detested *Horace* and *Polyeucte* but blazed with sympathy for *Le Misanthrope*. She had always made fun of everything ever since I had first known her; between the ages of twelve and fifteen her irony became systematic; she turned to ridicule not only the majority of the people we knew, but also established customs and conventional ideas. The *Maxims* of La Rochefoucauld were her bedside book and she never tired of repeating at every opportunity that men are guided by self-interest. I had no opinions about mankind in general and her studied pessimism made a vast impression on me. Many of her notions were subversive; she caused a scandal at the Cours Désir by defending, in a French composition, Alceste against Philinte, and another time when she placed Napoleon above Pasteur. Her audacity enraged certain of our teachers; others attributed it to her youth and were amused by it; to some she was a holy terror, while she was the favourite of others. I usually rated myself above her, even in French, in which I was superior to her in the 'groundwork' of my compositions; but I think she set no store by the first place; although her marks were not as good as mine, her free-and-easy attitude to her work gave it an indefinable quality which mine lacked, despite or perhaps because of my assiduity. She was said to have 'personality': that was her supreme advantage. The confused self-complacency I had indulged in had not given my character any very definite outlines; inside me, everything was shapeless and without significance. But in Zaza I could glimpse a presence, flashing as a spring of water, solid as a block of marble, and as firmly drawn as a portrait by Dürer. I compared this with my own interior void, and despised myself. Zaza forced me to make this comparison because she would often draw parallels between her nonchalance and my earnestness, her defects and my perfections, which she liked to poke fun at. I was not spared her sarcasm.

'I've no personality,' I would sadly tell myself. My curiosity embraced everything; I believed in an absolute truth, in the need for moral law; my thoughts adapted themselves to their objects; if occasionally one of them took me by surprise, it was because it reflected something that *was* surprising. I preferred good to evil and despised that which should be despised. I could find no trace of my own subjectivity. I had wanted myself to be boundless, and I had become as shapeless as the infinite. The paradox was that I became aware of this deficiency at the very moment when I discovered my individuality; my universal aspiration had seemed to me until then to exist in its own right; but now it had become a character trait: 'Simone is interested in everything.' I found myself limited by my refusal to be limited. Ideas and modes of conduct which had imposed themselves quite naturally upon me were in fact the reflections of my passivity and my lack of discrimination. Instead of being a pure mind set like a flawless jewel at the centre of everything, I took on flesh; it was a painful fall from grace. The face that was suddenly ascribed to me could only bring me disappointment for until then I had lived like God Himself, without a face. That is why I so readily accepted humiliation. If I was only one individual among many, any difference, instead of confirming my sovereignty, was liable to establish my inferiority. My parents had ceased to be dependable authorities; and I loved Zaza so much that she seemed to be more real than myself: I was her negative; instead of laying claim on my own characteristics, I had to have them thrust upon me which I supported with ill grace.

A book which I read about my thirteenth birthday provided me with a myth in which I believed for a long time. It was André Laurie's *Schoolboy in Athens*. Theagenus, an earnest, painstaking, and sensible schoolboy, was captivated by good-looking Euphorion; this young aristocrat, elegant, sensitive, refined, artistic, witty, and impertinent, dazzled his schoolfellows and teachers, though he was often reproached for his easy-going ways. He died in the flower of his youth, and it was Theagenus who fifty years later told their story. I identified Zaza with the handsome blond ephebe, and myself with Theagenus: there were obviously people who were gifted and people who were merely talented, and I classed myself irremediably in the latter category.

Yet my modesty was equivocal: the talented ones offered the gifted ones admiration and devotion. But in the end it was

Theagenus who survived his friend and wrote about him: he was both mind and memory, the essential Subject. If it had been suggested that I should be Zaza, I should have refused; I preferred owning the universe to having a single face. I persisted in the conviction that I alone would succeed in laying bare reality without either deforming or minimizing it. It was only when I compared myself with Zaza that I bitterly deplored my banality.

Up to a certain point I was the victim of a mirage; I felt myself from within, and I saw her from without: it wasn't a fair contest. I found it extraordinary that she could not touch or even look at a peach without shivers running down her spine, whereas my own horror of oysters was self-explanatory. But she was the only school-friend who could surprise me. Zaza was really a rather exceptional person.

She was the third of the nine Mabille children, and the second eldest daughter; her mother hadn't had time to fuss over her; she had always been involved in the life of her brothers, their friends, and cousins and had adopted their boyish ways; from an early age she had been considered as a grown-up person and charged with adult responsibilities. Madame Mabille, married at the age of twenty-five to a practising Catholic who was in addition her cousin, was at the time of Zaza's birth securely established in her position as mother of a family; a perfect specimen of a right-minded bourgeois upbringing, she sailed through life with all the assurance of those great ladies who, with their thorough grasp of etiquette, allow themselves on occasion to break all the rules; this was why she tolerated her children's harmless pranks: Zaza's spontaneity and naturalness reflected her mother's proud unselfconsciousness. I had been stupefied that Zaza should have dared, in the middle of a piano recital, to put her tongue out at her mother: it was because she counted on her support; over the heads of the assembled parents and teachers they were both laughing at conventions. If *I* had been guilty of such an incongruous act, my mother would have been deeply ashamed: my conformity was a reflection of her timidity.

Monsieur Mabille I did not altogether like. He was too different from my own father, who did not care for him either. He had a long beard and eyeglasses; he went to communion every Sunday and gave up a great deal of his leisure time to social work. His silken hair and his Christian virtues seemed to me to feminize him and lowered him in my estimation. At the beginning of our friendship,

Zaza had told me that he could make children cry with laughing when he gave readings of *Le Malade imaginaire*. A little later, she listened to him with a deferential interest when, in the long gallery at the Louvre, he expatiated on the beauties of Correggio, and again, coming out of a cinema after seeing *The Three Musketeers*, when he predicted that the moving pictures would be the death of art. She would movingly evoke for me the night of her parents' marriage, when, by the side of the lake, they had stood hand in hand listening to Offenbach's *Barcarolle* – 'Lovely night, O night of love. . . .' But gradually she began to talk in a different tone about her father. 'Papa is so *very* serious!' she told me one day, with some asperity. The elder daughter, Lili, took after Monsieur Mabille; she was as methodical, finicky, and categorical as he was, and was brilliant at mathematics: they got along famously together. Zaza didn't like this elder sister who was so positive and so preachy. Madame Mabille pretended to have the greatest esteem for this paragon but there was a secret rivalry between them and often their hostility came to the surface. Madame Mabille made no bones about her preference for Zaza: 'She's a living image,' she would say happily. For her part, Zaza showed a passionate preference for her mother. She told me that Monsieur Mabille had several times asked in vain for his cousin's hand in marriage; but Guite Larivière, impulsive, vivacious, beautiful, stood in awe of this former student of the Military Academy of Artillery and Engineering who was so serious and severe. But she led a very sheltered existence in the Basque country, where there were not many eligible young men; at the age of twenty-five, at the imperious insistence of her mother, she finally gave way and accepted him. Zaza confided in me also that Madame Mabille – to whom she attributed great reserves of charm, sensitivity, and imagination – had suffered from the lack of understanding of a husband who was as boring as an algebra text book; Zaza didn't tell me everything; I realize today that she was physically repelled by her father. Her mother had enlightened her at a very early age, and with a wicked crudity, about the realities of sex: Zaza had a precocious understanding of why Madame Mabille had hated the first night of her marriage and had loathed her husband's embraces ever since. She extended the repugnance she felt for him to the rest of his family. On the other hand, she adored her maternal grandmother who shared her bed whenever she came to Paris. At one time Monsieur Larivière had been a militant supporter

in provincial newspapers and revues of the ultramontane ideas of
Louis Veuillot; he had left on his death a few articles and an immense library. Zaza, who disliked mathematics as much as she did
her father, took up literature. But when her grandfather died, as
neither Madame Larivière nor Madame Mabille had any pretensions
to culture, there was no one to guide Zaza's tastes: she was forced
to think for herself. To tell the truth, her originality was very
limited; fundamentally, Zaza, like myself, reflected her environment. But at the Cours Désir and in our homes we were so narrowly bound by prejudice and convention that the least flash of
sincerity and the slightest trace of imagination was always something of a surprise.

What impressed me most about Zaza was her cynicism. I was
thunderstruck when, a few years later, she told me the reasons for
it. She was far from sharing the lofty opinion I had of her. Madame
Mabille had too many offspring, she performed too many 'social
obligations' and sat on too many committees to be able to give very
much of herself to her children; I believe her smiling patience concealed cold indifference; even when she was very small, Zaza had
felt herself to be more or less neglected; later her mother singled
her out for special but very limited affection; the passionate love
Zaza felt for her was a jealous rather than a happy devotion. I don't
know if a certain amount of spite had its part to play in her resentment against her father: she cannot have been indifferent to the preference her father showed for Lili. In any case, the third offspring
in a family of nine children can scarcely fail to regard herself as only
one among many; she benefits from a collective solicitude which
does not encourage her to think she is someone very special. None
of the Mabille children were shy or diffident; they thought too
highly of their family to feel any timidity in front of strangers; but
whenever Zaza, instead of behaving as a member of a clan, was left
to her own devices, she discovered in herself a host of faults: she
was ugly, ungraceful, not very nice, and nobody loved her. She
compensated for this sense of inferiority by making fun of everything. I did not notice it then, but she never made fun of my faults,
only of my virtues; she never drew attention to her gifts and her
successes; she only exposed her weaknesses. When I was fourteen,
during the Easter holidays she wrote to me that she hadn't the heart
to revise her physics notes, and yet that the idea of failing in the
next test grieved her deeply: 'You cannot understand how I feel,

because if you had to prepare for a test, instead of torturing yourself about not knowing anything, you would set to work to prepare yourself for it.' I was saddened by these words which poked fun at my hard-working, conscientious ways; but their veiled aggression seemed to indicate that Zaza was reproaching herself for her own indolence. If I irritated her, it was because she felt I was at the same time right and wrong; she defended in a joyless way the unfortunate child she considered herself to be against my maddening perfection.

There was also resentment in her scorn of mankind: she didn't rate herself very highly, but the rest of the world didn't seem to be worth rating highly either. She sought in heaven the love that was refused her upon earth; she was very devout. She lived in a more homogeneous environment than I did, in which religious values were given unanimous and emphatic support: the flat denial of theory in the actual practice of religion only served to give the lie a more scandalous flavour. The Mabilles gave money to charitable works. Every year, on the occasion of the national pilgrimage, they went to Lourdes: the boys served as stretcher bearers; the girls washed dishes in hospital kitchens. In their circle there was much talk of God, of charity, of ideals; but Zaza soon perceived that all these people only respected money and social position. This hypocrisy revolted her; she sought refuge from it in deliberate cynicism. I never realized how much torn and battered idealism lay behind what they called at the Cours Désir her paradoxes.

Zaza was much more informal with her other friends: she would address them as 'tu'. At the Tuileries she would play with anyone, she was very free-and-easy in her manners, and even rather impudent. Yet my relationship with her remained somewhat stiff and formal; there were no kisses, no friendly thumps on the back; we continued to address one another as 'vous', and we were reserved in our speech. I knew that she thought much less of me than I did of her; she preferred me to all her other schoolmates, but scholastic life did not count as much for her as it did for me; occupied as she was with her family, her home, her piano, her holidays. I was unable to tell what place I had in her scheme of things; at first I had not bothered too much about that; but now I was beginning to wonder; I was aware that my studious zeal and my docility exasperated her; how high an opinion did she have of me? There was no question of revealing my feelings to her, nor of trying to discover hers. I had succeeded in gaining an inner freedom from the set ideas with which adults clutter up their children's lives: I was more daring in my emotions, my dreams, my desires, and even in my use of certain words. But I never imagined that one could communicate sincerely, spontaneously, with someone else. In books, people make declarations of love and hate, they express their innermost feelings in fine phrases; but in life there are no significant speeches. What can be spoken is regulated by what can be done: if it 'isn't done', it isn't said. There could have been nothing more conventional than the letters we exchanged. Zaza used clichés and commonplace ideas a little more elegantly than I did; but neither of us expressed anything of what touched us most deeply. Our mothers read our correspondence: such a censorship certainly did not encourage us to pour out our souls. But even in our private conversations we used to observe unspoken and indefinable rules; we kept well within the bounds of modesty, for we were both of the opinion that our innermost feelings should not be exposed. So I was reduced to interpreting as best I could whatever indications I could find; the least praise from Zaza overwhelmed me with joy; the sarcastic smiles she so frequently gave me were a terrible torment. The happiness our friendship afforded me was blighted during those difficult years by the constant fear that I might incur her displeasure.

One year, in the middle of the summer holidays, her irony caused me to die a thousand deaths. I had been with my family to admire the waterfalls at Gimmel; I reacted with a dutiful enthusiasm to their rather standardized picturesqueness. Of course, as my letters were a reflection of my public life, I was careful to keep out of them the solitary joys of country life; so I decided to describe this collective excursion to Zaza, its beauties and my transports. The platitude of my style accentuated most unhappily the insincerity of my emotions. In her reply, Zaza maliciously insinuated that I had sent her by mistake one of my holiday tasks: I burst into tears. I felt that she was reproaching me with something more serious than the clumsy pomposity of my phrases: everywhere I went I dragged behind me the crippling shadow of the first-class pupil. This was partly true; but it was also true that I loved Zaza with an intensity which could not be accounted for by any established set of rules and conventions. I did not entirely correspond to the person she took me for; but I couldn't find a way of demolishing that image and revealing my true nature to Zaza; this misunderstanding drove me to despair. In my reply I pretended to take it all very lightly but at the same time reproached Zaza for being so naughty; she sensed that she had hurt me for she wrote asking to be forgiven by return of post: I had been the victim, she told me, of a fit of bad temper. This restored my equanimity a little.

Zaza did not suspect how much I idolized her, nor that I had adjured my pride in her favour. At a charity bazaar held in the Cours Désir, a graphologist examined our handwritings; Zaza's appeared to indicate a precocious maturity, sensitivity, culture, and remarkable artistic gifts; mine showed nothing better than infantilism. I accepted this verdict: yes, I was an industrious pupil, a good little girl, and nothing more. Zaza protested against it with a vehemence I found very comforting. She protested again in a short letter against another analysis, just as unfavourable, which I had sent to her, and sketched my portrait in these words: 'Rather reserved, a tendency to conform to convention and custom; but the warmest of hearts and an unequalled, kindly indulgence in overlooking the faults of her friends.'

It wasn't often we were so frank with one another. Was that my fault? The fact is that it was Zaza who spoke, very sweetly, of *my* reserve; would she have liked a freer relationship with me? My affection for her was fanatical, but she was very reticent towards me; perhaps it was I, after all, who was responsible for our excessive discretion.

Yet I found it very irksome. Though she was brusque and caustic in her manner, Zaza was sensitive; one day she came to school, her face ravaged with weeping because she had learnt the evening before of the death of a distant cousin. She would have been deeply touched by the devotion I felt for her: in the end I couldn't bear to think that she knew nothing about it. As it was impossible for me to say anything, I decided I must do something. It would be running a great risk: Mama would consider my plan ridiculous; or Zaza herself would think it odd. But the need to express my feelings was so great that for once I felt I must go forward with it. I revealed my plan to my mother, who approved it. I was to give Zaza for her birthday a bag which I would make with my own hands. I bought some blue and red silk brocaded in gold; it seemed to me the height of luxury. Following a pattern in *Practical Fashions*, I mounted it on a base of woven straw, and lined it with cerise satin; I enveloped my handiwork in tissue paper. When the day arrived, I waited for Zaza in the cloakroom; I handed her my gift; she threw me a stupefied look, then she blushed hotly and her whole face changed; for a moment we stood looking at one another, embarrassed by our emotion, and quite unable to find in our repertory of set responses a single appropriate word or gesture. The next day we met with our mothers. 'Now thank Madame de Beauvoir,' said Madame Mabille in her most affable tones, 'for all the trouble she must have taken.' She was trying to bring my unprecedented action within the range of polite grown-up reactions. I realized at that moment that I didn't like her any more. In any case, she failed in the attempt. Something had happened that could not be wiped out by polite social usage.

But I still wasn't able to relax. Even when Zaza was very friendly towards me, even when she seemed to enjoy being with me I was afraid of appearing importunate. She only let me have brief glimpses of that secret 'personality' which inhabited her; my notions of what her conversations with herself would be like became an almost religious obsession. One day I went to the rue de Varennes to get a book which she had promised to lend me; she wasn't at home; I was asked to wait for her in her room, for she was not expected to be long. I looked at the walls covered with blue paper, da Vinci's *Saint Anne*, the crucifix: Zaza had left open on her desk one of her favourite books: the *Essays* of Montaigne. I read the page she had left it open at and that she would continue reading when I wasn't there: but the printed symbols seemed to me as remote from my understanding as in the days when I didn't know the alphabet. I tried to see the room with Zaza's eyes, to insinuate myself into the internal monologue that was always going on inside her; but in vain. I could touch all the objects that were expressions of her presence; but they did not give her up to me; they revealed, but at the same time concealed her; it was almost as if they defied me ever to come close to her. Zaza's existence seemed so hermetically sealed that I couldn't get the smallest foothold in it. I took my book and fled. When I met her the next day, she seemed dumbfounded by my action: why had I rushed away like that? I couldn't explain it to her. I would not even admit to myself with what fevered torment I paid for the happiness she gave me.

*

The majority of the boys I knew seemed to me uncouth and of very limited intelligence; yet I knew that they belonged to a privileged category. If they had charm and a ready wit I was prepared to put up with them. My cousin Jacques had never lost his prestige in my eyes. He lived alone with his sister and an old nurse in the house in the boulevard Montparnasse and he often came to spend the evening with us. At thirteen he already had the assurance of a young man; his independent way of life, and his authority in discussion had turned him into a precocious adult and I thought it was quite natural that he should treat me as a little girl. My sister and I were delighted whenever we heard his ring at the door. One evening he arrived so late that we were already in bed; we rushed into the study in our nighties. 'What a way to behave!' my mother exclaimed. 'You're big girls now!' I was taken aback. I looked upon Jacques as a sort of elder brother. He helped me to do my Latin prose, criticized my choice of books, and recited poems to me. One evening, on the balcony, he declaimed Hugo's *Tristesse d'Olympio*, and I suddenly remembered, with a stab of the heart, that we had been 'engaged'. But now the only real conversations he ever had were with my father.

He was a day-boy at the Collège Stanislas, where he was a brilliant pupil; between the ages of fourteen and fifteen he became infatuated with his French literature teacher who taught him to prefer Mallarmé to Rostand. My father shrugged his shoulders in exasperation at this. As Jacques would run down *Cyrano* without being able to explain its weak points to me, and would recite obscure poems with great relish but without showing me why they were beautiful, I agreed with my parents that he was 'putting it on'. All the same, while deploring his tastes I admired the high-handed way he defended them. He knew a host of poets and writers of whom I knew nothing at all; the distant clamour of a world that was closed to me used to come into the house with him: how I longed to explore that world! Papa used to say with pride: 'Simone has a man's brain; she thinks like a man; she *is* a man.' And yet everyone treated me like a girl. Jacques and his friends read real books and were abreast of all current problems; they lived out in the open; I was confined to the nursery. But I did not give up all hope. I had confidence in my future. Women, by the exercise of talent or knowledge, had carved out a place for themselves in the universe of men. But I felt impatient of the delays I had to endure. Whenever I happened to pass by the Collège Stanislas my heart would sink; I tried to imagine the mystery that was being celebrated behind those walls, in a classroom full of boys, and I would feel like an outcast. They had as teachers brilliantly clever men who imparted knowledge to them with all its pristine glory intact. My old school-marms only gave me an expurgated, insipid, faded version. I was being crammed with an ersatz concoction; and I felt I was imprisoned in a cage.

In fact I no longer looked upon the ladies of the establishment as the august high-priestesses of Knowledge but as rather comical old church-hens. More or less affiliated to the Jesuit order, they parted their hair on the side while they were still 'novices' and in the middle when they had taken their final vows. They thought it their duty to show their devoutness in the eccentricity of their garb: they wore dresses of shot silk with leg-o'-mutton sleeves and whaleboned collars; their skirts swept the floor; their qualifications were Christian virtues rather than degrees and diplomas. It was considered a great triumph when Mademoiselle Dubois, a dark, bewhiskered lady, managed to scrape through a degree in English; Mademoiselle Billon, who was at least thirty, had been seen, all buttoned-up and blushing, at the Sorbonne, trying to get through the oral of her school-leaving certificate. My father made no secret of the fact that he found these pious old frauds a little backward. It exasperated him that I should be obliged, at the end of any composition in which I described an outing or a party, to 'thank God for a pleasant day'. He thought highly of Voltaire and Beaumarchais, and knew Victor Hugo by heart: he wouldn't allow that French literature came to a stop in the seventeenth century. He went as far as to suggest to my mother that my sister and I should attend the *lycée*; there we would enjoy a better and more liberal grounding and at much less cost. I rejected this proposal with all the vehemence I could muster. I should have lost all desire to go on living if I had been separated from Zaza. My mother supported my objections. But I was divided over this question too. I wanted to stay on at the Cours Désir and yet I didn't like it there any more. I went on working zealously, but my behaviour was changing. The lady in charge of higher studies, Mademoiselle Lejeune, a tall, gaunt woman with a ready tongue, was rather intimidating; but with Zaza and a few other fellow-pupils I used to make fun of the rest of our teachers' foibles. The assistant mistresses just couldn't keep us in order. We used to spend free time between classes in a large room known as 'the lecture-study room'. There we would talk and giggle and plague the life out of the poor creature left in charge whom we had nicknamed 'the old scarecrow'. My sister, who had thrown all discretion to the winds by now, had decided that she would behave in the most outrageous way. With a friend she had chosen herself, Anne-Marie Gendron, she founded the *Cours Désir Gazette*; Zaza lent her some hectograph jelly and from time to time I contributed to it; we turned out some bloodthirsty numbers. We were no longer given marks for good conduct; our mistresses lectured us and complained to our mother. She got rather worried, but as my father always laughed at our escapades she disregarded the complaints. I never dreamed of attaching any moral significance to our naughty pranks; as soon as I found out how stupid our schoolmistresses were, they could no longer speak with any authority on what was right and wrong.

Stupidity: at one time my sister and I used to accuse other children of stupidity when we found them dull and boring; now there were many grown-ups, and in particular our school-teachers, who came in for the charge. Unctuous sermons, all kinds of solemn twaddle, grand words, inflated turns of phrase, and any pompous affectation was 'stupidity'. It was stupid to attach importance to trifles, to persist in observing conventions and customs, to prefer commonplaces and prejudices to facts. The very height of stupidity was when people fatuously believed that we swallowed all the righteous fibs that were dished out to us. Stupidity made us laugh; it was one of our never-failing sources of amusement; but there was also something rather frightening about it. If this dunce-like dullness had won the day we would no longer have had the right to think, to make fun of people, to experience real emotions and enjoy real pleasures. We had to fight against it, or else give up living.

In the end my teachers got fed up with my insubordination and they let me know their displeasure. The Institut Adeline Désir took great care to distinguish itself from secular establishments where the mind is cultivated at the expense of the soul. At the end of the year, instead of awarding prizes for scholastic success – which would have run the risk of encouraging worldly rivalry among the pupils – we were presented at the end of March, in the presence of a bishop, with certificates and medals which were mainly rewards for industriousness and good behaviour and also for long attendance at the school. The ceremonies took place, with tremendous pomp, at the Salle Wagram. The highest distinction was called 'the certificate of honour' awarded to only a few pupils from each class who had excelled in everything. The rest only had a right to 'special mentions'. That year, after my name had reverberated in the solemn silence of the hall, I was startled to hear Madame Lejeune announce: 'Special mentions in mathematics, history, and geography.' From my assembled schoolmates came a murmur of consternation, and also of satisfaction, because not all of them were my friends. I took this affront without turning a hair. At the end of the ceremony, my history teacher came up to my mother: Zaza had a bad influence upon me; we would no longer be allowed to sit next to one another at school. I tried hard to keep a stiff upper lip, but in vain: my eyes filled with tears, to the great delight of Mademoiselle Gontran who thought I was weeping because I had only got a special mention; I was popping with rage because they were going to take me away from Zaza. But my distress had a more profound significance. In that sad corridor I realized vaguely that my childhood was coming to an end. The grown-ups still had me under their thumb, but peace had gone for ever from my heart. I was now separated from them by this freedom that was no source of pride to me, but that I suffered in solitary silence.

*

I no longer held sway over the world: the façades of buildings and the indifferent glances of the passers-by exiled me from life. That is why about this time my love of the countryside took on an almost mystical fervour. As soon as I arrived at Meyrignac all barriers seemed to be swept away and my horizon broadened. I lost myself in the infinite and at the same time remained myself. I felt on my eyelids the heat of the sun that shines for everyone but that here and now was lavishing its caresses on me alone. The wind went whirling round the poplars; it came from elsewhere, from everywhere; it went hustling through space, and I, too, was whirled away with it, without stirring from where I stood, right to the ends of the earth. When the moon arose in the heavens, I would be in touch with far-off cities, deserts, oceans, and villages which at that moment were bathed, as I was, in its radiance. I was no longer a vacant mind, an abstracted gaze, but the turbulent fragrance of the waving grain, the intimate smell of the heather moors, the dense heat of noon or the shiver of twilight; I was heavy; yet I was as vapour in the blue airs of summer and knew no bounds.

My experience of humanity was small; lacking insight and the appropriate words, I could not comprehend it all. But nature revealed to me a host of visible, tangible modes of existence which my own had never remotely resembled. I admired the proud isolation of the oak that dominated the landscape garden; I felt sorry for the communal solitude of blades of grass. I knew the innocence of morning and the melancholy of twilight, the triumphs and the defeats, the renewals and the expirations of life. One day, something inside me would find itself in harmony with the scent of the honeysuckle. Every evening I would go and lie among the same heather, and gaze at the shadowy blue undulations of the Monédières; every evening the sun would set behind the same hill: yet the pinks, the reds, the carmines, the purples, and the violets were never the same. From dawn to dusk there hummed over the unchanging plains a life that was everlastingly renewed. In the face of the changing sky, constancy was seen to be something more than routine habit, and growing-up did not necessarily mean denying one's true self.

Here, once again, I became unique and I felt I was needed: my own eyes were needed in order that the copper-red of the beech could be set against the blue of the cedar and the silver of the poplars. When I went away, the landscape fell to pieces, and no longer existed for anyone; it no longer existed at all.

Yet, much more strongly than in Paris, I could feel all around me the presence of God; in Paris He was hidden from me by people and their top-heavy preoccupations; here I could see blades of grass and clouds that were still the same as when He had snatched them out of primal Chaos, and that still bore His mark. The harder I pressed myself against the earth, the closer I got to Him, and every country walk was an act of adoration. His sovereign power did not cancel out my own authority. He knew all things after His own fashion, that is to say, in an absolute sense: but it seemed to me that He needed my eyes in order that the trees might have their colours. How could a pure spirit have experienced the scorching of the sun, the freshness of the dew, if not through the medium of my own body? He had created this earth for men, and he had created men in order that they might bear witness to its beauty: it was He who had given me the mission with which I had always felt myself to be somehow entrusted. Far from wishing to dethrone me, He assured me that I would go on reigning. Deprived of my presence, Creation sank into a shadowy slumber; by waking it to life again, I was accomplishing the most sacred of all my tasks, whereas grown-ups, the indifferent ones, took God's laws into their own hands. Every morning as I passed through the white gates and ran down to the underwoods, it was He Himself who was calling me. He was gazing upon me with high satisfaction as I gazed upon this world which He had created in order that I might gaze upon it.

Even when I was racked with hunger, even when I was weary with reading and meditating, I disliked resuming possession of my wretched carcase and returning to the enclosed spaces and the ossified timetables of grown-up life. One evening, however, I went too far. It was at La Grillière. I had read a long time by the edge of a small lake; when it grew too dark to read, I closed the book, which was about the life of St Francis of Assisi. Lying in the grass, I gazed up at the moon; it was shining down on an Umbrian landscape radiant with the first dews of night: I felt breathless with the soft beauty of the moment. I should have liked to snatch it as it fled and fix it for ever on paper with immortal words; there will be other hours like this, I told myself, and I shall learn how never to let it go. I lay flat on my back, unable to move, and with my eyes fixed on the sky. When eventually I opened the billiard room door, dinner was just coming to an end. There was a fine how-d'ye-do; even my father expressed himself very forcibly. Thinking to teach me a lesson, my mother ordered that next day I should not be allowed to go outside the boundaries of the estate. Frankly, I did not dare disobey. I spent the day sitting on the lawns or pacing up and down the avenues with a book in my hand and rage in my heart. Over there, outside, the waters of the lake were ruffling and smoothing, light was hardening and softening on the heath and the hills, but without me, without anyone to see: it was unbearable. 'If it were raining; if there were *some* reason for this silly prohibition,' I told myself, 'then I could resign myself to it.' Here, once more, boiling up inside me, was the rebelliousness that had expressed itself in furious convulsions during my early childhood; a word thrown out at random sufficed to disrupt my happiness or prevent the gratification of a desire; and this frustration of oneself and of the world didn't help anyone in any way. Fortunately, I didn't get another telling-off like that one. On the whole, as long as I was in time for meals, I could do what I liked with my time.

My holidays prevented me from confusing the joys of contemplation with boredom. In Paris, in museums, I would sometimes cheat; at least I knew the difference between forced admiration and sincere emotion. I also learnt that in order to enter into the secrets of things you first of all have to give yourself to them. Usually my curiosity was insatiable; I believed I could possess something as soon as I knew about it, and that I could get this knowledge in a superficial glance. But in order to make a small part of the countryside my own I wandered day after day along the country lanes, and would stand motionless for hours at the foot of a tree: then the least vibration of the air and every fleeting autumnal tint would move me deeply.

I returned to Paris with bad grace. I would go out on the balcony: there would be nothing but roofs; the heavens would be reduced to a geometrical pattern, the air was no longer a perfume and a caress, but a nothingness in a wilderness of space. The noises of the street did not speak to me. I would stand there with an empty heart, and with my eyes full of tears.

*

Back in Paris, I was again under grown-up supervision. I still accepted without criticism their version of the world. It would be impossible to imagine a more sectarian education than the one I received. School primers, text books, lessons, conversations: all converged upon the same point. I was never allowed to hear, even at a great distance, even very faintly, the other side of the question.

I learnt history as unquestioningly as I did geography, without ever dreaming that there might be more than one view of past events. When I was very small, we visited the Musée Grévin where I was very moved by the martyrs delivered up to the lions and by the noble countenance of Marie-Antoinette. The emperors who had persecuted the Christians, the stocking-knitters and the *sans-culottes* of the French Revolution seemed to me to be the most odious incarnations of Evil. Good was represented by the Church and by '*la France*'. In my lessons I was taught about Popes and Lateran Councils, but I was much more interested in the destiny of my country: her past, her present, and her future gave rise to numerous discussions at home; Papa enjoyed the works of Madelin, Lenôtre, and Funck-Brentano. I was made to read quantities of historical tales and romances, and the entire collection of *Memoirs* in Madame Carette's expurgated edition. About the age of nine, I had wept over the misfortunes of Louis XVII and admired the heroism of the insurgent Breton royalists. But I very soon dismissed the monarchy; I found it absurd that power should be given to hereditary rulers who were for the most part imbeciles. It would have seemed more natural to me if the Government had been entrusted to those who were most competent to govern. In our land, I knew, this was unfortunately not the case. We were fated to get scoundrels for our leaders, and so France, fundamentally superior to all other nations, did not occupy her rightful place in the world. Certain of Papa's friends maintained that England and not Germany was our hereditary enemy; but that was as far as their dissensions went. They agreed that the existence of any foreign country should be considered ludicrous as well as dangerous. '*La France*', a victim of Wilson's criminal idealism, her future threatened by the brutal realism of Boche and Bolshevik was heading for disaster because she lacked firm leadership. My father, who was steadily eating up his capital, saw ruin staring humanity in the face: Mama chorused her agreement. There was the red peril; there was the yellow peril: soon a new wave of barbarism was spreading from the four corners of the earth and from the lowest depths of society; revolution would precipitate the world into chaos. My father used to prophesy these calamities with a passionate vehemence that filled me with consternation; this future that he painted in such lurid colours was *my* future; I loved life: I couldn't accept that tomorrow it would be filled with hopeless lamentation. One day, instead of letting the flood of words and images of devastation roll over my head, I hit upon an answer: 'Whatever happens,' I said, 'it will be men who win the final victory.' One might have thought, to listen to my father, that there were deformed monsters waiting to tear humanity to pieces. But the two opposing sides would be composed of human beings! After all, I thought, it is the majority who will win the day; the dissatisfied will be in the minority; if happiness changes hands, that's no catastrophe. The Other Side had suddenly ceased to appear as Evil incarnate: I could not see why we should *a priori* prefer those interests which were said to be mine to

[128]

his interests. I breathed again. The world was not, after all, in danger.

It was mental distress that had provoked my outburst: I had found a way out of my despair because I ardently desired it and sought for it. But my security and my comfortable illusions made me insensitive to social problems. I was very far from disputing the established order of things.

To say the very least, property, it seemed to me, was a sacred right; I assumed that there was a consubstantial unity between the proprietor and his possessions, just as formerly I had considered words and their meanings to be integral parts of one another. When I said: *my* money, *my* sister, *my* nose, I was in all three cases consolidating a bond which no will could destroy because it existed above and beyond all conventional ideas. I was told that in order to construct the railway to Uzerche the State had expropriated a certain number of small farmers and landed gentry: I could not have been more horrified if it had shed their blood. Meyrignac belonged to my grandfather as absolutely as his own life.

On the other hand, I had to admit that the brute fact of wealth should not be allowed to confer special rights or any extrinsic credit upon its possessor. The Gospel exalts poverty. I respected Louise far more than many a rich lady. I was indignant that Madeleine refused to say good morning to the bakers who came in their carts to deliver bread at La Grillière. 'It is up to them to address me first,' she declared. I believed in the absolute equality of human beings. One summer at Meyrignac I read a book which recommended universal suffrage. Up went my head: 'But it's shameful that poor people should not be allowed to have the vote!' I cried. Papa smiled. He explained to me that a nation is a collection of private properties; and it is those who own them who naturally have the task of administering them. He ended by quoting Guizot's maxim: 'Get rich!' His exposition of the problem puzzled me. Papa had not succeeded in getting rich: would he have been willing to be deprived of his rights as a voter? If I protested against this particular injustice, it was in the name of the very set of values which he himself had taught me to observe. He did not hold that a man's qualities can be measured by the amount of money he has in the bank; he was always making fun of the 'new rich'. No, according to him, the élite were those who had intelligence, culture, and a sound education; they should be able to spell correctly and have 'the right ideas'. I readily agreed with him when he said his objection to universal suffrage was based upon the fact that the majority of the electorate were stupid and ignorant: only 'enlightened' people ought to have a say in the matter. I bowed to his logic which was supported by an empirical truth: 'enlightenment' is the prerogative of the bourgeoisie. Certain individuals from the lower classes might perform feats of intellectual prowess, but they would always retain something of their original lowly condition, and they are usually, in any case, people with 'wrong' ideas. On the other hand, every man who came from a good family had 'that certain something' which distinguished him from the common herd. I was not too shocked at the idea that personal merit depended on the chance of birth, since it was the will of God that decided what our fate would be. But in any case it seemed obvious to me that morally, and therefore absolutely, the class to which I belonged was far superior to the rest of society. Whenever I went with Mama to call on grandfather's tenant-farmers, the stink of manure, the dirty rooms where the hens were always scratching and the rusticity of their furniture seemed to me to reflect the coarseness of their souls; I would watch them labouring in the fields, covered in mud, smelling of sweat and earth, and they never once paused to contemplate the beauty of the landscape; they were ignorant of the splendours of the sunset. They didn't read, they had no ideals; Papa used to say, though quite without animosity, that they were 'brutes'. When he read me Gobineau's *Essay on the Inequality of the Human Races*, I promptly adopted his idea that the brains of the lower classes were made differently from ours.

I loved the country so much that the farmer's life seemed to me a very happy one. If I had ever had a glimpse into the labourer's way of life, I could hardly have failed to doubt the correctness of my assumptions; but I knew nothing of it. Before her marriage, Aunt Lili, with no work of her own, occupied her time with 'good works'. She sometimes took me with her to give toys to specially chosen under-privileged children; the poor did not seem to me to be very unhappy. There were many kindly souls who gave them charity and the sisters of Saint Vincent de Paul devoted themselves especially to their service. There were a few discontented ones among the poor: they were the would-be poor, who stuffed themselves with roast turkey at Christmas, or wicked ones who drank. Some books – Dickens's novels and Hector Malot's *Sans famille* –

described the hard life of the poor; I thought the miner's lot, cooped up all day in dark pits, and at the mercy of any sudden fall of rock, was terrible. But I was assured that times had changed. The workers worked much less, and earned much more; since the advent of trade unions, the real victims had been the employers. The workers, who were much luckier than we were, didn't have to 'keep up appearances' and so they could treat themselves to roast chicken every Sunday; their wives bought the best cuts in the markets and could even afford silk stockings. They were used to hard work and squalid homes: these things did not distress them as they would us. Their recriminations were not justified by the facts. 'Besides,' my father would say, raising his shoulders, 'they're not dying of starvation!' No, if the workers hated the bourgeoisie, it was because they were conscious of our superiority. Communism and socialism were the results of envy. 'And envy,' my father would add, 'is not a pretty thing.'

I only once came in contact with real destitution. Louise and her husband, the slater, lived in a room in the rue Madame, a garret right at the top of the house; she had a baby and I went to visit her with my mother. I had never set foot in a sixth-floor back before. The dreary little landing with its dozen identical doors made my heart sink. Louise's tiny room contained a brass bedstead, a cradle, and a table on which stood a small oil stove; she slept, cooked, ate, and lived with her husband and child between these four walls; all round the landing there were families confined to stifling little holes like this; the comparative promiscuity in which I myself had to live and the monotony of bourgeois life oppressed my spirits. But here I got a glimpse of a universe in which the air you breathed smelt of soot, in which no ray of light ever penetrated the filth and squalor: existence here was a slow death. Not long after that, Louise lost her baby. I cried for hours: it was the first time I had known misfortune at first hand. I thought of Louise in her comfortless garret without her baby, without anything: such terrible distress should have shaken the world to its foundations. 'It's not right!' I told myself. I wasn't only thinking of the dead child but also of that sixth-floor landing. But in the end I dried my tears without having called society in question.

It was very difficult for me to think for myself, for the standard of values I was taught was both monolithic and incoherent. If my parents had had differences of opinion, I could have compared those opinions. Or one firm line of argument would have given me something to get my teeth in. But brought up as I was on convent morals and paternal nationalism, I was always getting bogged down in contradictions. Neither my mother nor my teachers doubted for a moment that the Pope was elected by the Holy Spirit; yet my father thought His Holiness should not interfere in world affairs and my mother agreed with him; Pope Leo XIII, by devoting encyclicals to 'social questions' had betrayed his saintly mission; Pius X, who had not breathed a word about such things, was a saint. So I had to swallow the paradox that the man chosen by God to be His representative on earth had not to concern himself with earthly things. France was the elder daughter of the Roman Catholic Church; she owed obedience to her mother. Yet national values came before Catholic virtues; when a collection was being made at Saint-Sulpice for 'the starving children of Central Europe', my mother was indignant and refused to give anything for 'the Boche'. In all eventualities, patriotism and concern for maintaining the established order of things were considered more important than Christian charity. Telling lies was an offence against God; yet Papa could claim that in committing a forgery Colonel Henry had acted like an upright man. Killing was a crime, but the death-penalty must not be done away with. At an early age I was indoctrinated in the compromises of casuistry and sophistry, to make a clear distinction between God and Caesar and to render unto each his due; all the same, it was most disconcerting to find that Caesar always got the better of God. When we view the world at the same time through the verses of the Gospel and through the columns of the daily press, the sight tends to get blurred. There was nothing else I could do but to take refuge, with lowered head, under the wing of authority.

It was a blind submission. A dispute had broken out between *L'Action Française* and *La Démocratie Nouvelle*; having first made sure that they were ten to one, the royalists had attacked the supporters of Marc Sangnier and forced them to drink whole bottles of castor oil. Papa and his friends were highly amused by this episode. When I was very small I had learnt to laugh when the evil are discomfited; without really giving it a thought, I agreed with my father that the whole thing had been a most diverting lark. I made a laughing reference to it as I was walking up the rue Saint-Benoît with Zaza. Her face hardened: 'What a filthy thing to do!' she said disgustedly. I didn't know what to answer. Crestfallen, I realized that I had thoughtlessly copied my father's attitude and that I hadn't an idea of my own in my head. Zaza, too, was expressing her family's opinion. Her father had belonged to the democratic Catholic group *Le Sillon* before it had been denounced by the Church; he still thought that Catholics have social obligations and rejected the theories of Maurras; his was a fairly coherent position, one that a fourteen-year-old girl could rally round with a clear conscience; Zaza's indignation and her horror of violence was sincere. I, who had repeated my father's opinion parrot-fashion, hadn't a leg to stand on. I was hurt by Zaza's scorn, but what worried me much more was the difference of opinion between her father and mine. I didn't like to think that one of them might be wrong. I talked about it to Papa, but he merely shrugged his shoulders and said Zaza was only a child; this reply did not satisfy me. For the first time, I was driven to take sides: but I didn't know anything about the matter and I couldn't make a decision. The one conclusion I drew from this incident was that it was possible to be of another opinion than my father. One could not even be sure of what the truth was any more.

It was Vaulabelle's *History of the Two Restorations* which inclined me towards liberalism; I spent two summer holidays reading the seven volumes in grandfather's library. I wept over the defeat of Napoleon; I developed a hatred of monarchy, conservatism, obscurantism. I wanted men to be governed by reason and I was enthusiastic about democracy which I thought would guarantee them all equal rights and liberty of conscience. That was as far as I went.

But I was much less interested in remote political and social questions than in the problems that concerned me personally: morals, my spiritual life, my relationship with God. I began to think very deeply about these things.

*

All nature spoke to me of God's presence. But it seemed to me quite definitely that He was a total stranger to the restless world of men. Just as the Pope, away inside the Vatican, hadn't to bother his head about what was going on in the world, so God, high up in the infinity of heaven, was not supposed to take any interest in the details of earthly adventures. I had long since learnt to distinguish His law from secular authority. My insolence in class, and my furtive reading of banned books did not concern Him. As year followed after year, my growing piety was purified and I began to reject dry-as-dust morality in favour of a more lively mysticism. I prayed, I meditated, I tried to make my heart aware of the divine presence. About the age of twelve I invented mortifications: locked in the water-closet – my sole refuge – I would scrub my flesh with pumice-stone until the blood came, and fustigate myself with the thin golden chain I wore round my neck. My fervour did not bear fruit. In my books of piety there was much talk about spiritual progress and exaltation; souls were supposed to stagger up rugged paths and overcome obstacles; at one moment, they would be trudging across barren wildernesses and at another a celestial dew would fall for their refreshment: it was quite an adventure; in fact, whereas intellectually I felt I was moving ever onward and upward in my quest for knowledge, I never had the impression that I was drawing any closer to God. I longed for apparitions, ecstasies; I yearned for something to happen inside or outside me: but nothing came, and in the end my spiritual exercises were more and more like make-believe. I exhorted myself to have patience and looked forward to the day when, miraculously detached from the earth, I would find myself ensconced at the heart of eternity. Meanwhile I was able to go on living unconstrainedly on earth because my efforts set me up on spiritual peaks whose serenity could not be troubled by worldly trifles.

My complacency received a nasty shock. For the last seven years I had been making my confession to Abbé Martin twice a month; I would expatiate upon the state of my immortal soul; I would accuse myself of having taken Holy Communion without any true religious fervour, of not having thought often enough of God, and of having paid Him lip-service only in my prayers; he would reply to these ethereal shortcomings with a sermon couched in very elevated terms. But one day, instead of going through the usual rigmarole, he began to speak to me in a more familiar tone of voice: 'It has come to my ears that my little Simone has changed . . . that she is disobedient, noisy, that she answers back when she is reprimanded. . . . From now on you must be on your guard against these things.' My cheeks were aflame; I gazed with horror upon the impostor whom for years I had taken as the representative of God on earth; it was as if he had suddenly tucked up his cassock and revealed the skirts of one of the church-hens; his priest's robe was only a disguise for an old tittle-tattle. With burning face I left the confessional, determined never to set foot in it again: from that moment on, it would have been as repugnant to me to kneel before the Abbé Martin as before 'the old scarecrow'. Whenever I caught a glimpse of his black skirts swishing along a school corridor, my heart would begin to thump and I would run away: they made me feel physically sick, as if the Abbé's deceit had made me his accomplice in some obscene act.

I suppose he must have been very surprised; but probably he felt himself bound by the secret of the confessional; I never heard that he told anyone of my defection; he did not attempt to have it out with me. The break had been sudden, but complete.

God emerged blameless from this episode; but only just. If I had been so prompt in disowning my spiritual director, it was in order to exorcise the frightful suspicion which for a moment veiled the heavens in blackness: perhaps God Himself was as fussy and narrow-minded as an old church-hen; perhaps God was stupid! While the Abbé was talking to me, an idiot hand had fallen on the back of my neck, bending my head down until it pressed my face into the ground; till the day of my death, the dead hand of stupidity would force me to crawl through life, blinded by mud and dark; I should have to say good-bye for ever to truth, liberty, and all happiness: living would be a calamity and a disgrace.

I pulled myself away from that leaden hand; I concentrated all my revulsion on the traitor who had usurped the role of divine intermediary. When I left the chapel, God had been restored to His position of omniscient majesty; I had patched up heaven again. I went wandering under the vaulted roofs of Saint-Sulpice, seeking a confessor who would not alter the messages from on high by the use of impure human words. I tried a red-head, and then a dark-haired one whom I succeeded in interesting in my soul. He suggested a few themes for meditation and lent me a *Handbook of Ascetic and Mystical Theology*. But in the great bare church I could not feel at home as I did in the school chapel. My new spiritual director had not been given to me when I was a small girl; I had chosen him, rather casually: he was not a Father and I could not open myself completely to him. I had passed judgement on a priest, and despised him: no other priest would ever seem to me to be the sovereign Judge. No one on earth was the exact incarnation of God: I was alone before Him. And in the very depths of my being remained unanswered some disturbing questions: who was He? what did He really want? on whose side was He?

My father was not a believer; the greatest writers and the finest thinkers shared his scepticism; on the whole, it was generally the women who went to church; I began to find it paradoxical and upsetting that the truth should be *their* privilege, when men, beyond all possible doubt, were their superiors. At the same time, I thought there was no greater disaster than to lose one's faith and I often tried to insure myself against this risk. I had reached rather an advanced stage in my religious instruction and had followed lectures in apologetics; I had subtle arguments to refute any objection that might be brought against revealed truths; but I didn't know one that could prove them. The allegory of the clock and the clockmaker did not convince me. I was too ignorant of human suffering to find in it an argument against Providence; but there was no very obvious harmony in the world. Christ and a host of saints had manifested the supernatural here on earth: I realized that the Bible, the Gospels, the miracles, and the visions were vouched for only by the authority of the Church. 'The greatest miracle at Lourdes is Lourdes itself,' my father used to say. The facts of religion were convincing only to those who were already convinced. Today, I did not doubt that the Virgin had appeared to Bernadette in a blue and white robe: but tomorrow perhaps I would doubt it. Believers admitted the existence of this vicious circle since they declared that faith requires divine grace. I didn't suppose that God would play me a dirty trick and refuse me grace for ever; but I should have liked all the same to be able to get my hands on some irrefutable proof; I found only one: the voices of Joan of Arc. Joan belonged to historical fact; my father as well as my mother venerated her. She was neither a liar nor an illuminee, so how could one deny her witness? The whole of her extraordinary adventure confirmed it: the voices had spoken to her; this was an established scientific fact and I couldn't understand how my father managed to elude it.

One evening at Meyrignac I was leaning, as on so many other evenings, out of my window; a warm fragrance was rising from the stables up to the star-sprinkled sky; my prayer rose half-heartedly and then fell back to earth. I had spent my day eating forbidden apples and reading, in a book by Balzac – also forbidden – the strange idyll of a young man and a panther; before falling asleep I was going to tell myself some queer old tales which would put me in a queer state of mind. 'These are sins,' I told myself. It was impossible to deceive myself any longer: deliberate disobedience, systematic lies, impure imaginings – such conduct could hardly be described as innocent. I dipped my hands into the freshness of the cherry laurel leaves. I listened to the gurgling of the water, and I knew then that nothing would make me give up earthly joys. 'I no longer believe in God,' I told myself, with no great surprise. That was proof: if I had believed in Him, I should not have allowed myself to offend Him so light-heartedly. I had always thought that the world was a small price to pay for eternity; but it was worth more than that, because I loved the world, and it was suddenly God whose price was small: from now on His name would have to be a cover for nothing more than a mirage. For a long time now the concept I had had of Him had been purified and refined, sublimated to the point where He no longer had any countenance divine, any concrete link with the earth or therefore any being. His perfection cancelled out His reality. That is why I felt so little surprise when I became aware of His absence in heaven and in my heart. I was not denying Him in order to rid myself of a troublesome person: on the contrary, I realized that He was playing no further part in my life and so I concluded that He had ceased to exist for me.

This liquidation had been bound to happen. I was too much of an extremist to be able to live under the eye of God and at the same time say both yes and no to life. On the other hand it would have been repugnant to me to skip in bad faith from the profane to the sacred and to affirm my belief in Him when I was living without His presence. I could not admit any kind of compromise arrangement with heaven. However little you withheld from Him, it would be too much if God existed; and however little you gave Him, it would be too much again if He did not exist. Quibbling with one's conscience, haggling over one's pleasures – such petty bargaining disgusted me. That is why I did not attempt to prevaricate. As soon as I saw the light, I made a clean break.

My father's scepticism had prepared the way for me; I would not be embarking alone upon a hazardous adventure. I even felt great relief at finding myself released from the bonds of sex and childhood, and in agreement with those liberal spirits I admired.

[137]

The voices of Joan of Arc did not trouble me too much; I was intrigued by other enigmas: but religion had got me used to mysteries. And it was easier for me to think of a world without a creator than of a creator burdened with all the contradictions in the world. My incredulity never once wavered.

Yet the face of the universe changed. More than once during the days that followed, sitting under the purple beech or the silvery poplars I felt with anguish the emptiness of heaven. Until then, I had stood at the centre of a living tableau whose colours and lighting God Himself had chosen; all things murmured softly of His glory. Suddenly everything fell silent. And what a silence! The earth was rolling through space that was unseen by any eye, and lost on its immense surface, there I stood alone, in the midst of sightless regions of the air. Alone: for the first time I understood the terrible significance of that word. Alone: without a witness, without anyone to speak to, without refuge. The breath in my body, the blood in my veins, and all this hurly-burly in my head existed for no one. I got up and ran back to the gardens and sat down under the catalpa between Mama and Aunt Marguerite, so great was my need to hear a human voice.

I made another discovery. One afternoon, in Paris, I realized that I was condemned to death. I was alone in the house and I did not attempt to control my despair: I screamed and tore at the red carpet. And when, dazed, I got to my feet again, I asked myself: 'How do other people manage? How shall *I* manage too? . . .' It seemed to me impossible that I could live all through life with such horror gnawing at my heart. When the reckoning comes, I thought, when you're thirty or forty and you think: 'It'll be tomorrow,' how on earth can you bear the thought? Even more than death itself I feared that terror that would soon be with me always.

Fortunately, in the course of the scholastic year these metaphysical fulgurations were rare: I hadn't enough free time and solitude. My changed attitude did not affect my daily life. I had stopped believing in God when I discovered that God had no influence on my behaviour: so this did not change in any way when I gave Him up. I had always imagined that the logical necessity of moral laws depended on Him: but they were so deeply engraved on my spirit that they remained unaltered for me after I had abolished Him. It was my respect for her which gave my mother's rulings a sacred character, and not the fact that she might owe her authority to some supernatural power. I went on submitting myself to her decisions. Everything was as before: the concept of duty; righteousness; sexual taboos.

I had no intention of revealing my spiritual turmoil to my father: it would have put him in a terribly embarrassing situation. So I bore my secret all alone and found it a heavy burden: for the first time in my life I had the feeling that good was not necessarily the same thing as truth. I couldn't help seeing myself through the eyes of others – my mother, Zaza, my school-friends, my teachers even – and through the eyes of the girl I once had been. The year before, among the philosophy specialists, there had been an older pupil of whom it was rumoured that she was an 'unbeliever'; she worked well, she never expressed subversive notions, and she had not been expelled; but I would feel a sort of terror whenever I caught sight, in the school corridors, of her face which was all the more disturbing because of the fixed intensity of a glass eye. Now it was my turn to feel I was a black sheep. The awkwardness of my situation was aggravated by dissimulation: I still went to Mass and took Holy Communion. I would swallow the host with complete indifference, and yet I knew that, according to the faith, I was committing a sacrilege. I was making mine all the worse by concealing it; but how could I have dared confess it? I would have been pointed at with the finger of scorn, expelled from the school; I would have lost Zaza's friendship; and how terribly upset my mother would have been! I was condemned to live out a lie. It was no harmless fib: it was a lie that cast a shadow over my whole life, and some-times – especially with Zaza whose forthrightness I admired – it weighed upon my spirits like a secret disease. Once again I was the victim of a spell which I couldn't manage to exorcize: I had done nothing wrong, and I felt guilty. If the grown-ups had called me a hypocrite, a blasphemer, an unnatural and artful child, their verdict would have seemed to me at once horribly unjust and perfectly well-deserved. I could be said to be living a double life; there was no relationship between my true self and the self that others saw.

Sometimes I suffered such distress at feeling myself a marked person, an accused outcast, that I longed to fall into error again. I had to return the *Handbook of Ascetic and Mystical Theology* to Abbé Roulin. I went back to Saint-Sulpice, kneeled down in his confessional, and told him that I had not partaken of the sacra-ments for several months because I had lost my faith. Seeing the

Handbook and measuring the heights from which I had fallen, the Abbé was astounded, and with a disconcerting brutality asked me: 'What mortal sin have you committed?' I protested that I had not committed any sin. He did not believe me and advised me to pray hard. I resigned myself to the life of an outcast.

About this time I read a novel which seemed to me to translate my spiritual exile into words: George Eliot's *The Mill on the Floss* made an even deeper impression upon me than *Little Women*. I read it in English, at Meyrignac, lying on the mossy floor of a chestnut plantation. Maggie Tulliver, like myself, was torn between others and herself: I recognized myself in her. She too was dark, loved nature, and books and life, was too headstrong to be able to observe the conventions of her respectable surroundings, and yet was very sensitive to the criticism of a brother she adored. Her friendship with the young hunchback who lent her books moved me just as much as that between Jo and Laurie; I longed for her to marry him. But once again love broke with childhood. Maggie fell in love with a cousin's fiancé, Stephen, whose heart she captured quite unintentionally. Compromised by him, she refused to marry him out of loyalty to Lucy; village society would have excused a treachery sanctioned by marriage, but would not forgive Maggie for having sacrificed appearances to the voice of conscience. Even her brother disowned her. The only relationship I could imagine was a love-friendship one; in my view, the exchange and discussion of books between a boy and a girl linked them for ever; I couldn't understand the attraction Maggie felt for Stephen. But as she loved him, she should not have given him up. It was when she went back to the old mill, when she was misunderstood, calumniated, and abandoned by everyone that I felt my heart blaze with sympathy for her. I wept over her sorry fate for hours. The others condemned her because she was superior to them; I resembled her, and henceforward I saw my isolation not as a proof of infamy but as a sign of my uniqueness. I couldn't see myself dying of solitude. Through the heroine, I identified myself with the author: one day other adolescents would bathe with their tears a novel in which I would tell my own sad story.

I had long ago decided to devote my life to intellectual labours. Zaza shocked me when she declared, in a provocative tone of voice: 'Bringing nine children into the world as Mama has done is just as good as writing books.' I couldn't see any common denominator between these two modes of existence. To have children, who in their turn would have more children, was simply to go on playing the same old tune *ad infinitum*; the scholar, the artist, the writer, and the thinker created other worlds, all sweetness and light, in which everything had purpose. That was where I wished to spend my life; I was quite determined to carve out a place for myself in those rarefied spheres. As soon as I had given up all hopes of heaven, my worldly ambitions increased; I had to get on in life. Stretched out in a meadow, I could see at eye-level the endless waves of grass, each blade identical, each submerged in a miniature jungle that concealed it from all the rest. That unending repetition of ignorance and indifference was a living death. I raised my eyes and looked at the oak tree: it dominated the landscape and there was not another like it. That, I decided, is what *I* would be like.

Why did I decide to be a writer? As a child, I had never taken my scribblings very seriously; my real aim had been to acquire knowledge. I enjoyed doing French compositions, but my teachers objected to my stilted style; I did not feel I was a 'born' writer. Yet at the age of fifteen when I wrote in a friend's album the plans and preferences which were supposed to give a picture of my personality, I answered without hesitation the question 'What do you want to do later in life?' with 'To be a famous author.' As far as my favourite composer and my favourite flower were concerned I had invented more or less fictitious preferences. But on that one point I had no doubts at all; I had set my heart on that profession, to the exclusion of everything else.

The main reason for this was the admiration I felt for writers: my father rated them far higher than scholars, philosophers, and professors. I, too, was convinced of their supremacy; even if his name was well-known, a specialist's monograph would be accessible to only a small number of people; but everyone read novels: they touched the imagination and the heart; they brought their authors universal and intimate fame. As a woman, these dizzy summits seemed to me much more accessible than the lowlier slopes; the most celebrated women had distinguished themselves in literature.

I had always had a longing to communicate with others. In my friend's album I cited as my favourite hobbies reading and conversation. I was a great talker. I would recount, or try to, everything that had struck me in the course of the day. I dreaded night and oblivion; it was agony to condemn to silence all that I had seen, felt, and liked. Moved by the moonlight, I longed for pen and paper and the ability to describe my feelings. When I was fifteen I loved volumes of letters, intimate journals – for example the diary of Eugénie de Guérin – that attempted to make time come to a stop. I had also realized that novels, short stories, and tales are not divorced from life but that they are, in their own way, expressions of it.

If at one time I had dreamed of being a teacher it was because I wanted to be a law unto myself; I now thought that literature would allow me to realize this dream. It would guarantee me an immortality which would compensate for the loss of heaven and eternity; there was no longer any God to love me, but I should have the undying love of millions of hearts. By writing a work based on my own experience I would re-create myself and justify my existence. At the same time I would be serving humanity: what more beautiful gift could I make it than the books I would write? I was interested at the same time in myself and in others; I accepted my 'incarnation' but I did not wish to renounce my universal prerogative. My plan to be a writer reconciled everything; it gratified all the aspirations which had been unfolding in me during the past fifteen years.

*

I had always thought very highly of love. When I was about thirteen, in the weekly magazine *Le Noël* which I was given instead of *L'Étoile Noëliste*, I read an edifying little tale entitled *Ninon-Rose*. Pious little Ninon loved André, who loved her too; but her cousin Thérèse, in tears, her lovely long hair spread out over her nightdress, confided to her that she was consumed with a violent passion for André; after an inner conflict and a few well-chosen prayers, Ninon decided on self-sacrifice; she refused to accept André who, on the rebound, married Thérèse. But Ninon had her reward: she married another very worthy young man called Bernard. This story disgusted me. The hero of a novel had the right to be mistaken in the object of his devotion or about his own feelings; true love might well be born from a love that was false or incomplete – like that of David Copperfield for his girl-wife. But true love, from the moment it burst into passionate life, was irreplaceable; no self-sacrifice, however generous, should be allowed to come between it and its object. Zaza and I were bowled over by one of Foggezzaro's novels, *Daniel Cortis*. Daniel was an important Catholic politician; the woman he loved and who loved him in return was already married; there was a most exceptional degree of understanding between them; their hearts beat as one, and they had the same opinions about everything: they were made for one another. Yet even a platonic friendship would have given rise to unsavoury gossip, ruined Daniel's career and compromised the cause he served. Swearing to be faithful to one another 'until death and beyond', they parted for ever. The story harrowed me, and made me furious too. Daniel's career, the cause, and so on were all abstract things. I found it absurd and criminal that they should put them before love, happiness, life. Doubtless it was my friendship with Zaza which made me attach so much weight to the perfect union of two human beings; discovering the world together and as it were making a gift of their discoveries to one another, they would, I felt, take possession of it in a specially privileged way; at the same time, each would find a definite meaning in existence in the other's need. To give up love seemed to me to be as senseless as to neglect one's health because one believes in eternal life.

I was determined not to let any of the good things of this world slip through my fingers. When I gave up the idea of becoming a nun, I began to dream of love on my own account; I found I could envisage without repugnance being married to a man. Maternity was something I couldn't entertain, and I was astounded whenever Zaza started cooing over new-born infants with crumpled red faces: but I no longer thought it would be out of the question to spend the rest of my days with the man of my choice. My parents' house was no prison, and if I'd had to leave it without warning I should have been panic-stricken; but I had now ceased to look upon my eventual departure as an agonizing separation. I was feeling rather stifled in the family circle. That is why I was so vividly impressed by a film based on Bataille's *Le Berçail* which a chance invitation enabled me to see. The heroine was bored with her children and a husband as rebarbative as Monsieur Mabille; a heavy chain round her wrists symbolized her servitude. A lively, handsome young man came along and released her from the cares of house and home. The young woman, in a sleeveless linen dress, her hair blowing in the wind, was seen capering about the countryside hand in hand with her lover; they threw handfuls of hay in each other's faces – I felt I could almost smell it – and their eyes were always brimming with laughter: never had I felt, witnessed, or imagined such transports of gaiety. I don't know what twists and turns of the plot brought back the young woman, sadder and wiser, to the family fold, where her husband welcomed her with open arms; having repented of her outburst, she saw the heavy iron chain turn into a garland of roses. I was very sceptical about this miraculous transformation. But I had been dazzled by the revelation of unknown, unnamed delights which would one day be mine; they were liberty and physical pleasure. The grown-ups' mournful bondage frightened me; nothing unexpected ever happened to them; sighing, they put up with an existence in which everything was decided beforehand, and in which no one ever decided anything. Bataille's heroine had dared to make a decision, and the sun had smiled upon her. For a long time after that, whenever I turned my inward eye towards the uncertain years when I should be grown-up, the memory of a couple skipping about in a field made me quiver with hope.

In the summer of my fifteenth year, I went boating once or twice in the Bois de Boulogne with Zaza and some other school-friends. In one of the avenues I noticed a young couple walking ahead of me; the boy was resting his hand lightly on the girl's shoulder. Suddenly moved by the sight, I said to myself that it must be sweet to go through life with someone's hand on one's shoulder, a hand so well-known that one barely felt its weight, and so ever-present that loneliness would be banished for good. 'A well-matched pair'; I used to muse over those words. Neither my sister, who was too close to me, nor Zaza, who was too distant, had ever let me sense the true meaning of the phrase. After that, reading in the study, I would often look up from my book and wonder silently: 'Will I ever meet the one who is made for me?' My reading hadn't provided me with my ideal. I had felt very close to Hellé, Marcelle Tinayre's heroine. 'Girls like you, Hellé,' her father had told her, 'are fit to be the companions of heroes.' This prophecy had aroused my interest; but I found the bearded, ginger-haired missionary she finally married rather revolting. I had no particular type in mind for my future husband. On the other hand, I had a very precise idea of what our relationship would be; I would feel for him a passionate admiration. In this respect, as in all others, necessity must govern the choice. My chosen one must, like Zaza, impose himself upon me, prove he was the right one; otherwise I should always be wondering: why he and not another? Such a doubt was incompatible with true love. I should be in love the day a man came along whose intelligence, culture, and authority could bring me into subjection.

Zaza did not agree with me on this point; for her, too, love implied mutual esteem and understanding; but if a man was sensitive and imaginative, whether he was an artist or a poet, she said it didn't matter to her if he had had very little education or was even not very intelligent. 'But then you would not be able to discuss everything,' I objected. A painter, a musician would not have understood me completely, and a part of him would always be beyond my grasp. I wanted husband and wife to have everything in common; each was to fulfil for the other the role of exact observer which I had formerly attributed to God. That ruled out the possibility of loving anyone *different*; I should not marry unless I met someone more accomplished than myself, yet my equal, my double.

Why did I insist that he should be superior to me? I don't for one moment think I was looking for a father-image in him; I valued my independence; I would have a profession, I would write and have a life of my own; I never thought of myself as a man's female companion; we would be two comrades. Nevertheless the concept I had of our relationship was influenced indirectly by the feelings I had had for my father. My education, my culture, and the present state of society all conspired to convince me that women belong to an inferior caste; Zaza was doubtful about this because she much preferred her mother to Monsieur Mabille; but in my own case my father's prestige had strengthened that opinion: my whole existence was in part founded upon it. If in the absolute sense a man, who was a member of the privileged species and already had a flying start over me, did not count more than I did, I was forced to the conclusion that in a relative sense he counted less: in order to be able to acknowledge him as my equal, he would have to prove himself my superior in every way.

On the other hand I would think of myself as it were from within, as someone who was in the process of being created, and my ambition was to progress to the infinite of perfection; I saw the chosen one from outside, like a complete person; in order that he might always be at my own lofty level, I would provide him from the start with perfections that for me were still unrealized hopes;

from the very start he would be the model of all I wished to become; he would, therefore, be superior to me. Yet I was careful not to set too great a distance between us. I could not have accepted a man whose thoughts and work were an enigma to me; love would be a justification, not a limitation. The picture I conjured up in my mind was of a steep climb in which my partner, a little more agile and stronger than myself, would help me up from one stage to the next. I was grasping rather than generous; if *I* had had to drag someone along behind me, I should have been consumed with impatience. In that case, celibacy was preferable to marriage. A life in common would have to favour and not stand in the way of my fundamental aim, which was to conquer the world. The man destined to be mine would be neither inferior nor different, nor outrageously superior; someone who would guarantee my existence without taking away my powers of self-determination.

This scheme was the blueprint for my dreams during the next two or three years. I attached a certain importance to these dreams. One day I asked my sister, with a touch of anxiety: was I quite definitely ugly? Was there any chance of my growing up into a woman pretty enough to be loved? Accustomed to hearing my father declare that I was a man, Poupette did not understand my question; she loved me, Zaza loved me; what was I worrying about? To tell the truth, I was only very mildly concerned about my appearance. My studies, books, these things which were dependent upon my will remained the centre of my preoccupations. I was less interested in my grown-up destiny than in my immediate future.

At the end of my penultimate year at school I was fifteen and a half, and I went with my parents to spend part of the holidays at Châteauvillain. Aunt Alice was dead; we stayed with Aunt Germaine, the mother of Titite and Jacques. The latter was in Paris taking the orals of his school-leaving certificate. I was very fond of Titite; she was radiantly fresh and dewy; she had beautiful sensuous lips and one could sense the blood pulsing beneath her skin. Engaged to a childhood friend, a ravishing young man with immensely long eye-lashes, she awaited marriage with an impatience which she made no attempt to hide; certain aunts hinted that when she was alone with her fiancé she sometimes behaved badly: *very* badly. On the evening of our arrival, we both went after dinner for a stroll in the avenue beyond the garden. We sat down on a stone bench; we were silent; we never had much to say to one another. She pondered a moment, then stared at me inquisitively: 'Are your studies *all* you want out of life?' she asked me. 'Are you happy with things that way? You don't want anything more?' I shook my head. 'It's all I want,' I said. It was true: at the close of that year at school, I couldn't see much further than the next one with the school-leaving certificate that I had to pass at the end of it. Titite gave a sigh and returned to day-dreams about her fiancé which I was sure would be rather sloppy, despite my fondness for her. Jacques arrived next day; he had got through, and he was bursting with self-satisfaction. He took me off to the tennis court, suggested we should have a knock-up, trounced me, and then casually asked forgiveness for having used me as an Aunt Sally. I knew that I didn't interest him very much. I had heard him talk admiringly of girls who were pre-paring for their degree and at the same time went on playing tennis, going to parties, dancing, and keeping up with the latest fashions. But his contempt left no impression on me; not for an instant did I deplore my poor game or the rudimentary styling of my pink pongee dress. I was worth much more than the regimented students whom Jacques preferred to me, and he would find it out himself one day.

I was beginning to emerge from the difficult age; instead of re-gretting my childhood I turned towards the future; it was still far enough away not to alarm me and already I was dazzled by its brilliance. I was sitting on a block of grey granite beside the little lake I had discovered at La Grillière the year before. A mill was reflected in the water, across which broken cloud-reflections were drifting. I was reading Gaston Boissier's *Archaeological Walks* and was telling myself that one day I too would go rambling on the Palatine Hill. The clouds in the lake were tinged with pink; I got up but could not bring myself to go; I leaned against the hazel hedge; the evening breeze was caressing the spindle-trees; it was touching me, too, brushing and buffeting me, and I gave myself up to its gentle violence. The hazel leaves were rustling and I under-stood their mysterious whispers; I was expected: by myself. Bathed in the sunset glow, with the world crouching at my feet like a big friendly animal, I smiled to myself at the adolescent who would die on the morrow only to rise again in all her glory: no other life, no moment in any other life could hold all the promises which were thrilling my credulous heart.

*

At the end of September my sister and I were invited to Meulan where the parents of Poupette's best friend had a country house; Anne-Marie Gendron was one of a large family, quite a wealthy and well-integrated one; they never had any quarrels; there was never a voice raised in anger, but everywhere there were smiles and kind attentions. I found myself back in a paradise whose very memory I had forgotten. The boys took us boating on the Seine; the eldest daughter, who was twenty, took us to Vernon in a taxi. We followed the river road; I was responsive to the landscape's charms but even more so to those of Clotilde; she invited me that evening to come to her room and we had a talk. She had passed all her exams, read a little, and was studying the piano very hard; she spoke to me of her love for music, of Madame Swetchine's *Letters*, and of her family. Her desk was full of souvenirs: bundles of letters tied up with ribbon, notebooks – probably private diaries – concert programmes, photographs, and a water-colour done by her mother and given to Clotilde on her eighteenth birthday. It seemed to me a most enviable thing to have a past all to oneself: almost as enviable as having a personality. She lent me a few books; she treated me as an equal and gave me advice with all the tender solicitude of an elder sister. I developed a crush on her. I didn't admire her as I did Zaza and she was too ethereal to inspire in me obscure longings, as Marguerite had done. But I thought she was so romantic; she presented me with the attractive image of the girl I too should be very soon. She took us back to our parents; the door had hardly closed after her departure when a scene broke out: we had left a toothbrush behind at Meulan! In contrast with the serenely happy time I had had, the acrimonious atmosphere into which I was plunged on my return suddenly seemed suffocating. Leaning my head against the cupboard in the hall, I sobbed my heart out, and my sister did likewise: 'Here's a nice thing! They no sooner get home than they start to cry!' my father and mother exclaimed indignantly. For the first time I admitted to myself how painful to bear were the shouts, the recriminations, and the reprimands which I usually suffered in silence; all the pent-up tears of the past months were choking me: they had to flow some time. I don't know if my mother guessed that inwardly I was beginning to turn away from her; but I irritated her and she often got into a temper over something I had done or said. And so I looked to Clotilde as I would have looked to a big sister for consolation. I went to see her fairly often; I was enraptured by her pretty clothes, the tasteful decoration of her room, her sweetness and kindness, and her independence; I admired her for taking a taxi whenever we went to a concert – I thought this was the height of magnificence – and for making notes on her programme about the pieces she liked best. Zaza, and even more so Clotilde's own friends, were staggered by my friendship with her; it was customary to keep company only with girls of one's own age, give or take a year. One day I went to tea at Clotilde's with Lili Mabille and other 'young ladies'. I felt out of place and I was disappointed by the insipidity of the conversation. And then Clotilde was very pious: she couldn't possibly be my mentor, now that I was no longer a believer. I expect that she for her part found me too young; she saw to it that we met less frequently and I didn't make any effort on my side; after a few weeks we didn't see each other any more. Not long after that, with a great deal of sickening sentimentality, she made a suitably 'arranged' match.

At the start of the school year, grandpapa fell ill. All his undertakings had failed. His son had invented a kind of tin which could be opened with a small coin: grandpapa had wanted to exploit this invention but he had lost the patent. He took his competitor to court and lost the case. Disturbing words like 'creditors', 'banker's drafts', and 'mortgages' kept creeping into his conversation. Sometimes when I lunched at his house there would be a ring at the front door: he would lay a finger on his lips and we would hold our breath. His eyes would glaze over in his purpling face. One afternoon at home when he got up to go he started to mumble: 'Where's my umbrella?' When I saw him again he was sitting motionless in an armchair with his eyes closed; he could only move with great difficulty and dozed all day long. From time to time he would lift his eyelids: 'I've got an idea,' he would tell grandmama. 'I've got a good idea. We'll all be rich.' He soon became completely paralysed and never left his big bed with the twisted columns; his body became covered with bedsores which gave off a frightful smell. Grandmama nursed him and knitted children's garments all day long. Grandpapa had always been prone to catastrophe; grandmama accepted his fate with such philosophical resignation and they were both so old anyhow that their misfortune hardly touched me.

I was working even harder than ever. The imminence of the examinations and the hope that I would soon be at the university spurred me on. It was a great year for me. My face got into better shape, and I was no longer incommoded by my growing body; my secrets did not weigh so heavily. My friendship with Zaza ceased to be the torment it had been. I had regained confidence in myself; and Zaza was changing too: I didn't wonder why, but, by a stroke of irony, she became all dreamy and romantic. She began to like Musset, Lacordaire, and Chopin. She still inveighed against the pharisaism of her surroundings, but no longer extended her criticisms to the whole of humanity. From now on she spared me her sarcasms.

There was a very select little group of us at the Cours Désir. The school only prepared for the Latin–modern languages examinations. Monsieur Mabille wanted his daughter to have a good grounding in science; I myself liked things I could get my teeth into, like mathematics. An extra teacher was appointed who taught algebra, trigonometry, and physics. Mademoiselle Chassin was young, lively, and very competent; she didn't need to waste time on moral exhortations: we did serious work. She was very fond of us. Whenever Zaza stayed up in the clouds too long, Mademoiselle would say sweetly: 'Where are you, Elizabeth?' Zaza would start and smile. We had for classmates twins who were always in mourning and almost never said a word. I was enchanted by the intimate atmosphere of our classes. In Latin we had been allowed to skip a year and go on to a higher grade; the struggle to keep up with the pupils in the top class kept me on my toes. When I found myself back with my normal classmates in the year when I was to take my school-leaving certificate there was no longer the spice of novelty and Abbé Trécourt's knowledge seemed a little thin; he frequently made mistakes in translation; but this big fellow with the blotchy complexion was more forthcoming and more jovial than our old school-marms and we had a genuine affection for him which he obviously reciprocated. Our parents thought it would be fun if we also offered Latin–modern languages in our examination, and in January we began to learn Italian; we were soon able to translate *Cuore* and *le mie prigioni*. Zaza took German; but as my English teacher showed herself to be well-disposed towards me I followed her lessons with pleasure. On the other hand, we had to put up with the patriotic tub-thumping of Mademoiselle Gontran, our history teacher; and Mademoiselle Lejeune exasperated us by the narrowness and pettiness of her literary tastes. In order to broaden our horizons we read a great deal and had long discussions among ourselves. Often we would stubbornly defend our points of view in class; I don't know if Mademoiselle Lejeune was perspicacious enough to see through me but she now seemed to distrust me far more than Zaza.

We struck up friendships; we would meet to play cards and chatter; in summer we would go on Saturdays to an open-air tennis court in the rue Boulard. None of our other friends meant much to Zaza or myself. If the truth were told, the older pupils at the Cours Désir were not attractive. When, after eleven years' hard work, I won a silver-gilt medal, my father agreed without much enthusiasm to attend the prize-giving; he complained afterwards that he had never seen such a collection of ugly girls. A few of my schoolmates had quite pleasant features; but when we made public appearances we were done up like dogs' dinners: the severe hair-styles and the violent or sickly-sweet colours of our satin or taffeta dresses drained all the life from our faces. The thing that must have struck my father most forcibly was the depressed, mournful look those adolescents had. I was so accustomed to it that when a new girl arrived one day and I saw her laughing – it was a real, hearty laugh – I opened my eyes wide in astonishment; she was an international golf champion and she had travelled widely; her bobbed hair, her well-cut jumper and box-pleated skirt, her sporty manner, and her uninhibited voice were obvious signs that she had not been brought up under the influence of Saint Thomas Aquinas; she spoke perfect English and knew enough Latin to be able to present the subject for her school-leaving certificate at the age of fifteen and a half; Corneille and Racine bored her to tears. 'Literature makes me sick,' she told me. 'Oh, don't say that!' I protested. 'Why not?' she retorted. 'It's the truth.' Her gay personality enlivened the funereal 'lecture-study room'. Some things she found tedious, but there were other things in her life which gave her pleasure, and one felt that she had a future ahead of her. The air of sadness that emanated from my other schoolmates was due less to their appearance than to their hopeless resignation. Once they had passed their school-leaving certificate they would follow a few lecture-courses on history and literature, they would attend classes at the École du Louvre or the Red Cross where they would learn how to decorate china, make batik prints and fancy bindings, and occupy themselves with good works. From time to time they would be taken out to a performance of *Carmen* or for a walk round the tomb of Napoleon in order to make the acquaintance of some suitable young man; with a little luck, they would marry him. This was the elder Mabille girl's life; she did cooking and went to dances, acted as secretary to her father, and helped her sisters to make their clothes. Her mother dragged her from one meeting with a young man to another. Zaza told me that one of her aunts had a theory about 'the sacrament of love at first sight': at that very moment when the fiancés said 'yes' before the priest, they were filled with grace, and at once fell in love with one another. These tribal rites disgusted Zaza; she declared one day that she couldn't see any difference between a woman who married 'for convenience' and a prostitute; she had been taught that a Christian woman should respect her body: she would not be respecting it if she gave it to a man without love, for financial or family reasons. Her vehemence astounded me; it was as if she felt her own body was defiled by the ignominy of this bartering of human souls. The question did not arise for me. I would earn my own living, I would be free. But in Zaza's family you either had to get married or become a nun. 'Celibacy,' they used to repeat, 'is not a vocation.' She began to dread the future; was that the cause of her insomnia? She slept badly; often she would get up in the middle of the night and rub herself from top to toe, with eau de Cologne; in the morning, to get herself going, she would swallow quantities of black coffee and white wine. When she told me about these excesses, I realized that there were many things I did not know about her. But I encouraged her in her resistance to the family code and she was grateful to me for it: I was her only ally. We both agreed that many things were disgusting, and we both had a great longing for freedom and happiness.

Despite our differences, we often reacted to circumstances in the same manner. My father had received from his actor friend two free seats for a matinée at the Odéon; he made us a present of them; they were doing a play by Paul Fort, *Charles VI*. When I found myself alone with Zaza in a box, I was overjoyed. The three knocks sounded, the curtain rose, and we were watching a heavy melodrama; Charles went out of his mind; at the end of the first act, haggard-eyed, he was staggering round the stage in a long, incoherent monologue; I sank deeper and deeper into a gloomy despair that was as appallingly lonely as his own madness. I took a look at Zaza: she was white-faced. 'If it goes on like this let's leave,' I suggested. She agreed. When the curtain went up on the second act,

Charles, in shirt-sleeves, was struggling to get out of the clutches of masked and hooded men. We left the box. The attendant stopped us: 'Why are you leaving?' 'It's too horrible,' I said. She burst out laughing. 'But it isn't *real*, my pets. It's just play-acting.' We knew that: all the same, we had seen something frightful.

My understanding with Zaza and her good opinion helped me to free myself from the grown-ups and to see myself with my own eyes. But one incident reminded me how much I still depended on their judgement. It exploded unexpectedly just as I was beginning to enjoy a care-free existence.

Just as I did every week, I made a careful word-for-word translation of my Latin text; I wrote it in a column opposite the original. Then I had to put it into 'good French'. As it happened, this particular piece of prose had been translated in my text book on Latin literature, and with an elegance which I felt could not be equalled: in comparison, all the expressions which came to my mind seemed to be painfully clumsy. I had not made any mistake in the meaning; I was certain to get a good mark, and I had no ulterior motives; but the requirements of the object, the phrase itself, had to be satisfied: each sentence had to be perfect. It was repugnant to me to substitute my heavy-handed inventions for the ideal model furnished by the text book. There and then I copied it straight out of the book.

We were never left alone with the Abbé Trécourt; one of our old school-marms would sit at a little table near the window and supervise us; before he handed us back our translations, she entered our marks in a register. On that day the task had fallen to Mademoiselle Dubois, the one with the degree, whose Latin classes I would have normally attended the year before had not Zaza and I turned our noses up at them in favour of the Abbé's: she did not like me. I could hear her making a fuss behind my back; she was whispering furious protests. In the end she drafted a note which she placed on top of the pile of exercise books before giving them back to the Abbé. He wiped his eyeglasses, read the message, and smiled: 'Yes,' he said mildly, 'this passage from Cicero was already translated in your text books and many of you apparently noticed it. I have given the highest marks to those of you whose work showed the most originality.' Despite his indulgent tones, Mademoiselle Dubois' furious face, and the uneasy silence of my classmates filled me with terror. Whether through force of habit, absent-mindedness, or simple affection, the Abbé had given me the best mark. I had got 17. In any case, no one had got less than 12. Doubtless in order to justify his partiality he asked me to construe the text word by word: I kept my voice steady and did so without a mistake. He congratulated me and the tension eased a little. Mademoiselle Dubois didn't dare ask me to read out my final version; Zaza, sitting next to me, didn't so much as glance at it: she was scrupulously honest and I think refused to entertain any suspicions about me. But when the lesson was over certain of my other classmates started whispering together and Mademoiselle Dubois took me to one side: she felt she would have to inform Mademoiselle Lejeune of my perfidy. And so the thing I had often dreaded was finally going to happen: an action performed innocently and in secret would, by being brought to light, disgrace me. I still felt some respect for Mademoiselle Lejeune: the idea that she would despise me was torture. It was impossible to turn back the clock, to undo what I had done: I was marked for life! I had had a presentiment of danger: the truth can be unjust, unfair; all that evening and part of the night I tried to fight a way out of the trap into which I had so thoughtlessly fallen and which would not let me go. Usually I got round difficulties by running away from them, or keeping silent, or forgetting them; I rarely took any initiative; but this time I decided to fight it out. Lies would be needed to cover up the circumstances which conspired against me; so lie I must. I went to see Mademoiselle Lejeune in her study and I swore to her, with tears in my eyes, that I hadn't copied my Latin translation: only some involuntary recollections of the text book version had slipped into mine. Convinced that I had done nothing wrong, I defended myself with all the fervour of an injured innocent. But my tactics were absurd: I was guiltless, I should have taken my work with me as the chief evidence in my defence; but I merely gave my word. The principal did not believe me, told me so, and added impatiently that the subject was now closed. She did not tell me off, and she did not reproach me for what I had done: this indifference, and the crisp tone of her voice made me realize that she hadn't an ounce of affection for me. I had been afraid that my mistake would ruin the good opinion she had of me: but for a long time now I had had nothing more to lose. I recovered my equanimity. She had so categorically withheld her respect that I no longer wished for it.

During the weeks preceding the examination, my happiness was unalloyed. The weather was fine and my mother allowed me to go and study in the Luxembourg Gardens. I would sit in the 'English gardens', at the edge of a lawn, or near the Medici fountain. I was still wearing my hair down my back, caught together with a slide, but my cousin Annie, who often made me a present of her cast-off clothes, had given me that summer a white pleated skirt with a blue cretonne bodice; in my sailor-hat I fancied myself to be a real young lady. I was reading Faguet, Brunetière, and Jules Lemaître; I would sniff the fragrance of the lawns and feel I was as emancipated as the university students who strolled through the gardens. I would pass through the gates and go and rummage round the arcades of the Odéon; I felt the same thrill of delight there as I had felt at the age of ten in my mother's circulating library, the Bibliothèque Cardinale. Here there were displayed rows of leather-bound books, gilt-edged; their pages had been cut, and I would stand there reading for two or three hours without ever being asked to buy anything. I read Anatole France, the Goncourts, Colette, and whatever I could lay my hands on. I told myself that as long as there were books I could be sure of being happy.

I had also been given permission to sit up late: when Papa had left for the Café Versailles where he played bridge nearly every evening, and when Mama and my sister had gone to bed I would be left alone in the study. I would lean out of the window; the wind would bring me gusts of fragrance from the leafy trees; across the way, windows would be lighted. I would get Papa's opera glasses, take them out of their case and spy on the lives of strangers, just as I had used to do; I didn't care how trivial were the things I saw; I was – I still am – very conscious of the fascination of these little peepshows, these lighted rooms hanging in the night. My gaze would wander from house to house, and I would tell myself, deeply affected by the balmy airs of the summer evening: 'Soon I'll be living my own life . . . *really* living.'

I enjoyed my examinations. In the amphitheatres of the Sorbonne I rubbed shoulders with boys and girls who had been educated in schools and colleges and *lycées* which I had never even heard of: I was struggling free from the Cours Désir and facing up to the realities of life. Having been assured by my teachers that I had done well in the written examination, I approached the oral with complete self-confidence and took a great fancy to myself in my unfashionably long dress of sky-blue voile. In front of those important gentlemen who had gathered on purpose to evaluate my merits, I regained the self-conceit of childhood. The examiner in literature particularly flattered me by talking in quite a conversational manner; he asked me if I were a relative of Roger de Beauvoir; I told him that it was only a pseudonym; he questioned me about Ronsard; as I sat there displaying my learning I was admiring all the time the fine, thoughtful head which he inclined in my direction: at last, I was face to face with one of those superior men whose approbation I so earnestly desired! But in the Latin–modern languages oral the examiner gave me an ironic greeting: 'Well, mademoiselle! Have you come to pick up a few more diplomas?' I was rather disconcerted, and I suddenly realized that my performances might have appeared somewhat comical; but I held my own. I was given a pass with 'distinction', and my old schoolmarms, delighted to have this success to their credit, made much of me. My parents were over the moon. Jacques, peremptory as ever, had declared: 'You must pass with distinction, or else not at all.' He gave me his warmest congratulations. Zaza passed also, but at that period I was too much occupied with myself to bother much about her.

Clotilde and Marguerite sent me affectionate letters; my mother rather spoilt my pleasure in them by bringing them to me already opened and regaling me with a full description of their contents; but this custom was so well-established that I made no protest. By then we were at Valleuse, in Normandy, staying with some very prim and proper cousins. I didn't like their place: it was too well-groomed; there were no sunken lanes, no woods; the meadows were surrounded by barbed wire. One evening I crawled under a fence and lay down in the grass: a woman came up to me and asked if I wasn't feeling well. I returned to the garden, but I felt stifled there. With my father away, Mama and my cousins were all together like birds of a feather, all professing the same highly devout principles without asking any dissident voice to disturb their perfect harmony; speaking freely of spiritual matters in my presence, they seemed to involve me in a complicity which I didn't dare to challenge: I had the feeling that they were doing violence to my soul. We went by car to Rouen; the afternoon was spent visiting churches, of which there were very many, each one unleashing delirious admiration; the stone tracery in Saint Maclou caused their enthusiasm to rise to a paroxysm of ecstasy: what wonderful work!

[156]

what skill! what delicacy! I kept my peace. 'What! You don't think it's beautiful?' they asked me, scandalized. I found it neither beautiful nor ugly: I felt nothing at all. They urged me to look again. I gritted my teeth; I refused to let them thrust words into my mouth. All eyes were turned reproachfully upon my stubbornly silent lips; anger and distress had brought me to the verge of tears. In the end my cousin smoothed things over by explaining fatuously that at my age young people were often in a contrary mood; my torment was over.

Back in the Limousin, I found again the freedom I needed. When I had spent the whole day alone or with my sister, I was quite ready to play mah-jong with the family in the evening. I got my first real taste of philosophy by reading *Intellectual Life*, by Père Sertilanges, and Ollé-Laprune's *Moral Certainty* which bored me considerably.

My father had never tackled the study of philosophy; in my family, as in Zaza's, it was looked upon with suspicion. 'What a shame! You talk such good sense, and now they're going to teach you to talk nonsense!' one of Zaza's uncles had told her. But Jacques had been very interested in it. As for me, my hopes were always raised by anything new. I awaited the return to school with impatience.

Psychology, logic, moral philosophy, metaphysics: this was Abbé Trécourt's programme, four hours a week. All he did was to hand us back our essays, dictate a fair copy, and make us recite the chapter we had been asked to learn in the text book. Whatever the problem was, the author, the Révérend Père Lahr, made a rapid summary of human errors and instructed us in the truth according to Saint Thomas Aquinas. Nor did the Abbé himself bother much about the finer points of the subject. In order to confute idealistic theories he would cite the evidence of the sense of touch, and use this as an argument against the possibly illusory nature of human sight. He would pound on the table as he stated: 'What is, *is*!' The reading list he gave us was quite unappetizing: Ribot's *Attention*, Gustave Lebon's *Crowd Psychology*, and Fouillée's *The Power of Ideas*. Nevertheless I conceived a passion for philosophy. I found the problems that had intrigued me in childhood treated in books by serious gentlemen; suddenly the grown-up universe was no longer indisputably the only one; there was another side to it, a shady side; doubts were allowed to creep in: if only we went far enough, there'd be nothing left of it! We did not, of course, go too far, but even so it was rather extraordinary, after twelve years of dreary dogmatism, to find a discipline which asked questions and asked them of *me*. For suddenly it was I myself who was involved in these matters, and until then I had only been treated to commonplaces, as if I were a person of no account. Take my mind – where did it come from? Where did it get its powers? Condillac's statue made me pause, and gave me as dizzy flights of speculation as the old jacket I had when I was seven years old. I was flabbergasted to see the coordinates of the universe, too, begin to vacillate: Henri Poincaré's speculations on the relativity of space and time and measurement plunged me into infinities of meditation. I was deeply impressed by the pages in which he evokes the passage of mankind through the universe, the blind universe: no more than a flash in the dark, but a flash that is everything! For a long time I was haunted by the image of this great fire blazing down the sightless dark.

The thing that attracted me about philosophy was that it went straight to essentials. I had never liked fiddling detail; I perceived the general significance of things rather than their singularities, and I preferred understanding to seeing; I had always wanted to know *everything*; philosophy would allow me to appease this desire, for it aimed at total reality; philosophy went right to the heart of truth and revealed to me, instead of an illusory whirlwind of facts or empirical laws, an order, a reason, a necessity in everything. The sciences, literature, and all the other disciplines seemed to me to be very poor relations to philosophy.

Yet as day followed after day we did not seem to be learning anything very wonderful. But we managed to keep boredom at bay by the tenacity with which Zaza and I stated our opinions in class discussions. There was a particularly lively debate on the subject of the love which we call platonic and the love which we call – well, better just call it love. One of our classmates had cited Tristan and Isolde as platonic lovers. At this, Zaza burst out laughing: 'Platonic! Tristan and Isolde! Not on your life!' she declared, with a knowing air that disconcerted the whole class. The poor Abbé brought the lesson to a close by exhorting us all to make a 'sensible' match. 'After all,' he argued, 'you don't marry a young man simply because the colour of his tie suits him.' We decided to let him get away with that ridiculous remark. But we were not always quite so accommodating; when a subject interested us we discussed it with great intensity. We respected things, and believed that words like patriotism, duty, good, and evil had a meaning; we were simply trying to define that meaning; we weren't trying to destroy anything, but we liked to argue in a rational way. We thought it was bad enough to be called 'wrong-headed'. Mademoiselle Lejeune, who was present at all our philosophy lessons, declared that we were treading a dangerous and downward path. In the middle of our final year the Abbé had a little talk with each of us individually, and beseeched us not to let our hearts shrivel up; if we did, we would in the end resemble our schoolmistresses: they were saintly women, but it would be better if we did not follow in their footsteps. I was touched by his well-meant words, surprised by his aberration: I assured him that I had no intention of entering the religious confraternity. The thought of it filled me with a disgust which surprised even Zaza; despite her mockery, she still retained some affection for our old school-marms and I rather scandalized her when I told her that I would leave them without the slightest regret.

My school life was coming to an end, and something else was going to begin: what would it be? In *Les Annales* I read a lecture which set me day-dreaming; a former student at the teachers' training college for women at Sèvres was recalling her experiences there: she described the gardens in which beautiful young women, athirst for knowledge, went walking by moonlight, the sound of their voices mingling with the murmur of fountains. But my mother didn't like the idea of the École Normale Supérieure at Sèvres. And when I came to think about it, I hardly wanted to shut myself up with a lot of women away from Paris. So what should I do? I dreaded the arbitrary side of any choice. My father, who at the age of fifty had the painful prospect of an uncertain future ahead of him, wanted me to have some sort of security above everything else; he thought I should go into the Civil Service, which would provide me with a fixed salary and a pension on retirement. Someone recommended the School of Palaeography and Librarianship – l'École des Chartes. I went with my mother to an interview with a lady behind the scenes at the Sorbonne. We went along seemingly endless corridors lined with books; here and there were doors leading to offices full of filing cabinets. As a child I had always dreamed of working in this dusty ante-room of learning, and today I felt as if I were penetrating into the Holy of Holies. The lady we went to see described to us the attractions and also the difficulties of librarianship; I was put off by the thought of having to learn Sanskrit; I wasn't interested in dry-as-dust erudition. What I should have liked was to continue my study of philosophy. I had read in an illustrated magazine an article about a woman philosopher who was called Mademoiselle Zanta: she had taken her doctorate; she had been photographed, in a grave and thoughtful posture, sitting at her desk; she lived with a young niece whom she had adopted: she had thus succeeded in reconciling her intellectual life with the demands of feminine sensibility. How I should love to have such flattering things written one day about *me*! In those days the women who had a degree or a doctorate in philosophy could be counted on the fingers of one hand: I wanted to be one of those pioneers. From a practical point of view, the only career that would be open to me if I had a degree in philosophy was teaching: I had nothing against that. My father did not object to this plan; but he wouldn't hear of my giving private tuition in pupils' homes: I would have to get a post in a *lycée*. Why not? This solution was very much to my taste, and also set his mind at rest. My mother went in fear and trembling to tell my teachers of my decision; their faces went rigid with disapproval. They had given their lives to combating secular institutions and to them a state school was nothing better than a licensed brothel. In addition, they told my mother that the study of philosophy mortally corrupts the soul: after one year at the Sorbonne, I would lose both my faith and my good character. Mama felt worried. As a degree in classics held out greater possibilities – or so my father thought – and as there was a possibility that Zaza might be allowed to follow a few of the courses, I agreed to sacrifice philosophy for literature. But I was still determined to teach in a *lycée*. How scandalous! Eleven years of sermons, careful grooming, and systematic indoctrination, and now I was biting the hand that had fed me! It was with complete unconcern that I read in my teachers' eyes their opinion of my ingratitude, my unworthiness, my treachery: I had fallen into the hands of Satan.

In July, I passed in elementary mathematics and philosophy. The Abbé's teaching had been so feeble that my dissertation, which he would have marked at 16, only scraped through with 11. I made up for this in my science papers. On the eve of the oral, my father took me to the Théâtre de Dix-Heures, where I saw Dorin, Colline, and

Noël-Noël; I enjoyed myself immensely. How glad I was that I had finished with the Cours Désir! Yet a few days later, finding myself alone in the apartment, I was overcome by a strange uneasiness; I stood planted in the middle of the hall, feeling as utterly lost as if I had been transported to another planet! No family, no friends, no ties, no hope. My heart had died and the world was empty: could such an emptiness ever be filled? I was afraid. And then time started to flow again.

*

There was one respect in which my education had failed completely: despite all the books I had read, I was the most awful greenhorn. I was about sixteen when an aunt took my sister and me to the Salle Pleyel to see a film called *La Croisière jaune*. The house was full, and we had to stand at the back. I was surprised when I began to feel hands fumbling round my thin woollen coat, feeling me through the material; I thought somebody must be trying to pick my pockets or steal my handbag; I held on tightly to it; the hands continued to rub against me: it was absurd. I didn't know what to do or say: I just let them go on. When the film was over and the lights went up, a man wearing a brown trilby sniggered and pointed me out to a friend of his, who also started to snigger. They were laughing at me: why? I couldn't make it out at all.

A little later, someone – I can't remember who – sent me to a religious book-shop near Saint-Sulpice to purchase an article for a church youth club. A timid young fair-haired shop-assistant, wearing a long black overall, came forward and politely asked what I required. He walked away towards the back of the shop, beckoning me to follow; I went and stood beside him. He opened his overall, exposing something pink and erect; his face was devoid of expression and for a moment I stood there nonplussed; then I turned on my heels and fled. His preposterous gesture bothered me less than Charles VI's display of madness on the stage of the Odéon, but it left me with the feeling that the oddest things could happen to me without any warning. After that, whenever I found myself alone with a strange man – in a shop or on a platform of the Métro – I always felt a little apprehensive.

At the beginning of my philosophy course, Madame Mabille

[161]

persuaded Mama to let me take dancing lessons. Once a week Zaza and I would go to a dancing academy where girls and boys, under the supervision of an elderly lady, practised dance-steps. In those days I used to get myself up in a dress of sky-blue silk stockinette handed down to me from my cousin Annie, which fitted where it touched. All make-up was forbidden me. In our family, only my cousin Madeleine defied this ban on cosmetics. When she reached the age of sixteen she began to tart herself up discreetly. Papa, Mama, and Aunt Marguerite would point scandalized fingers at her: 'Madeleine! You've been putting powder on!' 'No, Aunt, I swear I haven't!' she would protest coquettishly, in an affected, babyish tone of voice. Along with the grown-ups, I laughed at her: any kind of artifice was always 'ridiculous'. Every morning they would harp on the same theme: 'It's no use trying to deny it, Madeleine, you've been putting powder on again; you can see it a mile off.' One day – she was then eighteen or nineteen – she got fed-up and retorted: 'Well, why shouldn't I?' She had finally admitted it: triumph for the grown-ups! But her reply gave me something to think about. In any case, we were far from living in a state of nature. In our family, the grown-ups claimed that 'make-up spoils the complexion'. But my sister and I often remarked to one another when we saw our aunts' raddled features that their prudence had not brought them any great reward. But I didn't attempt to argue them into letting me use cosmetics. So I used to arrive at the dancing academy in a dowdy old frock, with badly brushed hair, well scrubbed cheeks, and a shiny nose. I couldn't do anything with my body; I couldn't even swim or ride a bicycle: I felt as awkward and self-conscious as the day I had tried to show off my charms in the role of a Spanish dancer. I began to detest those dancing lessons, but for another reason. When my partner held me in his arms and held me to his chest, I felt a funny sensation that was rather like having butterflies in the stomach, but which I didn't find quite so easy to forget. When I got back home, I would throw myself in the leather arm chair, overpowered by a curious languor that I couldn't put a name to and that made me want to burst into tears. On the pretext that I had too much work, I gave up going to the dancing class.

Zaza was rather more sophisticated. 'When I think that our mothers are watching us dance, and never suspecting a thing, poor innocents!' she said to me one day. She used to tease her sister Lili and her older girl cousins: 'Go on! You're not going to tell me you'd enjoy it just as much if you were dancing among yourselves or with your brothers!' I thought she must connect the pleasure of dancing with something I had only the vaguest notions of – flirting. At the age of twelve, I had in my ignorance had an inkling of what physical desire and hugging and squeezing meant, but at seventeen, though in theory I was much better informed, I didn't even know what the trouble was all about.

I don't know whether there was a certain amount of self-deception in my ingenuousness: whatever it was, sexuality frightened me. Only one person, Titite, had ever made me realize that physical love may be enjoyed as the most natural thing in the world; her exuberant physique knew no shame, and when she used to recall the first night of her marriage, the desire that shone from her eyes made her even more beautiful. Aunt Simone insinuated that she had 'gone too far' with her fiancé; Mama wouldn't hear of it; I found their arguments quite beside the point; whether married or not, the embraces of these two good-looking young people did not shock me at all: they loved one another, and that was enough. But this isolated example was not sufficient to break down the taboos that had been erected round me. Not only had I never – since our holiday at Villers – set my foot on a bathing-beach or entered a public swimming-bath or gymnasium, so that in my mind nudity was confused with indecency; but in the environment in which I lived no open reference to bodily functions and no untoward physical act was allowed to tear aside the veil drawn over sex by custom and convention. How could adults, who kept their bodies so carefully covered up, and who restricted themselves to a cautious public exchange of words and gestures, how could they suddenly abandon themselves to the crude indecency of animal instincts and pleasures? During my last year at school, Marguerite de Théricourt came to tell Mademoiselle Lejeune of her forthcoming marriage: she was marrying a rich titled business associate of her father's, a man much older than herself, whom she had known since she was a baby. Everyone congratulated her, and she radiated a candid happiness. The word 'marriage' exploded in my brain and I was even more dumbfounded than the day when, in the middle of a lesson, a schoolmate had begun to bark like a dog. How could one superimpose the image of a pink, soft body lying with a naked man upon this well-behaved young lady with the studied smile standing there

[163]

in a smart hat and neatly buttoned gloves? I didn't go as far as to undress Marguerite in my mind's eye: but I saw her in a long, transparent nightdress, her hair spread out over the pillow, offering up her body. Such inconsequential immodesty verged on madness. Either sex was a brief disorder of the brain, or Marguerite was not the same well-bred young person who was escorted everywhere by a chaperone; appearances were deceptive, and the world I had been taught to believe in was a pack of lies. I was inclined to accept the latter hypothesis, but I had been deceived, and had deceived myself, too consistently and too long; my doubts could not disperse the illusion I had got so used to: the real Marguerite was the one before me wearing her hat and gloves. Whenever I imagined her half-naked and exposed to the eyes of a man, I felt myself whirled away in a hot storm of sensations which shattered every normal standard of morality and good sense.

At the end of July I went away on holiday. This time I discovered a new aspect of sexual life which was neither a calm sensual delight nor a disturbing deviation from common sense: it was more like childish depravity.

My Uncle Maurice, having existed entirely on fresh green salad for two or three years, had died of stomach cancer after the most atrocious sufferings. My aunt and Madeleine had mourned him long and loud. But eventually they found consolation and life at La Grillière became much gayer than it had been in the past. Robert was able to issue invitations freely to his friends. The scions of the local gentry had just discovered the motor-car and from as far as fifty miles away they would meet to go hunting and dancing. That year Robert was courting a young beauty of about twenty-five who was spending her holidays in a neighbouring town and was obviously dead-set on getting married; Yvonne came to La Grillière nearly every day; she rejoiced in a motley wardrobe; she had loads of hair, and such a fixed, unchanging smile that I was never quite able to decide whether she was deaf or daft. One afternoon in the drawing-room, where the dust-sheets had been removed at last from the furniture, her mother sat down at the piano, and Yvonne, dressed as a Spanish gipsy dancer, plied a fan and rolled her eyes and performed so-called Spanish dances surrounded by a circle of giggling young men and women. After this Andalusian idyll, there were more and more parties at La Grillière and at neighbouring houses. I enjoyed them like anything. Our parents did not take part in them; we could laugh and make as much of a rumpus as we liked. There were parlour games, musical chairs, round dances, and farandoles: dancing became just a game like anything else and no longer upset me. I even found one of my partners very charming; he was a medical student in his last year. Once, in a near-by country house, we stayed awake until dawn; we concocted onion soup in the kitchen; we went in a motor-car to the foot of Mont Gargan which we climbed to see the sunrise; we drank bowls of fresh milk and coffee at an inn; it was my first all-night do. In my letters to Zaza I told her of all this debauchery and she seemed a little scandalized that I should be taking so much pleasure in it and that my mother should have allowed me to. Neither my own virginity nor that of my sister was ever in danger; we were known as 'the babes'; obviously still a pair of innocents, sex-appeal was not our strong point. Yet the conversations that went on simply crackled with allusions and suggestions whose licentiousness shocked me. Madeleine told us that on our outings and at parties 'all kinds of things' went on in motor-cars and behind bushes. The young ladies were careful to remain young ladies. But Yvonne neglected to take this elementary precaution, and Robert's friends, who one after the other had done what they liked with her, were obliging enough to warn my cousin, and the marriage did not take place. The other girls knew the rules of the game, and stuck to them; but their prudence did not mean that they were unable to enjoy some very agreeable interludes. Doubtless these were not altogether illicit: those girls who were over-scrupulous trotted off to confession next morning; then, their souls washed free of sin, they could go on being themselves again. I should have very much liked to find out how it was that when two mouths came in contact people got voluptuous feelings: often, looking at the lips of a young man or a young woman, I would feel amazed, just as when I used to gaze at the live rail in the Métro or at a forbidden book – what *could* it be? The information Madeleine proffered was always rather odd: she explained to me that physical pleasure depends on one's personal tastes: her friend Nini couldn't do anything unless her partner kissed or tickled the soles of her feet. I wondered, with sickening curiosity, whether my own body contained hidden springs from which one day unpredictable sensations would suddenly leap to life.

Not for anything in the world would I have indulged in even

the most harmless experiment. The behaviour which Madeleine described I found revolting. Love, in my view, had nothing to do with the body; but I would not allow that the body should find release in furtive fumblings from which all love was absent. I didn't take my intransigence in this matter as far as Antoine Redier, the editor of the *Revue Française* where my father worked, who had in one of his novels drawn the touching portrait of a really young woman: she had once allowed a man to steal a kiss, and, rather than tell her fiancé of this dastardly act, she gave him up. I thought this story was a scream. But when one of my friends, the daughter of a general, told me, not without a certain sadness, that every time she went out dancing at least one of her partners kissed her, I blamed her for letting him. I thought it was sad, incongruous, and after all quite wrong to surrender one's lips to just anybody. Doubtless one of the reasons for my prudery lay in the disgust, mingled with terror, that the grown male usually inspires in virgins; above all I dreaded my own feelings and their unpredictable caprices; the disturbance I had felt during the dancing class exasperated me because it had come on without my wanting it to; I couldn't allow myself to think that by a mere contact, a pressure, a squeeze, I could be bowled over by the first man who wanted to take advantage of me. The day would come when I would swoon in the arms of a man: but I would choose the moment and my decision would be justified by the violence of my love. On this rationalist self-sufficiency were superimposed the myths I had been taught. I had cherished that immaculate host, my soul; my memory was still full of images of mud-stained ermine, of trampled lilies; if physical pleasure was not transmuted by the fires of passionate love, it was a defilement. On the other hand, I was an extremist; with me, it had to be 'all, or nothing'. If I loved a man, it would be for ever, and I would surrender myself to him entirely, body and soul, heart and head, past, present, and future. I refused to tamper with emotions and sensations which had no place in this scheme. To tell the truth I had no opportunity to test the firmness of these principles, because no seducer came along to try to get round them.

My behaviour conformed to the morality implicit in my environment; but with one important exception; I insisted that men should be subject to the same laws as women. Aunt Germaine had complained to my parents, in veiled terms, that Jacques knew too much about life. My father, the majority of writers, and the universal consensus of opinion encouraged young men to sow their wild oats. When the time came, they would marry a young woman of their own social class; but in the meanwhile it was quite in order for them to amuse themselves with girls from the lowest ranks of society – women of easy virtue, young milliners' assistants, work-girls, sewing-maids, shop-girls. This custom made me feel sick. It had been driven into me that the lower classes have no morals: the misconduct of a laundry-woman or a flower-girl therefore seemed to me to be so natural that it didn't even shock me; I felt a certain sympathy for those poor young women whom novelists endowed with such touching virtues. Yet their love was always doomed from the start; one day or other, according to his whim or convenience, their lover would throw them over for a well-bred young lady. I was a democrat and a romantic; I found it revolting that, just be-cause he was a man and had money, he should be authorized to play around with a girl's heart. On the other hand, I was up in arms in defence of the pure-hearted fiancée with whom I identified myself. I saw no reason why my future partner in life should per-mit himself liberties which I wouldn't allow myself. Our love would only be inevitable and complete if he had saved himself for me as I had saved myself for him. Moreover, our sexual life, and that of the whole world, should be in its very essence a serious affair; otherwise I should be forced to change my own attitude, and as I was at the moment unable to do so, I should have been thrown into the greatest confusion. Therefore, despite public opinion, I per-sisted in my view that both sexes should observe the same rules of chastity and continence.

*

At the end of September, I spent a week with a friend. Zaza had occasionally invited me to Laubardon; the difficult journey and my tender age had always militated against accepting. But now I was seventeen, and Mama agreed to put me on a train which would take me from Paris direct to Joigny, where my hosts would come to meet me. It was the first time I had travelled alone; I had put my hair up, I was wearing a little grey felt hat, I was proud of my inde-pendence, and slightly worried: at every station I was on the look-out: I should not have liked to find myself alone in a compartment with a strange man. Thérèse was waiting for me on my arrival. She was a melancholy adolescent who had lost her father and led an existence of perpetual mourning with her mother and half a dozen elder sisters. Pious and sentimental, she had decorated her room with yards and yards of billowing white muslin; Zaza hadn't been able to suppress a smile when she saw it. Thérèse envied me my comparative freedom and I believe that to her I was the incarnation of the gay outside world. She spent the summer in a huge brick château, rather grand, but very gloomy, surrounded by magnificent forests. In the high timber and on the flanks of hills covered with vineyards I discovered an entirely new kind of autumn: violet, orange, scarlet, with great splashes of gold all over it. When we went for walks, we talked about our studies and the new academic year that was about to begin: Thérèse had obtained permission to attend a few lectures on Latin and literature with me. I was determined to work hard. Papa would have liked me to take both literature and law, 'which would always come in useful', but I had skimmed through the Napoleonic Code at Meyrignac and this had put me off the study of law. Then my science teacher was urging me to try for the general mathematics paper, and I liked the idea: I would prepare for this certificate at the Institut Catholique. As for literature, it had been decided, at the instigation of Monsieur Mabille, that we would follow lectures in a college at Neuilly run by Madame Daniélou; in this way our connexions with the Sorbonne would be reduced to the minimum. Mama had had a talk with Mademoiselle Lambert, Madame Daniélou's principal assistant: if I went on working hard, I could easily go on to take my degree. I received a letter from Zaza: Mademoiselle Lejeune had written to her mother, warning her of the frightful crudities in the Greek and Latin classics; Madame Mabille had replied that she was more afraid of the influences that unbridled romanticism might have upon a young girl's imagination than of the healthy realism of the classics. Robert Garric, who was to be our literature professor, an ardent Catholic of a spiritual probity that was above suspicion, had assured Monsieur Mabille that it was possible to take a degree without being damned eternally. And so all my dearest wishes were being realized: a new life was opening out before me, but I would still be sharing it with Zaza.

A new life; a different life: I was even more excited than on the eve of my first day at school. Lying on dead leaves, my eyes dazed by the passionate colours of the vineyards, I kept repeating those austere words: degree, doctorate. And all barriers, all prison walls were being broken down. I was moving forwards, under an open sky, across the reality of life. The future was no longer just an impossible dream: I was touching it now. There would be four or five years of study, and then a whole way of life which I would build up with my own hands. My life would be a beautiful story come true, a story I would make up as I went along.

BOOK THREE

I INAUGURATED my new existence by ascending the stairs to the Bibliothèque Sainte-Geneviève. I took my seat, in the section reserved 'for ladies only', at a large table covered, like those in the Cours Désir, with black imitation leather, and I plunged straight into *The Human Comedy* and *The Memoirs of a Man of Quality*. Opposite me, her face shadowed by a huge hat covered with birds, a middle-aged lady was looking through old volumes of *The Official Gazette*; she was muttering and laughing to herself. In those days, anyone could use the library; all kinds of queer people and near-tramps used to take refuge there; they would talk to themselves, hum snatches of song, and gnaw at dry crusts of bread; there was one who used to walk up and down wearing a paper hat. I felt very far removed from the 'lecture-study room' at my old school: at last I had flung myself into the hurly-burly of real life. 'This is it! I'm a student now!' I gleefully kept reminding myself. I was wearing a tartan dress; it was new and made to measure, but I had taken up the hem myself; as I went about the library consulting the catalogue I felt I must be looking simply stunning.

On the syllabus that year were Lucretius, Juvenal, the Heptameron, and Diderot; if I had still been as ignorant as my parents would have liked on certain matters, the shock would have been a brutal one: they realized this. One afternoon, when I was alone in the study, my mother came in and sat down opposite me; she hesitated, blushed, and then said: 'There are certain things you ought to know!' I blushed too: 'I know all about that,' I hurriedly replied. She displayed no curiosity as to where I had obtained my knowledge, and to our mutual relief the conversation was not pursued any further. A few days later she called me into her room and asked me, with some embarrassment, 'how I stood from the religious point of view'. My heart began to pound: 'Well,' I said, 'for some time now I haven't believed in God.' Her face fell: 'My poor darling!' she said. She went to shut the door, so that my sister might not overhear the rest of our conversation; in a pleading voice she embarked on a demonstration of the truth of God's existence; then, with a helpless gesture, her eyes full of tears, she stopped suddenly. I was sorry to have hurt her, but I felt greatly relieved: at last I would be able to live without a mask.

One evening as I got off the bus I saw Jacques' car in front of the house; he had bought a small one a few months before. I took the stairs four at a time. Jacques was coming to see us less frequently than he used to do; my parents couldn't forgive his literary tastes, and probably he was rather sick of their heavy banter. According to my father, it was only the idols of his youth who had any talent; only intellectual snobbery could explain the success of modern French and foreign authors. He put Alphonse Daudet far above Dickens; whenever there was talk of the Russian novel he would despairingly shrug his shoulders. One evening, a student from the Conservatoire who was rehearsing with him a play by Monsieur Jeannot entitled *Return to Earth* impetuously declared: 'One must bow very low to the genius of Ibsen!' My father burst out laughing: 'You won't get *me* bowing to him!' Whether English, Slav, or Scandinavian, he thought all works of art from abroad were boring, badly constructed, and childish. As for the *avant-garde* writers and painters, they were cynical speculators in human folly. My father appreciated the naturalism of certain young actors like Gaby Morlay, Fresnay, Blanchard, and Charles Boyer. But he thought the experiments of Copeau, Dullin, and Jouvet were quite uncalled-for, and he detested 'those Bolshies', the Pitoëffs. He thought that anyone who didn't share his opinions was un-French and unpatriotic. So Jacques steered clear of discussion and argument; he was talkative, and a great charmer; he would exchange light banter with my father, and pay court to my mother in the gayest fashion: but he took care never to say anything important. I regretted this very much, because whenever by chance he dropped his guard he would say things that intrigued and interested me; I no longer found him at all pretentious; he knew far more than I did about the world, about human affairs, painting, and literature; I should have liked him to give me the benefit of his experience. That evening, as usual, he treated me like a little girl; but there was such kindness in his voice and in his smiles that I felt very glad simply to have seen him again. When I laid my head on my pillow that night, my eyes filled with tears. 'I weep, therefore I love,' I told myself, with rapturous melancholy. I was seventeen: it was the age for that sort of thing.

I thought I saw a way of raising myself in Jacques' esteem. He knew Robert Garric, who lectured on French literature at the Institut Sainte-Marie. Garric was the founder and director of a movement called Les Équipes Sociales whose aim was to bring culture to the lower social classes: Jacques was one of his adherents, and admired the man very much. If I could succeed in making my new professor take notice of me, he might praise me to Jacques, who might then stop regarding me only as an insignificant schoolgirl. Garric was just over thirty; he had thinning blond hair and spoke in a lovely manner; his voice had just a trace of Auvergne accent; his lecture-commentaries on Ronsard left me spellbound. I took infinite pains over my first essay for him, but only a Dominican nun, who wore ordinary clothes when she attended lectures, was complimented on her work; Zaza and I barely distinguished ourselves from the rest of the class: we both got eleven minus. Thérèse came a long way behind us.

The intellectual level at the Institut Sainte-Marie was much higher than that of the Cours Désir. Mademoiselle Lambert, who was in charge of the advanced students, filled me with respect. She had a degree in philosophy and was about thirty-five; a fringe of black hair gave a severe look to her face, in which her blue eyes had a piercing glitter. But I never had anything to do with her. I was a mere beginner in Greek, and I soon found out that my knowledge of Latin was very small: my professors took no notice of me. As for my fellow-students, I didn't find them any gayer than my former school companions. They got free board and lodging in return for teaching and keeping order in the secondary classes. The majority of them, already rather long in the tooth, were bitterly aware that they would never marry; their only chance of one day leading a decent existence was to pass their examinations: this became an obsession with them. I tried to talk to one or two of them but they had nothing to say.

In November I began to prepare for the general mathematics paper at the Institut Catholique; the girls sat in the front rows, the boys at the back; to me they all seemed to have the same narrow-minded look on their faces. I was bored by the literature lectures at the Sorbonne; the professors merely repeated in a flat voice the facts they had long ago written in their doctoral theses; Fortunat

Strowski would tell us about the plays he had seen during the past week; his jaded animation soon ceased to amuse me. To while away the time I would observe the young men and women students seated all round me on the amphitheatre benches: some of them intrigued and attracted me; when the lecture was over I would often follow with my eyes some unknown young woman whose elegance and grace astounded me: to whom was she going to offer that smile painted on her lips? Brushed in passing by these strange lives, I felt once more the intimate, obscure happiness that I had known as a child on the balcony of our flat in the boulevard Raspail. Only I didn't dare speak to anyone, and nobody spoke to me.

Grandpapa died at the end of the autumn, after lingering on interminably; my mother shrouded herself in black crêpe and had all my clothes dyed black. This funereal get-up did not improve my appearance; it set me apart, and I felt it condemned me to an austere way of life that was beginning to weigh heavily upon my spirits. The students, both boys and girls, used to parade up and down the boulevard Saint-Michel in laughing gangs; they went to cafés, theatres, cinemas. As for me, after reading learned tomes and translating Catullus all day, I would spend the evenings doing mathematical problems. My parents, by helping to push me, not into marriage, but into a career, were breaking with tradition; nevertheless they still made me conform to it; there was never any question of letting me go anywhere without them, nor of releasing me from family duties.

During the past year, my principal amusement had been my meetings and my conversations with my friends; but now, apart from Zaza, they all bored me stiff. I went three or four times to the study-circle they attended under the supervision of the Abbé Trécourt, but the dreary inanity of the discussions drove me away. My old schoolmates hadn't changed all that much; I hadn't either; but before, we had been bound by a common endeavour: our studies; while now our lives were going separate ways; I was pushing forward and developing all the time, whereas they, in order to adapt themselves to their role of marriageable young girls, were beginning to grow dull and stupid. From the outset, I was being separated from them by the diverse paths our future was taking.

I soon had to admit that this year was not bringing me all I had banked on getting. Cut off from my past, I felt out of place; my life seemed out of joint, and I had still not discovered any really

[174]

broad new horizons. Up to now, I had made the best of living in a cage, for I knew that one day – and each day brought it nearer – the door of the cage would open; now I had got out of the cage, and I was still inside. What a let-down! There was no longer any definite hope to sustain me; though this prison was one without bars, I couldn't see any way out of it. Perhaps there *was* a way out; but where? And when would I find it? Every evening I carried the rubbish bin downstairs; as I emptied out the peelings, the ashes and waste paper into the communal refuse bin, I would look up inquiringly at the patch of sky above the little yard; I would pause at the entry; shop-windows were ablaze with light, cars were dashing along the street, passers-by were passing by; outside, the night was alive. Then I would go back upstairs, loathing the greasy feel of the empty rubbish bin's handle. Whenever my parents went out to dinner, I would rush down into the street with my sister; we would wander aimlessly around, trying to catch an echo or a reflection of the brilliant festivities from which we were shut out.

My captivity seemed all the more unbearable because I no longer felt happy at home. Her eyes raised imploring heavenwards, my mother would pray for my salvation; she was always moaning about the error of my ways: we had completely lost touch with one another. At least I knew the reasons for her distress. But my father's reticence astonished and wounded me much more. He should have been taking some interest in my work, in the progress I was making; he might, I thought, have talked to me in a friendly way about the authors I was studying: but he was merely indifferent, and even vaguely hostile, in his attitude towards me. My cousin Jeanne was far from intelligent, but she was very amiable, always smiling and polite; my father never tired of telling everyone that his brother had a delightful daughter; then he would give a sigh. I was very put out. I couldn't understand what it was that had come between us and was to cast a heavy shadow over my youth.

*

In those days, people of my parents' class thought it unseemly for a young lady to go in for higher education; to train for a profession was a sign of defeat. It goes without saying that my father was a vigorous anti-feminist: I have already mentioned that he relished the novels of Colette Yver; he considered that a woman's place was in the home, that she should be an ornament to polite society. Of course, he admired Colette's literary style and the acting of Simone, but in the same way as he appreciated the beauty of the great courtesans – from a distance; he would not have received them in his house. Before the war, his future had looked rosy; he was expecting to have a brilliant career, to make lucrative investments, and to marry off my sister and myself into high society. He was of the opinion that in order to shine in those exalted spheres a woman should not only be beautiful and elegant but should also be well-read and a good conversationalist; so he was pleased by my early scholastic successes. Physically, I was not without promise; if in addition I could be intelligent and cultured, I would be able to hold my own with ease in the very best society. But though my father liked intelligent and witty women, he had no time for blue-stockings. When he announced: 'My dears, you'll never marry; you'll have to work for your livings,' there was bitterness in his voice. I believed he was being sorry for us; but in our hard-working futures he only saw his own failure; he was crying out against the injustice of a fate which condemned him to have daughters who could not keep up the social position he had given them.

He gave way to the inevitable. The war had ruined him, sweeping away all his dreams, destroying his myths, his self-justifications, and his hopes. I was wrong to think he had resigned himself to the situation; he never stopped protesting against his changed condition. Above all else he prized good education and perfect manners; yet whenever I was with him in a restaurant, in the Métro, or in a train I always felt embarrassed by the loudness of his voice, his gesticulations, and his brutal indifference to the opinion of others; he was trying to show, by this aggressive exhibitionism, that he belonged to a superior class. In the days when he used to travel first class he used every refinement of politeness to prove how well-bred he was; but in third class he would go to the other extreme and ignore the most elementary rules of civility. Nearly everywhere he went he affected a manner that was both bewildered and aggressive, which was intended to signify that his true place was really elsewhere. In the trenches he had quite naturally spoken the same language as his fellows; he was always happy to remind us that one of them had said: 'When Beauvoir says shit, it becomes a word fit for polite conversation.' In order to prove his distinction, he began to say 'shit' more and more often. Now he rarely associated with people other than those he considered to be 'common', and indeed out-commoned the common; as he was no longer looked up to by his equals, he took a bitter pleasure in being looked down upon by his inferiors. On rare occasions – when we went to the theatre, and his friend from the Odéon introduced him to some well-known actress – he would recover all his old airs and graces. But for the rest of the time he succeeded so well in appearing a nonentity that in the end no one but himself could be expected to know he was anything else.

At home, he would bewail the hard times we were having; whenever my mother asked him for housekeeping money, he made a violent scene; he would complain particularly about the sacrifices his daughters imposed upon him: my sister and I had the feeling that we were making unwarranted demands upon his charity. If he showed such bitter impatience with my troubles in 'the difficult age', it was because he already had a deep-seated resentment against me. I was not just another burden to be borne: I was growing up to be the living incarnation of his own failure. The daughters of his friends, his brother, and his sister would be 'ladies': but not me. Of course, when I passed my school-leaving examinations he rejoiced in my success; it flattered him and lifted a load off his mind: I should have no difficulty in making a living. But I didn't understand why such bitter vexation should cloud his happiness.

'What a pity Simone wasn't a boy: she could have gone to the Polytechnique!' I had often heard my parents giving vent to this complaint. A student at the Military Academy of Artillery and Engineering, they felt, was already 'someone'. But my sex debarred them from entertaining such lofty ambitions for me, and my father prudently envisaged a career in the Civil Service: yet he detested all government officials, whose taxes gobbled up his income, and he would tell me, with unconcealed resentment: 'At any rate, *you* will have a pension!' I made things worse for myself by expressing a desire to become a teacher: he approved my choice on practical grounds, but in his heart of hearts he was far from happy about it. He thought all teachers were low-minded pedagogues. At the Collège Stanislas one of his schoolfellows had been Marcel Bouteron, the great Balzac specialist; he used to speak of him with commiseration: he thought it ridiculous that one should spend one's life writing arid works of scholarship. He made more serious charges against schoolteachers; they belonged to the dangerous sect that had stood in defence of Dreyfus: the intellectuals. Blinded by their book-learning, taking a stubborn pride in abstract knowledge and in their futile aspirations to universalism, they were sacrificing the concrete realities of race, country, class, family, and nationality to those crack-pot notions that would be the death of France and of civilization: the Rights of Man, pacifism, internationalism, and socialism. If I joined their ranks, would I not be adopting their ideas? My father's native shrewdness turned me at once into a suspect. Later, I was surprised that, instead of prudently shunting my sister on to the same line as myself, he should have chosen for her the hazards of a career in art: he couldn't bear to think that he was driving both his daughters into the enemy camp.

Soon as I would be a traitor to my class; I had already renounced the privileges of my sex, and that was something else my father could not be reconciled to; he was obsessed by the 'well-bred young lady' idea: it was a fixation. My cousin Jeanne was the incarnation of this ideal: she still believed that babies were found under cabbages. My father had attempted to keep me in a state of blissful ignorance ; he used to say that even when I had reached the age of eighteen he would forbid me to read the *Tales* of François Coppée; he now accepted the fact that I read whatever I liked: but he couldn't see much difference between a girl who 'knew what's what' and the *Bachelor Girl* whose portrait Victor Marguerite had just drawn in a notorious book of that name. If I had only kept up the outward appearances, at least! He might have borne with an exceptional young woman for daughter if only she had taken pains not to appear in any way out of the ordinary: this I couldn't do. I had left the awkward age behind, and once more I found myself gazing approvingly at my reflection in the mirror; but I cut a poor figure in society. My friends, including Zaza, played their worldly roles with ease; they put in an appearance on their mothers' at-home days, served tea, smiled and smiled, and talked amiably about nothing; I found smiling difficult, I couldn't turn on the charm, make cute remarks, or any kind of concession to polite chit-chat. My parents would hold up to me as examples 'remarkably intelligent' girls who nevertheless were brilliant ornaments to their mothers' drawing-rooms. This used to exasperate me because I knew that their way of life had nothing in common with mine: they were mere amateurs; I was a professional. That year I was preparing for examinations in literature, Latin, and general mathematics, and I was learning Greek; I had set this heavy programme myself, for I found difficulties amusing: but precisely in order that I might be able to embark light-heartedly on such an undertaking, it was essential that my studies should not just represent an off-shoot of my life, but should be my entire life itself: the things people talked about did not interest me, I had no subversive ideas; in fact, I hardly had any ideas on anything; but all day long I would be training myself to think, to understand, to criticize, to know myself; I was seeking for the absolute truth: this preoccupation did not exactly encourage polite conversation.

On the whole, apart from when the news came that I had passed my exams, I was not an honour to my father; so he attached extreme importance to my diplomas and encouraged me to accumulate them. His insistence on this point convinced me that he was proud to have a brainy woman for a daughter; but the contrary was true: only the most extraordinary successes could have countered his dissatisfaction with me. If for example I had studied for three degrees at once, I would have become a sort of intellectual prodigy, a phenomenon who could not be judged by normal standards; my fate would no longer be a reflection of family failure, but could be explained away as the result of a strange and unaccountable gift.

I obviously didn't realize this contradiction in my father's personality: but I soon realized the one implicit in my own situation. I was obeying his wishes to the letter, and that seemed to anger him; he had destined me to a life of study, and yet I was being reproached with having my nose in a book all the time. To judge by his surly temper, you would think that I had gone against his wishes in embarking on a course that he had actually chosen for me. I kept wondering what I had done wrong; I felt unhappy and ill at ease, and nursed resentment in my heart.

*

The best part of the week was Garric's lecture. I was beginning to admire him more and more. It was rumoured at Sainte-Marie that he could have had a brilliant career at the University; but he had not a scrap of personal ambition; he never finished his thesis and devoted himself body and soul to his Social Welfare Groups; he lived the life of an ascetic in a working-class house in Belleville. He used to give fairly frequent propaganda lectures, and through Jacques' good offices my mother and I were admitted to one of them. Jacques took us into a suite of drawing-rooms, richly furnished, in which rows and rows of red plush chairs with gilded woodwork were set out; he found us seats and went off to greet his acquaintances; he seemed to know everybody: how I envied him! It was hot, I was stifling in my mourning garments and I knew no one. Then Garric walked on to the platform; I forgot myself, and everything else; I was spellbound by the authority in his voice. He explained to us that at the age of twenty he had discovered in the trenches the joys of a comradeship which overcame all social barriers; when, after the armistice, he became a student again, he was determined not to be deprived of that comradeship; the segregation which in civilian life separates young middle-class men from working chaps was something he felt like a personal mutilation; besides, he believed that everybody has a right to culture. He believed firmly in the truth of what General Lyautey had said in one of his Moroccan speeches: that beyond all differences, there is a common denominator which links all men. On the basis of this concept, he decided to set up a system of exchanges between students and working-class youths which would release the former from the egotistical solitude and the latter from their ignorance. By learning to understand and love one another they would work side by side to bring the classes together. To loud applause, Garric stated that it is impossible for any kind of social progress to emerge from a conflict whose motive force was class hatred: progress would only come through friendship. He had roped in a few friends who helped him to organize the first cultural centre at Neuilly. They obtained support and subsidies and the movement began to grow: there were now ten thousand members in groups all over France, all young men and women, and two hundred teachers. Garric himself was a firm Roman Catholic, but he did not intend to turn the movement into a religious mission; there were unbelievers among his collaborators; he believed that men should help one another on the human level. At the end, in a voice charged with emotion, he claimed that if people are well-treated they will be good; by refusing to offer the hand of friendship to the lower classes the bourgeoisie were making a grave mistake whose consequences would fall upon their own heads.

I drank in his words; they did not rock my universe to its foundations, they were not at variance with my own ideas, and yet they seemed to strike an absolutely new note. Of course, in my daily life, devotion to duty was always being cracked up, but it was not deemed necessary for such devotion to extend beyond the family circle, outside whose limits men were not regarded as our brothers. Working men in particular belonged to a species as dangerously foreign to our environment as the Boche and the Bolshevik. Garric had swept away these barriers: the world was now a great community in which all men were my brothers. I was thrilled by the movement's watchwords: I had to repudiate all barriers and all artificial divisions between the classes, renounce my own class, and step outside myself. I could not imagine a service more beneficial to humanity than the dissemination of sweetness and light. I promised myself that I would join one of the 'Groups'. But above all else I marvelled at the example which Garric gave me. At last I had met a man who instead of submitting to fate had chosen for himself a way of life; his existence, which had an aim and a meaning, was the incarnation of an idea, and was governed by its overriding necessity. That plain face with its lively but unassuming smile was the face of a hero, a superman.

I went back home in a state of exaltation; I was taking off my black coat and hat in the hall when I suddenly stood stock still; with my eyes fixed on the threadbare carpet, I heard an imperious voice within me saying: 'My life must be of service to humanity! Everything in my life must be of service!' I was stunned by the clear necessity of the call: innumerable tasks awaited me; it would need the whole strength of my being; if I allowed myself the slightest slackening of purpose, I would be betraying my trust and wronging humanity. 'Everything I do must be of service!' I told myself, with a tightening of the throat; it was a solemn vow, and I uttered it with as much feeling as if I had been pledging my whole future irrevocably in the face of heaven and earth.

I had never liked wasting time; yet now I reproached myself with having led an irresponsible existence, and henceforward I made scrupulous use of every minute. I slept less; my toilet was no more than 'a lick and a promise'; there was no longer any question of looking at myself in mirrors: I hardly ever brushed my teeth, and never cleaned my nails. I abjured all frivolous reading matter, idle gossip, and all forms of amusement; if my mother had not objected

I should have given up my Saturday morning games of tennis. I always brought a book to meals; I would be learning Greek verbs or trying to find the solution to a problem. My father got annoyed but I persisted, and in the end he gave up in disgust. When my mother was receiving friends, I refused to enter the drawing-room; sometimes she would fly into a temper, and I would give in; but I would sit perched on the edge of my chair, gritting my teeth, and with such a furious expression on my face that she very quickly sent me away again. In my family and among my friends there was great astonishment at my untidiness, my stubborn silences, and my lack of politeness; I soon got the reputation of being a kind of monster of incivility.

Without any doubt it was for the most part resentment that made me adopt this attitude; my parents did not find me to their liking, and so I deliberately made myself unpleasant. My mother dressed me badly and my father was always reproaching me with being badly dressed: so I became a slut. They were not attempting to understand me: so I took refuge in silence and odd behaviour; I wanted to make myself impervious to my surroundings. At the same time I was warding off boredom. My temperament was not suited to resignation; by taking to inordinate lengths the austerity that was my lot, it became a vocation; cut off from all pleasures, I chose the life of an ascetic; instead of dragging myself wearily through a monotony of days, I set out in stubborn silence, with set face, towards an invisible goal. I wore myself out with work, and my exhaustion gave me a feeling of fulfilment. My excesses also had a positive sense. For a long time now I had been promising myself that I would break away from the frightful banality of my daily life: Garric's example transformed this vague hope into grim determination. I refused to be patient any longer; without further ado I set my feet upon the way to heroic heights.

Every time I saw Garric, I renewed my vows. Sitting between Thérèse and Zaza, I would await, with bated breath, the moment of his appearance. My companions' indifference to him amazed me: I felt that one should be able to hear the beating of every heart. Zaza's admiration for Garric was not without reservation; it exasperated her that he should always arrive late. 'Punctuality is the politeness of kings,' she wrote on the blackboard one day. He would come in, sit down, and cross his legs under the table, exposing mauve sock-suspenders: she was critical of such free-and-easy manners. I couldn't understand why she fussed over these trifles, but I was glad she did, all the same; I couldn't have borne it if someone else had hung upon my hero's every word and smile with as much devotion as I did. I should have liked to know everything about him. In my childhood I had been trained in the techniques of meditation; I made use of them in attempts to imagine what I called, after an expression employed often by himself, his 'interior landscape'. But I had very little to go on: his lectures, and the rather hastily written reviews he wrote for *La Revue des Jeunes*; and in any case I was often too ignorant to be able to make the best use of my information. There was one writer whom Garric was always quoting: Péguy; who was he? Who was this Gide whose name he had uttered one afternoon, almost furtively, and with a smile that seemed to ask forgiveness for his audacity? After the class, he would go into Madame Lambert's study: what did they talk about? Would I one day be worthy to speak to Garric as to an equal? I occasionally lost myself in speculations. 'Girls like you, Hellé, are made to be the companions of heroes.' I was crossing the place Saint-Sulpice when suddenly this prophecy from my childhood blazed across the rainy twilight. Had Marcelle Tinayre foretold my future? Hellé, who at first had been dazzled by a rich, easy-going young poet, had eventually transferred her allegiance to a virtuous and noble-hearted missionary much older than herself. Today I felt that Garric's merits eclipsed Jacques' personal charm: had I met Mr Right? I hardly dared entertain the thought. It was somehow shocking to think of Garric being married. All I wanted was to have a small place in his life and I redoubled my efforts to gain his approval. I succeeded. A dissertation on Ronsard, the analysis of one of the *Sonnets à Hélène* and a lecture on d'Alembert earned me heady praise. With Zaza second, I went to the top of the class and Garric planned that we would take the literature paper at the beginning of the summer term.

Though she didn't realize how violent it was, Zaza thought my admiration for Garric was excessive; she worked steadily, went to a few parties and theatres, and devoted a great deal of time to her family; she was still in the same old rut; she had not heard the call to which I was responding with such fanatical fervour: I saw rather less of her. After the Christmas holidays, which she had spent in the Basque country, she was overtaken by a curious apathy. She still came to lectures, but there was a glazed look in her eyes; she didn't laugh any more, and hardly said a word; she was indifferent to her own life, and the interest I had in my own existence found no echo in her: 'All I want is to go to sleep and never wake up again,' she told me one day. I attached no importance to this statement. Zaza had often had fits of pessimism; I attributed this one to the fear she had of the future. This year of further education was only a brief respite for her; the fate she dreaded was gradually approaching and she probably didn't feel strong enough to make a stand against it; neither could she resign herself to it: and so she craved release from her cares in sleep. In my own mind, I reproached her with defeatism: I thought it already indicated an abdication of individuality and responsibility. For her part, she seemed to see in my optimism the proof that I was adapting myself easily to the established order of things. Both of us were cut off from life, Zaza by her despair, and I by my insane optimism; our personal solitudes did not bring us closer together: on the contrary, we became vaguely distrustful of one another and had less and less to say to each other.

My sister was very happy all that year; she was preparing to pass her school-leaving certificate with distinction; the Cours Désir lavished fond smiles upon her; she had a new friend whom she adored; she was only moderately concerned about my own existence and I assumed that in the near future she, too, would become a nice, quiet middle-class girl. 'Now, Poupette – *she'll* find a husband,' my parents confidently predicted. I still liked her but after all she was just a child: I couldn't talk to her about anything.

There was someone who might have helped me: Jacques. I now repudiated the tears I had shed so hastily over him that night; no, I didn't love him; if I did love somebody, it wasn't he. But I longed for his friendship. One evening when I was dining with his parents, just as we were called to take our seats at table we lingered a moment in the drawing-room, talking of this and that. My mother called me sharply to heel. 'I beg your pardon,' Jacques said with a faint smile, 'we were just talking about Charles Maurras' *Interior Music.* . . .' Sadly I drank my soup. How could I let him know that I no longer derided the things I didn't understand? If only he had talked to me about the new poems and books he liked, I would now have listened to him with deep respect. 'We were just talking about the *Interior Music.* . . .' I said that phrase over and over again, savouring its bitterness, with its after-taste of lingering hope.

I passed my literature paper with distinction. Garric congratulated me. Madame Lambert asked me into her study, looked me up and down and seemed to be sizing me up, then said I had a brilliant future ahead of me. A few days later, Jacques dined with us; towards the end of the evening he took me to one side and said: 'I saw Garric yesterday: we had a long talk about you.' He was interested to know how I was getting on with my studies and what my future plans were. 'I'll take you for a spin in the car round the Bois tomorrow,' he said without warning. How my heart thumped! I had succeeded in making Jacques interested in me! I'd brought it off! The next morning was fine and springlike and there I was bowling along in a car with Jacques round the lakes! He laughed: 'Watch how smartly I can pull up!' And I bumped my nose on the windscreen. So it was still possible, even at our age, to enjoy a childlike hilarity! We talked about our childhood: Châteauvillain, the *Popular Astronomy*, Old Charlie and the empty tin cans I used to collect for him. 'I really put you through the hoop, poor old Sim!' he told me happily. I also tried stumblingly to tell him of my difficulties and problems: he nodded his head gravely as I talked. About eleven o'clock he deposited me at the tennis court in the rue Boulard and smiled mischievously at me: 'You know,' he said, 'it's possible to be a smart young lady, even if you *have* got a degree.' Young ladies and gentlemen; smart young ladies and gentlemen – to be admitted to their ranks was the highest form of promotion. I strode triumphantly on to the tennis court: something had happened to me; something had begun. 'I've just come from a spin in the Bois de Boulogne,' I announced proudly to my friends. I described my outing with such gaiety and incoherence that Zaza cast me a suspicious look: 'What's the matter with you this morning?' she asked. I was happy.

When Jacques rang at our door the next week my parents were out; when that happened, he would usually joke with my sister and me for a few moments and then take himself off. But this time he stayed on. He recited one of Cocteau's poems and gave me advice about what I should read: he rattled off a score of names I had never heard before and recommended in particular a novel called, if I had heard aright, *Le Grand Môle*. 'Come round to the house tomorrow afternoon and I'll lend you some books,' he told me as he left.

It was Élise, the old housekeeper, who opened the door to me. 'Jacques isn't in, but he's left some things in his room for you.' He had scribbled a note: 'Please excuse me, Sim old thing, and take these books.' I found on his table a dozen volumes bound in paper covers whose colours were as sharp and fresh as those of boiled sweets: pistachio green Montherlant, a strawberry red Cocteau, lemon yellow Barrès, Claudels and Valéry in snowy white with scarlet letterpress. Again and again through the tissue-paper wrapping I read the titles: *The Potomak* (Cocteau), *Les Nourritures Terrestres* (Gide), *L'Annonce faite à Marie* (Claudel), *Le Paradis à l'ombre des épées*, *Du sang, de la volupté et de la mort* (Montherlant). Many were the books that had already passed through my hands, but these did not seem to belong to the common run of things: I expected extraordinary revelations from them. I was almost startled to find that when I opened them they contained words that I was familiar with.

They did not disappoint me: I was disconcerted, dazzled, transported. Apart from the rare exceptions I have mentioned, I regarded works of literature as historical monuments which I would explore with more or less interest, which I sometimes admired, but which did not concern me personally. But now, suddenly, men of flesh and blood were speaking to me with their lips close to my ear; it was something between them and me; they were giving expression to the aspirations and the inner rebellions which I had never been able to put in words, but which I recognized. I skimmed the cream of the Sainte-Geneviéve library; with fevered brow, my brain on fire, and my heart pounding with excitement, I read Gide, Claudel, Jammes. I exhausted the resources of Jacques' private library; I took out a subscription to the 'Maison des Amis des Livres', in which Adrienne Monnier, in a long dress of grey home-spun, held court; I was so greedy for reading matter that I couldn't be satisfied with the two-books-at-a-time rule: I would secretly slip half a dozen or so into my satchel; the difficulty was getting them back on the shelves, and I'm afraid I didn't get them all put back. When it was fine, I would go and read in the Luxembourg Gardens; I would walk in the sun round the fountains in a state of exaltation, repeating phrases I liked. Often I would install myself in the reading-room of the Institut Catholique which offered me a quiet spot to read in only a few steps from home. It was there, seated at a black desk among pious students and seminarists in long robes, that I read, with tears in my eyes, the novel that Jacques loved above all others and which was called not *Le Grand Môle* but *Le Grand Meaulnes*. I found release in reading as once I had done in prayer.

Literature took the place in my life that had once been occupied by religion: it absorbed me entirely, and transfigured my life. The books I liked became a Bible from which I drew advice and support; I copied out long passages from them; I learnt by heart new canticles and new litanies, psalms, proverbs, and prophecies and I sanctified every circumstance in my existence by the recital of these sacred texts. My emotions, my tears, and my aspirations were no less sincere on account of that: the words and the cadences, the lines and the verses were not aids to make-believe: but they rescued from silent oblivion all those intimate adventures of the spirit that I couldn't speak to anyone about; they created a kind of communion between myself and those twin souls which existed somewhere out of reach; instead of living out my small private existence, I was participating in a great spiritual epic. For months I kept myself going with books: they were the only reality within my reach.

My parents cast black looks upon them. My mother divided books into two categories: serious works and novels; she considered the latter to be an amusement which, if not sinful, was at least frivolous, and blamed me for wasting on Mauriac, Radiguet, Giraudoux, Larbaud, and Proust time which would have been better employed studying the geography of Baluchistan, the life of the Princesse de Lamballe, the habits of eels, the soul of Woman, or the Secret of the Pyramids. My father, having cast a rapid eye over my favourite authors, pronounced them to be pretentious, over-subtle, queer, decadent, and immoral; he was indignant with Jacques for having lent me, among other works, Marcel Arland's *Étienne*. My parents no longer had any way of censoring the books I read: but they often made explosive scenes about them. I was vexed by these attacks. The conflict that had been smouldering between us was beginning to leap into flame.

*

My childhood and adolescence had passed fairly smoothly; as year followed year, I felt surer of myself. But now it seemed that there had been a decisive break in the even course of my life; I would remember the Cours Désir, the Abbé, and my schoolmates but I could no longer recognize in myself the calm schoolgirl I had been a few months earlier; I now took more interest in my state of mind than in the world about me. I began to keep a private diary; I wrote this inscription on the fly-leaf; 'If anyone reads these pages, no matter who it may be, I shall never forgive that person. It would be a cheap and ugly thing to do. You are requested to take heed of this warning, despite its ridiculous pomposity.' In addition, I took the utmost care to keep it hidden from prying eyes. In it I used to copy out passages from my favourite books; there were self-communings and self-analyses in which I congratulated myself on the change that had taken place in me. Of what did that change actually consist? My diary gives very little indication; I passed over many things in silence, and I couldn't see things in their proper perspective then. Yet on re-reading it, a few salient facts emerge.

'I am alone. One is always alone. I shall always be alone.' I find this leitmotif running right through my diary. But I had never really believed it. I sometimes used to tell myself proudly: 'I am not as others are.' But I seemed to see in my difference the proof of a natural superiority which would one day be acknowledged by everybody. I was no rebel; I wanted to be someone, to do something, to go on progressing, ever onwards and upwards, as I had been doing since I was a little child; therefore I had to get out of the everyday rut I was in: but I believed it would be possible to rise above bourgeois mediocrity without stepping out of my own class. Its devotion to universal values was, I thought, sincere; I thought I was authorized to liquidate traditions, customs, prejudices, and all kinds of political and theological particularism in the light of reason, beauty, goodness, and progress. If I established myself in life by writing a work which would do honour to humanity, I would be congratulated for having trampled conformity in the dust; like Mademoiselle Zanta, I too would be accepted and admired. I made the brutal discovery that I had been wrong from the start; far from admiring me, people did not accept me at all; instead of weaving laurel crowns for me, people were banishing me from society. I was filled with anguish, because I realized that what people were reproaching me for, even more than for my present attitude, was the future that lay ahead of me: I would always be ostracized. I couldn't imagine the existence of environments other than my own kind; here and there a few individuals stood out from the common mass of people; but I never had a chance to meet any of them; even if I were to form one or two friendships they would never console me for the sense of exile I was already beginning to feel; I had always been made much of, and looked up to as the centre of excited comment; I loved being loved: the bleakness of my future terrified me.

It was my father who made me realize what it would be like; I had counted on his support, his sympathy, his approval: I was deeply disappointed when he withheld them from me. It was a far cry from my own high-flown ideas to his morose scepticism; his moral code insisted that institutions should be respected; as for individuals, they had no other purpose on earth than to keep out of trouble and enjoy life to the best of their abilities. My father often stated that one should have an ideal, and though he detested them, he admired the Italians because they had one in Mussolini: yet he never suggested what my ideal should be. But I didn't expect him to do as much as that for me. Considering his age and circumstances, I thought his attitude was a natural one, and it seemed to me that he might have been able to understand mine. On many points – the League of Nations, the Radical Coalition, and the war in Morocco – I had no opinion of my own and I agreed with everything he said about them. The points on which we disagreed seemed to me so unimportant that at first I made no effort to reconcile our differences.

My father regarded Anatole France as the greatest writer of the century; at the end of the summer holidays he had made me read *The Red Lily* and *The Gods Athirst*. I had not evinced much enthusiasm for these. But he persisted and gave me for my eighteenth birthday the four volumes of *The Literary Life*. France's hedonism filled me with indignation. All he looked for in art was the satisfaction of egotistical desires: how low can you get! I thought. I despised also the platitude of Maupassant's novels which my father considered to be works of art. I told him so politely, but he took it the wrong way: he was well aware that my tastes brought many things into question. He was more seriously annoyed when I attacked certain traditions. It was only with very bad grace that I attended the dinners and luncheons which several times a year reunited the whole blessed family at one cousin's or another's; only personal feelings are important, I claimed, and not chance ties of blood; but my father encouraged the cult of the family and he began to think that I was quite heartless. I couldn't accept his concept of marriage; he was less austere than the Mabilles, and admitted that love should play a fairly big part; but I couldn't separate love from friendship: he couldn't see what these two sentiments had in common. I couldn't accept that one of the partners should 'be unfaithful' to the other: if they didn't get along together, then they should separate. It exasperated me that my father should think it was quite all right for the husband to sabotage the marriage settlement. I was not a feminist to the extent of caring about politics: I didn't give twopence for women's right to the vote. But in my opinion men and women had a right to be considered equal as human beings, and I demanded that they should have exactly reciprocal benefits and privileges. My father's attitude towards 'the fair sex' wounded me deeply. Taken as a whole, the frivolity of bourgeois love-affairs and adulteries made me sick. My Uncle Gaston took my sister, a girl cousin, and myself to see an innocent little operetta by Mirande called *Passionately*; when we got back home I expressed my disgust with a vigour which took my parents by surprise: yet I could read Gide and Proust without batting an eyelid. Current notions of sexual morality scandalized me both by their indulgence and their severity. I was stupefied to learn from a small news item that abortion was a crime: what went on in one's body should be one's own concern; no amount of argument could make me see it any differently.

Our disputes soon took on an acrid note; if he had shown himself inclined to be tolerant I could have accepted my father for what he was; but I was still nobody, I was still trying to come to a decision about what I was to be, and by adopting opinions and tastes that were at variance with his own, it seemed to him as if I were deliberately disowning him. On the other hand, he could see much more clearly than I could the downward path I was treading. I was renouncing the hierarchies, the values, and the ceremonies which distinguish the élite; my critical attitude towards it was only serving, I thought, to rid it of futile relics of past times: it did, in fact, imply the liquidation of the élite. Only the individual seemed to me to be real and important: I would, in the end, inevitably be led to prefer society as a whole to my own class. After all, it was I who had opened fire; but I didn't realize this, and I couldn't understand why my father and the other members of my social class were condemning me. I had fallen into a trap; the bourgeoisie had persuaded me that its interests were closely linked with those of humanity as a whole; I thought that I could enlist the support of my own class in the pursuit of truths that would be valid for everyone: but as soon as I made my intentions clear, it was up in arms against me. I felt myself to be 'a voice crying in the wilderness'. Who or what had misled me? Why? And how? In any case, I was the victim of an injustice, and gradually my resentment turned to open rebellion.

No one would take me just as I was, no one loved me. I shall love myself enough, I thought, to make up for this abandonment by everyone. Formerly, I had been quite satisfied with myself, but I had taken very little trouble to increase my self-knowledge; from now on, I would stand outside myself, watch over and observe myself; in my diary I had long conversations with myself. I was entering a world whose novelty dumbfounded me. I learned to distinguish between distress and melancholy, lack of emotion and serenity; I learned to recognize the hesitations of the heart, its deliriums, the splendour of great renunciations and the subterranean murmurings of hope. I entered into exalted trances, as on those evenings when I used to gaze upon the sky full of moving clouds behind the distant blue of the hills. I was both the landscape and its beholder: I existed only through myself, and for myself. I was grateful for an exile which had driven me to find such lonely and such lofty joys; I despised those who knew nothing about them, and was astonished that I had been able to exist for so long without them.

At the same time I persisted in my determination to be of service to humanity. I attacked Renan in my diary. I protested that a great man is not an end in himself: he will only justify his existence if he contributes to the raising of the moral and intellectual standards of common humanity. My Catholic upbringing had taught me never to look upon any individual, however lowly, as of no account: everyone had the right to bring to fulfilment what I called their eternal essence. My path was clearly marked: I had to perfect, enrich, and express myself in a work of art that would help others to live.

I felt I should already be trying to communicate the experience of solitude which I was then undergoing. In April I wrote the first pages of a novel. In the character of Éliane, I described myself wandering in a park with some of my cousins; I picked up a beetle out of the grass. 'Let's see!' they cried. They thronged round me, but I struggled out of their grasp and ran away with the beetle jealously guarded in my hand. They ran after me; breathless, with pounding heart, I ran deeper and deeper into the woods until I shook them off; then I began to cry softly. Soon I dried my tears, and murmured to myself: 'No one will ever know.' I walked slowly back home. 'She felt sufficiently strong in herself to defend her one possession against blows and blandishments, and to keep her fist tightly closed all the time.'

This little fable expressed my most obsessive worry: how to defend myself against other people; for though my parents did not spare me their reproaches, they demanded my confidences. My mother had often told me how she had suffered from grandmama's coldness towards her, and that she hoped she could be a friend to her daughters; but how could she have talked to me as one woman to another? In her eyes I was a soul in mortal peril; I had to be saved from damnation: I was an object, not a woman. The firmness of her convictions forbade her to make the slightest concession. If she questioned me, it was not in order to come to an understanding with me on common ground: she was simply making an investigation. I always had the feeling, whenever she asked me a question, that she was spying on me through a keyhole. The very fact that she had renounced all her claims on me shut me up like a clam. This made her resentful towards me and she tried to break down my resistance by deploying a solicitude which only strengthened it. 'Simone would rather bite out her tongue than say what she's thinking,' she would remark in a tone of sharp vexation. That was quite true: I was prodigiously silent. I had given up arguing, even with my father; I hadn't the slightest chance of influencing his way of thinking – it was like beating my head against a brick wall. Once and for all, and just as radically as my mother, he had made up his mind about me, and for the worse; he no longer even tried to convince me of the error of my ways; all he wanted was to find fault with me. The most innocent conversations were full of hidden traps; my parents construed my words in their own idiom and ascribed to me ideas that had nothing in common with what I really thought. I had always fought against the tyranny of language, and now I found myself repeating Barrès' phrase: 'Why have words, when their brutal precision bruises our complicated souls?' As soon as I opened my mouth I provided them with a stick to beat me with, and once more I would be shut up in that world which I had spent years trying to get away from, in which everything, without any possibility of mistake, has its own name, its set place and its agreed function, in which hate and love, good and evil are as crudely differentiated as black and white, in which from the start everything is classified, catalogued, fixed and formulated, and irrevocably judged; that world with the sharp edges, its bare outlines starkly illuminated by an implacable flat light that is never once touched by the shadow of a doubt. I preferred to hold my tongue. But my parents wouldn't put up with that: they had to charge me with ingratitude. I was not nearly as heartless as my father thought, and I was deeply distressed; at night I wept on my pillow. It even came about that I burst into tears to their faces; they took offence at this and reproached me all the more with being a monster of ingratitude. I tried to pretend, to lie, to give soft answers, but I did it with ill grace: I felt I was being a traitor to myself. I decided I must 'tell the truth, the whole truth, and nothing but the truth': in that way I would avoid disguising and at the same time betraying my thoughts. This was not very clever of me, for I merely succeeded in scandalizing my parents without satisfying their curiosity. In fact, there was no possible solution to the situation. I was cornered; my parents could bear neither what I had to say, nor my dogged silence; when I took the risk and gave them certain explanations, they were staggered by them. 'You're taking the wrong view of life altogether; life isn't as complicated as all that,' my mother would say. But if I withdrew into my shell, my father would complain that I had no heart, that I was all brain and no feeling. There was talk of sending me abroad, all sorts of people were asked for advice and there was a general panic. I tried to put on protective armour by exhorting myself not to be afraid of blame, ridicule, or lack of understanding: it little mattered what opinion people had of me, whether well-founded or not. When I reached this state of indifference, I could laugh even when I least felt like laughing and agree with everything that was being said. But then I would feel so utterly cut off from my fellow-beings; I would gaze in the looking-glass at the person *they* could see: it wasn't *me*; I wasn't there, I wasn't anywhere; how could I find myself again? I was on the wrong track. 'Life is a lie,' I would tell myself in a fit of depression. In principle, I had nothing against lying; but from a practical point of view I found it exhausting to be always fabricating masks. Sometimes I used to think that my strength would fail me and that I would have to give in and become like all the others.

I found this idea all the more frightening because I was now returning their hostility. Formerly, when I had sworn never to be like them, I used to feel pity for them, and not animosity; but now they detested in me whatever distinguished me from them, the things to which I attached the greatest value: I moved on from commiseration to anger. How sure they were that they were right! They refused to admit any possibility of change or argument; they turned a blind eye to every problem. In order to understand the world and find myself I had to save myself from them.

It was very disconcerting, when I had thought I was making a triumphal progress, to realize suddenly that I was engaged in a bitter struggle; it gave me a shock from which I took a long time to recover; at any rate, books helped me to regain some of my crest-fallen pride. 'Family, I hate you! You dead homes and shut doors!' Ménalque's* imprecation re-assured me that by finding home dull I was serving a sacred cause. When I read the first books by Barrès I learnt that 'the free man' always arouses the ire of the 'barbarians', and that my first duty was to hold my own against them. So I was not suffering under some obscure misfortune; I was fighting the good fight.

Barrès, Gide, Valéry, Claudel: I took part in the devotions of a new generation of writers; and I read feverishly all the novels, all the essays of my older contemporaries. It was quite natural that I should have recognized myself in them because we were all in the same boat. Bourgeois like myself, they too felt ill at ease and out of place. The war had destroyed their security without freeing them from the trammels of class distinction; they were in revolt, but only against their parents, their family, and tradition. Sick of the 'bull' they had had to put up with during the war, they were now claim-ing the right to look things squarely in the face and call a spade a spade. As they had no intention of overthrowing society they con-tented themselves with studying the states of their precious souls in the minutest detail: they preached 'sincerity towards oneself'. Re-jecting all clichés and commonplaces, they disdainfully refused to accept the wisdom of their elders whose failure they had witnessed, but did not attempt to find another to take its place; they preferred to insist that one should never be satisfied with anything: theirs was a worship of disquiet. Every smart young man was an apostle of disquiet; during Lent in 1925 Father Sanson had preached in

* From Gide's *Les Nourritures terrestres* (Translators note).

Notre-Dame on 'Human Disquiet'. Out of disgust with an outworn morality, the most daring went as far as to question the existence of Good and Evil: they were admirers of Dostoyevsky's 'possessed' creatures; Dostoyevsky became one of their idols. Certain of them practised a disdainful aestheticism; others rallied round the flag of the immoralists.

I was in exactly the same position as these unhinged young men from respectable homes; I, too, was breaking away from the class to which I belonged: where was I to go? There was no question of sinking to the level of the 'lower orders'; one could, one ought to help them to rise above their inferior condition, but just at that period in my diary I was confusing my disgust for the epicurism of Anatole France with the crass materialism of the workers who 'crammed the cinemas'. As I couldn't imagine any place on earth that would suit my temperament, I gaily accepted the idea that I would never settle anywhere. I dedicated myself to the cult of Disquiet. Since childhood I had been questing for absolute sincerity. All around me people deplored falsehood, but were careful to avoid the truth; if I found so much difficulty in speaking freely now, it was because I felt it was repugnant to make use of the counterfeit coinage that was current in my environment. I lost no time in embracing the principles of immoralism. Of course, I did not approve of people stealing out of self-interest or going to bed with someone for the pure pleasure of it; but if these became quite gratuitous acts, acts of desperation and revolt – and, of course, quite imaginary – I was prepared to stomach all the vices, the rapes, and the assassinations you might care to mention. Doing wrong was the most uncompromising way of repudiating all connexions with respectable people.

A refusal to use hollow words, false moralizing and its too-easy consolations: the literature of those days was presenting this negative attitude as a positive ethical system. It was turning our disquiet into a crusade; we were seeking for salvation. If we had renounced our class, it was in order to get closer to the Absolute. 'Sin is God's empty place,' Stanislas Fumet wrote in *Our Baudelaire*. So immoralism was not just a snook cocked at society; it was a way of reaching God. Believers and unbelievers alike used this name. According to some, it signified an inaccessible presence, and to others, a vertiginous absence; there was no difference, and I had no difficulty in amalgamating Claudel and Gide; in both of them,

God was defined, in relationship to the bourgeois world, as the *other*, and everything that was other was a manifestation of something divine. I could recognize the thirst that tortured Nathanaël as the emptiness at the heart of Péguy's Joan of Arc and the leprosy gnawing at the flesh of Violaine; there is not much distance between a superhuman sacrifice and a gratuitous crime, and I saw in Sygne the sister of Lafcadio. The important thing was to use whatever means one could to find release from the world, and then one would come within reach of eternity.

A small number of young writers – Ramon Fernandez, Jean Prévost, and others – turned from these mystical ways in order to try to build a new humanism; I did not follow them. Yet the year before I had read Henri Poincaré with excitement; I was glad to be alive; but humanism – unless it were revolutionary, and the sort that was talked about in the *Nouvelle Revue Française* was not – implies that one can attain the universal and still be a bourgeois: and I had just made the brutal discovery that such a hope was a trap. From then on, I only attached a relative value to my intellectual life, as it had failed to reconcile me with everyone whose respect I wanted. I invoked a superior authority which would allow me to challenge outside judgements: I took refuge in 'my inmost self' and decided that my whole existence would be subordinate to it.

This change of attitude led me to look upon the future with a different eye: 'I shall have a happy, fruitful, and fame-crowned life,' I told myself when I was fifteen. Finally I decided a merely fruitful life would do. It still seemed to me very important to serve humanity, but I didn't expect any reward as the opinions of others would not count any more. This renunciation was not hard to make, for fame had only been an uncertain shadow at the end of a long future. As for happiness, I had known what it is, and I had always wanted it. I did not find it easy to give it up. If I decided to abjure happiness, it was because I felt it would always be withheld from me. I could not separate it from love, friendship, tenderness, and I was setting out on an 'irremediably solitary' enterprise. In order to find happiness, I should have had to go back, to go down in my own estimation: I asserted that all happiness is in itself a fall from grace. How could happiness be reconciled with disquiet? I loved Meaulnes, Alissa, Violaine, and Marcel Arland's *Monique*: I would follow in their footsteps. Besides, there was no ban on being joyful; I was often visited by joy. I wept many tears during that term, but I also enjoyed tremendous revelations.

*

Although I had passed my literature examination, I had no intention of forgoing Garric's lectures: I went on sitting at his feet every Saturday afternoon. I didn't cool off: I felt the world would no longer have been habitable if I hadn't someone to admire. Whenever I happened to leave Neuilly without Zaza or Thérèse, I used to walk home; I would go along the avenue de la Grande Armée; I used to enjoy playing a game which in those days did not have a great element of risk attached to it: I had to walk straight across the place de l'Étoile without stopping. Then I would push my way through the crowds parading up and down the avenue des Champs-Élysées. And all the time I would be thinking of that man, so different from all others, who lived in an unknown, almost exotic district, Belleville. He was not filled with 'disquiet', but he wasn't half-asleep like most people: he had found the right road; no home, no profession, no routine; there was no waste in his life: he was alone, he was free; from morning to night he was active, blazing a trail, illuminating the dark of ignorance. How I longed to be as he was! I cultivated the 'group spirit' and looked upon all the passers-by with love in my heart. When I read in the Luxembourg Gardens and someone came and sat beside me and started a conversation, I eagerly entered into it. At one time I had been forbidden to play with strange little girls, and now I took pleasure in trampling that old taboo in the dust. I was particularly happy when I had contacts with 'the people', for then it seemed to me that I was putting Garric's instructions into practice. His existence illuminated all my days.

Yet the joy he brought me was soon shot through with anxiety. I was still listening to him talk about Balzac, Victor Hugo: I had to admit that I was trying to resuscitate a past that was now dead; I was a listener, but no longer his pupil: I no longer belonged to his life. 'And in a few weeks I shan't see him any more!' I kept telling myself. I had lost him already. I had never lost anything valuable: when things took their leave of me, I had ceased to attach any importance to them; this time, I was being forced to part with something very precious, and I refused to allow it to happen. No, I said, I will *not*. But my own wishes were without any weight. How could I win the day? I informed Garric that I was going to join one of the Groups, and he thanked me warmly; but he never had anything to do with the feminine sections of the movement. Next year I should probably never meet him again. I found the prospect so unbearable that I began thinking up all kinds of wild ideas; couldn't I pluck up enough courage to speak to him, write to him, tell him that I couldn't live without him? If I ventured to do so, I wondered, what would happen? 'I'll be able to see him again when the autumn term starts.' This hope had a slightly calming effect. And yet, even while I strove to hold on to him, I was all the time allowing Garric to slip into the background of my life. Jacques was becoming more and more important to me. Garric was a remote idol; but Jacques was concerned about my problems, and I found it pleasant to talk to him. Soon I had to admit that he had first place in my heart.

In those days I preferred to wonder about things rather than to understand them, so I didn't try to 'place' Jacques or to explain him. It is only now that I find I can tell his story without too much incoherence.

*

Jacques' paternal grandfather had married my grandfather's sister, the bewhiskered great-aunt who wrote little pieces for *La Poupée Modèle*. He was ambitious, and a gambler; he had endangered his fortune in wild speculations. The two brothers-in-law had had a furious quarrel over money matters, and although my grandfather had himself plunged from one bankruptcy into another he used to declare with virtuous aplomb in the days when I called Jacques my fiancé: 'None of my grand-daughters shall ever marry a Laiguillon.' When Ernest Laiguillon died, the stained-glass works was still a going concern; but it was said in the family that if poor Charlie had not met a premature death in that frightful road accident, he would probably have ruined the business in the end: like his father, he was excessively enterprising, and always had a quite unreasonable faith in his lucky star. It was my Aunt Germaine's brother who undertook to look after the business until his nephew reached his majority; he administered it with the utmost prudence, because, unlike the Laiguillons, the Flandins were provincials with very limited views, who were satisfied with small returns.

Jacques was two years old when he lost his father; he took after him; he had his gold-flecked eyes, his sensuous mouth, his alert expression; his grandmother Laiguillon idolized him and treated him as the head of the family almost before he could talk: he was to protect Titite and Mama. He took this role very seriously, and his sister and mother worshipped him. But after being a widow for five years, Aunt Germaine married again – a civil servant who lived at Châteauvillain; she took up residence there and gave birth to a son. At first she kept her elder children with her. Then, in the interests of their education, Titite went as a day-boarder to the Cours Valton, and Jacques to the Collège Stanislas; they lived in the apartment in the boulevard Montparnasse, looked after by old Élise. How did Jacques take this abandonment by his mother? Few children were more desperately driven to wear a mask than this little lord, dethroned, exiled, abandoned. He evinced the same ever-smiling regard for his step-father and his half-brother as for his mother and sister; the future was to prove – very much later – that only his affection for Titite was sincere; he probably didn't admit to himself that he felt resentful: but it was not without significance that he used to bully his grandmother Flandin and always manifested towards his mother's side a scorn which verged on hostility. The name of Laiguillon on the shopfront in fine stained-glass letters had to his mind all the splendour of a coat of arms; but if he took such ostentatious pride in it, it was also because he was avenging himself on his mother by acknowledging the superiority of his paternal ancestry.

He had not succeeded in replacing the young husband in his mother's home; to compensate for this, he boldly laid claim to his inheritance at the age of eighteen; having submitted scornfully to the provincial guardianship of his uncle, he now proclaimed himself to be the sole director of the business. That was the explanation for his youthful self-importance. No one ever knew what mental distress, what jealousies, rancours, and perhaps terrors he knew in those lonely top-floor workshops where the dust of the past was a foretaste of his future. But certainly his bounce, aplomb, and bragging concealed a grave distress.

A child is a rebel: he wanted to be calm and respectable as a grown man. He didn't have to fight for his freedom, but had to protect himself from it: he imposed upon himself standards and prohibitions which a living father might have dictated to him. He was exuberant, devil-may-care, insolent, and at the college he often got into hot water for his bad behaviour; he laughed one day as he showed me in one of his exercise-books a teacher's comment which reproached him for making 'divers odd noises in Spanish'; he did not set himself up as a Little Lord Fauntleroy: he was a grown-up whose maturity allowed him to infringe any discipline which he felt was too childish. At the age of twelve he improvised a comic charade at home, and dumbfounded his audience with a moral fable on marriages of convenience; he took the part of a young man who refuses to marry a girl without a dowry. 'If I am to set up a home,' he explained, 'I must be able to guarantee my children sufficiently easy circumstances.' When he was an adolescent, he never questioned the established order. How could he have rebelled against a phantom shade which he alone kept from falling into nothingness? A good son and a considerate brother, he remained faithful to the role that had been assigned to him by a voice from beyond the tomb. He used to make a great display of his respect for bourgeois institutions. One day, talking about Garric, he told me: 'He's a good sort; but he should marry and have a profession.' 'Why?' I asked. 'A man should have a profession.' He took his future responsibilities very much to heart. He attended lecture-courses on decorative art and law, and began learning the business in the musty smelling ground-floor offices; business and law bored him, but he liked to draw; he learnt wood-engraving and he was passionately interested in painting. Only there could be no question of him taking it up as a profession; his uncle, who knew nothing about the fine arts, ran the business very well; Jacques' work would not differ in any way from that of all small business men. He found consolation for this in taking up again his father and grandfather's ambitious projects; he wasn't going to be contented with a modest clientele of country priests; Laiguillon stained-glass windows would be of a high artistic quality that would be the wonder of the world, and the little factory would become an important business. His mother and my parents were worried: 'He'd do far better to leave the management of the business to his uncle,' said my father. 'He'll ruin the firm.' The fact was that in Jacques' eagerness there was something suspect; his eighteen-year-old's seriousness was too much like the grown-upness he had shown when he was only eight not to seem put on. He strained after conformity as if he had never belonged by right of birth to the caste he claimed kinship with. This was because he had failed to become an effective substitute for his father: he could only hear his own voice, and this lacked all authority. He carefully avoided any dispute about the propriety of his acts, all the more so as he never really thought very deeply about them. Never did his super-ego coincide with the personage he so boisterously incarnated: the elder Laiguillon.

I realized this flaw in his personality. I came to the conclusion that Jacques, too, had taken up the one attitude which seemed to me to be permissible: he, too, was a seeker crying aloud in the wilderness. No amount of vehement language could convince me of the sincerity of his ambition; nor could his more measured tones make his resignation seem real. Far from associating with 'respectable' people, he went as far as to refuse to employ all the stratagems of anti-conformism. His blasé, sulky face, his evasive eyes, the books he had lent me, his half-confidences – everything convinced me that he lived with his face turned towards an uncertain future. He liked *Le Grand Meaulnes*, and had made me love it: I identified him with Meaulnes. I saw in Jacques the perfect incarnation of Disquiet.

I went to dine fairly frequently at his home in the boulevard Montparnasse. I didn't mind these evenings out. Unlike the rest of my family, Aunt Germaine and Titite did not consider that I had turned into a monster; when I was with them in the great drawing-room with the shaded lights which had been familiar to me since my childhood, I took up the threads of my life again: I no longer felt branded nor banished. I used to have little confidential chats with Jacques which seemed to draw us even closer together. My parents did not disapprove of our association. Their attitude towards Jacques was ambiguous: they held it against him that he hardly ever came to our house now, and that he spent more time with me than with them; they accused him, too, of ingratitude. Yet Jacques was certain to be comfortably off in life: what a catch it would be for a girl without a dowry if he were to marry me! Every time my mother mentioned his name, she allowed herself a discreetly controlled smile: I was furious that they should be trying to transform into a bourgeois business deal an understanding based on a common refusal to recognize bourgeois views; all the same, I found their official recognition of our friendship very convenient because it authorized me to be alone with Jacques.

[201]

It was generally towards the end of the afternoon that I rang at the street door; I would go up to the apartment. Jacques would greet me with an eager smile. 'I hope I'm not disturbing you?' 'You never disturb me.' 'How's things?' 'They're always going well when I see you.' His kindness used to warm my heart. He would take me into the long, pseudo-medieval gallery where his work table stood; there was never very much light there, as the windows were of stained glass; I liked that semi-darkness, and the trunks and chests of massive wood. I would sit on a sofa covered with crimson velvet; he would pace up and down with a cigarette dangling from a corner of his mouth, and screwing up his eyes a little as if trying to catch a glimpse of his thoughts in the whorls of smoke. I would give back the books I had borrowed, and he would lend me others; he would read to me Mallarmé, Laforgue, Francis Jammes, Max Jacob. 'Are you going to initiate her into modern literature?' my father had asked him, in a primly ironical tone. 'Nothing would give me greater pleasure,' Jacques had replied. He took this task to heart. 'When all's said and done, I've introduced you to quite a few beautiful things!' he would tell me sometimes with a touch of pride. He guided my taste with a good deal of discrimination. '*C'est chic d'aimer Aimée!*' he told me when I brought back one of Jacques Rivière's novels; our comments rarely went much further than that; he hated making heavy weather of anything. Often, when I asked him to explain something, he would smile and quote Cocteau: 'It's like a railway accident; something you feel but can't explain in words.' When he sent me to the Studio des Ursulines – with my mother, when there was a matinée – to see an avant-garde film, or to the Atelier theatre to witness Dullin's last spectacular production, he would simply say: 'It shouldn't be missed.' Sometimes, he would give me a minute description of a single detail: a yellow light at the corner of a backcloth, or a hand slowly opening on the screen; his voice, amused and rapt, would suggest the infinite. But he also gave me very precious hints on how to look at a picture by Picasso; he flabbergasted me because he could identify a Braque or a Matisse without seeing the signature: that seemed to me like magic. I was dazed by all the new things he revealed to me, so much so that I almost had the feeling that he was the author of them all. I more or less attributed to him Cocteau's *Orpheus*, Picasso's *Harlequins*, and René Clair's *Entr'acte*.

What was he really doing? What were his plans, his pre-occupations? He didn't seem to do much work. He liked driving about Paris at night; he occasionally frequented the brasseries of the Latin Quarter, the bars in Montparnasse; he described the bars to me as fabulous places in which something was always happening. But he wasn't very satisfied with his way of life. Striding up and down the gallery, rumpling his beautiful golden-brown hair, he would confess to me with a smile: 'It's frightful to be so compli-cated! I simply get lost in my own complications!' Once he told me very seriously: 'D'you see, what I need is to have something to believe in!' 'Isn't it enough just to live?' I answered. I believed in life. He shook his head: 'It's not easy to live if you don't believe in anything.' And then he changed the subject; he would give himself only in small doses, and I never asked for more. In my conversa-tions with Zaza, we never touched on the essence of things; with Jacques, if we got anywhere near it, it seemed quite natural to do so in the most round-about manner. I knew that he had a friend, Lucien Riaucourt, the son of a great Lyon banking family, with whom he used to spend whole nights talking; they would keep walking each other back home, from the boulevard Montparnasse to the rue de Beaune and back again; sometimes Riaucourt stayed at Jacques' place and slept on the red velvet sofa. This young man had met Cocteau and had outlined a play he was writing to Dullin himself. He had published a book of poems, with woodcuts by Jacques. I felt very humble beside these great figures. I thought myself very lucky to have a small place in the background of Jacques' life. He told me that he did not usually get on well with women; he loved his sister, but found her too sentimental: it was really extraordinary for him to be able to have friendly conversa-tions with a girl as he did with me.

I think he would have liked nothing better than to bring me a little closer into his life. He used to show me his friends' letters, and would have liked to introduce me to them. One afternoon I went with him to the races at Longchamps. Another time he wanted to take me to see the Russian Ballet. My mother put her foot down: 'Simone may *not* go out with you in the evenings.' Not that she had any doubts about my losing my virtue; before dinner, I could spend hours alone in the flat with Jacques: but after dinner, any place, unless it was exorcized by the presence of my parents, was automatically a den of vice. So our friendship was restricted to exchanges of unfinished sentences broken by lengthy silences and readings from our favourite authors.

*

The term came to an end. I passed my examinations in mathematics and Latin. It was good to go so fast, and to succeed; but I quite decidedly had no liking for the exact sciences, nor for dead languages. Mademoiselle Lambert advised me to go ahead with my original plan: it was she who gave the philosophy lectures at Sainte-Marie; she would be glad to have me as a student; she assured me that I would obtain my degree without any difficulty. My parents made no objection. I was very satisfied with this decision.

Although during the previous few weeks the figure of Garric had rather faded into the background of my life, I nevertheless felt I would die when I took my leave of him in a gloomy corridor in the Institut Sainte-Marie. I went to hear one more of his lectures: it was in a hall in the boulevard Saint-Germain and Henri Massis and Monsieur Mabille also spoke. It was Monsieur Mabille who spoke last: his words seemed to have difficulty in penetrating his beard and whiskers, and Zaza's cheeks were hot with embarrassment. I couldn't take my eyes off Garric. I felt my mother looking at me in some perplexity, but I didn't even try to restrain the adoration in my gaze. I was learning by heart that face which was about to be extinguished for ever. The presence of a person is so complete, his absence so final; there seemed to be nothing between the two extremes. Monsieur Mabille stopped talking, the speakers left the platform; it was all over.

But I still clung on. One morning I took the Métro to an unknown part, so far off that I felt I must have crossed a frontier without showing my papers: the place was Belleville. I walked down the long street where Garric lived; I knew the number of his house; I moved towards it, hugging the walls: if he were suddenly to see me there, I was ready to sink through the ground with shame. For a brief moment I paused in front of his house, gazed up at the mournful brick façade, and stared at the door through which he passed every morning and evening; I went on my way; I looked at the shops, the cafés, and the square; *he* knew them all so well that

he didn't even see them any more. What had I come here for? I
went home empty-handed.

I was sure that I would see Jacques again in October and I said
good-bye to him without regret. He had just failed his law examination and was feeling a little depressed. In his last handshake and
in his final smile he put so much warmth that I was overcome with
emotion. I wondered anxiously if perhaps he hadn't taken my com-
posure for indifference. This thought distressed me. He had given
me so much! I was thinking less of the book, the pictures, the films
than of that light in his eyes, like the touch of a hand, whenever I
talked to him about myself. I suddenly wanted to thank him, and
straight away I wrote him a little note. But my pen hovered over
the envelope: should I send it? Jacques set the greatest store on restraint in human relationships. With one of those mysterious smiles
that might have meant anything, he had once quoted to me Goethe's
phrase, in Cocteau's version: 'I love you: is that any business of
yours?' Would he find my modest effusions embarrassing? Would
he perhaps mutter to himself: 'Is that any business of yours?' Yet
if my letter might bring him a little comfort, it would be cowardly
not to send it. I hesitated, held back by that fear of ridicule that had
paralysed my childhood; but I wasn't going to act like a child any
more. I added a hasty postscript: 'Perhaps you will think I'm ridiculous but I would be ashamed of myself if I never dared to be.'
And I went and put the letter in the letter box.

My Aunt Marguerite and my Uncle Gaston, who with their children were spending the season at Cauterets, had invited my sister
and me to join them. A year earlier, I would have been enraptured
by the mountain landscape: but now I had withdrawn into myself
and the world outside no longer had any effect on me. And besides,
I had had too intimate a relationship with nature to be willing to see
it brought down to the level of a summer attraction, as it was here.
It was served up to me on a plate, and I was not allowed the necessary leisure or solitude to get close to it: if I couldn't give myself up
to it, it would give me nothing. Pine forests and mountain torrents
meant nothing to me. We went on excursions to the Gavarnie
amphitheatre and the Lac de Gaube, where my cousin Jeanne took
snapshots: all I saw were mournful dioramas. These uselessly
elaborate surroundings could not distract me from my grief any
more than could the hideous spectacle of the hotels planted along
the village streets.

For I was unhappy. Garric had disappeared for ever. And how did I stand with Jacques? In my letter I had given him my address at Cauterets; as he would obviously not want his reply to fall into my parents' hands he would write to me here, or not at all. Dozens of times every day I went to look in pigeon-hole number 46 behind the hotel desk: nothing. Why? I had felt a carefree confidence in our friendship; now I wondered: did I mean anything to him? Had he found my letter childish? Or uncalled-for? Was it simply that he had forgotten me? What torture! And how I wished I could brood over it in peace and quiet! But I never had a minute to myself. I was sleeping in the same room with Poupette and Jeanne; we always went out together; all day long I had to keep a ceaseless watch on myself, and other peoples' voices were constantly assailing my ears. At La Rallière, over a cup of hot chocolate, and in the evenings at the hotel the lady guests and the gentlemen guests chattered away; it was the holidays, they were all reading something and they all kept talking about what they were reading. One of them would say: 'It's very well written, but parts of it are rather dull.' Another would announce: 'Parts of it are rather dull, but it's very well written.' Occasionally, someone, with a far-off look in his eyes and a carefully modulated voice, would say: 'It's a curious work.' Or, in rather severer tones: 'It's not everybody's taste.' I used to wait for night-time in order to indulge in the luxury of tears; the next day, the letter would still not have arrived; once again I would start waiting for night, my nerves on edge, and my emotions in a very prickly state. One morning in my room I burst into tears; I don't know how I managed to reassure my flustered aunt.

Before going on to Meyrignac, we spent two days at Lourdes. It gave me a shock. Confronted with that ghastly parade of the sick, the moribund, the lame, and the goitrous, I made the brutal discovery that the world was not just an expression of the human soul. Human beings had bodies and their bodies were full of suffering. As I followed a procession, indifferent to the squalling of hymns and the sour body-smells of church-hens on the loose, I began to feel ashamed of my self complacency. This human misery was the only truth. I felt vaguely envious of Zaza who, when she went on a pilgrimage to Lourdes, washed the dirty dishes in hospitals. How could one forget oneself, give oneself utterly? And for what? Tragedy, disguised by grotesquely smiling masks of hope, was here too completely devoid of meaning to make the scales fall from my eyes. For a day or two I supped on horrors; then I took up the threads of my own worried existence again.

I spent a miserable holiday at Meyrignac. I wandered around the chestnut plantations weeping my heart out. I felt I was absolutely alone in the world. That year, my own sister was like a stranger to me. My aggressively self-critical attitude had offended my parents, who now regarded me with suspicion. They read the novels I had brought with me and discussed them with Aunt Marguerite: 'It's morbid, it's perverted, it's not natural,' I used to hear them saying; their pronouncements used to wound me as much as their comments on my black moods or their wild guesses as to what was in my mind. With more leisure than they enjoyed in Paris, they bore even less patiently with my silences, and I didn't make things any better by giving way once or twice to reckless outbursts of temper. Despite all my efforts, I still remained very vulnerable. Whenever my mother nodded her head saying: 'You're in a bad way, my girl,' I flew into a rage; but if I succeeded in mastering my temper and gave her a soft answer, she would give a sigh of fatuous satisfaction and say: 'There, now, that's better!' which only served to exasperate me all the more. I was fond of my parents, and in this environment where we had been so happy together I felt our lack of contact even more painfully than in Paris. In addition I had nothing to do; I had only been able to get hold of a small number of books. Reading a book on Kant, I developed a passion for critical idealism which confirmed me in my rejection of God. In Bergson's theories about 'the social ego and the personal ego' I enthusiastically recognized my own experience. But the impersonal voices of the philosophers didn't bring me the same consolation as those of my favourite authors. I could no longer feel their elder-brotherly presences about me. My sole refuge was my diary; when I had chewed over my boredom and sadness in it, I could begin again to feel bored and sad.

One night, at La Grillière, just as I had laid myself to sleep in a vast country bed, I was overwhelmed by a terrible anguish; I had on occasion been terrified by the thought of death, to the point of tears and screams; but this time it was worse. Life was already tilting over the brink into absolute nothingness; at that instant I felt a terror so violent that I very nearly went to knock on my mother's door and pretend to be ill, just in order to hear a human voice. In the end I fell asleep, but I retained a horrified memory of that awful attack of nerves.

When we got back to Meyrignac, I toyed with the idea of writing; I preferred literature to philosophy, and I wouldn't have been at all pleased if someone had prophesied that I would become a kind of female Bergson; I didn't want to speak with that abstract voice which, whenever I heard it, failed to move me. What I dreamed of writing was a 'novel of the inner life'; I wanted to communicate my experience. I hesitated. I could feel within me 'masses of things to say'; but I realized that writing is an art and that I was not an expert. All the same I jotted down a few subjects for novels and finally I made a decision. I composed my first work. It was the story of an attempt to escape that came to nothing. The heroine was the same age as myself, eighteen; she was spending her holidays with her family in a country house where she was awaiting the arrival of her fiancé whom she loved in a conventional manner. Until then she had been satisfied with the banality of her existence. Suddenly she discovered that there was 'something else'. A musician, a genius, awoke in her a realization of the real things in life: art, sincerity, disquiet. She felt that she had been living a lie; a strange, feverish longing took possession of her. The musician went away. The fiancé arrived. From her room on the first floor she could hear the joyous cries of welcome; she hesitated: was she going to keep, or lose for ever, what the musician had given her a glimpse of? Her courage failed her. She went downstairs and smilingly entered the drawing-room where the others were awaiting her. I had no illusions about the value of this tale; but it was the first time I had made myself put my own experience into words, and I took pleasure in writing it.

I had sent a little note to Garric, the sort a pupil sends to a teacher, and he had replied with a postcard, the sort a teacher sends to a pupil; I no longer thought about him very much. By his personal example he had encouraged me to uproot myself from my past, from my environment: condemned to solitude, I had followed him headlong into the heroic life. But it was a hard road, and I would certainly have preferred my life sentence to be put off for a while; my friendship with Jacques seemed to authorize me to go on hoping. Lying in the heather or wandering the country lanes it was always his face I saw before me. He hadn't replied to my letter but in time my disappointment died away, softened by memories of his welcoming smiles, our complicity, and of the velvet hours I had spent in his company. I was so weary of crying that I allowed myself a few day-dreams. I would light the lamp, I would sit on the red velvet sofa: I would feel at home. I would look at Jacques: he would be mine. Without any doubt, I was in love with him; why should he not be in love with me too? I began to make plans for our future happiness. If I had renounced all thoughts of personal happiness, it could only be because I thought I couldn't have him; but as soon as it began to seem possible, I started to long for happiness again.

Jacques was good-looking; his was a boyish, fleshly beauty; yet he never once caused me the least physical disturbance or aroused in me the faintest sexual desire; perhaps I was mistaken when I noted in my diary, not without some astonishment, that he had made some tentative gesture of affection and something inside me had recoiled: it signified that at any rate in my imagination I kept my distance. I had always looked upon Jacques as an elder brother, rather remote and grand; my family, whether hostile or well-disposed towards our relationship, never ceased to bait us; doubtless that is why my love for him was the kind I would have had for an angel.

My love owed the irremediable nature which I at once attributed to it to the fact that we were cousins and childhood friends. I had bitterly reproached Jo March and Maggie Tulliver with having betrayed their childhood loves: by loving Jacques I felt I was living out my destiny. I would recall our former 'engagement', and the stained-glass plaque he had made me a present of; I rejoiced in the fact that we had been separated in adolescence, because it had given me the rapturous joy of discovering him all over again. This idyllic match was obviously to be made in heaven.

In truth, if I believed it to be inevitable, it was because, without consciously realizing it, I felt it would provide the ideal solution to all my difficulties. Though thoroughly detesting the sameness of bourgeois life, I still felt a little nostalgia for those evenings in the black and red study in the days when I couldn't imagine myself ever leaving my parents. The Laiguillon's house, that beautiful apartment with its thick-pile carpets, the airy drawing-room, and the shadowy gallery were already my own hearth and home; I would read side by side with Jacques, and I would think of 'the two of us' just as in former days I had thought of 'the four of us'. His mother and sister would lavish their affection upon me and my parents would be kinder to me: I should become once more a person universally loved and I would take my place again in that society from which I had felt myself exiled for ever. Yet I would not give up my new ideas; with Jacques beside me, happiness would never mean just closing our eyes to reality; day would lovingly follow day, but all the time we would be pursuing our search; we would lose our way together, without ever going astray from one another, joined for ever by a common disquiet. So I would find my salvation in peace of heart and not in mental anguish. Exhausted by tears and boredom, I suddenly staked my whole future on this one chance. I waited in a fever of impatience for our return to Paris, and my heart seemed to thump to the rhythm of the train that took us back there.

*

When I found myself back in our old apartment with the threadbare carpets it was a brutal awakening for me: I hadn't come to earth beside Jacques, but at home; I was going to spend a whole year between these walls, I had a sudden vision of a long succession of days and months; what a wilderness! I had made a clean sweep of all my old friends, comrades, and pleasures; Garric was lost to me for ever: I would see Jacques at the most two or three times a month, and nothing encouraged me to expect from him any more than what he had already given me. So once more I should know the misery of joyless awakenings; in the evenings, there would be the refuse bin to empty; there would be more weariness and boredom. In the stillness of the chestnut groves, the delirious fanaticism which had helped me to get through the past year had finally exhausted itself; it would all be the same as before, only without that kind of madness which had helped me to bear it.

I was so frightened that I wanted to run straight away to see Jacques: only he could help me now. As I have said, my parents looked upon him with mixed feelings. That morning my mother forbade me to go and see him, and made a violent attack on him and on the influence he had over me. I still didn't dare disobey or tell any outright lies. I still used to tell my mother what my plans were for the day; in the evening I had to give her a full account of how I had passed my time. I gave in. But I was choking with fury and vexation. For weeks I had been looking forward eagerly to this meeting, and here I was being debarred from it by a whim of my mother's! I was horrified to realize the extent of my dependence. Not only had I been condemned to exile, but I was not even allowed the freedom to fight against my barren lot; my actions, my gestures, my words were all rigidly controlled; they tried to fathom every thought, and could with one word bring to nought the plans on which I had set my heart: there was no way out for me. During the past year I had been more or less able to adapt myself to my fate because I was so taken aback by the great changes that were going on inside me; but now this spiritual adventure was over and I again fell into a depression. I had become a different person, and I should have had a different world about me; but *what* kind? What was I really looking for? I couldn't even imagine what it would be like. This passivity filled me with despair. There was nothing for it but to wait. How long? three years? four years? That's a long time when you're eighteen. And if I spent them in prison, in chains, when I came out I would still find myself just as alone, without love or hope or anything. I would teach philosophy in some provincial school: what good would that do me? What about writing? My attempts at Meyrignac were quite worthless. If I remained where I was, a victim of the same monotonous routines, the same boredom, I would never make any progress: I would never write a book. No, there was no single ray of hope anywhere. For the first time in my existence I believed sincerely that it would be better to be dead.

After a week, I was given permission to go and see Jacques. When I arrived at his front door, I was overcome by panic: he was my only hope, and all I knew about him was that he had not replied to my letter. Had he been touched or irritated by it? How would he receive me? I walked two or three times round the block: I felt more dead than alive. The bell-push embedded in the wall frightened me: it had the same deceptively harmless appearance as the dark hole in which as a child I had so imprudently poked my finger. I pressed it. As usual, the door opened automatically and I went up-stairs. Jacques smiled at me, and I sat down on the crimson sofa. He handed me an envelope with my name on it: 'Here, take this,' he said. 'I didn't send it to you because I wanted this to be just be-tween us two.' He had blushed right up into his hair. I opened the envelope. At the top of the letter he had written: 'Is it any business of yours?' In it he congratulated me for not being afraid of appearing ridiculous; he assured me that he had often thought of me 'in the long, warm, lonely afternoons'. He gave me advice. 'If you were more human you would shock your family much less; and in the end it's better to be like that: I was going to say more self-respecting. . . . The secret of happiness and the very height of artistic achievement is to be like everybody else, yet to be like no one on earth.' He closed with this: 'Will you look upon me as your friend?' A great sun rose in my heart. And then Jacques began to speak, using little disjointed phrases, as the dusk was falling. Things weren't going at all well, he told me, not well at all. He was in a mess, really fed up; he had always thought he was a fairly decent person: he didn't believe that any longer; he despised himself; he no longer knew what he could do about himself. I listened, touched by his humility, enraptured by his confidences, and overwhelmed by his depression. When I left him, my heart was in a whirl. I sat down on a bench in the street to fondle and gaze at the present he had given me: a sheet of fine, thick, deckle-edged paper covered with signs in violet ink. Certain bits of his advice surprised me: I didn't feel I was inhuman; I wasn't trying deliberately to shock people; I didn't in the least want to be like everybody else; but I was touched that he should have taken the trouble to compose these beautifully cadenced sentences for me. Again and again and again I read the inscription: 'Is it any business of yours?' It clearly meant that Jacques cared for me much more than he had ever admitted before; but there was something else which proved definitely that he didn't love me: he wouldn't have sunk to such depths of despair if he had been in love with me. My mistake was obvious, and I resigned myself to the inevitable: it was not possible to reconcile love and disquiet. Jacques had brought me back to reality; cosy chats by the fire, lamplight on lilac and roses were not for us. We were too clear-headed and too demanding ever to let ourselves be lulled into the false security of love. Jacques would never abandon his tormented pursuit of the truth. He had reached the end of his despair, to the point of turning back on himself in disgust: I would have to follow him along that thorny path. I called upon Alissa and Violaine to support me, and plunged headlong into self-renunciation. 'I shall never love anyone else, but love is impossible between us two,' I decided. I did not disown the conviction that had impressed itself upon me during the holidays: Jacques was my destiny. But the reasons why I linked my fate with his would not allow him to bring me happiness. I had a part to play in his life: but it was not to invite him to sleep away his disquiet; I had to fight against his discouragement and help him to carry on his search. I undertook the task immediately. I wrote him a fresh letter in which I quoted scores of reasons for going on living drawn from the best authors.

It was natural that he should not reply, as we both wanted our friendship to be 'just between us two'. All the same, I ate my heart out. When I dined with his family, I was watching all evening for a conspiratorial twinkle in his eyes. Nothing. He played the fool even more exuberantly than usual: 'Will you stop this clowning!' his mother laughed. He seemed so carefree and so indifferent to me that I was certain that this time I had missed the target: he had read with exasperation the dissertation which I had so ungraciously flung at his head. 'A painful, painful evening in which his mask concealed with too hermetic a fixity his real face. . . . I wish I could vomit up my heart,' I wrote next morning in my diary. I decided to go to ground, to forget him. But a week later, my mother, who had been told by his family, informed me that Jacques had again failed his examination: he seemed very cast down; it would be a kindness if I would go and see him. I immediately prepared my spiritual first-aid kit and ran to succour him. He really did look like a broken man; sunk in his armchair, unshaven, without a tie, hardly 'decent' almost, he didn't raise the flicker of a smile. He thanked me for my letter, though without much warmth I thought. And he told me again that he was good for nothing, that he was utterly worthless. He had led a stupid life all summer, he was spoiling everything, he was a failure, he was disgusted with himself. I tried to console him, but my heart wasn't in it. When I left, he whispered: 'Thank you for coming,' in a voice charged with meaning which moved me deeply: none the less I went back home feeling very low. This time, I couldn't paint Jacques' distress in glowing colours; I didn't know *what* he'd been doing exactly all the summer, but I assumed the worst: gaming, drinking, and what I vaguely called debauchery. There must be a good explanation for such behaviour: but I found it disillusioning to have to excuse him. I recalled the great fantasy of love and admiration that I had built round him when I was fifteen and I compared it sadly with the present state of my affection for Jacques: no, I did not admire him any more. Perhaps all admiration was self-deception; perhaps in the depths of every human heart one found only the same unreliable pretence; perhaps the one link possible between two souls was compassion. This pessimistic view did nothing to console me.

Our next meeting threw me into fresh perplexity. He had pulled himself together; he was laughing, and making quite rational plans for the future in a calm, meditative way. 'One day I'll get married,' he suddenly threw out. This little phrase racked my heart. Had he uttered it casually or on purpose? In the latter case, was it a promise or a warning? It was impossible to think of any other woman but myself as his wife: yet I found that the idea of marrying him revolted me. I had been toying with the idea all summer; but now, when I contemplated the possibility of this marriage which my parents so ardently desired, I wanted to run away. I no longer regarded it as a way out but as a blind alley. For several days I lived in terror.

The next time I went to Jacques, he had some friends with him; he introduced them to me and the young men went on talking among themselves about bars and barmen, money difficulties and obscure intrigues; I was glad that they went on talking in my presence; yet their conversation depressed me. Jacques asked me to wait while he took his friends back to their homes in his car; at the end of my tether, I flung myself on the sofa and sobbed my heart out. I had calmed down when he returned. His face had altered and once more I could feel a tender concern in his voice. 'You know, a friendship like ours is something quite exceptional,' he told me. He walked with me along the boulevard Raspail and we paused a long while in front of a shop window in which a ghostly white painting by Foujita was displayed. He was leaving next day for Châteauvillain where he was to spend three weeks. I was relieved to think that during the whole of that time my last memory of him would be tinged with the sweetness of this twilight walk.

Still my agitation did not decrease: I didn't know what to make of myself. At times Jacques was everything to me; at others absolutely nothing at all. I was surprised to feel almost a kind of hatred for him sometimes. I asked myself: 'Why is it only in moments of regret, expectation, and pity that I feel my greatest surges of tenderness?' The thought of a love shared between us chilled my heart. If the need I had of him died, I felt myself diminished; but I noted in my diary: 'I need *him* – which doesn't mean I need to *see* him.' Our conversations, instead of stimulating me as they had done the year before, sapped my strength. I preferred to think of him at a distance rather than be with him.

Three weeks after his departure, I was crossing the place de la Sorbonne when I saw his car standing outside the Café d'Harcourt. What a shock! I knew that his life didn't belong entirely to me; we used to speak of it in oblique terms; I was only on the fringes of his existence. But I liked to think that in our conversations he showed his real self; this little car at the kerb proclaimed that the contrary was true. At that moment, at every moment in his life, Jacques existed as a creature of flesh and blood, but for other people, not for me; against the great mass of weeks and months, our brief timid meetings counted for very little. He came to our house one evening; he was charming; and I felt bitterly disappointed. Why? I was more and more in the dark. His mother and sister were staying in Paris and I no longer had any chance of meeting him alone. I felt we were playing at hide-and-seek and that perhaps in the end we would never find each other again. Did I love him or didn't I? Did he love me? My mother told me repeatedly with a wry smile what he had said to his mother: 'Simone is very pretty; it's such a pity that Aunt Françoise dresses her so badly.' This criticism was no concern of mine: all I remembered was that he liked my face. He was only nineteen; he had to pass his exams, and then do his military service; it was quite natural that he should not talk about marriage except in a vaguely allusive way; this reserve did not belie the warmth of his greetings, his smiles, his handclasps. He had written to me: 'Is it any of your business?' In the affection shown to me that year by Aunt Germaine and Titite there was a kind of conspiracy: his family and my own seemed to regard us already as practically engaged. But what was he really thinking? He sometimes looked so utterly indifferent to me! At the end of November we dined at a restaurant with our parents. He joked and chattered away: his presence completely masked his absence, disguised his real self too completely: I didn't know where I was in this masquerade. I wept half the night.

A few days later, for the first time in my life, I saw someone die: my Uncle Gaston, suddenly carried off by an intestinal occlusion. His death-throes lasted a whole night. Aunt Marguerite sat holding his hand, and saying things he couldn't understand. His children, my parents, my sister, and I were with him when he died. He gave the death-rattle, and vomited up some blackish stuff. When he stopped breathing his jaw sagged, and a scarf was tied round his head to keep it up. My father was sobbing openly: I had never seen him weep before. The violence of my own despair surprised everyone, including myself. I was very fond of my uncle, and I cherished the memory of our early morning hunting expeditions at Meyrignac; I was very fond of my cousin Jeanne and I couldn't bring myself to say: she's an orphan. But neither these regrets nor my compassion could explain the storm of grief that swept over me during the next two days: I couldn't bear to think of that despairing glance which my uncle had cast at his wife just before he died, and in which the irreparable was already an accomplished fact. Irreparable; irremediable: these words were hammering in my brain, till I thought my head would burst; and there was another answering them: inevitable. Perhaps one day I, too, would see that look in the eyes of a man whom I had loved all my life.

It was Jacques who brought me comfort. He seemed so moved by my ravaged eyes and was so affectionate that I dried my tears. In the course of a luncheon at his grandmother Flandin's, she told me: 'It wouldn't be you if you weren't hard at work.' Jacques gazed at me tenderly: 'I hope she would still be herself even if she didn't.' And I thought to myself: 'I was wrong to doubt him: he really does love me.' I dined at his house the following week, and he told me in a confidential aside that he had got out of the mess he was in but that he was afraid he was becoming very middle-class. And then, immediately the meal was over, he went off on his own. I invented excuses for him, but not one of them really satisfied me; if he'd cared anything at all for me, he wouldn't have shot off like that. Could he really be relied upon for anything? He certainly seemed to me to be lacking in stability and very fickle; he kept throwing himself away on small-time friendships and got involved in trivial and bothersome little affairs; he had no thought for the problems that tormented me; he was lacking in intellectual conviction. Again I felt bewildered and confused: 'Will I ever be able to set myself free from him, despite my occasionally rebellious feelings towards him? I love him, I am madly in love with him; yet I don't even know if he is really the one for me.'

The fact is that there were many differences between Jacques and me. That autumn, when I drew a word-portrait of myself, the first thing I noted was what I called my 'serious side'. 'An implacable, austere seriousness, for which I can find no reasonable explanation, but that I submit to as if it were a burden I *have* to bear.' Since my infancy I had always been headstrong, self-willed, a creature of extremes, and proud of it. Others might stop half-way in their quest for faith or in the expression of their scepticism, their desires, their plans: I despised their half-heartedness. I always carried my emotions, my ideas, my enterprises to the bitter end; I didn't undertake anything lightly; and now, as in my earliest childhood, I wanted everything in my life to be justified by a kind of absolute necessity. This stubbornness, I realized, deprived me of certain qualities; but there was never any question of departing from my fixed intention; my 'serious side' was the whole of me, and I wanted very much to remain a 'whole' person.

It was not his easy-going attitude, his paradoxical and irregular behaviour with which I reproached Jacques; I believed he was more artistic, more sensitive, more spontaneous, and more gifted than myself; at times I would recall the story of Theagenus and Euphorion and I was prepared to set on a pedestal high above my own humbler qualities the special grace with which he seemed to be imbued. But contrary to my experience with Zaza, in whom I could see nothing to find fault with, certain aspects of Jacques' character bothered me: 'His predilection for set formulas; his enthusiasms which are often too extravagant for their objects; his rather affectedly disdainful criticisms of certain things.' He was lacking in depth and perseverance, and sometimes – this seemed to me a much graver flaw – in sincerity. I sometimes felt exasperated by his elusiveness; and on occasion I suspected him of simply making cynical use of his scepticism in order to spare himself the least effort. He kept complaining that he didn't believe in anything; I kept racking my brains to provide him with objects he *could* believe in; it seemed to me a sacred task to work hard for one's own development and enrichment; this was the sense in which I took Gide's precept: 'Make yourself indispensable'; but if I reminded Jacques of this, he would simply shrug his shoulders: 'You might as well go to bed and sleep your head off, for all the truth there is in *that* statement.' I would urge him to write; I was sure he had some fine books in him. 'What's the use?' he would reply. What about drawing and painting? He had the gifts. He still replied: 'What's the use?' He countered all my suggestions with those three little words. 'Jacques still persists in wanting to build on absolute foundations; he should study Kant; he won't get anywhere like this,' I

[217]

naïvely noted in my diary one day. Yet I had a grave suspicion that Jacques' behaviour had nothing to do with metaphysics, and most of the time I was severely critical of his attitude: I did not approve of idleness, thoughtlessness, or inconsistency. On his side, I felt that my good intentions often exasperated him. It would be possible in a friendship to overcome these divergencies; but they made the prospects of a life in common very formidable.

I should not have worried so much about it if I had been aware of a simple opposition in our characters; but I realized that something else was at stake: the future course of our lives. On the day when he mentioned marriage, I made a long inventory of the things that separated us: 'He is content to enjoy beautiful things; he accepts luxury and easy living; he likes being happy. But I want my life to be an all-consuming passion. I need to act, to give freely of myself, to bring plans to fruition: I need an object in life, I want to overcome difficulties and succeed in writing a book. I'm not made for a life of luxury. I could never be satisfied with the things that satisfy him.'

There was nothing startling about the luxury of the Laiguillon home: what I was really rejecting, and what I reproached Jacques with accepting, was the bourgeois status. Our understanding was based on an ambiguity which explains the incoherence of my emotions. In my view, Jacques was freeing himself from his class because he, too, was suffering from a deep disquiet; what I did not realize was that this deep disquiet was the means which that bourgeois generation was employing in order to effect its own cure; yet I felt that at the very moment when marriage ought to have delivered him from the bonds of class, Jacques would at last coincide exactly with the *persona* of a young business man and head of a family. In fact, all he wanted was to play with conviction the role assigned to him by birth, and he was counting on marriage as Pascal had counted on holy water, to give him the faith he lacked. I was still not clearly conscious of all this at that time, but I understood that he looked upon marriage as a solution and not as a point of departure. There would be no question of us storming the heights together: if I became Madame Laiguillon I would be dedicated to 'home life'. Perhaps that would not be absolutely incomparable with my personal aspirations? I distrusted all compromises, and that one in particular seemed to me to be dangerously suspect. If I were to share Jacques' existence I would find it hard to hold my own against him, for already I found his nihilism contagious. I tried to challenge his authority by having recourse to the evidence of my own passions and wishes: I often succeeded. But in moments of discouragement I was inclined to think he was right. Once under his influence and in order to gratify his desires wouldn't I let myself be driven to sacrifice everything I thought worthwhile? I rebelled at the thought of such a personal mutilation. That is why all that winter my love for Jacques was such a painful one; either he was throwing away his talents, and I was hurt to see him drifting away from me; or he was trying to seek a certain stability in a bourgeois self-sufficiency which might have brought him closer to me if I hadn't looked upon it as a fall from grace. I couldn't follow him in his disordered ways, yet I didn't want to live with him in an order I despised. We neither of us had any faith in conventional values; but I was determined to find some I could believe in, or else invent new ones; he could see as far as that; he wavered between dissipation and the depths of despair, and it was only by an acceptance of bourgeois values that he was able to pull himself together: he never thought of changing his way of life, but only of adapting himself to it. But I wanted to find a way out of it.

I often used to feel how incomparable we were, and I would mournfully tell myself: 'He alone is happiness and life! Ah! happiness! And life, that should be everything to me!' Yet I couldn't bring myself to exclude Jacques from my heart. He set off on a month's trip over the whole of France: he was going to see priests and look at churches, trying to find buyers for the Laiguillon stained-glass windows. It was winter, and very cold: I began again to long for the warmth of his presence, for a peaceful love, a place of my own, that would also be a home to us both. I no longer conducted self-interrogations. I was reading Mauriac's *Good-bye to Adolescence*; I was learning long languid passages of it by heart and I would recite them to myself in the streets.

If I persisted in this love, it was mainly because despite my hesitations I always retained a deep affection for Jacques: he was charming, and a charmer, and his engaging manners, which, though capricious, were very real, had conquered more than one fond heart; my own was quite defenceless: an intonation, a glance was enough to unleash in me a bewildered gratitude. Jacques' intellect no longer dazzled me; I no longer needed his help in understanding books and paintings; but I was always moved by his confidences and his bouts of humility. All the others – narrow-minded young people and smug adults – thought they knew everything, and whenever they said 'I don't understand!' they never thought it might be themselves who were at fault. How grateful I was to Jacques for his lack of set ideas! I wanted to help him as he had helped me. Even more than by our childhood's past I felt myself bound to him by a sort of pact which made his 'salvation' even more important than my own. I believed all the more firmly in this predestined bond because I didn't know a single man, whether young or old, with whom I could even begin to have a serious conversation. If Jacques wasn't made for me, then no one was, and I would have to go back to a solitude which I found very bitter and hard to bear.

At those moments when I re-dedicated myself to the service of Jacques, I would raise a statue to him again in my mind: 'Everything that comes to me from Jacques seems like a game, a lack of courage, a cowardice – and then, after all, I realize the truth in what he says.' His scepticism was proof of his lucidity; in truth, it was I who was lacking in courage whenever I tried to shut my eyes to the sad relativity of human ends; but he dared to admit that nothing was worth the effort. Did he waste his time in bars? That was because he was trying to escape from his despair, and sometimes he encountered a kind of poetry there. Instead of reproaching him for his excesses, I should admire him for his prodigality: he resembled that king of Thule whom he liked to take as an example and who didn't hesitate to throw his most beautiful golden goblet into the ocean for the sake of a sigh. I wasn't capable of such refinements, but this didn't mean that I was unable to recognize their value. I was convinced that one day Jacques would express such things in a book. He didn't altogether discourage my hopes: from time to time he would announce that he had found a simply wonderful title. I had to wait, give him credit. I practised these self-deceptions in the enthusiasm of his painful recoveries from dissipation and depression.

The main reason for my desperate eagerness to save him was that apart from this love my life seemed desolately empty and futile. Jacques was only what he was; but from a distance he became something more, became everything to me, everything I did not possess.

It was to him I owed pains and pleasures whose violence alone saved me from the deserts of boredom in which I found myself bogged down.

*

Zaza returned to Paris at the beginning of October. She had had her lovely black hair cut short, and her new hair-style threw into pleasant relief her rather thin face. Dressed in the style of St Thomas Aquinas, comfortably, but without elegance, she always wore a little cloche hat pulled right down to her eyebrows, and very often gloves too. On the day of our first reunion, we spent the afternoon on the *quais* along the Seine and in the Tuileries; she had that serious and even rather sad air which she now seemed to carry about with her permanently. She told me that her father had taken a new situation; Raoul Dautry had been given the post of head engineer on the State railways, a post Monsieur Mabille had been expecting to get; annoyed by this, he had accepted a proposition which the Citroën firm had long been making him: he would earn an enormous salary. The Mabilles were going to move to a luxurious apartment in the rue de Berri; they had bought a car; they would have to go out to dinner and give dinners in return much more frequently than before. Zaza didn't seem to be exactly enraptured by all this; she spoke impatiently about the social life she had to put up with, and I understood that it was not of her own choosing that she kept going to weddings and funerals, baptisms, First Communions, teas, luncheons, charity bazaars, family conclaves, engagement parties, and dances; she still judged her environment with the same severely critical eye as before: perhaps even more so. Before the holidays I had lent her some books; she told me that they had given her a lot to think about; she had read *Le Grand Meaulnes* three times over: she had never been moved so much by any other novel. She suddenly seemed very close to me and I talked to her a little about myself: she thought as I did about many things. 'I've got Zaza back!' I joyfully told myself when I left her as dusk was falling.

We got into the habit of going for a walk together every Sunday morning. It would hardly have been possible for us to have an intimate talk either at her house or mine; and we were completely ignorant as to the purpose of cafés: 'But what are all those people there for? Haven't they got homes?' Zaza asked me once as we were passing the Café de la Régence. So we used to tramp up and down the Champs-Elysées or the paths of the Luxembourg Gardens; if it was fine, we would sit on the iron seats at the edge of a lawn. We borrowed the same books from Adrienne Monnier's library; we read with passionate interest the correspondence between Alain Fournier and Jacques Rivière; she far and away preferred Fournier; I was fascinated by Rivière's methodical rapacity. We would discuss and comment on our daily lives. Zaza was having serious trouble with Madame Mabille who reproached her with spending too much time on studying, reading, and music and neglecting her 'social duties'; she thought the books Zaza liked were very dubious works; she was worrying. Zaza still felt the same devotion for her mother as before, and she couldn't bear to think she was causing her pain. 'Yet there are some things I *don't* want to give up!' she told me in an anguished voice. She was afraid there might be even graver conflicts in the future. After being dragged from one interview to another with 'suitable parties' her sister Lili, who was now twenty-three, would one day get herself married off; and then it would be Zaza's turn. 'I won't let them do it to me!' she declared. 'But then I shall have to have a row with Mama!' Though I didn't talk to her about Jacques or my new views on religion, I too confided many things in her. But on the day after that night I had spent weeping my heart out, following the dinner with Jacques and our parents, I felt unable to wander round alone until the evening; I went and rang at Zaza's door and as soon as I found myself alone with her I burst into tears. She was so dumbfounded that I told her everything.

As usual, I used to pass the better part of my days working. That year Mademoiselle Lambert was lecturing on logic and on the history of philosophy and I started studying for the examinations in both these subjects. I was glad to be reading philosophy again. I was still as keenly aware as in my childhood of the inexplicable nature of my presence here on earth; where had I come from; where was I going? I often thought about these things with a kind of stupefied horror and used to fill my diary with long self-communings; it seemed to me that I had been taken in by 'a conjuring trick whose secret, though childishly simple, cannot be guessed'. I was hoping, if not to elucidate the mystery, at least to get to closer grips with it. As my philosophical equipment consisted only in what the

Abbé Trécourt had taught me, I began by groping my way blindly through the systems of Descartes and Spinoza. These sometimes bore me up to lofty heights, out into the infinite: I would see the earth like an ant-hill at my feet, and even literature became a futile jabbering of voices; sometimes they seemed no more than clumsy scaffoldings constructed on air without any relationship to reality. I studied Kant, and he convinced me that no one could ever put me wise to things. His *Critique* seemed to me to be so very much to the point and I took so much pleasure in getting the hang of it that for the moment I couldn't find it in my heart to be saddened by it. Yet if it failed to explain the mystery of the universe and of my own existence, I really didn't know what could be the point of philosophy; I was only moderately interested in doctrines which I already took exception to. I did a dissertation on 'Descartes and the Ontological Fallacy' which Mademoiselle Lambert thought very mediocre. All the same, she had decided to take an interest in me, and this flattered me very much. During her logic lectures, I whiled away the time by watching her face, her mannerisms, her clothes. She always wore simple blue dresses that were at the same time rather studied in their effect; I found the cool ardour of her expression rather boring, but I was always startled by her smile which would transform the severe mask into a human face. It was rumoured that she had lost her fiancé in the war and that after this affliction she had withdrawn from worldly life. She inspired passion in certain breasts: she was even accused of abusing her hold over certain students who, out of love for her, formed part of the 'inner circle' which she presided over with Madame Daniélou. Then after having lured these devoted young things she was said to reject their advances. It didn't matter to me what she did. In my view, it was not enough just to think or just to live; I gave my complete allegiance only to those who 'thought their lives out': Mademoiselle Lambert did not 'live' her life. She gave lectures and was working on a thesis: I thought such an existence was very arid. Nevertheless I liked going to see her in her study, which was of the same blue as her dresses and her eyes: there was always a tea-rose in a crystal vase on her table. She would recommend books; she lent me *La Tentation d'Occident* by a young unknown called André Malraux. She would ask me very searching questions about myself, without making me feel scared. She thought it was quite natural that I should have lost my faith. I talked to her about many things, and about the state of my heart: did she think that one should resign oneself to a life of conjugal love and happiness? She gave me a rather anxious look: 'Do you really believe, Simone, that a woman can find fulfilment without love and marriage?' There was no doubt that she, too, had her problems; but it was the only time she referred to them; her task was to help me resolve my own. I listened to her advice without having much faith in it; I couldn't forget that she had a stake in Heaven; but I was grateful to her for having such a deep concern about me and her faith in me was very comforting.

In July I had put my name down for the Social Service Groups. The woman in charge of the women's sections, a huge purple-faced individual, made me the head of the Belleville group. At the beginning of October she called a meeting of officers to give us our instructions. The young women I met at this gathering were depressingly like my ex-schoolmates at the Cours Désir. I had two assistants, one of whom was to teach English, the other gymnastics; they were close on thirty and never went out in the evenings without their parents. Our group had its headquarters in a sort of community centre administered by a tall, dark, rather handsome girl of about twenty-five; she was called Suzanne Boigue and I got on well with her. But my new activities gave me very little satisfaction. On one evening a week for two hours I would talk about Balzac or Victor Hugo to young working girls; I would lend them books and we would have discussions; they were fairly numerous, and regular attenders; but they mainly came in order to meet one another and to keep in with the centre, which provided them with more material benefits. There was also a men's section, and the young men and women were brought together fairly frequently at social gatherings and dances; dancing and flirtation attracted them much more than study circles. I thought this was quite natural. My students were working all day long in fashion workshops or tailoring establishments; the knowledge, of a rather spasmodic nature, which was doled out to them had no bearing on their own experience and was of no use to them at all in their work. I saw nothing wrong in making them read *Les Misérables* or *Le Père Goriot*; but Garric was much mistaken if he imagined that I was providing them with Culture; and it was distasteful to me to follow instructions which called upon me to talk to them about human dignity or the value of suffering: I would have felt I was having them on. As for friendship, here too Garric had misled me. The atmosphere

[224]

at the centre was a fairly happy one; but between the young people of Belleville and those who, like myself, had come to teach them there was neither intimacy nor anything in common. We came together to pass the time, that was all. My disillusionment extended itself to Garric. He came to give a lecture and I spent a good part of the evening with him and Suzanne Boigue. I had passionately wanted to have a chance to speak to him one day, as one grown-up to another: our conversation seemed utterly pointless now. He chewed over the same old ideas: friendship was to take the place of hatred; instead of thinking from the point of view of parties, trade unions, and revolutions we had to orientate our thinking from the point of view of trade, family, and region; the great problem was to preserve the dignity of man. I listened to him with only half my attention. My admiration for him had died at the same time as my faith in his work. A little later, Suzanne Boigue asked me to take over a correspondence course for sick children in the sanatorium at Berck: I accepted. I found this work, because of its modest aim, to be more effective. Nevertheless I concluded that action is a deceptive solution: by pretending to devote oneself to the welfare of others one was providing oneself with too easy a way out. I had no idea that action could take forms far different from the kind I was condemning. Because if I felt that the Groups were something of a humbug, I was all the same a victim of that humbug. I thought I was in real contact with 'the people'; they seemed to be friendly, deferential, and willing to collaborate with their privileged superiors. This fake experience only served to aggravate my ignorance.

From a personal point of view, what I appreciated most in my work for the Groups was that it allowed me to spend an evening away from home. I had once more become very intimate with my sister; I would talk to her about love, friendship, happiness, and its snares; about joy and the beauties of the inner life; she read Francis Jammes and Alain Fournier. On the other hand, my relationship with my parents did not get any better. They would have been sincerely grieved if they had guessed how much their attitude affected me: but they didn't. They considered my tastes and my opinions to be a challenge to common sense and to themselves, and they counter-attacked on all sides. Sometimes they called in the help of their friends; they would then all join in denouncing the charlatanism of modern artists, the intellectual snobbery of the public, the decadence of France, and the civilized world; during these broadsides, all eyes would be directed towards me. Monsieur Franchot, a brilliant talker, well up in literature and the author of two novels which he had had published at his own expense, asked me one evening in a sarcastic tone of voice what beauties I could possibly find in Max Jacob's *Cornet à dés*. 'Ah!' I snapped, 'it cannot be penetrated at a casual reading.' They all burst out laughing and I must admit that I had given them reason to: but in such cases I had no other alternative but to take refuge in either pedantry or coarseness. I tried hard not to let myself be drawn, but my parents wouldn't allow me to sham dead. Convinced that I was being worked upon by baleful influences, they would question me suspiciously: 'And what's so extraordinary about your Mademoiselle Lambert?' my father would demand. He held it against me that I had no family feeling and preferred the company of strangers to his own. My mother admitted in principle that one might like friends one had chosen oneself better than distant relatives, but she thought my feelings towards Zaza were excessive. On the day when I went without warning to weep my heart out at Zaza's, I told my parents of the visit: 'I called in to see Zaza.' 'But you saw her last Sunday!' my mother cried. 'You've no need to go running to her all the time!' There was a lengthy scene. Another bone of contention was the books I read. My mother could not resign herself to the inevitable; she turned pale as she glanced through Jean-Richard Block's *La Nuit Kurde*. She let everybody know what a trial I was to her – my father, Madame Mabille, my aunts, my cousin and her friends. I couldn't bring myself to ignore the air of mistrust I felt all around me. How long the evenings seemed, and the Sundays! My mother said that a fire could not be made in my bedroom fireplace; so I put up a card table in the drawing-room, where there was an oil heater, but the door was always open. My mother would come in and out, coming and going and leaning over my shoulder all the time: 'What's that you're doing? What's that book you're reading?' Endowed with considerable energy for which she could find no outlet, she believed in being merry and bright. Singing, laughing, joking, she would try to bring back the happy bursts of merriment which used to fill the house in the days when my father didn't go out every evening and everyone was in a good humour. She wanted me to join in, and if I did not show any inclination to do so she would start to worry: 'What are you thinking about?

What's the matter with you? What are you looking like that for? Of course, I'm only your mother, you won't tell me anything . . .' When at last she went to bed, I was too exhausted to take advantage of the peace and quiet. How I should have liked just to go to the cinema! I would stretch out on the carpet with a book, but my head would feel so heavy that often I would fall asleep on the floor. I would drag myself off to bed, sick at heart. I would wake next morning feeling listless and bored, and my days would seem to crawl with a mournful slowness. I had had my fill of books: I had read too many that were everlastingly repeating the same old thing; they didn't bring me any fresh hope. I preferred killing time in the picture galleries in the rue de la Seine or the rue de la Boétie: painting took me out of myself. I used to try hard to get away from myself. Sometimes I would lose myself in the glowing embers of the setting sun; I would look at pale yellow chrysanthemums blazing against a pale green lawn; at the moment when the street lamps came on and changed the leafy trees of the Carrousel into a stage set at the Opéra, I would listen to the fountains playing. There was no lack of good will; it only needed a ray of sunlight to set my heart dancing. But it was autumn, it was drizzling; my joys were rare and soon past. Then boredom would return, and despair. The last year, too, had begun badly; I had been counting on mixing happily with the rest of the world, and I had been kept in my cage, then sent into exile. I had made shift by working hard, but in a negative way: the break with my past, with my environment; I had also made some great discoveries: Garric, Jacques' friendship, books. I had felt a renewed confidence in the future, and soared high into the heavens, seeking a heroic destiny. What a let-down! Once more the future was now and all promises should have been carried out already, without any need to wait. I had to be of service: to what? To whom? I had read, thought, and learnt much; I told myself that I was ready; I was rich; but nobody wanted anything from me. Life had appeared to me so full; I had sought with fanatical ardour to use my whole self in replying to its endless calls: it was empty; not one voice had asked for me. I felt strong enough to lift the whole world on my shoulders: and I couldn't find a single pebble that needed moving. My disillusionment was bitter: 'I *am* so much more than what I can *do*!' It was not enough to have renounced fame and happiness; I no longer even wished for my existence to be a fruitful one; I no longer wished for anything: I was

[227]

learning the painful lesson of 'the sterility of being'. I was working in order that I might have a profession; but a profession is a means: towards what end? Marriage? What would that mean? Whether it was bringing up children or correcting exercises, it was all the same old song; it was absolutely useless. Jacques was right to say: what's the use? People resigned themselves to pointless existences: not me. Mademoiselle Lambert, just like my mother, spent her days in aimless activity; as long as they were doing something, it didn't matter what they did. 'But *I* want to be driven by a force so exacting that it doesn't leave me time to bother about anything!' I didn't find any such force, and in my impatience I universalized my particular case: 'Nothing has any need of me, nothing has need of anybody, because nothing has any need to exist.'

And so I discovered within me that 'new *Weltschmerz*' denounced by Marcel Arland in an article in the *Nouvelle Revue Française* which had made a great stir. Our generation, as he saw it, could find no consolation for the absence of God; it was discovering, to its great distress, that apart from Him life was nothing but a series of occupations. I had read this essay a few months earlier with interest but without any particular concern; at that time I was quite happy to do without God and if I made use of His name it was only in order to designate a void which to me had all the splendour of the plenitude of grace. I still had absolutely no desire to know of His existence, and it even seemed to me that if I had believed in Him I should have detested Him. Groping my way along paths whose every twist and turn He knew, buffeted by the chance winds of His grace, petrified by His infallible judgement, my existence could only have been a stupid and pointless ordeal. No amount of sophistry could have convinced me that the Omnipotent had any need of my miserable life: or if He did, it would only be to play a joke on me. In earlier days, when the grown-ups' amused condescension used to transform my life into a puerile piece of play-acting, I would be convulsed with rage: and today, too, I would have refused no less violently to let myself become the ape of God. If I had rediscovered in Heaven, amplified to infinity, the monstrous alliance of fragility and implacability, of caprice and artificial necessity which had oppressed me since my birth, rather than worship Him I would have chosen damnation. His eyes gleaming with a malicious benevolence, God would have stolen everything from me – the earth, my life, other people, and my own self. I thought it great good luck that I had been able to get away from Him.

But then why was I always repeating in a desolate voice that 'all is vanity'? In fact, the sickness I was suffering from was that I had been driven out of the paradise of childhood and had not found my place in the world of men. I had set myself up in the absolute in order to gaze down upon this world which was rejecting me; now, if I wanted to act, to write a book, to express myself, I would have to go back down there: but my contempt had annihilated it, and I could see nothing but emptiness all around me. The fact is that I had not yet put my hand to the plough. Love, action, literary work: all I did was to roll these ideas round in my head; I was fighting in an abstract fashion against abstract possibilities and I had come to the conclusion that reality was of the most pitiful insignificance. I was hoping to hold fast to something, and, misled by the violence of this indefinite desire, I was confusing it with the desire for the infinite.

My poverty and my helplessness would have worried me less if I had had the least suspicion of how ignorant and narrow minded I still was; a job of work would have made the necessary demands upon me. I could have made inquiries about one; and others would no doubt have come along. But the worst of living in a prison without bars is that you aren't even aware of the screens that shut out the horizon; I was wandering through a thick fog, believing it to be transparent. I didn't even know that the things I was missing were there.

I wasn't interested in history. Apart from Vaulabelle's book on the two Restorations, the memoirs, stories and chronicles which I had been made to read all seemed to me, like Mademoiselle Gontran's history lessons, a jumble of meaningless anecdotes. What was happening at the present day hardly merited my attention either. My father and his friends used to talk politics without stopping and I knew that everything was in a bad way; I had no wish to poke my nose into such a gloomy mess. The problems that were bothering them – the recovery of the franc, the evacuation of the Rhineland, the airy utopias of the League of Nations – seemed to me to be of the same order as family quarrels and money troubles; they were no concern of mine. Jacques and Zaza didn't care twopence about them; Mademoiselle Lambert never mentioned them; the *NRF* writers – I hardly ever read any others – never touched on them,

[229]

excepting sometimes Drieu la Rochelle, though he wrote in such hermetic terms I couldn't understand him. In Russia, perhaps, things were going on: but it was very far away. The Groups had muddled my ideas about social questions, and philosophy wouldn't have anything to do with them. At the Sorbonne, my professors systematically ignored Hegel and Marx; in a big book on the progress of conscience in the western world, Brunschvig had devoted a bare three pages to Marx, whom he placed on the same level as one of the obscurest reactionary thinkers. He was teaching us about the history of scientific thought, but no one was teaching us about the adventure of humanity. The incomprehensible uproar going on in the world might be of interest to specialists; it was not worthy of the philosopher's attention, for, when he had got to the point where he knew that he knew nothing and that there was nothing worth knowing, he knew everything. That is why I was able to write in January: 'I know everything; I've gone all the rounds.' The subjective idealism to which I was now giving my allegiance deprived the world of its solidity and originality: it is hardly surprising that even in my imagination I could find nothing to hold on to.

So everything was conspiring to convince me of the inadequacy of human affairs: my own position, the influence of Jacques, the ideologies I was being taught, and the literature of the period. The majority of writers kept harping on 'our disquiet' and offered me a despairing lucidity. I took this nihilism to its logical conclusion. All religions, all morals were shams; so was the worship of oneself. I considered – not without reason – that the fevers I had formerly so complacently whipped up were artificial, and I threw Gide and Barrès overboard. In every plan I made I suspected an escape; work became a distraction just as futile as any other. One of Mauriac's young heroes looked upon his pleasures and his friendships as 'branches' supporting him precariously above the void: I borrowed this word from him. One had the right to clutch at branches, but on condition that one didn't confuse the relative with the absolute, defeat with victory. I judged others by these standards; the only people who existed for me were those who, without cheating, looked this all-consuming nothingness in the face. All ministers, Academicians, much-decorated gentlemen, and all big-wigs I considered *a priori* to be barbarians. A writer ought to feel he was damned; any kind of success was suspect, and I used to wonder if the very fact of writing something didn't imply a failure: only the silence of Valéry's Monsieur Teste seemed to me to express with dignity humanity's absolute despair. And so, in the name of the absence of God, I resurrected the ideal of a withdrawal from the world – a withdrawal that His existence had first inspired me to choose. But this asceticism led nowhere, gave no hope of salvation. The most honest attitude to take, after all, was to do away with oneself; I had to admit this, and I admired those who committed suicide for metaphysical reasons; yet I had no intention of resorting to suicide myself: I was far too afraid of death. When I was alone in the house, I would sometimes have to fight against my fear as I had done at the age of fifteen; trembling, with clammy hands, and feeling utterly distraught, I would cry: 'I don't want to die!'

And already death was slowly eating my life away. As I was not engaged on any sort of work, time became decomposed into instants that cancelled each other out indefinitely; I could not resign myself to this 'multiple and fragmentary death'. I would copy out whole pages of Schopenhauer and Barrès, and the verses of Madame de Noailles. I found death all the more frightful because I could see no point in living.

And yet I loved life passionately. It needed very little to restore my confidence in it, and in myself: a letter from one of my pupils at Berck, the smile of a Belleville working girl, the confidence of a fellow-student at Neuilly, a look from Zaza, a thank-you, a kind word. As soon as I felt I was useful and loved, the horizon brightened and again I would begin to make fresh resolutions: 'Be loved, be admired, be necessary; be somebody.' I was more and more certain that I had 'masses of things to say': and I would say them. On my nineteenth birthday, I wrote in the library at the Sorbonne a long dialogue between two voices, both of which were mine: one spoke of the vanity of all things, of disgust and weariness; the other affirmed that life, even a sterile existence, was beautiful. From day to day, from one hour to the next I would pass from depression to exaltation. But all through that autumn and winter the dominating thing in me was an anguished fear that one day I would again find myself 'broken by life'.

These oscillations of mood and all these doubts filled me with terror; I was bored to suffocation and my heart was sore. Whenever I cast myself into despair, it was with all the violence of my youth and strength, and moral pain could rack my body with as much savagery as physical suffering. I wandered around Paris, mile after mile after mile, staring at unknown vistas through eyes swimming in tears. Made hungry by my long tramp, I would go into a cake shop, eat a bun, and recite in an ironic tone Heine's famous line: 'Whatever tears one may shed, in the end one always blows one's nose.' On the *quais* of the Seine I would try to rock away my misery by sobbing out the lines by Laforgue:

'O, well-belovèd, it's too late now, my heart is breaking,
    A break too deep for bitterness, and I have wept so long . . .'

I liked to feel the tears singeing my eyes. But at certain moments, with all my defences down, I would seek refuge in the side-aisles of a church in order to be able to weep in peace; there I would prostrate myself with my head in my hands, suffocated by the bitter-smelling dark.

*

Jacques returned to Paris at the end of January. The day after his return he came to see us. My parents had had photographs taken of me for my nineteenth birthday, and he asked me for one; never had I heard such tender inflexions in his voice. I was trembling when, a week later, I rang at his door, for I was dreading some brutal relapse into indifference. I was enchanted by our meeting. He had started a novel, which he was calling *Les Jeunes Bourgeois*, and he told me: 'It's because of you I'm writing it.' He also told me that he would dedicate it to me: 'I feel I owe it to you.' For the next few days, I was walking on air. The week after, I talked to him about myself; I described my boredom, and told him how I could no longer see any meaning in life. 'There's no need to look so hard,' he told me gravely. 'One must simply live from day to day.' A little later, he added: 'One must have the humility to recognize that one can't face life alone; it's easier to have someone else to live for.' He smiled at me: 'The solution would be to cultivate our egos together.'

I kept dwelling on that phrase, that smile; I was no longer in any doubt: Jacques loved me; we would be married. But there was something very wrong: my happiness didn't last any longer than three days. Jacques came back to see us; I spent a very happy evening with him, and after he had left I broke down: 'I've got everything a girl could want to make her happy, yet I feel I want to die! Life is here, waiting for me, waiting for us to seize it with both hands. I'm frightened: I am alone, I shall always be alone. . . . If only I could run away – where to? Anywhere. It would be like a terrible cataclysm, sweeping us away.' For Jacques, marriage was obviously an end in itself, and I didn't want to put an end to anything, at least not so soon. For another month I tussled with my feelings. At moments I was able to persuade myself that I could live alongside Jacques without mutilating myself; and then terror would seize me again: 'What? Imprison myself in the limitations of another human being? I would feel only horror for a love that held me prisoner, and would not let me go. I have a longing to snap this link between us, to forget it all, to start a fresh life all over again. . . . Not yet; I'm not ready: I don't want to sacrifice myself, the whole of myself.' Yet I kept feeling great surges of love for Jacques, and it was only occasionally and briefly that I admitted to myself: 'He's not the one for me.' I preferred to protest that I was not made for love or for happiness. I wrote about it in my journal, in a queer way, as if the facts were inescapable and unalterable, as if I were at liberty to reject or accept them, but incapable of modifying their application. Instead of telling myself: 'Every day I feel less certain of being able to find happiness with Jacques,' I wrote: 'I dread happiness more and more,' and 'The prospect of saying yes or no to happiness causes me equal distress.' Again: 'It's when I feel I love him most that I hate all the more the love I have for him.' I was afraid that my affection for him would trap me into becoming his wife, and I savagely rejected the sort of life that awaited the future Madame Laiguillon.

Jacques for his part was often capricious. He would turn on ingratiating smiles for me; he would tell me: 'There are some people who are quite irreplaceable,' looking at me with eyes full of meaning; he would ask me to come back and see him soon: then he would receive me very coldly. At the beginning of March he fell ill. I paid him several visits: there were always uncles, aunts, and grandmothers round his bed. 'Come back tomorrow and we'll be able to talk in peace,' he told me once. I felt even more worked-up than usual that afternoon as I made my way towards the boulevard Montparnasse. I bought a bunch of violets which I pinned on the collar of my dress; I had some difficulty in getting them fixed, and in my distraction I lost my purse. There was nothing much in it, but it was enough to make me arrive at Jacques' in a very nervous state. I had been thinking all day of the heart-to-heart talk we would have in his shaded room. But when I got there he was not alone: Lucien Riaucourt was sitting at his bedside. I had already met him. he was an elegant casual young man, a good talker. They went on chatting together about the bars they frequented and the people they met there; they arranged to go out together during the coming week. I felt I was completely superfluous and unwelcome: I didn't have money, I didn't go out in the evenings; I was only a poor little student, quite incapable of taking any part in Jacques real existence. Besides, he was not in the best of humours; he was sarcastic towards me, almost aggressive; I made my escape as soon as possible and he was obviously relieved to see me go. I was shaking with fury; I hated him. What was there so very special about him after all? There were hosts of other men who were just as good as he. I had been badly mistaken in thinking he was a sort of Grand Meaulnes. He was fickle, egotistical, and only out for his own enjoyment. I stormed along the boulevards, telling myself I would cut myself off from his life completely. The next day I relented: but I had made up my mind not to set foot in his house for a good long time. I kept my word, and six weeks went by before I saw him again.

*

Philosophy had neither opened up the heavens to me nor anchored me to earth; all the same, in January, when I had mastered the first difficulties, I began to take a serious interest in it. I read Bergson, Plato, Schopenhauer, Leibniz, Hamelin, and, with passionate enthusiasm, Nietzsche. I was excited by a host of problems: the values of science; life, matter, time, art. I had no fixed ideas of my own, but at least I knew that I rejected Aristotle, St Thomas Aquinas, Maritain, and also all empirical and materialist doctrines. In the main, I favoured critical idealism of the kind expounded to us by Brunschvig, although on certain points he left me far from satisfied. I acquired a taste for reading again. In the boulevard Saint-Michel, students found a happy hunting-ground in the Librairie Picard: I would stand there looking through the *avant-garde* magazines which in those days came and went like the flowers that bloom in the spring. I spent hours there reading Aragon and Breton; surrealism bowled me over. All this 'disquiet' had got a little stale in the end; I preferred the outrageous jokes of pure negation. The destruction of art, morals, language; the systematic derangement of the senses, suicidal despair – I was delighted by all these excesses.

I wanted to talk about these things; I wanted to talk about all sorts of things with people who, unlike Jacques, wouldn't let their sentences trail away at the ends. I was eager to find new acquaintances. At the Institut Sainte-Marie, I sought the confidences of my fellow-students: but quite definitely there was not one of them who interested me. At Belleville, I began to take much greater pleasure in talking to Suzanne Boigue. She had chestnut-coloured hair, very severely cut, a broad forehead, very light blue eyes, and she had a certain dashing air. She earned her living as director of the centre I have been talking about; her greater age, her independence, her responsibilities, and her authority all contributed to her importance. She was a believer, but she gave me to understand that the relations she had with her Maker were not altogether satisfactory. We had almost the same taste in books. And I was gratified to observe that she, too, was not taken in by the Groups, nor by the idea of 'action' in general. She confessed to me that she, too, wanted to live her life to the full; she, too, despaired of ever finding more than a drug in the activities of daily life. As we were both hale and hearty young women, our disillusioned conversations, far from depressing, re-invigorated me. On leaving her, I would stride purposefully through the Buttes Chaumont park. Just as I did, she wanted to find her rightful place in the world. She went to Berck to meet a sort of female saint who had devoted her life to 'the bedridden'. On her return, she declared forcefully: 'I'm not cut out to be a saint.' At the beginning of the spring, she was smitten with a young and pious fellow-worker in the Groups; they decided to get married. Circumstances would compel them to wait two years; but, as Suzanne Boigue informed me, when you're in love, time doesn't count. She was radiant. I was stupefied when, a few weeks later, she announced that she had 'broken it off' with her fiancé. The physical attraction between them was too strong, and the young man was scared by the intensity of their kisses. He had asked Suzanne not to see him any more, in order to preserve their chastity; they would keep themselves for one another, but at a distance. She had preferred to call the whole thing off. I thought it was all very queer, and I was never able to discover the ins and outs of the affair. But

I was touched by Suzanne's disappointment, and by her efforts to overcome it.

The students I tried to get friendly with at the Sorbonne were all, I thought, both male and female, without any interest: they kept rushing about in noisy groups, laughing their heads off; they weren't interested in anything and were quite complacent about their indifference. But in the history and philosophy lectures I noticed a young man, much older than myself, who had very serious blue eyes; dressed entirely in black, and wearing a black felt hat, he never spoke to anyone excepting a little thin-faced dark girl; he was always smiling at her. One day in the library he was translating some of Engel's letters when some students at his table began to kick up a disturbance; his eyes flashed, and in a curt voice he asked for silence in such an authoritative manner that he was instantly obeyed. 'He must be somebody!' I told myself, highly impressed. I managed to get into conversation with him, and after that, whenever the little dark girl wasn't there, we would talk together. One day I walked a little way with him along the boulevard Saint-Michel: that evening, I asked my sister if I had acted improperly; she reassured me that I hadn't and I did it again. Pierre Nodier was a member of the 'Philosophies' group to which belonged Mohrange, Friedmann, Henri Lefebvre, and Politzer; thanks to a generous subsidy from the father of one of the group, a rich banker, they had started a magazine; but their patron, infuriated by an article in it against the war in Morocco, had withdrawn his support. A little later the magazine was revived under a new name, *L'Esprit*. Pierre Nodier brought me two numbers: it was my first contact with left-wing intellectuals. But I didn't feel at all out of my depth: I could recognize the idiom to which the literature of the period had accustomed me; these young men, too, were talking about soul, salvation, joy, eternity; they declared that all thought should be 'concrete' and 'carnal', but they said so in abstract terms. According to them, philosophy could not be distinguished from revolution, in which lay humanity's final hope; but in those days Politzer believed that 'in the interests of truth, historical materialism is not inseparable from revolution': he believed in the value of the idealist Idea, on condition that it was apprehended in its concrete totality, with no intermediary stage of abstraction. They were interested above all in the manifestations of the Spirit; economy and politics to their mind could only play subordinate roles. They condemned capitalism because it had destroyed 'the sense of being' in man; they considered that through the uprisings of the peoples of Asia and Africa 'History is coming to be the servant of Wisdom'. Friedman pulled to pieces the ideology of the young bourgeois intellectuals; their disquiet and lack of responsibility were puerile: but he wanted a new mystique to take its place. It was a question of giving back to men 'the eternal part of themselves'. They didn't look upon life from the point of view of necessity or labour; they were turning it into a romantic dream. 'There *is* life, and all our love goes out to it,' wrote Friedmann. Politzer defined it in a phrase which caused a sensation: 'The triumphant, brutal life of the sailor who stubs out his cigarette on the Gobelins tapestries in the Kremlin terrifies you, and you don't want to hear about it: and yet *that* is life!' They weren't far removed from the surrealists, many of whom were in fact being converted to the Revolution. It attracted me, too, but only from a negative point of view; I began to hope that society would be turned topsy-turvy, but I didn't understand the workings of society any better than before. And I remained indifferent to the great events which were taking place in the world. All the newspapers — even *Candide* — were devoting columns and columns to the revolution that had broken out in China: it didn't make me bat an eyelid.

Yet my conversations with Nodier were beginning to broaden my mind. I used to ask him lots of questions. He was very willing to answer them and I found these conversations so profitable that I asked myself sadly: why wasn't I fated to love a man like this, who would share my liking for study and the exchange of ideas, and whom I could love with my head as well as my heart? I was very sorry when, towards the end of May, he said good-bye to me outside the Sorbonne. He was leaving for Australia where he had found a post; the little dark girl was to follow him out there. Shaking my hand for the last time, he said, in a voice charged with meaning: 'I wish you every good thing in life.'

At the beginning of March, I passed my examinations in the history of philosophy with flying colours, and on that occasion made the acquaintance of a group of left-wing students. They asked me to sign a petition: Paul Boncour had tabled an army bill decreeing the mobilization of women, and the magazine *Europe* was organizing a protest campaign. I was in a quandary. I was all for the equality of the sexes; and in case of danger, wasn't it one's duty to do all one could to defend one's country? When I had read the text of the bill, I said: 'But this is very patriotic!' The large young man who was sending round the petition sniggered: 'Who wants patriotism?' This was a question I had never asked myself: I didn't know how to reply. They explained to me that the new law, if it came into force, would result in a general mobilization of freedom of conscience, and that decided me: after all, freedom of thought was sacred; and then all the others were signing: so I signed too. I didn't have to be asked twice when it was a question of petitioning for the reprieve of Sacco and Vanzetti; their names didn't mean anything to me, but I was assured that they were innocent: besides, I disapproved of the death penalty.

My political activities didn't go any further and my ideas remained hazy. One thing I knew: I detested the extreme right. One afternoon, a handful of brawling young men had entered the Sorbonne library shouting: 'Down with wops and Jews!' They were carrying stout canes, and had turned out a few of the darker-skinned students. This triumph of violence and stupidity had shocked and angered me. I detested conformity, all forms of obscurantism, and wanted men to be governed by reason; therefore I was interested in the left. But I disliked all labels: I hated people to be catalogued. Several of my fellow-students were socialists; I thought the word had an evil ring; a socialist couldn't possibly be a tormented soul; he was pursuing ends that were both secular and limited: such moderation irritated me from the outset. The Communists' extremism attracted me much more; but I suspected them of being just as dogmatic and stereotyped as the Jesuits. Nevertheless, about May I struck up a friendship with an ex-student of Alain who was a communist: in those days, such an unlikely conjunction caused no surprise. He praised Alain's lectures, outlined his ideas to me, lent me his books. He also introduced me to Romain Rolland and I became a firm believer in pacifism. Mallet was interested in many other things: in painting, the cinema, the theatre, even the music hall. There was a fire in his eyes and in his voice, and I enjoyed talking to him. I noted in my diary, with some astonishment: 'I've found out that it's possible to be intelligent *and* take an interest in politics.' In fact, he didn't know much about the theory of politics and didn't teach me anything. I continued to rate social questions lower than problems of metaphysics and morals: what was the use of bothering about suffering humanity if there was no point in its existence?

This obstinate refusal prevented me from deriving any benefit from my meeting with Simone Weil. While preparing to enter the Normale – the training-college in Paris for professoriates – she was taking the same examinations as myself at the Sorbonne. She intrigued me because of her great reputation for intelligence and her bizarre get-up; she would stroll round the courtyard of the Sorbonne attended by a group of Alain's old pupils; she always carried in the one pocket of her dark-grey overall a copy of *Libres Propos* and in the other a copy of *Humanité*. A great famine had broken out in China, and I was told that when she heard the news she had wept: these tears compelled my respect much more than her gifts as a philosopher. I envied her for having a heart that could beat right across the world. I managed to get near her one day. I don't know how the conversation got started; she declared in no uncertain tones that only one thing mattered in the world today: the Revolution which would feed all the starving people of the earth. I retorted, no less peremptorily, that the problem was not to make men happy, but to find the reason for their existence. She looked me up and down: 'It's easy to see you've never gone hungry,' she snapped. Our relationship did not go any further. I realized that she had classified me as 'a high-minded little bourgeois', and this annoyed me, just as I used to be annoyed whenever Mademoiselle Litt attributed certain tastes I had to the fact that I was only a child; I believed that I had freed myself from the bonds of my class: I didn't want to be anyone else but myself.

I don't really know why I had anything to do with Blanchette Weiss. She was short and stout, and in a face bursting with self-sufficiency her two malevolent little eyes were always darting here and there; but I was fascinated by her gift of the gab and her command of philosophical jargon; she rattled off student gossip and metaphysical speculations with a volubility which I mistook for intelligence. As finite modes are unable to communicate without the intervention of the infinite, therefore all human love, she explained, is sin; she considered herself entitled to assume the absolute authority of the infinite in her disparagement of all the people she knew. I was amused to learn from her something about the ambitions, the little foibles, the weaknesses and vices of our professors, and our fellow-students. 'I have the soul of a Proustian caretaker,' she declared complacently. Rather inconsistently, she charged me with clinging to my nostalgia for the absolute: 'Now me, I create my own system of values,' she stated. What could they be? On this point she was somewhat vague. She attached the greatest importance to her inner life: I agreed with her there; she disdained wealth; so did I; but she explained to me that in order to be able to keep one's mind off money it was necessary to have enough for one's needs, and that she would probably consent to a marriage of convenience: I was disgusted. I also found that she suffered from a curious kind of narcissism; all curled and bedizened she thought she looked the living image of Clara d'Ellébeuse. Despite all this, I had such a longing to have someone I could 'exchange ideas' with that I used to see her fairly frequently.

But Zaza was still my only real friend. Unfortunately her mother was beginning to look upon me with a rather jaundiced eye. It was under my influence that Zaza preferred studying to domestic life, and I was lending her scandalous books. Madame Mabille detested Mauriac: she took his portrayals of bourgeois homes as a personal insult. She didn't trust Claudel, whom Zaza liked because he helped her to reconcile heaven and earth. 'You would be better occupied reading the Fathers of the Church,' Madame Mabille bad-temperedly remarked. She came several times to our house to complain to my mother about me and made it quite clear to Zaza that she wished we would see less of each other. But Zaza stood firm; our friendship was one of those things she would not give up. We used to see each other very often. We used to study Greek together; we would go to concerts and art exhibitions. Sometimes she would play the piano for me – Chopin and Debussy. We often went for long walks. One afternoon, having screwed an unwilling permission out of my mother, Zaza took me to a hairdresser and I had my hair cut off. I didn't gain much by this, because my mother was furious that I had forced her hand, and refused to allow me the luxury of having my hair set. From Laubardon where she was spending the Easter holidays, Zaza sent me a letter which moved me to the depths of my being: 'Since the age of fifteen I had lived in great moral solitude; it hurt me to feel so lost and isolated: you have broken that solitude.' This didn't prevent her from being plunged just then 'in the depths of despair'. She wrote: 'Never have I felt so overwhelmed by myself.' She added: 'I've lived too long with my eyes turned towards the past and unable to tear myself away from the wonder of my childhood memories.' Again I took this for granted. I thought it was natural that one should be unwilling to grow up.

It was a great relief to me not to see Jacques any more; I was no longer torturing myself over him. The first rays of spring sunshine were taking the nip of winter out of my blood. While I continued to work hard, I decided that I would have a little amusement. I went fairly often to the cinema in the afternoons; I usually went to the Studio des Ursulines, the Vieux-Colombier, and the Ciné-Latin; this was a little hall with wooden seats situated behind the Panthéon; a piano accompanied the films; the seats weren't dear and they showed revivals of the best films of the last few years; it was there that I saw *The Gold Rush* and many other Chaplin films. On certain evenings my mother would accompany my sister and me to the theatre. I saw Jouvet in *Le Grand Large*, in which Michel Simon was making his first appearance, Dullin in *La Comédie du bonheur* and Madame Pitoëff as St Joan. I used to look forward to these outings for days; they irradiated my week. I can tell how much importance I attached to them when I think of how hardly the austerity of the first two terms weighed upon me. Now, during the daytime, I would visit all the exhibitions, and go for long prowls round the galleries of the Louvre. I would wander all over Paris, my eyes no longer brimming with tears, but looking at everything. I loved those evenings when, after dinner, I would set out alone on the Métro and travel right to the other side of Paris, near Les Buttes Chaumont, which smelt of damp and greenery. Often I would walk back home. In the boulevard de la Chapelle, under the steel girders of the overhead railway, women would be waiting for customers; men would come staggering out of brightly lit bistros; the fronts of cinemas would be ablaze with posters. I could feel life all round me, an enormous, ever-present confusion. I would stride along, feeling its thick breath blow in my face. And I would say to myself that after all life is worth living.

I began to have ambitions again. Despite my friendships and my uncertain love-affair, I still felt very much alone; there was no one who knew me or loved me completely, for myself alone; no one was, nor, I thought could anyone ever be 'someone definite and complete' to me. Rather than go on suffering because of this, I again took refuge in pride. My isolation was a sign of my superiority; I no longer had any doubts about that: I was somebody, and I would do great things. I thought up themes for novels. One morning in the library at the Sorbonne, instead of doing Greek translation, I began 'my book'. I had to study for the exams in June; I hadn't enough time; but I calculated that next year I would have more free time and I made a promise to myself that I would then without more ado write my very own book 'It is to be a work,' I told myself in my diary, 'which will *tell all.*' I often insisted in my journal on this necessity to 'tell all', which makes a curious contrast with the paucity of my experience. Philosophy had increased my tendency to seize the essence, the root, the totality of things; and as I was living in a world of abstractions I believed that I had discovered, once and for all, the truth of life. From time to time I would suspect that there was more to it than I had so far discovered: but only very occasionally. My superiority over other people came precisely from the fact that I didn't let anything get past me: the peculiar value of my work would be the result of this exceptional privilege.

Sometimes I would have scruples; I would recall that all is vanity: but I would disregard them. In imaginary dialogues with Jacques I would challenge his 'What's the use?' I had only one life to live, I wanted it to be a success, nobody would stop me, not even he. I did not abandon my view of the absolute; but as there didn't seem to be much to be gained in that quarter I decided not to bother about it. I was very fond of Lagneau's phrase: 'I have no comfort but in my absolute despair.' As I was going to continue to exist, once this despair had been established I had to live as best I could here below, that is, do what I liked.

I was rather surprised to find I could so easily do without Jacques, but the fact is that I didn't miss him at all. My mother told me at the end of April that he was surprised not to see me any more. I went to see him: I didn't feel anything. It seemed to me that this affection could no longer be called love, and I even found it rather tiresome. 'I no longer even want to see him. I can't help it if he makes me tired, even when he's at his best.' He was no longer writing his novel; he would never write it. 'I should feel I had prostituted myself,' he told me haughtily. A drive in his car and a conversation in which he seemed to be sincerely ashamed of himself brought me closer to him again. After all, I told myself, I have no right to blame him for an inconsequence which is that of life itself: it leads us to certain conclusions and then reveals their emptiness. I reproached myself for being so severe with him. 'He is better than his life,' I decided. But I was afraid lest in the end his life should leave its stains upon him. Sometimes I would be filled with dire foreboding: 'I feel bad when I think about you, Jacques; I don't know why, but your life is a tragic one.'

*

The June examinations were approaching; I was ready for them and tired of working; I relaxed a little. I indulged in my first escapade. On the pretext that there was a charity performance at Belleville, I got permission from my mother to stay out until midnight, and twenty francs. I took a seat in the gallery for a performance of the Russian Ballet. When twenty years later I suddenly found myself alone at two o'clock in the morning in Times Square, I was less dazzled than I was that evening up in the gods in the Théâtre Sarah-Bernhardt. Below me, silks, furs, diamonds, perfumes, and the chatter of a brilliant, packed house. Whenever I went out with my parents or the Mabilles, an impenetrable glass would be interposed between me and the world: but now, here I was revelling in one of those great nocturnal festivities whose reflected glow I had so often gazed at longingly in the heavens. I had wormed my way in, unknown to all my acquaintances, and the people I was rubbing shoulders with didn't know who I was. I felt invisible and endowed with the power to be everywhere at once, like a sprite. That evening they were dancing Sauguet's *La Chatte*, Prokofieff's *Pas d'acier*, *The Triumph of Neptune*, and all kinds of other marvels. Scenery, costumes, music, dancing: the whole thing astounded me. I don't think I'd ever been so dazzled and enchanted by anything since I was five.

I went again. I don't know on what pretexts I got hold of the money, but in any case it was always the Groups which furnished me with alibis. I went back twice to the Russian Ballet: I was surprised to hear gentlemen in evening dress singing Stravinsky's *Oedipus* with words by Cocteau. Mallet had talked to me about Damia's snow-white arms, and about her voice: I went to hear her at the Bobino. Singers, conjurers, acrobats – everything was new to me and I applauded everything.

On the days preceding the exams, between papers, and while we were waiting for the results, certain of my fellow-students – among them Jean Mallet and Blanchette Weiss – used to while away the time in the courtyard of the Sorbonne. We would play ball, perform charades, and 'Chinese portraits'; there would be gossip and discussion too. I joined this little band. But I felt ill at ease with the majority of the students I came in contact with: the looseness of their morals scared me. Though in theory I was inured to every kind of depravity, in reality I was still extremely prudish. If I was told that so-and-so and someone else were 'going together' I used to shrivel up. Whenever Blanchette Weiss, pointing out to me a student from the Normale, confided in me that he was 'that way inclined', I shuddered. Bachelor-girl students – above all those who were 'like that' – filled me with horror. I had to admit that these reactions were the result of my upbringing, but I refused to fight against them. Coarse jokes, rude words, free-and-easy behaviour, and bad manners disgusted me. Yet I felt no sympathy at all for a little male coterie to which I was introduced by Blanchette Weiss; she had a certain tact, and knew a few students of good family who, reacting against the lack of tone in the Normale, had acquired affected and stilted manners. They used to invite me to tea in the back rooms of cake-shops: they did not frequent the cafés, and in any case would never have been seen there with young women. I was flattered by their interest in me, but I quelled this surge of vanity, because I classed them among the Barbarians; they were only interested in politics, in social success, and in their future careers. We would sit sipping tea, as if we were in a drawing-room, and the conversation would oscillate disagreeably between pedantry and the latest society news.

One afternoon in the courtyard of the Sorbonne I vehemently contradicted on some subject or other a young man with a long, dark face: he looked at me in surprise and declared that he couldn't find an answer to my objection. From then on he used to come every day to carry on our argument. He was called Michel Riesmann and was finishing his second year in the *khâgne*.* His father was an important person in the official art world. Michel claimed to be a disciple of Gide, and paid homage to Beauty. He believed in literature and was busy finishing a short novel. I scandalized him by professing a great admiration for surrealism. I thought he was

---

* Usually spelt *cagne*, and meaning the class preparing to compete for entrance to the training-college for the professoriate (Translator's note).

moth-eaten and boring, but perhaps there was a sensitive soul hidden away behind his pensive ugliness; besides, he used to urge me to write and I needed encouragement. He sent me a ceremonious and artistically handwritten letter, proposing that we should correspond during the holidays. I agreed. Blanchette Weiss and I also arranged to write to one another. She took me home to tea. I had strawberry tarts in a luxurious apartment in the avenue Kléber, and she lent me collections of poems by Verhaeren and Francis Jammes magnificently bound in leather.

I had spent the year moaning over the vanity of human aims: but I had pursued my own with tenacious zeal. I passed in general Philosophy. Simone Weil headed the list followed by me, and then by a student from the Normale called Jean Pradelle. I also passed my certificate in Greek. Mademoiselle Lambert was exultant, my parents smiled upon me; at the Sorbonne, at home, everyone congratulated me. I was very happy. These successes confirmed the good opinion I had of myself, they assured me a brilliant future, I attached great importance to them and not for anything in the world would I have thrown them away. Nevertheless I didn't forget that all success cloaks a surrender, and I thought my tears were justified. I kept repeating to myself with furious intensity the phrase which Martin du Gard puts into the mouth of Jacques Thibault: '*This* is what they've brought me to!' I had been reduced to the *persona* of a brilliant, gifted student, when I was really only the pathetic absence of the Absolute! There was a certain self-deception in my tears; yet I don't think they were just play-acting. In the hurly-burly accompanying the end of the summer term, I was bitterly conscious of the emptiness in my heart. I went on longing passionately for that something else which I couldn't put a name to because I refused to give it the only name I knew for it: happiness.

*

Jean Pradelle, who was pretending to be vexed at being beaten by a couple of girls, said he wanted to meet me. He was introduced to me by a fellow-student whom I had got to know through Blanchette Weiss. He was a little younger than me, and he had already spent a year at the Normale as a day-student. He too looked as if he came from a good family, though he wasn't at all stuck-up. He had a limpid, rather beautiful face, with thick, dark lashes, and the gay, frank laugh of a schoolboy; I liked him at once, and I met him a fortnight later at the rue d'Ulm where I had gone to see the results of the entrance examination for the Normale: some friends of mine, among them Riesmann, had sat for it. Pradelle took me into the gardens of the Normale. For a mere student from the Sorbonne it was a rather awe-inspiring place and as I chatted with him I had a good look round me. I met Pradelle there again the next morning. We listened to a few of the philosophy orals, then went for a walk in the Luxembourg Gardens. We were on holiday; all my friends, and almost all of his, had already left Paris: we got into the habit of meeting one another every day beside the statue of some queen or other. I would always arrive on the dot: it gave me so much pleasure to see him running towards me, laughing, pretending to be embarrassed, that I was almost grateful to him for being late.

Pradelle was a good listener; he had a meditative air and would reply in a grave voice: what a find! I hastened to lay bare my soul to him. I made an aggressive attack upon the Barbarians, and he surprised me by refusing to agree with me; he had lost his father, and got on perfectly well with his mother and sister and did not share my horror of family life. He was not averse to parties and sometimes went dancing: why not? he asked me with an innocent air which disarmed me. My manichaeism postulated a small band of the chosen in a great mass of people unworthy of consideration; according to him, there was some good, some evil in everyone: there wasn't all that much difference between people. He disapproved of my uncompromising attitude, and his indulgence offended me. Apart from this, we had many views in common. Brought up, like myself, in a pious home, and now an unbeliever, he had been branded by Christian morality. At the École Normale he was classed among the *talas** (Holy Willies). He disapproved of his fellow-students' coarse manners, their indecent songs, rude jokes, brutality, debauchery, and cynical dissipations. His taste in books was almost the same as mine, with a predilection for Claudel and a certain disdain for Proust whom he didn't consider to be 'essential'. He lent me Jarry's *Ubu-Roi*, which I couldn't really appreciate because I couldn't find in it a trace of my own obsessions. What I thought was most important was that he, too, was anxiously seeking for the truth: he believed that one day it would be revealed

* Slang term probably a contraction of '*talapoin*' (priest) (Translator's note).

to him through the medium of philosophy. We discussed this hotly for a whole fortnight. He told me that I had been too eager to choose despair and I reproached him with grasping at straws: all the systems had something wrong with them. I demolished them one after the other; he finally gave in on every point, but retained his confidence in rational humanity.

In fact, he wasn't as rationalist as all that. Much more than I did, he still felt a nostalgia for his lost faith. He considered that we had not studied Catholicism sufficiently deeply to have the right to reject its claims: they ought to be re-examined. I objected that we knew even less about Buddhism; why should we be prejudiced in favour of the religion of our mothers? He quizzed me with a critical eye and accused me of preferring the search for truth to the truth itself. As I was fundamentally very self-willed, but superficially very suggestible, his objurgations, added to those which Mademoiselle Lambert and Suzanne Boigue had discreetly loaded upon my head, gave me a pretext for getting myself worked up. I went to see a certain Abbé Beaudin, whom even Jacques had spoken of with admiration, and who specialized in the refloating of intellectuals marooned on the rocks of perdition. I happened to be carrying a copy of a book by Julien Benda and the Abbé began with a brillant attack on it which left me completely indifferent. Then we exchanged a few guarded words. I left him, feeling ashamed of my conduct, which I knew to be pointless from the start, for I knew that my unbelief was as solid as a rock.

I soon realized that despite our affinities there were wide divergencies between Pradelle and myself. I could not recognize my personal anguish in his purely cerebral disquiet. I summed him up pretty quickly as 'uncomplicated, un-mysterious, a well-behaved scholar'. Because of his seriousness and philosophical earnestness I admired him more than Jacques; but Jacques had something that Pradelle hadn't got. Wandering in the Luxembourg Gardens, I told myself that after all if one of them had wanted to marry me, neither would have suited my requirements. The thing which still made me feel attached to Jacques was that flaw which split him apart from his environment, but nothing solid could be built on a flawed personality, and I wanted to construct a system of thought, a work of art. Pradelle was, like me, an intellectual: but he had remained perfectly adapted to his class and its way of life, and accepted bourgeois society with an open heart; I could no more accommodate myself to his sunny optimism than I could to Jacques' nihilism. Besides, they were both, though for different reasons, a bit scared of me. 'Do men marry women like me?' I used to wonder with a tinge of melancholy, for in those days I made no distinction between love and marriage. 'I'm so sure that the one who would really be all to me, who would understand the whole of me, and be fundamentally the brother and the equal of myself, simply doesn't exist.' What was cutting me off from other people was a certain violence of temperament which only I seemed to possess. This set-to with Pradelle strengthened me in my conviction that I was destined to a life of solitude.

Yet as far as just being friends was concerned, we got on well together. I appreciated his love of truth, his honesty; he didn't get feelings mixed up with ideas and under the influence of his impartial attitude I realized that with me states of mind and moods had very often been substitutes for thought. He forced me to think hard, to keep to the point; I no longer felt proudly that I knew everything; on the contrary: 'I know nothing, nothing; I not only have no answer to give, but I haven't even found a satisfactory way of propounding the question.' I promised myself that I would practise no more self-deceit, and I begged Pradelle to help me guard against all falsehood; he was to be 'my living conscience'. I decided that I would consecrate the years to come to an unrelenting search for truth. 'I shall work and slave till I find it.' Pradelle performed a valuable service for me in reviving my interest in philosophy. And perhaps an even more valuable one in teaching me how to be gay again: I knew no one else from whom I could have learnt the art of gaiety. He bore so lightly the weight of the whole world that it ceased to weigh upon me, too; in the Luxembourg Gardens, the blue of the morning sky, the green lawns and the sun all shone as they used to in my happiest days, when it was always fine weather. 'The branches just now are growing thick and putting out new shoots; they mask completely the abyss, the void which lies beneath.' This meant that I was taking a joy in living and that I was forgetting my metaphysical anxieties. As Pradelle was walking back home with me one day, we met my mother; I introduced him to her; she liked him: people always liked him. This set a seal on our friendship.

*

Zaza had got her certificate in Greek. She left for Laubardon. At the end of July I received a letter from her which took my breath away. She was desperately unhappy and told me why. Only now did she speak of that adolescence which she had lived through with me and of which I had known nothing at all. Twenty-five years ago, a cousin of her father's, faithful to the Basque tradition, had gone to seek his fortune in the Argentine; he had amassed a considerable amount of wealth there. Zaza had been eleven when he had returned to his native hearth, about half a mile from Laubardon; he had married, and had a son of the same age as Zaza; this was a 'sad, lonely, shy little boy' who had taken a great liking to her. His parents sent him to a boarding-school in Spain; but in the holidays the two friends would meet again and it was then that they had gone on those rides through the pine forests about which Zaza used to speak with such enthusiasm. When they were fifteen, they realized that they were in love with one another; André, lonely, exiled from the land of his birth, only had her in all the world; and Zaza, who thought herself ugly, ungraceful, unwanted, threw herself into his arms; they exchanged kisses that bound them passionately to one another. From then on, they had written to each other every week, and in the physics lessons and under the jovial eye of Abbé Trécourt she had dreamed only of André. The parents of the two children had quarrelled – André's were much richer than Zaza's – though they had never interfered with the friendship between them; but when the parents realized that the children were growing up, they intervened. There was no question of André and Zaza ever being able to marry, so Madame Mabille decided that they must stop seeing one another.

During the New Year holidays in 1926 [Zaza wrote] I was allowed to spend a single day here to see André and to tell him that all was over between us. But despite all the cruel things I had to say, I couldn't help letting him see how dear he was to me, and this final parting bound us closer than ever to one another.

She added, a little further on:

When they forced me to break with André, I suffered so much that several times I was on the verge of committing suicide. I remember how one evening, watching the train come into the Métro station, I nearly threw myself on the rails in front of it. I no longer had the slightest desire to go on living.

Since then eighteen months had gone by; she had not seen André again, and they had not written to one another. Suddenly, on returning to Laubardon, she had met him again.

For the last twenty months we had known nothing of one another, and our paths had been so different that in our sudden coming together there was something quite baffling, almost painful. I see with great clarity all the difficulties and all the sacrifices which must result from a love between two such ill-assorted people as he and I, but I can't act in any other way, I can't give up the dream of my youth and all its cherished memories, I cannot let down someone who has need of me. André's family and my own are as dead-set as possible against our coming to an understanding of this nature. He is leaving in October to spend a year in the Argentine, and then will return to France to do his military service. So there are still many difficulties ahead of us, and a long separation; and if our plans succeed we shall have to live at least ten years in South America. So you see it's a rather gloomy prospect. I am going to have to speak to Mama this evening; two years ago, she gave her refusal in the most uncompromising terms, and already I feel upset at the thought of the conversation I must have with her. You see, I love her so much that the hardest thing of all for me is to cause her all this pain and to go against her wishes. When I was little, I always used to say in my prayers: 'Let no one ever suffer on my account.' Alas! What an impossible wish!

I read this letter ten times at least, with a lump in my throat. Now I understood the change that had come over Zaza at the age of fifteen – her air of not always being with us, her romanticism, and also her strange precognition of what love must be: she had already felt the pulse of love in her body, and this was why she had laughed when someone had claimed that the love of Tristan and Iseult was 'platonic', why the thought of an 'arranged' marriage filled her with such horror. How little I had known of her! 'I'd like to go to sleep and never wake up again,' she had said, and I had taken no notice; yet I knew only too well into what depths of black despair the heart can be plunged. I couldn't bear to think of Zaza neatly dressed in her hat and coat and gloves standing on the edge of a platform in the Métro and fixing a fascinated gaze on the gleaming rails.

I received another letter a few days later. The talk with Madame Mabille had gone off very badly. She had again forbidden Zaza ever to see her cousin. Zaza was too much of a Christian to dream of disobeying her mother: but never had this prohibition seemed more frightful than then, with only half a mile separating her from the boy she loved. The thing that tormented her more than anything was the thought that he was suffering because of her, when night and day she was thinking of no one but him. I was stunned by this unhappiness which surpassed anything I had ever known. It had been agreed that I would spend three weeks with Zaza that year in the Basque country, and I was impatient to be with her.

*

When I arrived at Meyrignac, I felt 'calmer than I've ever been during the last eighteen months'. All the same, a comparison with Pradelle did not favour Jacques, and I was able to think of him without trying to excuse his lapses: 'Ah! all that frivolity, that lack of seriousness, all that talk about bars, bridge, and money! There are fine things in him, finer than in anyone else I know: but there is also something pitiful, a failure . . .' I felt detached from him, and just sufficiently attached to Pradelle for his existence to irradiate my days without their being darkened by his absence. We wrote often to one another. I also wrote frequently to Riesmann, Blanchette Weiss, Mademoiselle Lambert, Suzanne Boigue and Zaza. I had set up a table in the attic under a skylight, and in the evenings, by the light of a small oil lamp I would cover page after page. Thanks to the letters I was receiving – particularly Pradelle's – I no longer felt lonely. I also had long conversations with my sister; she had just passed her school-leaving certificate in philosophy, and all that year we had been very close to one another. I told her about everything, excepting my attitude to religion. She looked up to Jacques as much as I did, and she had adopted my myths. Detesting, as I had done, the majority of her schoolfellows and the Cours Désir, as well as the prejudices current in our environment, she had gleefully taken up arms against 'the Barbarians'. Perhaps because she had not had such a happy childhood as mine, she rebelled much more boldly than I had done against the conventions that lay so heavily upon our spirits. 'It's silly of me, I know,' she told me one evening with an embarrassed look, 'but I don't like Mama to open the letters I receive: I no longer have any pleasure in reading them.' I told her that this bothered me, too. We took our courage in our hands: after all, we were seventeen and nineteen; we went and begged our mother not to censor our correspondence. She replied that it was her duty to watch over the safety of our souls, but in the end she gave in. It was an important victory.

The tensions between my parents and myself had on the whole slackened a little. I spent my days in peace and quiet. I was studying philosophy and thinking of writing something. I hesitated a long time before deciding what to do. Pradelle had convinced me that my first task was to search for the truth: would not the writing of books be an escape from that task? And wasn't there a fundamental contradiction in my enterprise? I wanted to write about the vanity of things; but the writer is a traitor to his despair as soon as he writes a book: perhaps it would be better to imitate the silence of Monsieur Teste. I was afraid, also, if I started to write, that I would be driven to wish for success, fame, things I despised. These abstract scruples did not carry enough weight to make me stop writing. I consulted many of my friends by letter, and, as I had hoped, they encouraged me to begin. I started a vast novel; the heroine was to live through all my own experiences: she was to be awakened to the meaning of 'the true life', enter into conflict with her environment, then be disillusioned by everything: action, love, knowledge. I never knew what the ending was because I hadn't the time and I gave up halfway through.

The letters I was then receiving from Zaza didn't strike the same note as those of July. She had noticed, she told me, that in the course of the last two years her intellectual development had been considerable; she had matured, she had changed. During her brief meeting with André she had got the impression that he had not made any progress; he was still very young, and a little frustrated. She was beginning to wonder if her love wasn't just 'an obstinate pursuit of dreams which one doesn't wish to see vanish away, a lack of sincerity and courage'. She had surrendered, probably too completely, to the influence of *Le Grand Meaulnes*. 'I found in it a love, a cult of the dream which has no basis in reality and which perhaps put me well out of my course, far away from my real self.' She certainly did not regret her love for her cousin: 'This emotion, experienced at the age of fifteen, was my real awakening to life; from the day I fell in love, I understood at once an infinity of things; nothing, or almost nothing, seemed to be ridiculous any more.' But she had to admit that after the parting in January 1926 she had artificially prolonged this past existence 'by will-power and the power of the imagination'. In any case, André had to go and spend a year in the Argentine: it would be time to make a decision when he returned. For the moment, she was sick and tired of thinking about it all; she was spending a very lively and sociable holiday at Laubardon, and at first she had found it terribly exhausting; but now, she wrote, 'all I want to do is amuse myself'.

This sentence astonished me and in my reply I reproached her gently for taking this attitude. Zaza put up a spirited defence: she knew that a feverish search for amusement doesn't solve anything:

Not long ago [she wrote] a great excursion to the Basque country was organized among our friends; I had such a longing for solitude that I cut my foot open with an axe in order to get out of the expedition. I had a week lying on a chaise-longue and a great deal of commiseration, but at least I had a little time to myself, and the right not to talk and not to amuse myself.

I was staggered. I knew only too well how desperately one can long for solitude and 'the right not to talk'. But I should never have had the courage to cut my foot. No, Zaza was neither half-hearted nor resigned to her fate: there was a hidden violence in her which frightened me. Not one of her words was to be taken lightly, for she was much more sparing of them than I was. If I hadn't made her tell me, she wouldn't even have mentioned this incident to me.

I didn't want to keep anything more from her: I confessed to her that I had lost my faith; she had suspected it, she replied; she, too, during the past year, had gone through a religious crisis.

When I compared faith with the usages of my childhood, and the Catholic dogma with all my new ideas, there was such a disproportion, such a disparity between them that I felt I was standing on the edge of an abyss. Claudel was a great help to me and I can never tell you how much I owe to him. And I still believe in the way I did when I was six years old, with my heart far more than with my head, and by renouncing absolutely all rational ideas. Theological discussions nearly always seem to me to be absurd and grotesque. Above all, I believe that God cannot be apprehended, for He is hidden away from us, and that the faith He gives us is a supernatural gift, a grace accorded only by Him. That is why I cannot but pity with all my heart those who are deprived of this grace, and I believe that if they are sincere and athirst for the truth that truth will one day be revealed to them. . . . Moreover [she went on] faith does not bring eternal relief from spiritual hunger and thirst; it is as difficult to find peace of mind when one believes as when one does not believe; but one has the hope that one will know peace in another life.

So she not only accepted me as I was, but she took great care not to appear in the least way superior; if she could see a ray of hope in Heaven, that didn't prevent her, here on earth, from groping blindly in the same darkness as myself, and we still went on side by side towards the truth.

On the 10th of September I left in high spirits for Laubardon. I boarded the train at Uzerche, early in the morning, and got out at Bordeaux, for I had written to Zaza that 'I couldn't ride through the Mauriac country without stopping'. For the first time in my life I found myself walking along in a strange town. There was a great river, misty quaysides, and the plane trees already smelt of autumn. In the narrow streets, there was a constant play of light and shade; and then the broad avenues, stretching out towards the Esplanades. I felt sleepy and enchanted as I went floating, light as a feather, through the autumn city. In the public park, among the clumps of scarlet cannas, I dreamed dreams of an adolescent disquiet. I had been given instructions: I was to have a cup of hot chocolate in a cake shop in the allée de Tourny. I had my lunch in a restaurant called Le Petit Marguery near the station: never before had I been in a restaurant without my parents. Then a train took me along a dead-straight line bordered with endless pine forests. I loved trains. Leaning out of the window, I surrendered my face to the wind and the flying cinders and swore never to be like travellers who always huddled together in the fug of their dusty compartments.

It was evening when I arrived. The park at Laubardon was much less beautiful than the one at Meyrignac but I thought the house was pleasant, with its tiled roof and its walls covered with Virginia creeper. Zaza took me to the bedroom which I was to share with her and Geneviève de Bréville, a blooming, well-behaved girl who according to Madame Mabille could do no wrong. I remained alone in the room for a moment to unpack and freshen up. Sounds of crockery and children's voices came from downstairs. I wandered aimlessly round the room. I saw an exercise book bound in shiny black cloth lying on a side table and I opened it out of idle curiosity; it was Geneviève's, and I read: 'Simone de Beauvoir is arriving to-morrow. I must admit that the thought fills me with dismay, because frankly I do not like her.' I was taken aback; this was a new and disagreeable experience; I had never dreamt that anyone could feel an active dislike for me; this enemy face which Geneviève saw was mine, and it rather frightened me. I didn't have much time to think about it, for there came a knock at the door: it was Madame Mabille. 'I'd like to have a word with you, Simone dear,' she began; I was surprised by the friendly way she spoke to me, for of late she had hardly looked upon me with a kindly eye. With an air of embarrassment, she fingered the cameo on the velvet ribbon round her neck, and asked me if Zaza 'had told me how things stood'. I said yes. She didn't seem to know that her daughter's feelings were changing, and began to explain to me why she was so much against them. André's parents were against the marriage, and besides they belonged to a very rich, dissipated and vulgar set which would not do at all for Zaza: it was absolutely essential for her to forget her cousin, and Madame Mabille was counting on me to help her to do so. I detested being involved in a conspiracy with her; yet her appeal touched me because it must have cost her a great deal to beg for my collaboration. I assured her, with some embarrassment, that I would do my best.

Zaza had put me in the picture; at the beginning of my stay, there were never-ending picnics, tea-parties, and dances; the house was thrown open to everyone; droves of cousins and friends came to lunch and tea, to play tennis or bridge. Or else we would go to dances at the big houses in the neighbourhood, driven in the Citroën by Madame Mabille, Lili, or Zaza. There were frequent festivities in the nearby country town; I attended pelota games, I went to watch young Basque farmhands, white-faced with fear, planting rosettes in the sweating hide of skinny cows: sometimes a steel-tipped horn would rip open their lovely tight white trousers, and everyone would laugh. After dinner, someone would sit down at the piano and the whole family would join in the singing; there were parlour games, too: charades and versifying to set rhymes (bout rimés). The mornings were taken up with domestic chores. Flowers were picked and arranged in vases, and everybody took a hand with the cooking. Lili, Zaza, and Bébelle would make cakes, buns, shortbread, and brioches for afternoon tea; they helped their mother and grandmother to bottle tons of fruit and vegetables; there were always peas to be shelled, French beans to be strung, nuts to be cracked and plums to be stoned. The provision of food-stocks became a harassing and lengthy business.

I hardly ever saw Zaza, and I felt rather bored. And although I was quite insensitive to other people's feelings about me, I realized that the Mabilles and their friends didn't think much of me. Badly dressed, and caring little about my personal appearance, I couldn't bring myself to curtsy to the old ladies, I couldn't control the violence of my gestures or the pitch of my laughter. I hadn't a penny and was making plans for a career: that was shocking enough; but to make matters worse I was to be a teacher, in a *lycée*, too! For generations these people had been fighting a losing battle against undenominational education: in their eyes I was heading for an ignominious future. I held back my tongue as much as possible, and kept a check on myself, but in vain: every word I said, and even my silences, caused consternation. Madame Mabille forced herself to be friendly. Monsieur Mabille and old Madame Larivière politely ignored me. The eldest son had just entered a training college for the priesthood; Bébelle aspired to a religious vocation: they took no notice of me. But the youngest children found me vaguely odd, they had a vague grudge against me. Lili made no secret of her disapproval. This paragon of all the virtues, perfectly adapted to her environment, had an answer to everything: I only had to ask a question, and she was up in arms. When I was about fifteen or sixteen, during a dinner at the Mabilles' I had expressed my astonishment that, although all people are made in the same way, the taste of tomato or herring is not the same to everybody: Lili had made fun of me. I did not make such naïve remarks now, but my reticence was enough to irritate her. One afternoon in the garden we were discussing women's suffrage; it seemed logical to everyone that Madame Mabille should be allowed the vote rather than some drunken workman. But Lili claimed to know on the best authority that among the working classes women were bigger 'reds' than the men; if they were allowed to vote, the cause of the righteous would suffer. This argument was considered decisive. I didn't say anything, but among the chorus of approving voices, my own silence was highly subversive.

Almost every day the Mabilles had a visit from their cousin, the du Moulins de Labarthète. The daughter, Didine, was very friendly with Lili. There were three sons: Henri, a financial examiner with the heavy features of an ambitious rake; Edgar was an officer in a cavalry regiment; and Xavier, a twenty-year-old seminarist: he was the only one I thought at all interesting; he had delicate features, pensive eyes, and caused his family some anxiety on account of what they called his 'aboulia' – a lack of will-power. On Sunday mornings, stretched out in an armchair, he would take so long to make up his mind whether or not to go to Mass that he quite often missed it altogether. He read and meditated; he looked quite out of place in this environment. I asked Zaza why she hadn't struck up a friendship with him. She appeared to be very disconcerted: 'It would never have entered my head. That sort of thing's not possible in our house. The family wouldn't understand.' But she quite liked him. In the course of a conversation Lili and Didine were asking one another, with rather overworked stupefaction, how sensible people could possibly doubt the existence of God. Lili talked about the clock and the Great Clockmaker, all the time looking me straight in the eye; against my better judgement I decided to mention Kant. Xavier supported my views: 'You see what happens when you haven't studied philosophy!' he said. 'That sort of argument wouldn't satisfy you if you had, Lili!' Lili and Didine beat a hasty retreat.

The most hotly debated subject at Laubardon was the conflict which just then was setting *L'Action Française* and the Church at each other's throats. The Mabilles adamantly declared that all good Catholics should submit to the wishes of the Pope; the Labarthètes – all except Xavier, who would not commit himself – were for Maurras and Daudet. As I listened to their voices raised in passionate argument I felt left out of things. It made me feel very unhappy. In my diary I had claimed that there were many people who 'simply did not exist'; in fact, everyone I met was of some account. I quote here from my journal: 'Had a fit of despair while talking to Xavier du Moulin. He understood only too well the gulf that lies between them and myself, and the sophistry they employ to trap me.' I cannot remember now the reason for this outburst which obviously remained a secret between us both; but the meaning of it is clear: I couldn't light-heartedly accept the fact that I was different from the others, who treated me more or less openly as a black sheep. Zaza was fond of her family; I had been fond of them too, and the past still weighed heavily upon my conscience. Besides, my childhood had been too happy to be able to whip up hatred or even animosity in my heart: I just didn't know how to defend myself against other people's ill-will.

Zaza's friendship would have given me courage if we had been able to talk, but even at night there was a third person with us; as soon as I was in bed I tried to go to sleep. When Geneviève thought I had dropped off, she would enter into long discussions with Zaza.

She kept wondering if she were really treating her mother kindly enough; she sometimes made her feel impatient: was that awfully wrong of her? Zaza would give the briefest possible replies. But however deaf an ear she turned to these girlish effusions, they compromised her, and she became a stranger to me; I told myself, with a lump in my throat, that despite everything she believed in God, in her mother's authority and in her duties; once more I began to feel very much alone.

Fortunately Zaza managed to arrange a private conversation with me. Had she suspected what I had been feeling? She told me discreetly but unmistakably that her liking for Geneviève was of the lowest order; the latter imagined that she was her intimate friend, but in fact Zaza could not reciprocate her feelings. I felt relieved. Then Geneviève left and as the holidays were drawing to a close there was much less social activity. I had Zaza to myself. One night, when everybody was asleep, we put warm shawls on over our long calico night-dresses and crept down into the garden; we sat under a pine tree and talked for a long time. Zaza was quite certain now that she no longer loved her cousin; she recounted their idyll for me in its most intimate details. It was then that I learnt what her childhood had been, and of her great feeling of having been utterly deserted, which I had had no inkling of. 'I loved you,' I told her; she was taken aback; she admitted that in the hierarchy of her friendships I had occupied only a minor place, though none of her childhood friends had in fact meant very much to her. In the night sky, a brown old moon was slowly foundering under the horizon. We talked of days gone by, and were saddened by the ignorance of our childhood hearts; she was grief-stricken at the thought that she had ignored me and caused me pain; for my own part, I found it bitter to have to tell her these things only now, when they had ceased to have any real meaning: I no longer preferred her above all others. Yet there was a certain relief in being able to exchange these regrets with one another. We had never been so close, and the last part of my stay at Laubardon was very happy. We would sit and talk in the library, surrounded by the collected works of Louis Veuillot and Montalembert and bound numbers of the *Revue des Deux Mondes*; we talked about Francis Jammes, Laforgue, Radiguet, and about ourselves. I read Zaza a few pages of my novel: she was nonplussed by the dialogues, but she urged me to go on with it. She told me that she, too, would like to write something later on, and I encouraged her to do so. When the day came for my departure, she went in the train with me as far as Mont-de-Marsan. We sat on a bench eating little cold dry omelettes and took leave of one another without sadness, for we were soon to meet again in Paris.

*

I was at the age when one believes in the value of epistolary outpourings. From Laubardon I wrote to my mother asking her to trust me, and assuring her that later I would really be 'somebody'. She sent me a very nice reply. But on my return to our apartment in the rue de Rennes, my heart failed me for a moment: there were still another three years to be spent within these four walls! However, the last term had left me with some pleasant memories and I encouraged myself to take an optimistic point of view. Mademoiselle Lambert wanted me to take over part of her school-leaving certificate class at Sainte-Marie; she was to hand over the lessons in psychology to me; I had jumped at the chance to earn a little money and to get some teaching practice. I was planning to complete my degree in philosophy in April, and my degree in literature in June; these would not require much work, and I would have time to write and read and investigate more profoundly the great problems of existence. I drew up a vast plan of studies with timetables in which every minute in my day was accounted for; I took a childlike pleasure in getting the future all cut and dried and I almost recaptured the feeling of busy good intentions and simmering activity which I had known in my schooldays with the arrival of October. I hurried to see my friends at the Sorbonne. I raced across Paris, from Neuilly to the rue de Rennes, from the rue de Rennes to Belleville, casting appreciative glances at the little piles of dead leaves at the edge of the pavements.

I went to see Jacques, and mapped out my system to him; one had to consecrate one's life to a search for its meaning: meanwhile, one must never take anything for granted but base one's standards on acts of love and free-will that were to be indefinitely repeated. He heard me out with good grace but shook his head: 'No one could ever live like that.' When I persisted, he smiled: 'Don't you think that's all a bit too abstract for young people like us?' he asked me. He was hoping that his own existence would for some time to come still be a great game of chance. During the days that followed, I would think he was right, and then that he was wrong. I would decide that I loved him, then that I decidedly did not love him. I felt put out. I let two months go by without seeing him.

In the Bois de Boulogne, I walked round the lake with Jean Pradelle; we watched the autumn, the swans, the people in rowing-boats; we took up our discussions where we had left off: with a diminished ardour. I thought a lot of Pradelle, but oh, how untormented he was! His tranquillity offended me. Riesmann made me read his novel, which I thought puerile, but when I read him a few pages of mine he found it insufferably boring. Jean Mallet still talked to me about Alain, Suzanne Boigue about the state of her affections, Mademoiselle Lambert about God. My sister had recently entered a school of applied arts where she was very unhappy. Zaza was cultivating the virtue of obedience and spent hours in the large shops picking over samples of material with her mother. Boredom once more descended upon me, and solitude. When I had told myself that day in the Luxembourg Gardens that it was to be my lot, there was so much gaiety in the air that I didn't feel too bad about it; but now, seen through the fogs of autumn, the future frightened me. I should never love anyone, no one is ever big enough for one's love; I should not know the joys of a family hearth; I should spend my days in a small provincial room which I would leave only in order to give my lessons: what a barren existence! I no longer even hoped to have a true understanding with another human being. Not one of my friends would take me as I was, without reserves; Zaza prayed for me, Jacques thought I was too abstract, Pradelle deplored my rank obstinacy and the way I kept working myself up. What alarmed them was the most firmly rooted of my convictions: my refusal to accept that mediocre existence which they, in one way or another, said yes to, and my frantic efforts to escape from it. I tried to content myself. 'I'm not like other people; I'll have to try to accept that,' I would keep telling myself; but I couldn't content myself. Cut off from everybody, I no longer had any link with the world: it was becoming a spectacle that did not concern me personally. One after the other I had renounced fame, happiness, and the wish to serve others; now I was not even interested in living. At moments I completely lost all sense of reality: the streets, the cars, the passers-by were only so many shadows among which my own anonymous presence floated aimlessly. I would sometimes tell myself, fearfully but proudly, that I was mad: it's a very short step between utter loneliness and madness. There were plenty of reasons why I should have lost my wits. For two years I had been struggling to get out of a trap but without finding a way; I kept bumping into invisible obstacles: in the end it must affect my brain. My hands remained empty; I tried to offset my disillusionment by repeating to myself both that one day I would possess everything and that it would not be worth anything anyway: I got all muddled by these contradictions. Above all, I was bursting with health and youthful vigour, and I was confined to home and library: all that vitality which I was unable to make use of unleashed its futile whirlwinds in my head and heart.

The earth was nothing to me any more; I was 'outside life'. I didn't even want to write any more; the horrible vanity of all things had me by the throat again; but I had had enough of suffering and weeping in the past year; I built a new hope for myself. In moments of perfect detachment when the universe seems to be reduced to a set of illusions and in which my own ego was abolished, something took their place: something indestructible, eternal; it seemed to me that my indifference was a negative manifestation of a presence which it was perhaps not impossible to get in touch with. I was not thinking of the Christian God: I was more and more disgusted by Roman Catholicism. But all the same I was influenced by Mademoiselle Lambert, by Pradelle who affirmed that it was possible to attain to true 'being': I read Plotinus and books about mystical psychology; I began to wonder if, beyond the limitations of reason, certain experiences were not susceptible to revealing the absolute to me; I was seeking fulfilment in this desert of abstraction in which I was reducing the inhospitable world to sand. Why shouldn't a mystical theology be possible? 'I want to touch God or become God,' I declared in my journal. All through that year I abandoned myself intermittently to these deliriums.

Yet I was fed-up with myself. I almost gave up keeping my diary. I was busy. At Neuilly, as at Belleville, I got on well with my pupils, and was amused by the rest of the teaching staff. At the Sorbonne, no one attended the lectures in sociology and psychology, so insipid did they seem to us. I only went to the demonstrations which, with the help of a few madmen, Georges Dumas gave every Sunday and Tuesday morning at Sainte-Anne. Maniacs, paranoiacs, schizophrenics, and people suffering from dementia praecox paraded on a platform; he never told us anything about their case-histories or their mental conflicts; he hardly even seemed to be aware that things were going on in their minds. He contented himself with demonstrating that their anomalies were based on the patterns which he had outlined in his Treatise. He was clever at choosing the questions which would provoke the effects he required, and the malice in his waxen old face was so infectious that we had difficulty in repressing our laughter: it was almost as if madness were an enormous lark. Even seen from this angle, it fascinated me. Lunatics, imbeciles; hallucinated, demented, moonstruck, hilarious, tormented, possessed creatures – *these* people were different.

I also went to hear Jean Baruzi, the author of a thesis that was very well thought of on St John of the Cross; he treated all the major problems by fits and starts. Black-haired, dark-skinned, his eyes flashed sombre fires in the dark night of the soul. Every week his trembling voice would be drawn out of abysmal silences, promising us harrowing illuminations in the weeks to come. The students at the Normale did not go to his lectures, which were attended by certain outsiders, among whom were René Daumal and Roger Vailland. They were writers in avant-garde magazines; the former was said to be a deep thinker, the other to have a lively intelligence. Vailland liked shocking people and his very appearance was striking. His smooth skin was stretched tightly on a face that was all profiles: from the front, all that could be seen was his adam's apple. The blasé expression on his face belied his youth: he looked an old man who had been regenerated by some devil's magic philtre. He was often seen in the company of a young woman, with his arm laid negligently round her neck. He would introduce her as 'my woman'. In a magazine called *Le Grand Jeu* I read a violent diatribe by him against an army sergeant who had punished a private for having bestial relations with a sow. Vailland claimed that all men, both civil and military, had the right to perform bestial acts. I wondered about it. As I have already mentioned, I had a bold imagination, but I was easily shocked by reality. I did not attempt to get into conversation with Daumal or Vailland, who ignored me.

I struck up only one new friendship: with Lisa Quermadec, a boarder at Sainte-Marie who was reading for a degree in philosophy. She was a frail little Breton girl with a lively, rather boyish face and short-cropped hair. She detested Neuilly and the mysticism of Mademoiselle Lambert. She believed in God, but thought that those who claimed to love Him were boasters or snobs: 'How can you love someone you don't know?' she asked. I liked her very much, but her rather bitter scepticism did not add to the gaiety of life. I went on with my novel. I undertook for Baruzi an enormous dissertation on 'the personality' in which I displayed the sum total of my knowledge and my ignorance. Once a week I went to a concert, alone or with Zaza: I heard the *Sacre du Printemps* twice, and was enraptured by it. But on the whole I was no longer very interested in anything. I was disappointed with the second volume of letters between Rivière and Fournier: the fevers of their youth were extinguished by trivial worries, spite, bitterness. I wondered if the same degradation lay in wait for me.

I went back to see Jacques. He paced up and down the gallery with the same smiles and gestures as before, and the past came to life again. I returned frequently to see him. He would talk and talk and talk; the twilight would fill with cigarette smoke and shimmering words would tremble in the blue coils of air; somewhere, in unknown places, one could meet people who were unlike any others, and things happened – funny things, or rather tragic, sometimes very beautiful things. *What* things? When the door closed behind me, the words died away. But the next week again I would surprise in his gold-flecked eyes the glow of Adventure. Adventure, escape, getting away from it all: perhaps that was the answer! It was the answer given by Marc Chadourne in *Vasco* which had a considerable success that winter and which I read with almost as much enthusiasm as *Le Grand Meaulnes*. Jacques had never crossed the seven seas; but many young novelists – among them Philipe Soupault – declared that one could go on marvellous voyages without ever leaving Paris; they would describe the bewildering poetry of those bars in which Jacques spent his nights. I began to feel in love with him again. I had gone to such lengths of indifference and even disdain that this return of passion astounds me. Yet I think I know the explanation for it. At first the past had a great deal to do with it: I loved Jacques because I had loved him in the past. And then I was weary of feeling loveless and full of despair: I was overtaken by a longing for tenderness and security. Jacques showed me a kindness that was now invariable; he put himself out to please me, he entertained me. Even so, all that would not have sufficed to draw me back to him. What really decided me was his great discomposure; he felt uncertain and out of place; when I was with him, I felt less ill at ease than when I was with people who accepted life blindly; nothing, I thought, was more important than to say no to life; I therefore concluded that he and I were of the same species, and once again I linked my destiny with his. However this did not give me much comfort; I knew how different we were and I was no longer counting on love to deliver me from loneliness. I had the feeling that I was suffering a calamity, rather than moving forward of my own free will towards the happiness I longed for. I celebrated my twentieth birthday with a melancholy tirade: 'I shall not go to the South Seas. I shall never read St John of the Cross again. There is no sadness; nothing surprises me any more. Dementia praecox would be a way out. What if I tried to live? But I was brought up at the Cours Désir.'

I, too, would have liked to try that 'hazardous and useless' existence whose attractions Jacques and the younger novelists were praising all the time. But how could I introduce the unexpected into my daily life? Very occasionally my sister and I managed to spend an evening away from our mother's vigilant eye; Poupette often took drawing lessons in the evening at La Grande Chaumière, and this provided a convenient pretext when I, too, had a good excuse for going out in the evenings. With the money I was earning at Neuilly we would go to see an avant-garde play at the Studio des Champs-Élysées, or we would go and stand in the promenade at the Casino for Maurice Chevalier. We would walk the streets, talking about our lives and about Life; adventure, unseen but ever-present, rubbed shoulders with us everywhere. These pranks used to raise our spirits; but we couldn't repeat them often. The monotony of daily life continued to weigh heavily upon me: 'Oh! deadly awakenings, life without longing, without love; all over, finished already, and so quickly; frightful *boredom*. Things can't go on like this! What do I want? What can I do? Nothing, nothing, nothing. My book? Vanity of vanities. Philosophy? I'm fed up to the teeth with it. Love? Too tired. Yet I'm only twenty. I want to *live*!'

It couldn't last: It didn't last. I would go back to my book, to philosophy, to love. And then it would start all over again: 'Always this never-ending conflict! A ready acknowledgement of my own powers, of my superiority to all of *them*; keenly aware of all I could do; but this feeling of complete futility in everything! No, it can't go on like this.'

But it did go on. And after all, perhaps it would go on like this for ever. Like a lunatic pendulum I swung frantically from apathy to wild happiness. At night I would climb the steps to the Sacré-Cœur, and I would watch Paris, that futile oasis, scintillating in the wilderness of space. I would weep, because it was so beautiful, and because it was useless. I would run down the narrow little streets of the Butte laughing at all the lights. I would fall into an arid despondency of heart, and then be bounced up into happiness again. It was wearing me out.

I became more and more dissatisfied with my friends. Blanchette Weiss quarrelled with me, I never knew why: she suddenly, without any explanation, turned her back on me and did not reply to the letter in which I asked her what was the matter. I learnt later that she thought I was a mischief maker and accused me of being jealous of her to the extent of spoiling the books she had lent me by chewing their leather bindings. My friendship with Riesmann had cooled off. He had invited me to his house. There, in an immense drawing-room full of works of art I had met Jean Baruzi and his brother Joseph, author of an esoteric novel; there was also a celebrated official sculptor whose works disfigured the whole of Paris, and other academic personalities: the conversation filled me with consternation. Riesmann himself annoyed me with his aestheticism and his sentimentality. The others, the ones I liked, the ones I loved – the one I loved – did not understand me; they weren't good enough for me; their existence, their presence did not solve anything.

Solitude had long ago plunged me into pride. My head was completely turned. Baruzi handed me back my dissertation with copious praise; he gave me an interview after the lecture and, in his voice with the dying fall, sighed out the hope that it might be the basis for an important work. I got swelled-headed: 'I am sure that I shall reach loftier heights than any of them. Is this pride? If I didn't have genius, it would be; but if I *have* got genius – as I sometimes believe; as I am sometimes *quite sure* – then it simply means that I recognize clearly my superior gifts,' I wrote complacently in my diary. The next day I went to see Charlie Chaplin in *The Circus*; when I came out of the cinema I went for a walk in the Tuileries; an orange sun was foundering in a pale blue sky and making the windows of the Louvre flash with fire. I remembered other dusks and suddenly I felt stunned by that necessity which I had been calling out for so desperately all this time: I was to write my book. This was no new project. Yet because I wanted things to happen to me, and they never did, I turned my emotion into an event. Once again, I uttered vows to heaven and earth. Nothing was ever, under any circumstances, to stand in the way of my writing a book. The fact is that I was no longer calling my decision into question. I also promised myself that from now on I would wish for happiness, and obtain it.

*

It was spring again. I passed my examinations in moral science and psychology. The thought of taking up philology was so distasteful to me that I gave it up. My father was bitterly disappointed: he would have liked me to take two degrees; it would have been the smart thing to do; but I wasn't sixteen any more: I stood my ground. I had an inspiration. My final term was vacant; why not start on my diploma straight away? In those days it was not against regulations to present oneself for the diploma in the same year as the degree; if I made sufficient progress, there was nothing to stop me preparing for it on my return next October, and taking it at the same time: in this way I would gain a year! So that within eighteen months I would have finished with the Sorbonne, finished with life at home; I would be free, and a new life would begin! I did not hesitate. I went to see Monsieur Brunschvig who could see no reason why I shouldn't carry out my plan, as I already had the certificate in science and an adequate knowledge of Greek and Latin. He advised me to do my thesis on 'The Concept in Leibniz' and I agreed.

But loneliness continued to lower my spirits. It got worse at the beginning of April. Jean Pradelle went to spend a few days at Solesmes with some friends. I met him, the day after his return, at Adrienne Monnier's bookshop-library, to which we were both subscribers. In the main room Adrienne Monnier, garbed in her monkish robes, would receive celebrated authors: Fargue, Prévost, Joyce; the little rooms at the back were always empty. We sat down there on a couple of stools and talked. In a rather hesitant voice, Pradelle confided in me that at Solesmes he had taken Holy Communion: when he had seen his friends approaching the Lord's Table, he had felt left out, excluded, abandoned; he had accompanied them to the Table next day, after having gone to confession; he had decided that he was still a believer. I listened to him with a lump in my throat: I felt abandoned, shut out, betrayed. Jacques could find refuge in the bars of Montparnasse, Pradelle at the foot of the cross: there was no one left to stand beside me. This desertion made me weep at nights.

Two days later, my father left for La Grillière; he wanted to see his sister for some reason or other. The groaning locomotives, the red glow of smoke in the sooty night made me think of the awful finality of farewells. 'I'm coming with you,' I suddenly announced. My mother protested that I hadn't even a toothbrush with me, but in the end my wish was granted. During the whole journey, leaning out of the window, I drank in the darkness and the wind. I had never seen the country in the spring; I went walking to the song of the cuckoo, among primroses and campanulas; I felt moved by memories of childhood, by my life, by my death. The fear of death had never left me; I couldn't get used to the thought; I would still sometimes shake and weep with terror. By contrast, the fact of existing here and now sometimes took on a glorious splendour. During those few days, the silence of nature often plunged me into joy and horror. I went even further. In those woods and meadows undisturbed by man, I thought I touched that superhuman reality I aspired to. I knelt down to pick a flower, and suddenly I felt riveted to the earth, with all the weight of the heavens on my shoulders; I couldn't move: it was both an agony and an ecstasy which brought eternity within my grasp. I returned to Paris, convinced that I had passed through a mystical experience, and attempted to bring it on again. I had read in St John of the Cross: 'In order to go the way thou knowest not, thou must go the way thou knowest not.' Reversing this phrase I saw in the obscurity of my ways a sign that I was moving towards fulfilment. I would descend into the very depths of my being, and rise entire towards a zenith in which I embraced the Whole. There was no lack of sincerity in these divagations. I had lost myself in so deep a solitude that at moments I became a stranger to this world, and I was dumbfounded by its strangeness: objects had no meaning; neither did faces, nor my own body: as I couldn't recognize anything, it was very tempting to let myself believe that I had attained the Unknown. I cultivated these states with the utmost complacency. All the same, I didn't want to take myself in; I asked Pradelle and Mademoiselle Lambert what they thought about it all. His reply was categorical: 'Not of the slightest interest.' She was a little more tactful: 'It's a sort of metaphysical intuition.' I came to the conclusion that one can't base one's life on such giddy notions and I did not try to bring them on again.

I was still very busy. Now that I had my degree, I had the entry to the Victor Cousin library, stuck away in a remote corner of the Sorbonne. It contained an enormous collection of philosophical works, and practically no one went there. I spent my days in that library. I was writing away at my novel. I was reading Leibniz and books that would be useful in the preparation of my diploma. In the evenings, exhausted by study, I would languish in my room. I should have found great consolation in not being able to quit the earth if only I had been allowed to walk about it in freedom. How I longed to plunge into the night, to listen to jazz, to rub shoulders with people! But no, I was 'cribbed, cabined and confined!' I felt suffocated, I was eating my heart out, I wanted to hammer my head against those prison walls.

*

Jacques was was about to sail for Algeria where he would do his military service. I saw him frequently, and he was friendlier than ever. He talked to me a lot about his friends. I knew that Riaucourt was having an affair with a young woman called Olga; Jacques painted their relationship in such a romantic light that for the first time I felt favourably disposed to the idea of indulging in an illicit love affair. He also referred to another, very beautiful woman called Magda whom he would have liked me to meet. 'We both paid dearly for that affair,' he said. Madga was one of those disturbing characters one met at night in the bars. I didn't wonder what role she had played in Jacques' life. I didn't wonder about anything. I was now certain that Jacques thought a great deal of me, that he wanted me, and that I could live with him in complete happiness. I dreaded our coming separation; but I hardly gave a thought to it, so happy was I about this closer contact it had given me with Jacques.

A week before Jacques' departure I dined with him, together with our parents. His friend Riquet Bresson called for him after the meal; Jacques proposed to take me with them to see a film called *L'Équipage.* My mother, vexed that there had been no mention of marriage, no longer looked with favour upon our friendship; she refused to let me go; I pleaded with her, and my aunt spoke up in my favour: in the end, seeing how things were, my mother allowed herself to be swayed.

We didn't go to the cinema. Jacques took me to the Stryx, a bar in the rue Huyghens where he was one of the 'regulars'; he hoisted me up on a tall bar-stool between himself and Riquet. He called the barman by his Christian name, Michel, and ordered a dry Martini for me. I had never even set foot in a café before, and now here I was in a bar, at night, with two young men; this was something really extraordinary for me. The pale or violently coloured bottles, the bowls of olives and salted almonds, the little tables – it all filled me with wonder; and the most astonishing thing was that this was one of Jacques' familiar haunts. I quickly knocked back my cocktail, and as I had never touched alcohol before, not even wine, which I didn't like, I was soon pretty high. I called Michel by his Christian name and played the fool. Jacques and Michel sat at a small table to play poker-dice and pretended not to know me. I accosted the other customers, most of whom were stolid young Swedes. One of them treated me to a second Martini which on a signal from Jacques I poured behind the counter. To keep the ball rolling I smashed a few glasses. Jacques was laughing, and I was walking on air. Then we went to The Vikings. Out on the street I linked arms with Jacques and Riquet, giving my right arm to Jacques: the left arm didn't seem to exist at all, and I marvelled at this physical intimacy with Jacques which symbolized the fusion of our souls. He taught me to play poker-dice and had me served with a gin fizz with very little gin: I lovingly surrendered to his watchful care. Time no longer existed: it was already two o'clock when I found myself tossing off a crème de menthe at the counter in the Rotonde. All around me swarmed faces from another world; miracles happened at every corner, like explosions. I felt myself bound to Jacques by an indissoluble complicity, as if we had committed a murder, or crossed the Sahara together on foot.

He left me outside number 71 in the rue de Rennes. I had the key to the door. But my parents were waiting up for me; my mother was in tears, and my father's face wore its most forbidding expression. They had just come back from the boulevard Montparnasse where my mother had rung and rung at the door until my aunt stuck her head out of a window: my mother had yelled that she wanted her daughter back, and that Jacques had dishonoured me. I explained that we had been to see *L'Équipage* and had then called at the Rotonde for a coffee. But my parents refused to calm down, and though I was now less disturbed by their outbursts I too burst into tears and screamed with rage. Jacques had arranged to meet me next day on the terrace of the Select. Filled with consternation by my reddened eyes and by the tale his mother had told him, he gazed into my eyes more tenderly than ever; he objected to the accusation that he had treated me in a disrespectful manner: 'I have too much real regard for you to do that,' he told me. And I felt even closer to him than I had during our orgy of the night before. I asked him if he felt sad to be saying good-bye to Paris. 'It's *you* I don't want to say good-bye to,' he replied. He took me to the Sorbonne in his car. I got out. We took a long last look at one another. 'Come on, now,' he said, and the emotion in his voice really shook me: 'I'm going to see you again, aren't I? We're not saying good-bye for ever.' He let in the clutch, and I was standing at the edge of the pavement, not knowing where to turn. But the memory of those last moments gave me the strength to face the months of separation. 'Here's to next year,' I thought to myself, and went to read Leibniz.

*

'If ever you feel like going for a spin, get in touch with Riquet,' Jacques had told me. I sent Bresson a note and one evening I went to meet him at the Stryx: we talked about Jacques, whom he admired; but the bar was empty, and nothing happened. Nothing much happened that other evening when I went to the bar at the Rotonde for an apéritif; there were a few young people talking to one another in intimate tones; the deal tables, the rustic chairs and the red and white checked curtains made the place seem no more mysterious than the back room of a cake-shop. Yet when I tried to pay for my sherry-cobbler, the tall red-headed barman refused my money; this incident – which I never managed to fathom – had a faint touch of the miraculous and I felt greatly encouraged. By leaving home in good time and arriving late at my class, I managed to spend an hour at The Vikings on the evenings when I went to Belleville. Once I drank two whole gin fizzes: it was too much for me; I brought them up in the Métro; when I walked into the centre my knees were like water and my forehead was bathed in a cold sweat: they thought I was ill and made me lie down on a divan, praising me for my courage in turning out. My cousin Madeleine came to spend a few days in Paris: I jumped at the opportunity. She was twenty-three, and my mother gave permission for us to go alone to the theatre every evening: in fact, we had made up our minds to visit a few dens of vice. Our plans nearly fell through because, just before we left home, Madeleine put a little rouge on my cheeks as a joke: I thought it looked very pretty, and when my mother ordered me to wash it off, I protested. She probably thought it was Satan's cloven hoof-mark she saw on my cheeks; she exorcized me by boxing my ears. I gave in, with very bad grace. However, she let me go out and my cousin and I wended our way towards Montmartre. For a long while we wandered under the light of the neon signs; we couldn't make up our minds. We slunk into a couple of bars, both of them dead as dairies, and then we found ourselves in the rue Lepic, in a frightful little hole where young women of easy virtue awaited their customers. Two of them came and sat at our table; they were startled to see us there, for we were obviously not offering any competition. We stayed there for some time, both of us bored to death: the place made me feel sick.

Yet I wasn't to be put off. I told my parents that the centre at Belleville was getting up an entertainment for the 14th of July, that I was rehearsing my pupils in a play and that I would have to be out several nights a week; I told them that I was giving the money I spent on gin fizzes towards the upkeep of the centre. I often went to the Jockey in the boulevard Montparnasse: Jacques had told me about it, and I liked the highly coloured posters on the walls, where Chevalier's straw hat and Chaplin's boots kept company with Greta Garbo's smile; I loved the shining bottles, the little striped flags, the smell of tobacco and alcohol, the voices, the laughter, the saxophone. The women amazed me: I had no words to describe the material of their dresses, the colour of their hair; I couldn't imagine any shop in which one might buy such gossamer-fine silk stockings, such very high-heeled shoes, such vivid red lipstick. I would listen to them arguing with men about their rates for the night or for a short time or for the various refinements of pleasure they had to offer. My imagination didn't react: I had set up a blockage in it. At first especially, I didn't think of the people around me as creatures of flesh and blood, but as allegories: Disquiet, Futility, Stupidity, Despair, Genius perhaps, and certainly Vice in all its masks. I remained convinced that sin is the absence of God and I would perch

[271]

on my bar-stool with all the fervour which made me kneel, as a child, before the Holy Sacrament: it was the same presence I was in touch with; jazz had taken the place of the deep-toned organ, and I used to be on the look-out for adventure as I had once waited upon the coming of ecstatic illumination. Jacques had told me: 'Anything you do in a bar – no matter what it is – will make things happen.' And so I did whatever came into my head. If a customer came in with his hat on, I would shout 'Hat!' and throw his headgear up at the ceiling. From time to time I would smash a glass or two. I would hold forth, accosting 'regulars' whom I naïvely tried to mystify: I would give myself out to be a model, or a tart. With my dingy old frock, my woollen stockings, my sensible shoes and my face ignorant of make-up, I never deceived anyone. 'You've not got the right touch, dearie,' an old cripple with thick horn-rimmed spectacles told me. 'You're a little middle-class girl who wants to play at being a bohemian,' said a man with a hook nose who wrote love-serials for the papers. I protested violently. The cripple drew something on a piece of paper: 'There you are; if you want to be a professional, that's what you have to do, and have it done to you as well.' I didn't lose my nerve. 'It's very badly drawn,' I remarked icily. 'It's good enough,' he retorted. He opened his flies, but this time I had to turn my eyes away. '*That* doesn't interest me.' They all laughed. 'You see!' cried the serial-writer. 'A real tart would have said: that's nothing much to brag about!' With the help of alcohol, I coolly swallowed their obscenities. Besides, they left me alone. Occasionally someone would offer me a drink or invite me to dance, nothing more: apparently I didn't incite them to lubricity.

My sister joined me several times on these evenings out; in order to give herself a 'low-class' appearance she would wear her hat on one side and pull her skirts up over her crossed knees. We would talk loudly and laugh at the tops of our voices. Or we would enter a bar separately, pretending not to know one another and then we would start to fight: we would tear each other's hair, scream insults at one another, and feel very gratified if such an exhibition diverted the public for a few minutes.

On the evenings when I stayed at home, I could hardly bear the silence of my room; again I sought release in mysticism. One night I summoned God, if He really existed, to show Himself to me. He didn't, and I never addressed another word to Him. In my heart of hearts, I was very glad He didn't exist. I should have hated it if what was going on here below had had to end up in eternity.

Anyhow, there was now one place on earth where I felt at home: I became one of the regulars at the Jockey, I saw familiar faces there, and I liked being there more and more. All I needed was one gin fizz, and my loneliness evaporated: then all men were brothers and we all understood one another, everybody loved everybody else. No more problems, no more regrets and tensions: I was filled with the ever-present here and now. I would dance in arms that held me tight, and my body would have presentiments of escapes and abandonments that were easier and more satisfying than my mystical spasms; far from taking offence as I had at the age of sixteen, I would find comfort in the warmth of a strange hand on the back of my neck, stroking me with a gentleness which resembled love. I didn't know the first thing about the people around me, but that didn't matter: I was in a new world; and I had the feeling that at last I had put my finger on the secret of freedom. I had progressed since the days when I had hesitated to walk in the street beside a young man: I merrily defied convention and authority. The attraction that bars and dance-halls had for me was based in great part on their illicit character. Never would my mother have set her feet in such places; my father would have been deeply shocked to find me there, and Pradelle grieved; it gave me a feeling of great satisfaction to know that I was so totally at odds with authority.

I gradually grew bolder. I allowed men to accost me in the streets, and went to drink in bars with strangers. One evening I got in a car that had followed me all along the street. 'Like to go for a spin to Robinson?' the driver suggested. He was not at all attractive, and what would become of me if he left me stranded ten miles out of Paris, at midnight? But I had certain principles: 'Live dangerously. Refuse nothing,' said Gide, Rivière, the surrealists, and Jacques. 'All right,' I said. At the place de la Bastille, sitting outside a café, we drank cocktails in glum silence. When we got back into the car, the man put his hand on my knee: I pushed him violently away. 'What's up? You get yourself picked up off the street, and now you don't want nobody to touch you?' His voice had a nasty sound. He stopped the car and tried to kiss me. I ran off, followed by a flood of oaths. I caught the last Métro. I realized that I had got off lightly; but I was pleased that I had performed a truly gratuitous act.

Another evening, in a pin-table saloon in the avenue de Clichy, I played miniature football with a young thug whose cheek was marked with a long pink scar; we tried the rifle range too, and he insisted on paying every time. He introduced me to a friend and they treated me to a coffee. When I heard my last bus starting up, I bade them a hasty farewell and ran after it. They caught up with me just as I was going to jump on the platform; they took hold of me by the shoulders. 'That's a nice way to treat your friends!' The conductor was hesitating, with his arm raised to pull the bell; then he pulled it and the bus rumbled away. I was white with fury. The two boys assured me that I'd behaved badly: you don't just drop your friends like that. We made it up and they insisted on accompanying me home, on foot. I made it quite clear to them that they were not to expect anything of me, but they persisted. At the rue Cassette, at the corner of the rue de Rennes, the young thug with the razor-slashed cheek put his arm round my waist. 'When am I going to see you again?' 'Whenever you like,' I said weakly. He tried to kiss me; I struggled to get free. Four policemen on bicycles came riding past; I didn't dare call out to them but my companion released me and walked on a little way towards the house. When the police passed, he took hold of me again: 'You won't turn up! You've been having us on! I don't like that sort of thing. I'm going to teach you a lesson.' He looked nasty: he was going to strike me or kiss me full on the mouth, and I don't know which I feared the more. His friend intervened: 'Here, let's settle this nicely. He's grousing 'cos you cost him a bit of money, that's all.' I turned over the contents of my handbag. 'I don't want her fricking money!' the other replied. 'I want to teach her a lesson.' All the same, he took my entire fortune in the end: fifteen francs. 'Not even enough to get meself a bit of skirt!' he sulked. I let myself into the house: I'd really had a fright.

*

The academic year was coming to an end. Suzanne Boigue had spent several months with one of her sisters in Morocco; there she had met Mr Right. The wedding-breakfast took place in a big suburban garden; the husband was good-looking, Suzanne was exultant, and happiness seemed to me to be very desirable. Yet I didn't feel unhappy: Jacques' absence and the certainty of his love kept my heart

at rest; its peace was no longer threatened by the shocks of unexpected meetings or the hazards of one of his moods. I went boating in the Bois with my sister, Zaza, Lisa, and Pradelle: my friends
got on well together, and when they were all with me I didn't so
much regret not getting on with them so well as individuals. Pradelle introduced me to a friend from the Normale for whom he had
a great admiration: it was one of these who, at Solesmes, had persuaded him to take Holy Communion. He was called Pierre Claraut
and was a supporter of *L'Action Française*; he was short and dark,
and looked like a cricket. He was going to present himself the
following year for the selective examination for teachers of philosophy, and so we would be fellow-competitors. As he had a hard,
haughty, self-confident air I promised myself that on my return to
the Sorbonne in October, I would try to find out what was underneath that rebarbative exterior. I went with him and Pradelle to hear
the orals of the competition: there was a crowd to hear the lesson
presented by Raymond Aron, for whom everybody foretold a brilliant future as a philosopher. They also pointed out to me Daniel
Lagache who was going in for psychiatry. To everyone's surprise,
Jean-Paul Sartre had failed in the written examination. I thought
the competition seemed difficult, but my courage didn't fail me: I
would work harder than I'd ever worked before, but within a year,
I would be through with it: I already felt as if I were free at last.
I think, too, that it had done me a great deal of good to have a good
fling, to amuse myself and have a change of air. I had regained my
self-confidence to such an extent that I no longer even kept a diary:
'All I want is an ever greater intimacy with the world, and to put
that world into a book,' I wrote to Zaza. I was in great good humour
when I arrived in the Limousin, and I received a letter from Jacques
into the bargain. He talked about Biskra, the little donkeys, the
dappled shade, the summer; he recalled our meetings: 'Those were
the only times I stood to attention in those days.' And he promised
that 'next year we'll have some good times together'. My sister,
who was less experienced than I was at deciphering cryptograms,
asked me what this last phrase meant. 'It means we're going to get
married!' I triumphantly replied.

What a wonderful summer it was! No more tears, no more solitary effusions, no more epistolary tempests. The countryside overwhelmed me as it had done when I was five and twelve, and there
was enough blue and to spare to fill the skies. I knew now what was

the hidden promise in the scent of the honeysuckle, and the meaning of the morning dew. In the country lanes, over the ripening corn and among the spiny gorse and the warm heather I caught innumerable glimpses of my former pains and happinesses. I went for many walks with my sister. Often we would go bathing, in our petticoats, in the beer-brown waters of the Vézère; then we would dry off in the long grass that smelt of mint. She would draw and I would read. Even outside distractions did not bother me. My parents had renewed an old friendship with some friends who were spending the summer in a neighbouring château; they had three grown-up sons, all very handsome young men who were destined for the Bar; we sometimes went over to play tennis with them. I was very happy. Their mother gave Mama a delicate hint that she would only consider girls with dowries as future daughters-in-law: this made my sister and me roar with laughter, because we were far from coveting the attentions of such well-behaved young gentlemen.

That year again I was invited to Laubardon. My mother had been quite willing for me to meet Pradelle in Bordeaux; he was spending his holidays in the region. It was a delightful day we spent together. Pradelle certainly meant a great deal to me. And Zaza even more so. I got out of the train at Laubardon and my heart was dancing.

In June Zaza had achieved the rare feat of passing at the first go her certificate in philology. And yet this year she had devoted only very little time to her studies. Her mother's demands on her attendance and services were becoming more and more tyrannical. Madame Mabille considered that thrift was a cardinal virtue; she would have thought it immoral to buy in a shop products that could be made at home – cakes, jams, underwear, dresses, and coats. During the spring and early summer months she often got up at six in the morning to go to the fruit and vegetable markets with her daughters in order to get stuff cheap. Whenever the little Mabilles needed a new outfit, Zaza had to go and ransack a dozen shops, bringing back from each of them a swatch of samples which Madame Mabille would compare, taking into account the quality and price of the material; after a lengthy deliberation, Zaza would go back to the shop to buy the required cloth. These tasks, and the boring social duties which had increased in number since Monsieur Mabille's promotion, exasperated Zaza. She couldn't bring herself to believe that by trotting off to shops and tea-parties she was observing faithfully the precepts of the Gospel. Doubtless it was her Christian duty to obey her mother in everything; but in a book on Port-Royal she had been struck by a phrase of Pierre Nicole's which suggested that obedience might also be a trap set by the Devil. By allowing herself to be diminished and her intelligence to be misused, was she not acting contrary to God's will? How could she know for certain what His will might be? She was afraid of the sin of pride if she surrendered to her own judgement, and of being cowardly if she gave in to pressure from outside. This doubt exacerbated the conflict which had been raging in her mind for some time: she loved her mother, but she also loved many things that her mother did not like. She would often quote to me that phrase from Ramuz: 'The things I love do not love each other.' The future did not offer much comfort. Madame Mabille refused point-blank to allow Zaza to take her diploma the year after; she was afraid her daughter might become an intellectual. As for love, Zaza no longer had any hope of finding it. In my family circle it sometimes – but very rarely – happened that someone married for love: that had been what my cousin Titite had done. But Madame Mabille said: 'The Beauvoirs should not be judged by accepted standards.' Zaza was much more deeply involved than I was in the rigid formalities of a class whose marriages were all arranged; now all these people who allowed themselves to be married off without a murmur were a dismally mediocre lot. Zaza was ardently in love with life; that is why the prospect of a joyless existence at times robbed her of all desire to go on living. As in her childhood, she used paradoxes to protect herself against the false idealism of her environment. Having seen Jouvet play the part of a drunkard in *Le Grand Large* she declared that she was in love with him and pinned his photograph over her bed; his irony, his dry wit, his scepticism at once found an echo in her. In a letter she sent me at the beginning of the holidays, she confided in me that she sometimes dreamed of renouncing this world completely. 'After brief moments of intellectual as well as physical love of life, I am suddenly so struck by a feeling of the vanity, the futility of it all that I feel everything and everybody withdrawing from me; I feel such utter indifference for the whole of creation that I already seem to be half-dead. The renunciation of self, of existence, of everything; the renunciation made by those who try to begin the life of the hereafter here on earth – if you only knew how much it tempts me. I've often thought that this desire to find liberty in "bondage" was the sign of a vocation; at other times, life and the things of life become so important to me that I feel life in a convent would be a mutilation and that this is not what God wants of me. But whatever may be the path I shall tread, I could never go whole-heartedly for life as you do; even at the moments when I live with the greatest intensity I still have the taste of nothingness in my mouth.'

This letter had frightened me a little. Zaza reassured me in it that my lack of faith did not come between her and me. But if ever she entered a convent she would be lost to me; and to herself, I thought.

On the evening of my arrival I had a disappointment; I wasn't sleeping in Zaza's room, but in Mademoiselle Avdicovitch's; she was a Polish student who had been engaged as a governess for the period of the holidays; she was looking after the three youngest Mabilles. My only consolation was that I found her charming: Zaza had talked to me about her in her letters; she liked her very much. She had pretty blonde hair, blue eyes that were both languorous and gay, a broad, full mouth and a quite exceptional attractiveness which I then hadn't the face to call by its right name: sex-appeal. Her gauzy dress revealed a pair of deliciously rounded shoulders; in the evenings she would sit down at the piano and sing Ukrainian love-songs with a coquetry that enchanted Zaza and me, but which scandalized everybody else. At bedtime, I was startled to see her putting on a pair of pyjamas instead of a nightdress. She opened up her heart to me at once. Her father had a large sweet factory at Lwow; while studying at the university, she had taken part in the struggle for Ukrainian independence and had spent a few days in prison. She had left home to complete her studies, first in Berlin, where she had spent two or three years, then in Paris; she was attending lectures at the Sorbonne and receiving an allowance from her parents. She had wanted to use the holidays to advantage by going to live with a French family: the experience had flabbergasted her. I realized next morning the extent to which she shocked the conventional Mabilles; she was so graceful and feminine that beside her Zaza and I and Zaza's friends seemed like young novices. In the afternoon, she would amuse herself by telling everybody's fortune with cards, including Xavier du Moulin's; without regard to the dignity of his cloth, she flirted discreetly with him: he appeared to be not indifferent to her advances, and smiled at her a great deal. She gave him the whole works, and foretold that he would very soon meet the queen of hearts. The mothers and elder sisters were outraged; behind her back, Madame Mabille accused Stépha of not keeping her place. 'Besides, I'm sure she's no lady,' she said. She blamed Zaza for being too friendly with this foreigner.

As for myself, I wonder why she invited me: probably in order not to cross her daughter too much; but she did her best to make a private conversation between Zaza and myself impossible. Zaza used to spend her mornings in the kitchen: it broke my heart to see her spending hours covering jam pots with greaseproof paper, assisted by Bébelle or Mathé. During the day, she wasn't alone for a minute. Madame Mabille was increasing the numbers of parties and outings in the hope of getting Lili settled: she was already beginning to get a bit long in the tooth. 'This is the last year I'm going to bother with you: what I've gone through for you! All those interviews with eligible young men! Well, it's your sister's turn next,' she had publicly declared during a dinner at which Stépha was present. Already there were well-set-up young men from the Polytechnique who had intimated to Madame Mabille that they would be glad to marry her younger daughter. I couldn't help wondering if after all Zaza would let herself be persuaded that her Christian duty was to set up house; but I could no more see her accepting the dullness of a dutiful marriage than the stultifying deadness of a convent.

A few days after my arrival, all the well-to-do families in the neighbourhood were invited to an immense picnic on the banks of the Adour. Zaza lent me her dress of pink tussor. She was wearing a white silk dress with a green sash and a jade necklace; she had lost weight. She had frequent migraines, and slept badly; to cheer herself up a little she dabbed some rouge on her cheeks; despite this artifice, she looked ill and sad. But I loved her face and it hurt me to see her offering it to anybody with perfect amiability: she played with deceptive ease her role of a young society lady. We arrived in good time; gradually the guests began driving up, and every one of Zaza's smiles, every nod stabbed at my heart. I busied myself, with the others, laying out the tablecloth on the grass and unpacking hampers of crockery and food; I turned the handle of a machine which made ice-cream. Stépha took me to one side and asked me to explain to her Leibniz's philosophical system: for an hour or so I forgot my boredom. But after that the day dragged heavily along. There were pickled eggs, pastry horns filled with savouries, aspics, and puff biscuits, plates of cold meat-balls, galantines, pâtés, cold jellied chicken, hot stews, potted meats, candied fruits, tarts, raised pies, and marzipan fruits: all the ladies of the household had performed their social duties with the utmost zeal. We stuffed ourselves with food, we laughed without much real gaiety; we talked for the sake of talking: nobody seemed to be having any fun. Towards the end of the afternoon, Madame Mabille asked me if I knew where Zaza was; she set off to look for her, and I followed. We found her taking a dip in the Adour at the foot of a waterfall; she had used as a bathing costume a voluminous cloak of rough tweed. Madame Mabille scolded her, but in a playful way: she didn't waste her authority on peccadilloes. I realized that Zaza had felt in need of solitude and violent sensations, and perhaps of purification too, after that long and sticky afternoon, and I felt reassured: she was not yet ready to let herself sink into a contented, matronly slumber.

Yet I realized that her mother had a great hold over her. Madame Mabille pursued a clever policy with her children: when they were very small, she would treat them with playful indulgence; later, she would allow them to have their own way in little things, so that when it was a question of getting them to do something her credit was unimpaired. She could on occasion bring into play vivacity and a certain charm; she had always shown a particular affection for her younger daughter, who had been taken in by her smiles: love as much as respect paralysed her attempts at rebellion. But one evening she let herself go. Madame Mabille declared in the course of dinner, in a very cutting voice: 'I don't understand how a believer could have anything to do with unbelievers.' I was horrified to feel the blood mounting to my cheeks. Zaza indignantly retorted: 'No one has the right to judge anyone else. God leads people by the paths He chooses for them.' 'I am not judging anyone,' Madame Mabille replied icily. 'We must pray for lost souls; but we must not let ourselves be contaminated by them.' Zaza was choking with anger, and that, too, reassured me. But I felt that the atmosphere at Laubardon was more hostile than in the preceding year. Later, in Paris, Stépha told me that the children used to snigger at me because I was so badly dressed: they sniggered, too, on the day Zaza lent me one of her dresses without saying why. I was not vain about my appearance and I never noticed people's reactions to it: I was indifferent to all kinds of affronts. Nevertheless, I sometimes felt my heart sink with misery. Stépha was curious to see Lourdes, and I felt even more alone while she was away. One evening after dinner, Zaza sat down at the piano; she played some Chopin; she played well; I sat looking at her helmet of black hair with its touchingly white, straight parting and told myself that it was this passionate music which really expressed her true self; but there was that mother and all that family between us, and perhaps one day she would disown her real self, and I would lose her. I felt such piercing sadness that I got up, left the room and went to bed in tears. The door opened; Zaza entered and came over to my bed, leaned over me and kissed me. Our friendship had always been such an undemonstrative one that her action overwhelmed me with joy.

Stépha came back from Lourdes; she had brought a big box of caramels for the children. 'It's very kind of you, Mademoiselle,' said Madame Mabille in frosty tones, 'but you might have saved yourself the expense: the children do not need presents from you.' Stépha and I pulled Zaza's family and friends to pieces, and that consoled me a little. Moreover, that year, too, the end of my stay was happier than the beginning. I don't know whether or not Zaza had spoken about it to her mother, or whether she just handled things rather cleverly, but I was able to see her alone; again we went for long walks and we talked. She talked about Proust, whom she understood much better than I did; she told me that when she read him a great desire to write came over her. She assured me that next year she would not allow herself to be bullied into a dull routine: she would read a lot, and we would talk. I had an idea which appealed to her: on Sunday mornings we would all meet to play tennis – Zaza, my sister, and I, Jean Pradelle, Pierre Clairaut, and one of their friends.

Zaza and I agreed on almost everything. She believed that, provided one is not doing harm to others, there is nothing reprehensible in the conduct of unbelievers: she did not reject Gide's immoralism; vice did not shock her. On the other hand, she failed to imagine how one could worship God and yet knowingly break His commandments. I found this attitude, which was practically in line with my own, to be quite logical, for I felt others should be allowed every freedom; but in my own case and in that of those near and dear to me – Jacques in particular – I continued to apply the standards of Christian morality. It was not without some misgiving that I heard Stépha roar with laughter one day as she said: 'Good Lord! How naïve Zaza is!' Stépha had declared that even in strictly Catholic circles no young man is a virgin when he marries. Zaza had protested that if one believes, one lives according to one's belief. 'Just look at your du Moulin cousins,' Stépha had said. 'But they take Holy Communion every Sunday!' Zaza had replied. 'I can assure you that they would not allow themselves to live in a state of mortal sin.' Stépha had not tried to take the matter any further; but she told me that she had many a time met Henri and Edgar in Montparnasse – which she visited frequently – and in no unmistakable company: 'You've just got to look at their faces!' she told me. Indeed they didn't look like angelic little choirboys. I thought of Jacques: he had quite another kind of face, he was altogether different; it was impossible to think of him popping in and out of bed with women all the time. All the same, by revealing some of Zaza's naïveté, Stépha was challenging my own experience. It was something very ordinary for her to frequent bars and cafés in which I used to go hunting secretly for extraordinary experiences: she certainly saw them from a different angle to me. I realized that I took people as they were; I didn't suspect them of having any other self than the official one; Stépha had opened my eyes to the fact that this rigid society had its darker corners. The conversation upset me.

That year, Zaza did not accompany me to Mont-de-Marsan; I walked round the town thinking about her as I waited for my train. I had decided to fight with all my strength to prevent her life becoming a living death.

BOOK FOUR

THE beginning of this academic year was unlike any other. By deciding to enter for the competition, I had at last escaped from the labyrinth in which I had been going round in circles for the last three years: I was now on my way to the future. From now on, every day had its meaning: it was taking me further on my road to final liberation. I was spurred on by the difficulty of the enterprise: there was no longer any question of straying from the straight and narrow path, or of becoming bored. Now that I had something definite to work for, I found that the earth could give me all I wanted; I was released from disquiet, despair, and from all my regrets. 'In this diary, I shall no longer make note of tragic self-communings, but only of the events of every day.' I had the feeling that after a painful apprenticeship my real life was just beginning, and I threw myself into it gladly.

In October, while the Sorbonne was closed, I spent my days in the Bibliothèque Nationale. I had obtained permission to have my lunch out: I would buy bread and rillette and eat them in the gardens of the Palais Royal while watching the petals of the late roses fall; sitting on the benches, navvies would be munching thick sandwiches and drinking cheap red wine. If it was raining, I would take shelter in the Café Biard with bricklayers eating out of mess-tins; I was delighted to escape from the ritual of family meals; by reducing food to its essential elements I felt I was taking another step in the direction of freedom. I would go back to the library; I was studying the theory of relativity, and was passionately interested in it. From time to time I would look up at the other readers and lean back proudly in my armchair: among these specialists, scholars, researchers, and thinkers I felt at home. I no longer felt myself to be rejected by my environment; it was I who had rejected it in order to enter that society – of which I saw here a cross-section – in which all those minds that are interested in finding out the truth communicate with each other across the distances of space and time. I, too, was taking part in the effort which humanity makes to know, to understand, to express itself: I was engaged in a great collective enterprise which would release me for ever from the bonds of loneliness. What a victory! I would settle down to work again. At a quarter to six, the superintendent's voice would solemnly announce: 'Gentlemen – we shall – very soon – be – closing.' It was always a surprise, after leaving my studies, to come back to the shops outside, the lights, the passers-by, and the dwarf who sold bunches of violets near the Théâtre Français. I would walk slowly, giving myself up to the melancholy of evening and of my return home.

Stépha came back to Paris a few days after me and often came to the library to read Goethe and Nietzsche. With her roving eye and ready smile, she was too attractive to men and they were too much interested in her for her to be able to get much work done. She would have barely taken her place beside me when she would put her coat over her shoulders and go outside to have a chat with one of her boy friends: the teacher studying German, the Prussian student, the Romanian doctor. We used to lunch together and although she was not well-off she would treat me to cakes at a *pâtisserie* or a good cup of coffee at the Bar Poccardi. At six o'clock we would stroll along the boulevards, or most often have tea in her room. She had a bright blue room in a hotel in the rue Saint-Sulpice; she had hung reproductions of Cézanne, Renoir, and El Greco on the walls, together with some drawings by a Spanish friend who wanted to be a painter. I liked being with her. I loved the soft feel of her fur collar, her little toques, her dresses, her scent, her warbling voice, her loving gestures. My relationships with my other friends – Zaza, Jacques, Pradelle – had always been extremely formal. But Stépha would take my arm in the street; in the cinema she would hold hands with me; she would kiss me on the slightest provocation. She used to tell me all kinds of stories about herself, was enthusiastic about Nietzsche, indignant about Madame Mabille and made fun of the men who were in love with her: she could do imitations very well and would intersperse her stories with bits of acting which amused me vastly.

She was trying to get rid of a religious hangover. At Lourdes, she had gone to confession and taken Holy Communion; back in Paris she had bought a small missal at the Bon Marché and had gone to pray in one of the chapels in Saint-Sulpice: but it hadn't worked. For a whole hour she had paced up and down in front of the church without being able to make up her mind whether to go back inside or to walk away. With her hands behind her back, her forehead deeply furrowed and stamping backwards and forwards in her room, she mimed this spiritual crisis so exuberantly for me that I didn't know whether to take her seriously or not. In fact, the divinities she really worshipped were Thought, Art, and Genius; at a pinch, intelligence and talent would do instead. Every time she tracked down an 'interesting' man, she would arrange to have herself introduced to him and then would do her utmost to 'get him under my thumb'. It was, she explained to me, the 'eternal feminine' in her. She preferred intellectual conversations and comradeship to these flirtations; once a week she would argue for hours at the Closerie des Lilas with a group of Ukrainians who were journalists or engaged on vague studies in Paris. She saw her Spanish friend every day; she had known him for years, and he had asked her to marry him. I often met him in her room; he lived in the same hotel. He was called Fernando. He was a descendant of one of those Jewish families that had been driven out of Spain by the Inquisition four centuries ago; he had been born in Constantinople and had studied in Berlin. Prematurely bald, with a rounded face and skull, he would talk with romantic intensity about his *daimón*, but he was capable of irony, and I liked him very much. Stépha admired him because, though he hadn't a penny, he managed somehow to go on painting, and she shared all his ideas: these were unshakeably internationalist, pacifist, and even, in a Utopian sense, revolutionary. The only reason she hesitated to marry him was that she wanted to keep her freedom.

I introduced them to my sister, whom they at once took to their hearts, and to my friends. Pradelle had broken his leg; he was limping when I met him at the beginning of October on the terrace in the Luxembourg Gardens. Stépha thought he was too quiet, and her volubility bewildered him. She got on better with Lisa, who was now living in a students' hostel, the windows of which overlooked the Petit Luxembourg. She made a scanty livelihood by giving lessons; she was studying for a science certificate and preparing a thesis on Maine de Biran; but she had no intention of entering for the competitive examination; her health was too weak. 'My poor brain!' she used to say, holding her little cropped head in her hands. 'When I think it's all I have to rely on, and that I have to get everything from it! It's not natural! One of these days it's going to give way!' She wasn't interested in Main de Biran, in philosophy, or in herself: 'I often wonder,' she told me with a frosty smile, 'what pleasure you can get in seeing *me*!' I was always pleased to see her, because she never let herself be taken in, and her mistrustful turn of mind often made her very perspicacious.

I often talked to Stépha about Zaza, who was having an extended holiday at Laubardon. I had sent her a few books from Paris, including *The Constant Nymph*; Stépha told me that Madame Mabille had flown into a temper and had declared: 'I hate intellectuals!' Zaza was beginning to cause her serious concern: it would not be easy to make her accept a marriage of convenience. Madame Mabille regretted ever having let her attend the Sorbonne; she felt it was now urgently necessary to get her daughter in hand, and she would have very much liked to have her somewhere where she would not be under my influence. Zaza wrote to me that she had mentioned our plan for playing tennis to her mother, and that she was up in arms against it: 'She declared that she didn't hold with that sort of student behaviour and that I was not to go to a game of tennis organized by a girl of twenty where I would come into contact with young men whose families she had never met. I'm not mincing my words; I prefer that you should realize the state of mind that I have to contend with all the time but which my concept of Christian duty obliges me to respect. But today I'm so upset about it I could weep; the things I love do not love each other; and taking refuge in moral principles I have been listening to opinions that I cannot stomach . . . I made an ironical offer to sign a statement saying I would undertake never to marry Pradelle, Clairaut, or any of their friends, but that didn't make matters any better.' In her next letter, she told me that in order to make her break completely with the Sorbonne her mother had decided to send her to Berlin for the winter, just as in former times the local gentry used to pack their sons off to South America in order to put an end to some scandalous or embarrassing affair.

Never had I written Zaza such expansive letters as in those last weeks; never had she confided so frankly in me. Yet when she came back to Paris in the middle of October our friendship got off to a bad start. When she was not with me, she could write to me about her difficulties and her dislikes and I felt I was her ally; but in fact her attitude was an equivocal one: she still retained all her love and respect for her mother, and remained loyal to her background. I could no longer accept such a division of personality. I had got the measure of Madame Mabille's hostility, and had understood that there could be no possible compromise between the two camps to which we belonged: the 'orthodox' Catholics wanted to annihilate the 'intellectuals' and vice versa. By not coming over to my side, Zaza was throwing in her lot with enemies who were set on destroying me, and that made me feel resentful towards her. She dreaded the journey she was being compelled to make, and was worrying herself sick; I showed my resentment by refusing to share her worries; I let myself go in a great burst of high spirits which disconcerted her. I professed a great intimacy with Stépha, and began to imitate her by laughing and chattering in her own over-exuberant way; Zaza was often shocked by our conversations; she frowned when Stépha declared that the more intelligent people were, the more internationally-minded they became. In reaction against our 'Polish student' manners, she set out deliberately to play the part of the 'well-bred young French girl', and my apprehensions increased: perhaps in the end she would go over entirely to the enemy; I no longer dared speak freely to her, and so I preferred to meet her when I was in the company of Pradelle, Lisa, my sister, and Stépha rather than alone. She certainly sensed this distance between us; she was absorbed in the preparations for her departure. We said good-bye to one another, without regrets, at the end of November.

Lectures started again. I had skipped a year, and, except for Clairaut, knew none of my new fellow-students; there was not one amateur, not one dilettante among them: they were all, like me, grim professionals intent on getting through the competition. I thought they looked a forbidding lot, with their air of great self-importance. I decided to ignore them. I went on working hell for leather. I followed all the lectures in the competitive examination course at the Sorbonne at the École Normale, and, whenever my timetable allowed, I would go and study at Sainte-Geneviève, at the Victor Cousin, or the National libraries. In the evenings I would read novels or go out. I had grown up; I would soon be leaving: that year my parents gave me permission from time to time to go out to the theatre in the evenings, alone or with a friend. I saw Man Ray's *Star-fish*, all the programmes at the Ursulines, Studio 28, and Ciné Latin, all the films with Brigitte Helm,

Douglas Fairbanks, and Buster Keaton. I frequented the left-wing theatres. Under Stépha's influence, I took more pride in my personal appearance. She had told me that her boy friend who was studying German thought I was wrong to spend all my time studying: twenty is too young for a blue-stocking, and if I went on like this I'd turn into an ugly little spinster. She had protested against his judgement, but had taken it to heart; she didn't want her best friend to look like an old frump; she assured me that I could do something with a body like mine, and insisted that I should show it off to its best advantage. I began to pay regular visits to the hairdresser and to take an interest in buying a hat or making a dress. I made friends. Mademoiselle Lambert no longer interested me. Suzanne Boigue had followed her husband to Morocco; I was quite pleased to see Riesmann again and I took a fresh liking to Jean Mallet who was working as assistant master at the Lycée de Saint-Germain and was preparing a thesis under the guidance of Baruzi. Clairaut often used to come to the Nationale. Pradelle had great respect for him and had convinced me of his exceptional qualities. He was a Catholic, a Thomist, and a follower of Maurras; when he talked to me, with his eyes boring into mine, and using a categorical tone of voice that impressed me deeply, I would wonder if I hadn't misjudged St Thomas and Maurras; I still disliked their doctrines; but I should have liked to know how one looked at life and how one felt within oneself when one adopted them: Clairaut intrigued me. He assured me that I was bound to succeed in the competition: 'Apparently you succeed in everything you undertake,' he told me, and I felt very flattered. Stépha, too, encouraged me: 'You'll have a wonderful life. You'll always get just what you want.' So I sailed along, confident that I was under a lucky star and feeling very pleased with myself. It was a lovely autumn, and whenever I raised my head from my books I was grateful to the heavens for their smile.

All the time I was trying so hard not to be a little book-worm, I was thinking of Jacques; I devoted entire pages of my diary to him, and wrote him long letters that I never posted. When I met his mother at the beginning of November, she was very affectionate towards me; Jacques, she informed me, was always asking her for news of 'the only person in Paris who interests me'; she smiled at me in a conspiratorial manner as she uttered these words.

I was working hard, and amusing myself too: I felt my balance had been restored, and it was with a certain wonder that I recalled the pranks I had got up to in the summer. Those bars and dance-halls where I had whiled away my evenings now only filled me with disgust, and even with a kind of horror. This virtuous revulsion had the same roots as my former dissipation: despite my rationalist mentality, the things of the flesh remained taboo to me.

'How idealistic you are!' Stépha often told me. She took great care not to shock me. One day, Fernando, pointing to a sketch of a naked woman on the walls of his room, told me mischievously 'Stépha posed for that.' I didn't know where to look, and she cast an indignant glance at him: 'Don't say such stupid things!' He hurriedly admitted that he only meant it as a joke. Not for one moment did I think that Stépha might be what Madame Mabille had called her – 'not a lady', which meant, of course, 'not a virgin'. Nevertheless she made some gentle attempts to open my eyes a little: 'But I'm telling you, dear, physical love is very important, for men especially. . . .' One night, as we were coming out of the Atelier, we saw a crowd gathered in the place Clichy; a policeman had just arrested an elegant young man whose hat was lying in the gutter; he was white-faced and trying to struggle free; the crowd were booing him: 'Dirty touting pimp. . . .' I thought I was going to faint, and dragged Stépha away; the lights, the noises of the boulevard, the painted women, everything made me feel like screaming. 'But Simone, that's life!' In her brisk, matter-of-fact voice, Stépha explained to me that men aren't angels. Of course, 'all that' was rather 'disgusting', but after all it was a fact, and even a very important fact; she supported her claims with a host of examples. Her stories made me rigid with disapproval. All the same, from time to time I tried to be frank with myself: where did these resistances and prohibitions stem from? 'Is it my Catholic upbringing which has left me with such a fixation on purity that the slightest allusion to fleshly things causes me this indescribable distress? I think of Alain Fournier's Colombe, who drowned her-self in a lake before she would sully her purity. But perhaps that is pride?'

Obviously I did not hold that one should languish in perpetual virginity. But I was sure that the wedding-night should be a white mass: true love sublimates the physical embrace, and in the arms of her chosen one the pure young girl is briskly changed into a radiant young woman. I loved Francis Jammes because he painted physical passion in colours as simple and as clear as the waters of a mountain torrent; I loved Claudel above all because he celebrates in the body the miraculously sensitive presence of the soul. I refused to read to the end of Jules Romains' *Le Dieu des corps* because in it physical pleasure was not described as an expression of the spirit. I was exasperated by Mauriac's *Souffrances du chrétien* which the *NRF* was publishing just then. In the former triumphant, in the latter humiliated, I found that in both of them the flesh was given too much importance. I was indignant with Clairaut who, in his reply to a questionnaire in *Les Nouvelles Littéraires*, denounced 'the rag-bag of the flesh and its tragic tyranny', and also with Nizan and his wife who claimed that married couples should enjoy complete sexual licence.

I justified my repugnance in the same way as when I was only seventeen years old: all is well if the body obeys the head and the heart, but it must not take the first step. This argument was all the more illogical because Romains' heroes were 'spontaneous' lovers and the Nizans were apostles of sexual freedom between man and woman. Moreover the reasonable prudery I felt at seventeen had nothing to do with the mysterious 'horror' which so often used to chill my heart. I did not feel directly threatened; sometimes I had been momentarily seized by a physical urge: at the Jockey for example, in the arms of certain dancers; or at Meyrignac, when, lying with my sister in the long grass, we would be locked in one another's arms; but I enjoyed these intoxicating sensations which made me feel in tune with my body; it was curiosity, and sensuality that made me want to discover the resources and secrets of my body; I waited without apprehension and even without impatience the moment when I would become a woman. It affected me in a rather round-about way: through Jacques. If physical love was only an innocent game, there was no reason why he shouldn't indulge in it; but then our conversations ought not to carry much weight with him beside the joyous and violent delights he had known with other women; I admired the pure and lofty tone of our relationship: but in fact it was incomplete, insipid, lacking in body, and the respect Jacques showed me was dictated by the most conventional morality; I was assigned the thankless role of the little girl cousin, of whom one is quite fond – what distance lay between such a green girl and a man rich in the full possession of all a man can experience! I didn't want to submit to such an inferior position.

I preferred to look upon debauchery as a defilement; then I could allow myself to hope that Jacques had not been contaminated by it; if he had, then I didn't envy him – I pitied him; I would rather forgive him his weaknesses than be exiled from his pleasures. Yet this prospect also frightened me. I yearned for the transparent confusion of our souls; if he had committed murky deeds, I was robbed of his past and even of his future, for our story, wrong from the start, would never fit in with the one I had invented for us. 'I don't want life to obey any other will but my own,' I wrote in my journal. Here I think lay the root of my anguish. I knew almost nothing of physical reality; in my class of society it was masked by conventions and rituals; these tedious formalities bored me, but I didn't attempt to seize the root of existence; on the contrary, I found escape in the clouds; I was a soul, a pure, disembodied spirit; I was only interested in people's souls and spirits. The advent of sexuality destroyed this angelic concept; it suddenly revealed to me, in all their dreadful unity, sexual appetite and sexual violence. I had had a shock, in the place Clichy, because I had felt the most intimate link between the pimp's revolting trade and the policeman's brutality. It was not I but the world that was at stake: if men had bodies that were heavy and racked with lust, the world was not the place I had thought it was. Poverty, crime, oppression, war: I was afforded confused glimpses of perspectives that terrified me.

Nevertheless, in the middle of November I returned to Montparnasse. I suddenly wearied of books, student gossip, cinemas. Was this any way to live? Was it my real self that was living in this way? There had been tears, frenzies, adventure, poetry, love – a life filled with emotions: I didn't want to let them die. That evening, I was to go with my sister to *L'Œuvre*; I met her at the Café du Dôme and took her off to the Jockey. As the believer at the end of a period of spiritual drought plunges into the smell of incense and candles, I lost myself in the fumes of alcohol and tobacco. They very soon went to our heads. Reverting to our old ways, we exchanged loud-mouthed insults and knocked each other about a bit. I wanted my heart to be rent beyond recall, and I took my sister to the Stryx. There we found Bresson and one of his friends, a middle-aged man who flirted with Poupette and bought her bunches of violets while I talked to Riquet; he warmly defended Jacques: 'He's had some hard knocks,' he told me, 'but he's always risen above them.' He assured me that there was great strength behind his apparent weaknesses, and great sincerity beneath his mask of flippancy; that he could talk of grave and painful things while sipping a cocktail – and with what lucidity he had seen through everything! 'Jacques will never be happy,' he concluded admiringly. My heart sank: 'And what if some woman were to give him her all?' I asked. 'It would just humiliate him.' Fear and hope clutched at my throat again. All the way along the boulevard Raspail I sobbed into my bunch of violets.

I loved tears, hope, fear. The next morning, when Clairaut, fixing me with his steady gaze, told me: 'You'll do a thesis on Spinoza; there's no greater thing in life than to marry and write a thesis,' I took offence. Marriage and a career were two ways of throwing in the sponge. Pradelle agreed with me that work can also be a drug. I was deeply grateful to Jacques whose memory had delivered me from my brutish enslavement to my books. Doubtless many of my friends at the Sorbonne were of greater intellectual worth than he, but that didn't matter too much. Clairaut's, Pradelle's futures seemed to me to be already mapped out; Jacques' very existence, and that of his friends, appeared to me like a series of throws in a game of dice; perhaps in the end they would destroy or ruin themselves. I preferred such risks to sinking deeper and deeper into a rut.

Once or twice a week during the next month I went to the Stryx with Stépha, Fernando, and a Ukrainian journalist who was a friend of theirs and who preferred to spend his free time learning Japanese; I also took my sister, Lisa, and Mallet. I don't quite know where I found the money that year, because I was no longer giving any lessons. Probably I saved something out of the five francs a day which my mother gave me for my lunches, and I managed to scrape up a bit here and there. In any case, my budget was based on the assumption that I would indulge in these orgies. I wrote in my diary: 'Glanced through Alain's *Eleven Chapters on Plato* at Picard's. It costs eight cocktails: too dear.' Stépha would dress up as a barmaid and help Michel to serve the clients, with whom she could joke in four languages, and sing Ukrainian folksongs. With Riquet and his middle-aged friend we talked about Giraudoux, Gide, the cinema, life, women, men, friendship, love. We would then saunter down towards Saint-Sulpice in a noisy gang. The next morning I would make a note: 'Wonderful evening!' But I would intersperse my account with parentheses which struck quite a different note. Riquet had said about Jacques: 'He'll marry one day, out of sheer impetuosity, and perhaps he'll make a good father: but he'll always regret it.' These prophecies did not unduly worry me; what disturbed me was that Jacques should have led practically the same sort of life as Riquet during the past three years. The latter spoke about women with a freedom which offended me: could I still go on believing that Jacques was a brother of Le Grand Meaulnes? I very much doubted it. After all, I had created this image of him in my mind quite without his authorization, and now I was beginning to think that perhaps he did not in the least resemble it. But I would not give in. 'All that is very hurtful to me. I have visions of Jacques that hurt me.' All in all, if work was a narcotic, alcohol and gambling were no better. My place was neither in bars nor libraries: then where was it? I could see no other salvation than in books; I planned a new novel; its protagonists would be a heroine who would be myself and a hero who would resemble Jacques, with 'his overweening pride and his mad urge to self-destruction.' But I couldn't get rid of my uneasiness. One evening, I saw Riquet, Riaucourt, and his friend Olga in a corner of the Stryx; I thought Olga looked very elegant. They were talking about a letter they had just received from Jacques; they were sending him a post-card. I couldn't help asking myself: 'Why does he write to *them*, never to me?' I walked all one afternoon along the boulevards with my heart sunk in despair, then wound up weeping in a cinema.

The next day, Pradelle, who was on excellent terms with my parents, came to dine at our house and then we left for the Ciné Latin. We got right to the rue Soufflot; then I suddenly suggested that he should come with me to the Jockey; he agreed, without enthusiasm. We sat down at a table like two good and sober customers, and while I drank my gin fizz I tried to explain to him who Jacques was, for I had only mentioned him to Pradelle in passing. He listened to me in a detached way. He was obviously embarrassed. I wondered if he was shocked that I frequented this sort of place. I asked him. No, but personally he found them depressing. That's because he hasn't known that utter loneliness and despair which justifies all derangements. Yet as I sat beside him, at a distance from the bar where I had so often behaved with such eccentric abandon, I could look upon the place with a fresh vision: he had seen through it at once, and extinguished all its poetry. Perhaps I only brought him here in order to hear him say aloud what I kept whispering quietly to myself: 'What are you doing here?' In any case, I at once told myself he was right, and even began to look upon Jacques with a more critical eye: why did he waste his time killing his finer feelings? I gave up my life of debauchery. My parents went to spend a few days in Arras and I did not take advantage of their absence. I refused to go to Montparnasse with Stépha; I even rejected her offers with some acerbity. I stayed at home and read Meredith.

I gave up wondering about Jacques' past; after all, if he had made mistakes, the heavens weren't going to fall. Now I hardly bothered to think about him; he had kept silent too long; and the silence in the end was beginning to resemble hostility. When at the end of December his grandmother Flandin gave me the latest news about him, I couldn't have cared less. Yet as I disliked giving anything up I supposed that on his return our love for each other would revive again.

*

I went on working furiously; every day I spent from nine to ten hours at my books. In January I did my teaching practice at the Lycée Janson de Sailly under the supervision of Rodrigues, a very sweet old gentleman: he was president of the League of Civil Liberties and killed himself in 1940 when the Germans entered France. My fellow-pupils were Merleau-Ponty and Lévi-Strauss; I knew them both a little. The former I had always admired from a distance. The latter's impassivity rather intimidated me, but he used to turn it to good advantage. I thought it very funny when, in his detached voice, and with a dead-pan face, he expounded to our audience the folly of the passions. There were foggy mornings when I felt it was ridiculous to discourse upon the life of the emotions to forty boys who obviously couldn't care less about it; but when the weather was fine, I used to take an interest in what I was saying, and I used to think that in certain eyes I could catch glimmers of intelligence. I recalled my former emotions when I used to pass by the Collège Stanislas: all this had seemed so far away, so inaccessible – being in a classroom full of boys! And now here I was out in front of the class, and it was I who was giving the lessons. I felt that there was nothing in the world I couldn't attain now.

I certainly didn't regret being a woman; on the contrary it afforded me great satisfaction. My upbringing had convinced me of my sex's intellectual inferiority, a fact admitted by many women. 'A lady cannot hope to pass the selective examination before the fifth or sixth attempt,' Mademoiselle Roulin had told me; she had already had two. This handicap gave my successes a prestige far in excess of that accorded to successful male students: I felt it was something exceptional even to do as well as they did: in fact, I hadn't met a single man student who seemed at all out of the ordinary; the future was as wide open to me as it was to them: they had no advantage over me. Nor did they lay claim to any; they treated me without condescension, and even with a special kindness, for they didn't look upon me as a rival; girls were judged in the contest by the same standards as the boys, but they were accepted as supernumeraries, and there was no struggle for the first places between the sexes. That is why a lecture I gave on Plato brought me unreserved compliments from my fellow-students – in particular from Jean Hippolyte. I was proud of having won their esteem. Their friendliness prevented me from ever taking up that 'challenging' attitude which later was to cause me so much dismay when I encountered it in American women: from the start, men were my comrades, not my enemies. Far from envying them, I felt that my own position, from the very fact that it was an unusual one, was one of privilege. One evening Pradelle invited to his house his best friends and their sisters. Poupette went with me. All the girls retired to Mademoiselle Pradelle's room; but I stayed with the young men.

Yet I did not renounce my femininity. That evening my sister and I had paid the utmost attention to our appearance. I was in red, she in blue silk; actually we were very badly got-up, but then the other girls weren't all that grand either. In Montparnasse I had caught glimpses of elegant beauties; but their lives were too different from mine for the comparison to overwhelm me; besides, once I was free, with money in my pocket, there would be nothing to stop me imitating them. I didn't forget that Jacques had said I was pretty; Stépha and Fernando had high hopes of me. I liked to look at myself, just as I was, in mirrors; I liked what I saw. In the things we had in common, I fancied that I was no less ill-equipped than other women and I felt no resentment towards them; so I had no desire to run them down. In many respects I set Zaza, my sister, Stépha, and even Lisa above my masculine friends, for they seemed to me more sensitive, more generous, more endowed with imagination, tears, and love. I flattered myself that I combined 'a woman's heart and a man's brain'. Again I considered myself to be unique – the One and Only.

The person who took first place in my affections was my sister. She was now taking a commercial art course at an establishment in the rue Cassette where she was very happy. At a concert organized by the school, she dressed up as a shepherdess and sang some old French songs; I thought she was ravishing. Sometimes she would go out for the evening to some party, and when she came home – blonde, pink-cheeked, animated, in her blue tulle dress – our room seemed to light up. We went together to the art exhibitions, to the Salon d'Automne and the Louvre; in the evenings she attended drawing-classes in a studio in Montmartre; I would often go to collect her there and we would walk back home across Paris, carrying on the conversation which had begun when we had first learned to talk; we would continue it in bed before falling asleep, and again the next day as soon as we found ourselves alone together. She played her part in all my friendships, my admirations, and enthusiasms. With Jacques as a hallowed exception, there was no one I was more attached to than to her; she was too close to me to be able to help me in living, but I used to think that without her my life would have lost all its savour. Whenever my feelings took a tragic turn, I would tell myself that if Jacques died I would kill myself, but that if *she* were to vanish from the face of the earth, I shouldn't need to kill myself in order to die.

I used to spend quite a lot of time with Lisa, as she had no friends and was always free. One rainy December morning she asked me, as we were leaving one of Laporte's lectures, to go back to the hostel with her. I wanted to go home and work, and so I refused. In the place Médicis, just as I was about to get on the bus, she said in a funny voice: 'All right then. I'll tell you all about it on Thursday.' I pricked up my ears: 'Tell me now.' She took me to the Luxembourg Gardens; there was no one in the dripping avenues. 'You mustn't tell anyone; it's too stupid.' She hesitated: 'Well, here it is: I should like to marry Pradelle.' I sat down on the wire at the edge of the lawn and stared at her, dumbfounded.

'I like him so much!' she declared. 'And I've never liked anyone before!' They were both preparing for the same examination in science, and were attending some of the same philosophy lectures; I hadn't noticed anything special between them when we all went out together; but I knew that Pradelle, with his thick dark lashes and his welcoming smile, made girls fall head over heels in love with him; I had learnt from Clairaut that at least two of his friends' sisters were eating their hearts out for him. For a whole hour in the deserted gardens, under the trees dripping with wet, Lisa talked to me about this new radiance that life had taken on for her. How fragile she looked, in her threadbare coat! I thought her face was attractive under the little hat that looked like an inverted flower, but I doubted whether her rather bony grace would appeal to Pradelle. That evening, Stépha reminded me of how he had appeared bored and had changed the conversation one day when we were talking about Lisa's loneliness and sadness. I tried to sound him. He had just come from a wedding, and we had a bit of an argument: he thought these ceremonies had a certain charm, whereas I thought this public exhibition of a private affair was sickening. I asked him if he ever thought about getting married himself. Vaguely, he replied; but he had very little hope of really loving any woman; he was too exclusively attached to his mother; he even reproached himself for a certain aridity in his feelings towards his friends. I spoke to him about that great upsurge of tenderness which sometimes made my eyes fill with tears. He shook his head: 'All that's a bit exaggerated.' He himself never exaggerated anything and I was struck by the thought that he would be a difficult person to love. In any case, Lisa obviously meant nothing to him. She told me sadly that at the Sorbonne he did not show the slightest interest in her. We spent the whole of one afternoon at the bar of the Rotonde talking about love and about our loves; from the dance-floor came the strains of a jazz-band and there were voices whispering in the semi-darkness. 'Unhappiness is a habit of mine,' she said. 'You're just born like that.' She had never had anything she wanted. 'And yet, if only I could hold that head between my hands, it would all have been worth it, for always.' She thought of looking for a job in the colonies, of leaving for Saigon or Antananarivo.

I always had fun with Stépha; Fernando was often there when I went up to see her in her room; while she made cocktails with curaçao he would show me reproductions of Soutine and Cézanne; his own painting, though still rather clumsy, pleased me, and I too admired him for dedicating his whole life to painting without bothering about material difficulties. Sometimes the three of us would go out together. We were enthusiastic about Charles Dullin's performance as Volpone; but we were very critical of Baty in Gantillon's *Départs* at the Comédie des Champs-Élysées. At the end of my morning lectures, Stépha would invite me to lunch at the Knam; we would eat Polish dishes to the accompaniment of a Polish orchestra and she would ask me for advice: should she marry Fernando? I used to tell her yes; never had I seen such complete understanding between a man and a woman: they corresponded exactly to my idea of the ideal couple. She was hesitant: there were so many 'interesting' people in the world! This word exasperated me a little. I didn't feel much attracted by those Romanians and Bulgarians with whom Stépha waged the battle of the sexes. At times my patriotism would come to the fore. One day we were lunching with a German student in a restaurant inside the Bibliothèque Nationale. Blond, with the ritual duelling-scars on his cheeks, he talked in a vindictive manner about the greatness of the Fatherland. I suddenly thought: 'Perhaps one day he'll be fighting against Jacques and Pradelle,' and I felt a sudden urge to leave the table.

But I struck up a friendship with the Hungarian journalist who burst into Stépha's life towards the end of December. He was very tall and massively built, and in his broad face his thick lips seemed to have difficulty in smiling. He used to talk with great self-satisfaction about his father by adoption who was director of the biggest theatre in Budapest. He was working on a thesis about French melodrama, and was a passionate admirer of French culture, Madame de Staël and Charles Maurras; except for Hungary, he thought all the countries of Central Europe were inhabited by barbarians, particularly the Balkans. He flew into rages whenever he saw Stépha talking to a Romanian. It didn't take much for him to lose his temper: then his hands would shake, his left foot would tap the floor convulsively, and he would have difficulty in getting his words out: I was embarrassed by this lack of self-control. He irritated me too because he was always mouthing the words: refinement, grace, delicacy. He was far from stupid, and I would listen curiously to his disquisitions on cultures and civilizations.

But on the whole I didn't care much for his conversation, and this used to annoy him: 'If you only knew how witty I can be in Hungarian!' he told me one day, in a voice that was at once furious and frustrated. When he tried to get round me in order to make me plead his case with Stépha, I sent him packing. 'It's idiotic!' he snarled, his voice full of hatred. 'All girls love acting as go-betweens when one of their friends has a man interested in her.' I told him roundly that his love for Stépha was nothing to do with me, that it was an egotistical desire for possession and domination; moreover, I couldn't trust it: was he prepared to spend the rest of his life with her? His lips trembled: 'If you were given a Dresden china figure, you would throw it on the ground to see if it would break or not!' I made no secret of the fact to Bandi – as Stépha called him – that I was Fernando's ally in this affair. 'I detest that Fernando!' Bandi told me. 'For one thing, he's a Jew!' I was shocked.

Stépha was rather sorry for him; she thought he was fairly brilliant, and wanted to 'get him under her thumb', but he pursued her with too much persistency. I realized, on this occasion, that I was, as she had told me, naïve. One evening I went with Jean Mallet to the Théâtre des Champs-Élysées to see Podrecca's *Piccolo Teatro* which was playing for the first time in Paris. I noticed Stépha there; Bandi had his arm round her, and she was not trying to disengage herself. Mallet was very fond of Stépha, whose eyes he liked to compare to those of a tiger with a dose of morphine: he suggested we should go and say hullo to her. The Hungarian quickly withdrew his arm; she smiled at me without the least embarrassment. I realized then that she treated her boyfriends with rather less severity than she had given me to understand, and I felt angry with her for what seemed to me to be disloyalty, because I didn't know what was meant by 'flirting'. I was very glad when she finally decided to marry Fernando. Bandi made several violent scenes at that: he would follow her home to her room, despite all her orders to let her alone. Then he calmed down. She stopped coming to the Nationale. He still used to invite me to coffee at Poccardi's but he never talked about her to me again.

After that he settled in France as correspondent to a Hungarian newspaper. Ten years later, on the eve of the declaration of war, I met him at the Dôme. He was going to join up next day in a regiment composed of foreign volunteers. He handed over to me for safe keeping an object which he prized very highly: it was a travelling clock in the form of a glass sphere. He confessed to me that he was a Jew, an illegitimate child, and a sexual maniac: he could only love women weighing more than fifteen stone; Stépha had been the one exception in his life: he had hoped that, despite her small stature, she would be able to give him, thanks to her intelligence, an illusion of immense size. The war swept him away; he never came back for his clock.

*

From Berlin Zaza wrote me long letters from which I read extracts to Stépha and Pradelle. When she left Paris she had called the Germans 'Huns', and it was with great trepidation that she set foot in enemy territory:

My arrival at the Fiobel Hospiz was rather awful; I was expecting a women's hostel, but found it was a great caravanserai full of enormous Huns, all quite respectable; when I entered my room the *Mädchen*, as Stépha had told me, handed me a bunch of keys for the wardrobe, the room door, entrance door and finally the street door, in case I should want to come in after four o'clock in the morning. I was so exhausted by the journey, so bewildered by the extent of my freedom and by the immensity of Berlin that I hadn't the courage to go down to dinner and sought refuge, soaking my pillow with tears, in a curious bed without any sheets which consisted only of one huge eiderdown. I slept for thirteen hours, went to Mass in a Roman Catholic church, walked wide-eyed round the streets, and by midday my morale had improved. I've got more used to things by now; there are moments when I'm suddenly seized by an unreasonable longing for my family, for you, for Paris, a sharp and painful stab of homesickness; but I like life in Berlin, I've not had any difficulty with anyone, and I feel that the three months I'm to spend here are going to be most interesting.

She got no help from the French colony, which was composed entirely of the Diplomatic Corps: there were only three French students in Berlin and people found it very surprising that Zaza should have come to spend a term in Germany attending lectures at the University.

The consul, in a letter of recommendation he gave me for a German professor, ended with a sentence which amused me very much: 'I beg of you to give the warmest encouragement to Mademoiselle Mabille's most praiseworthy initiative.' You'd think I'd flown over the North Pole!

She soon decided to mix with the natives.

On Wednesday I got to know the Berlin Theatre in the most unexpected company. Just think – as Stépha would say – about six o'clock I see the manager of the Hospiz, tall old Herr Pollack, coming up to me and saying with his most amiable smile: 'My dear little French lady, would you care to come to the theatre with me this evening?' A little bewildered by this, I inquired about the moral propriety of the performance, and considering old Herr Pollack's serious and dignified air I decided to accept. By eight o'clock we were hurrying through the streets of Berlin, talking away like old friends. Every time it was a question of paying for anything the tall Hun would say graciously: 'You are my guest, it's free.' During the third interval, emboldened by a cup of coffee, he told me that his wife never came to the theatre with him, that she didn't share his tastes at all and had never tried to give him any pleasure during the thirty-five years of their marriage, excepting two years ago, because he was at death's door; but, as he told me in German, one can't always be at death's door. I was very amused, and found old Herr Pollack much more fun than Sudermann, whose *Die Ehre*, a problem play in the style of Alexandre Dumas fils, was being given. On leaving the Trianon Theatre, in order to put the crowning touch to this very German evening, my Hun absolutely insisted on going to eat sauerkraut and sausages!

Stépha and I laughed at the thought that, rather than let Zaza take part in a game of mixed doubles Madame Mabille had banished her to Berlin; and now Zaza was going out alone in the evening, with a man, a stranger, a foreigner, a Boche! She had, of course, made inquiries about the moral propriety of the play. But judging by later letters she had soon found her feet. She was attending lectures at the University, going to concerts, theatres, museums, she had formed friendships with students and with one of Stépha's friends, Hans Miller, whose address Stépha had given her. At first he had found Zaza so stiff and starchy that he had told her jokingly: 'You handle life with glacé kid gloves.' She had been very mortified by this: she had decided to take her gloves off.

I am seeing so many new people, places, countries, all so different from what I've known that I can feel all my prejudices getting lamentably lost, and I no longer really know if I have ever belonged to a certain background, nor what it could have been. I sometimes lunch in the morning at the Embassy with diplomatic celebrities, sumptuous ambassadresses from Brazil or Argentina, and in the evening find myself dining alone at Aschinger's, a very popular cheap restaurant, rubbing shoulders with a fat office worker or some French or Chinese student. I am not hemmed in by any group, no stupid reasons are suddenly given me for not being able to do something interesting; there's nothing impossible and nothing that is 'not done', and I accept with wonder and confidence all the new and unexpected things that each day brings me. At first, I was bothered about questions of form: I used to wonder and ask people if things were 'done' or 'not done'. People would smile at me and say: 'But people do just as they like', and I took the lesson to heart. Now I'm worse than any Polish girl student, I go out alone at all hours of the day and night, I go to concerts with Hans Miller, and I walk the streets with him until one o'clock in the morning. He seems to find all that so natural that I feel embarrassed at still feeling astonished by it.

Her ideas too were changing; her chauvinism was melting away.

What amazes me more than anything here is that in general all the Germans are pacifists, and – even more amazing – francophiles. The other day at the cinema I saw a film with pacifist tendencies which showed the horrors of war: everybody applauded it. It appears that last year, when *Napoleon* was shown and had a great success here, the orchestra played the *Marseillaise*. On one evening in particular, at the Ufa Palace, people applauded it so much that it had to be played three times, to general and prolonged applause. I should have been startled if, before leaving Paris, I had been told that I should be able without embarrassment to talk to a German about the war; the other day, Hans Miller told me about the time when he had been a prisoner of war, and ended by saying: 'Perhaps you were too young to remember, but the things that were done, on both sides, were frightful; such things must never happen again!' Another time, as I was talking to him about Giraudoux' *Siegfried et le Limousin*, and telling him that he would be interested in the book he replied – but the German words expressed his feelings so much more energetically: 'Is it a "political" or a "human" book? We've had enough talk about nations, races; now we want to hear a little about man in general.' I believe that ideas of this kind are widespread among German youth.

Hans Miller spent a week in Paris; he went out with Stépha and told her that since her arrival her friend had been transformed; given a cold reception by the Mabilles, he was astonished at the abyss which separated Zaza from the rest of her family. She, too, was more and more aware of this. She wrote and told me that she had wept for joy when she had seen her mother's face at the window of the carriage in the train bringing her to see Zaza in Berlin; yet the thought of returning home frightened her. Lili had finally given her hand to a student from the Polytechnique, and according to Hans Miller's report, the house was upside down.

I feel that at home everybody is already completely absorbed in sending out wedding invitations, receiving congratulations and gifts, choosing the ring, the trousseau, the colour of the bridesmaids' dresses (I don't think I've forgotten anything); and this great flood of formalities doesn't make me feel very much like going back home; I've so much lost touch with all that sort of thing! And really life is wonderfully interesting here. . . . When I think of my return, it's chiefly of the great joy I shall have in seeing you again; that's what I feel most. But I must confess that I am afraid to resume the existence I was leading three months ago. The very respectable formalism which governs the lives of most of the people in 'our class' I now find quite unendurable, all the more so when I recall the not-so-distant past when, without realizing it, I was still impregnated by it; and I fear that when I step back into the picture I shall become imbued with that spirit once again.

I don't know if Madame Mabille realized that Zaza's stay in Berlin had not had the result she had expected; in any case, she was preparing to take her daughter in hand again. Meeting my mother at a party to which she had gone with Poupette, she had addressed her rather stiffly. My mother spoke Stépha's name: 'I do not know Stépha. I know a Mademoiselle Avdicovitch who was governess to my children,' was Madame Mabille's stuffy reply, to which she had added: 'You may bring up Simone as you wish. *I* have other principles.' She had complained of my influence upon her daughter, and had concluded: 'Fortunately, Zaza loves me very much.'

*

The whole of Paris had flu that winter and I was in bed when Zaza returned to Paris; seated by my bedside, she described Berlin, the Opera, the concerts, the museums to me. She had put on weight and got some colour in her cheeks: Stépha and Pradelle were struck, as I was, by her metamorphosis. I told her that in October I had been upset by her reserve; she assured me gaily that she had turned over a new leaf. Not only had many of her ideas changed, but instead of meditating on death and aspiring to the life of a nun she was bursting with a new vitality. She was hoping that her sister's departure would make existence much easier for her. Yet she lamented Lili's fate: 'It's your last chance!' Madame Mabille had told her. Lili had run to seek advice from all her friends. 'Accept him,' all the resigned young married women and the spinsters who couldn't get a husband had told her. Zaza's heart sank whenever she heard the two fiancés talking together. Yet without quite knowing why, she was now certain that no such future lay in store for her. For the moment, she felt she wanted to work seriously at her violin, to read a lot and extend her cultural background; she was thinking of doing a translation of a novel by Stefan Zweig. Her mother didn't dare deprive her too abruptly of her new-found freedom; she gave her permission to go out two or three times in the evening with me. We went to see the Russian Ballet in *Prince Igor*. We saw Al Jolson in *The Jazz Singer*, the first talking film, and attended a meeting organized by the 'Effort' group where films by Germaine Dulac were shown: afterwards there was a lively debate on pure cinema and talking films. Often in the afternoons while I was working at the Nationale I would feel a gloved hand on my shoulder: Zaza would smile down at me from under her pink felt cloche and we would go for a coffee or take a walk. Unfortunately she left for Bayonne, where for a whole month she kept a sick cousin company.

I missed her very much. The newspapers were saying that such severe cold had not been known in Paris for the last fifteen years; there were ice-floes bumping down the Seine; I no longer went out walking, and I worked too hard instead. I was finishing for a professor called Laporte a dissertation for my diploma on Hume and Kant; from nine in the morning till six in the evening I was glued to my desk at the Nationale: I hardly took half an hour off for a sandwich; sometimes I would half-doze in the afternoons, and sometimes I even fell sound asleep. In the evenings, at home, I tried to read: Goethe, Cervantes, Chekhov, Strindberg. But I had headaches. I sometimes wanted to weep for weariness. And philosophy, at least as it was taught at the Sorbonne, was not at all comforting. Bréhier gave excellent lectures on the Stoics; but Brunschvig kept repeating himself; Laporte pulled every system except Hume's to pieces. He was the youngest of our professors; he had a little moustache, wore white spats, and followed women in the street: once he had accosted one of his own students by mistake. He handed me back my dissertation with a fairly good mark and some ironic comments: I had made the mistake of preferring Kant to Hume. He invited me to his home, in a fine apartment on the avenue Bosquet, to talk to me about my work. 'Great qualities; but very antipathetic. Style obscure; a false profundity: when one thinks of what one has to say in philosophy!' He considered all his colleagues one by one, particularly Brunschvig, then all the old masters. The philosophers of antiquity? They were stupid fools. Spinoza? A monster. Kant? An impostor. That left only Hume. I objected that Hume didn't solve any of the practical problems: he shrugged his shoulders: 'There *are* no practical problems.' No. One must simply look upon philosophy as an amusement, and one had the right to prefer other forms of entertainment. 'So that after all it's all a matter of convention!' I suggested. 'Ah, no Mademoiselle, now you're exaggerating,' he countered with sudden indignation. 'I know,' he added, 'that scepticism isn't fashionable. All right: go and find yourself a more optimistic doctrine than mine.' He accompanied me to the door: 'Delighted you came! You're bound to get through the examination,' he concluded, with an air of distaste. His attitude was probably healthier but less comforting than the vaticinations of Jean Baruzi.

I tried to snap out of my depression. But Stépha was preparing her trousseau and getting her flat ready, and I hardly ever saw her now. My sister was far from cheerful, Lisa was in despair, Clairaut distant, Pradelle always the same; Mallet had been ploughed in his diploma. I tried to take an interest in Mademoiselle Roulin and other friends. I did not succeed. During one long afternoon I went on a great Journey from Assyria to Egypt, from Egypt to Greece in the galleries of the Louvre; when I came out I found a dark, wet Paris evening. I wandered about, thoughtless, loveless. I despised myself. I thought of Jacques, but from a long way off, as if he had been something I was proud of and had lost. Suzanne Boigue, who had come back from Morocco, received me in a brightly lit, discreetly exotic flat; she was beloved and happy, and I envied her. The thing that oppressed me most was to feel myself in some way diminished: 'I feel as if I'd lost absolutely everything and the worst part of it is that I cannot bring myself to feel sorrow about it. . . .

I am inert, driven hither and thither by the occupations and the day-dreams of the moment. No part of me is engaged; I no longer cling either to an idea or to an affection by that tight, cruel, and inspiring rein which for so long attached me to so many things; I'm interested in everything *in moderation*; oh! I'm so reasonable now, I no longer even feel that dreadful anguish about my own nothingness.' I clung on to the hope that this state would only be a passing one; in four months' time, when the selective examination was over, I could once more begin to take an interest in my life; I would begin to write my book. But I should have appreciated some outside help: 'Longing for a new affection, an adventure, anything, so long as it's something different!'

The poetry of the bars had been dissipated. But after a day spent at the Nationale or in the Sorbonne, I didn't feel at all like being cooped up in the house. Where could I go? Again I started roaming round Montparnasse, one evening with Lisa, another with Fernando and Stépha. My sister had struck up a friendship with one of her fellow-students, a bold, pretty, athletic seventeen-year-old whose mother kept a sweet-shop; she was called Gégé, and she went out as much as she liked in the evenings. I often found them together in the Dôme. One evening we decided to go to the Jungle, which had just opened up opposite the Jockey; but we were short of funds. 'Not to worry,' said Gégé. 'Wait for us over there: we'll fix things.' I went into the night-club on my own and took my place at the bar. Poupette and Gégé, sitting on a bench in the street, kept moaning dramatically: 'If only we had that extra twenty francs!' A passer-by took pity on them. I have no idea what sort of yarn they spun, but soon they were perched beside me mopping up gin fizzes. Gégé knew how to lead men on. Drinks were bought for us, and we were invited to dance. A female dwarf called Chiffon whom I had already heard at the Jockey sang songs and kept up a flow of obscenities, lifting up her skirts and exhibiting thighs all marbled over with bites and bruises, inflicted on her, so she told us, by her lover. In one sense, it was very refreshing. We picked up our old habits. One evening at the bar in the Jockey I met some old acquaintances with whom I reminisced over the gay times we had had in the past; a young Swiss student, one of the regulars at the Nationale, paid me a great deal of attention; I drank and felt amused. Later that night, a young doctor who had been observing our trio with a critical eye asked me if I came there to study human nature; when my sister left at midnight, he congratulated me on her good behaviour, but he told me reproachfully that Gégé was too young to go to night-clubs. About one o'clock, he offered to take us home in a taxi; first we dropped Gégé, and my discomfiture at finding myself alone with him in the taxi during the rest of the ride obviously amused him. I was flattered by his interest in me. A meeting with a stranger or an unexpected incident was enough to put me in a good temper again. But the pleasure I took in these brief encounters does not explain why I should have succumbed again to the fascination of these haunts of vice. I expressed my surprise in my diary: 'Jazz, loose women, sexy dancing, bad words, drink, physical intimacies: how is it I'm not shocked, but willingly accept things that in any other situation I could never accept, and bandy lewd expressions with strange men? How does it come about that I like these things, have such an incongruous passion for them; and why does this passion have such a strong hold over me? What am I looking for in these places with their curious, dubious charm?'

A few days later, I had tea with Mademoiselle Roulin, and was bored stiff. When I left her, I went straight to the Européen; I paid four francs for a seat in the balcony among the loose women and even looser men; there were couples locked in each other's arms; others were kissing; heavily scented tarts swooned with ecstasy as they listened to the crooner with the slick black hair, and their riotous laughter made the comic's dirty jokes seem even dirtier. I was too excited; I laughed and felt happy. Why? I wandered a long time on the boulevard Barbes, watching the whores and pimps – no longer with horror, but with a sort of envy. Again I was surprised at myself: 'There is within me I know not what yearning – maybe a monstrous lust – ever-present, for noise, fighting, savage violence, and above all for the gutter. . . . What is there to prevent me today from becoming a morphinomaniac, and alcoholic, and heaven knows what else? Perhaps all that's lacking is the opportunity, a little greater hankering for everything I shall never know. . . .' At times I was shocked by this 'perversion', by these 'baser instincts' which I discovered in myself. What would Pradelle have thought – he who used to accuse me of putting life on a pedestal? I reproached myself with being two-faced, hypocritical. But I never once thought of denying my nature: 'I want life, the whole of life. I feel an avid curiosity; I desperately want to burn myself away, more brightly than any other person, and no matter with what kind of a flame.'

I was on the verge of admitting the truth to myself: I was fed up with being a disembodied spirit. Not that I was tormented by lust, as I was at the onset of puberty. But I guessed that the violence of the flesh and its crudity would have saved me from this ethereal insipidity that was atrophying my life. There was no question of my indulging in sexual experiments; my own prejudices, as well as my feelings towards Jacques, forbade me to do so. I frankly detested the Roman Catholic religion; watching Lisa and Zaza fighting for their lives against 'this self-martyring religion', I was more and more thankful that I had escaped from its clutches; in fact, I was still contaminated by it; the sexual taboos still haunted me to such an extent that I longed to become a drug-addict or an alcoholic, but never for a moment did I contemplate sexual indulgence. Reading Goethe, and the book about him by Emil Ludwig, I protested against his moral code. 'That place, so calmly intended for the gratification of the senses – without heartbreak, without any discomposure – shocks me,' I wrote. 'The worst kind of debauchery, provided it be a defence, a provocation, provided it be the means used by a Gide to find spiritual nourishment, moves me deeply; Goethe's amours irritate me.' Either physical love was identified with love itself, in which case it becomes self-explanatory, or it was a tragic fall from grace, and I hadn't the courage to attempt it.

*

Decidedly, I was a creature of the seasons. That year again, at the first whisper of spring, I blossomed forth, I sniffed up with greedy gaiety the smell of warm tarmac. I did not relax; the examination was drawing near and there were many gaps in my knowledge that had to be filled in; but sheer fatigue forced me to take rests, and I made the most of them. I walked with my sister on the banks of the Marne, I took renewed pleasure in talking to Pradelle under the chestnut trees in the Luxembourg Gardens; I bought myself a little red hat which made Stépha and Fernando smile. I took my parents to the Européen and my father treated us to ices on the terrace of the Café Wepler. My mother went fairly frequently with

[308]

me to the cinema; I saw Barbette with her at the Moulin Rouge, and found him – or her – not nearly as extraordinary as Cocteau made out. Zaza returned from Bayonne. We visited the newly opened galleries of French painting in the Louvre; I didn't like Monet, Renoir I appreciated with some reserve, I admired Manet very much, and Cézanne I worshipped because I thought I saw in his paintings 'the descent of the spirit to the heart of the senses'. Zaza more or less shared all my tastes. I attended her sister's wedding and wasn't too bored.

During the Easter holidays I spent every day at the Nationale; there I used to meet Clairaut whom I still found rather pedantic but who continued to intrigue me; had this dry, dark little man really suffered from the 'tyranny of the flesh'? Whatever the answer, it was quite certain that he was much preoccupied by this question. Several times he brought the conversation round to Mauriac's article. How much sexual pleasure is permissible between a Christian husband and wife? And between fiancés? He asked Zaza this question one day, and she flew into a temper: 'It's only priests and old maids who ask that kind of thing!' she retorted. A few days later, he told me he had gone through a harrowing personal experience. At the beginning of the academic year, he had become engaged to a friend's sister; she admired him enormously, and she was of a passionate nature: if he hadn't kept a firm rein on her, heaven knows what her impetuosity might not have involved them in! He had explained to her that they should save themselves for their wedding-night, and that in the meantime only the chastest of kisses were permissible. She had persisted in offering him her open mouth, and he had kept on turning his away; at the end she had got fed-up with him and had broken off the engagement. He was obviously obsessed by this set-back. He argued about marriage, love, and women with a maniacal intensity. I thought his story was rather ridiculous, for it reminded me of Suzanne Boigue's first affair. But I felt flattered that he had confided in me.

The Easter holidays came to an end; in the gardens of the École Normale, aflower with lilacs, laburnums, and pink hawthorn, I was delighted to meet my fellow-students again. I knew almost all of them. Only Sartre's little band, which included Nizan and Herbaud, remained closed to me; they had no truck with anybody else; they only attended certain lectures, and always sat apart from the rest of us. They had a bad reputation. It was said of them that they were unsympathetic. Violently opposed to the 'Holy Willies' among their fellow-students, they belonged to a clique composed mainly of Alain's ex-pupils and well known for its brutality: its members threw water-bombs on distinguished students at the Normale returning home at night in evening dress. Nizan was married and had travelled; he sported plus-fours and I found the eyes behind his heavy horn-rimmed glasses very intimidating. Sartre wasn't bad to look at, but it was rumoured that he was the worst of the lot, and he was even accused of drinking. Only one of them I thought seemed fairly accessible: Herbaud. He too was married. When he was with Sartre and Nizan, he ignored me. When I met him on his own, he would exchange a few words with me.

He had given a talk in January in one of Brunschvig's lectures, and during the discussion that had followed everyone had found him very amusing. I was very conscious of the charm of his mocking voice, and of the ironical twist he gave to his mouth. Weary of gazing upon the grey mass of students, I found his pink face with its baby-blue eyes very refreshing; his blond hair seemed as tough and springy as grass. One morning he had come to work in the Nationale, and despite the elegance of his blue overcoat, his light-coloured scarf, and his well-cut suit, I had found something of the country boy about him. I had a sudden inspiration: contrary to my usual habits, I went to lunch in the restaurant in the library; he cleared a place for me at his table as naturally as if we'd arranged to meet there. We talked about Hume and Kant. I passed him in the ante-room outside Laporte's study; the professor said in ceremonious tones: 'Well, au revoir, Monsieur Herbaud'; and I thought to myself regretfully that he was a married man, inaccessible, and totally unaware of my existence. One afternoon I had noticed him in the rue Soufflot in the company of Sartre and Nizan; a woman in a grey coat was on his arm: I felt shut out. He was the only one of the three to attend Brunschvig's lectures; just before the Easter holidays, he sat down beside me in the lecture-room. He had drawn *Eugène* figures inspired by those which Cocteau created in *Le Potomak*, and composed acidulous little poems. I found him very amusing, and I was overjoyed to find someone at the Sorbonne who liked Cocteau. In a way, Herbaud reminded me of Jacques; he, like Jacques, often used a smile instead of a word and seemed to live elsewhere than in books. Every time he had come to the Nationale he had greeted me in a friendly manner, and I had racked my brains to find something intelligent to say to him: unfortunately I had been quite unable to do so.

Nevertheless when Brunschvig started his lectures again after the holidays, Herbaud once more came and sat beside me. He dedicated a 'Portrait of the Average Student', a few other drawings and some poems to me. He made the abrupt announcement that he was an individualist. 'I am too,' I replied. 'What? You!' He stared at me mistrustfully. 'But I thought you were a Catholic, a Thomist, and devoted to good works?' I protested against this, and he was pleased that we had come to an understanding. He gave me a disjointed running commentary on our precursors, praising Sylla, Barrès, Stendhal, and other 'individualists' including Alcibiades, for whom he had a weakness; I no longer remember all he talked about, but I found him more and more amusing; he seemed to be absolutely sure of himself and didn't take himself in the least bit seriously: it was this mixture of arrogance and irony which delighted me. When he said, as he left, that he hoped we would have many more talks, I was over the moon, and wrote in my journal that evening: 'He has a kind of intelligence that goes straight to my heart.' I was already prepared to throw over Clairaut, Pradelle, Mallet, and all the rest of them for Herbaud. It was obviously a case of a new broom sweeping clean; I knew that I was very soon won over by people, and sometimes this made me drop them all the more quickly. All the same, I was surprised by the violence of my new enthusiasm: 'Meeting with André Herbaud; or with myself...? Who else has ever made such a strong impression on me? Why am I overwhelmed by this meeting, as if something had *really* happened to me at last?'

Something *had* happened to me, something which indirectly was to shape the whole of my life to come: but I wasn't to know that till later.

From then on, Herbaud became one of the regulars at the Nationale; I used to keep the chair next to mine for him. We used to lunch in a sort of tea-room on the first floor of a cake-shop; I could only just afford the 'special', but he used to insist on stuffing me with strawberry tarts. Once, at the Fleur-de-Lys in the square Louvois, he treated me to what I thought was a sumptuous spread. We would stroll together in the gardens of the Palais Royal, and sit beside the fountain; the wind would ruffle the jet of water and sprinkle cold drops on our faces. I would suggest that we go back to work. 'Let's go and have a coffee first,' Herbaud would say. 'If you don't have one, you'll work badly, then you'll fidget and prevent me from reading.' He would take me to Poccardi's, and when I used to stand up after draining my cup, he would say: 'What a pity!' He was the son of a schoolteacher from somewhere near Toulouse and he had come to Paris to study for the Normale. That is how he had met Sartre and Nizan; he often talked to me about them; he admired Nizan's smooth, gay distinction, but he had more to do with Sartre, who he said was prodigiously interesting. He despised our other fellow-students, individually and *en masse*. He thought Clairaut was a stuffy pedant and never spoke to him. One afternoon Clairaut came over to me with a book in his hand: 'Mademoiselle de Beauvoir,' he began, in a quizzing, inquisitorial tone, 'what do you make of Brochard who is of the opinion that Aristotle's God would be able to experience sexual pleasure?' Herbaud cast him a disdainful look: 'I should hope so, for His sake,' he haughtily replied. In our early days together, we used to talk chiefly about the little world we both belonged to: our friends, our professors, the competition. He told me about the subject that students would suggest – it was a traditional joke – for their theses: 'The difference between the notion of concept and the concept of notion.' He had invented others: 'Of all the authors in your syllabus, which one do you prefer, and why?' And: 'Body and soul: resemblances, differences; advantages and disadvantages of.' In fact, he only had the most tenuous association with the Sorbonne and the Normale; his life was elsewhere. He talked to me a little about it. He spoke to me about his wife who in his view was every feminine paradox incarnate; about Rome, which they had visited on their honeymoon, and the Forum, which had moved him to tears; about his system of morality and the book he wanted to write. He used to bring me magazines like *Detective* and the *Autocar*; he would take a passionate interest in a cycle-race or in a crime novel; he made my head swim with his anecdotes, with unexpected juxtapositions. He could handle everything – bombast and dry wit, lyricism and cynicism, naïveté and insolence – with such happy ease that nothing he said ever seemed banal. But the most irresistible thing about him was his laugh: when he gave vent to his laughter, it was as if he had just unexpectedly dropped in on a strange planet and was making a rapturous discovery of its prodigious comicality;

whenever he exploded in laughter, everything seemed to me to be novel, surprising, deliciously funny.

Herbaud didn't resemble any of my other friends, whose faces were all so commonsensical that they almost ceased to exist as faces. Actually, there was nothing seraphic about Jacques' face, but a certain bourgeois icing masked some of its abundant sensuality. It would have been impossible to reduce Herbaud's face to a symbol; the jutting jaw, the broad, liquid smile, the blue irises set in their lustrous corneas; his flesh, his bone-structure, and his very skin made an ineffaceable impression and were self-sufficient. Herbaud had more than a face: he had an unmistakable body, too. Walking under the leafy trees, he told me how much he detested death, and that he would never submit to being ill or old. How proud he was of the young red blood pulsing in his veins! I would watch him come striding through the gardens with his rather awkward grace; I would look at his ears, transparent in the sun as pink sugar-candy, and I knew that I had beside me not an angel, but a real man. I was tired of saintliness and I was overjoyed that he should treat me – as only Stépha had done – as a creature of the earth. Because he was not interested in my soul; his liking for me was not based just on an evaluation of my good points, but being spontaneous and undemanding, accepted the whole of me, just as I was. The others talked to me in a deferential, or at any rate in a grave and reserved way. Herbaud laughed as he spoke to me, put his hand on my arm and used to shake his finger at me in mock warning when he called me, 'My poor young friend!' He would make all kinds of remarks about my appearance – friendly, joking remarks, always unexpected.

I did not think much of him as a philosopher. I noted, rather incoherently, in my diary: 'I admire his ability to have his own theories about everything. Perhaps because he does not know much about philosophy. I like him enormously.' He was, in fact, ignorant of any philosophic discipline, but what mattered much more to me was that he opened up paths that I longed to explore without as yet having the courage to do so. The majority of my friends were believers, and I kept evading the issue by trying to find a compromise between their point of view and my own; I didn't dare disassociate myself from them too much. But Herbaud made me want to wipe out the past that separated me from him: he frowned upon my association with the 'Holy Willies'. Christian asceticism was repugnant to him. He professed deliberate ignorance of meta-physical soul-searching. He was anti-religious, anti-clerical, anti-nationalist, and anti-militarist; he had a horror of all mysticisms. I gave him my dissertation on 'The Personality' to read, for I was overweeningly proud of it; he pulled a face as he handed it back to me; he felt it smacked of Catholicism and romanticism: he exhorted me to get them out of my system as soon as possible. I accepted his advice with open arms. I had had enough of 'Catholic complications', spiritual dead-ends, miraculous make-believes; I felt it was time for me to get my feet back on the ground. That is why, when I got to know Herbaud, I had the feeling of finding myself: he was the shadow thrown by my future. He was neither a pillar of the Church, nor a book-worm, nor did he spend his time propping up bars; he proved by personal example that one can build for oneself, outside the accepted categories, a self-respecting, happy, and responsible existence: exactly the sort of life I wanted for myself.

*

This brand-new friendship added greatly to the gaiety of spring. There's only one spring-time in the year, I kept telling myself, and you're only young once: I mustn't fritter away any of my youthful spring-times. I was finishing the final draught of my diploma thesis; I was reading books on Kant; but I'd broken the back of my work, and I felt sure of success; this too helped the spring to go to my head. I used to spend mirthful evenings with my sister at the Bobino, the Lapin Agile, and the Caveau de la Bolée, where she would sketch the patrons. At the Salle Pleyel, I heard the Layton and Johnstone festival with Zaza; with Riesmann I visited an exhibition of paintings by Utrillo; I applauded Valentine Tessier in *Jean de la Lune*. I read with admiration Stendhal's *Lucien Leuwen*, and with curiosity *Manhattan Transfer*, which was far too contrived for my taste. I would sit in the sun in the Luxembourg Gardens; in the evenings I would wander beside the jet-black waters of the Seine, while my heart felt it was brimming over with the lights, the scents of Paris, and my own overwhelming happiness.

One evening at the end of April I met my sister and Gégé at the place Saint-Michel: after drinking a few cocktails and listening to some jazz records in a bar that had just opened in that district, we went on to Montparnasse. The fluorescent blue of the neon signs reminded me of the convolvulus of my childhood. At the Jockey, familiar faces smiled at me and once again the voice of the saxophone quietly broke my heart. I caught sight of Riquet. We talked: about *Jean de la Lune*, and, as always, about friendship and love; he bored me; what a difference there was between him and Herbaud! He took a letter out of his pocket and I saw it was in Jacques' handwriting. 'Jacques is changing,' he said. 'He's ageing. He won't be back in Paris until the middle of August.' He added, impetuously: 'In ten years from now, he'll be doing fantastic things.' I didn't turn a hair. I felt as if my heart were dead.

But when I awoke next morning I was on the brink of tears. 'Why does Jacques write to other people and never to me?' I went to Sainte-Geneviève, but I couldn't get started on my work. I read the *Odyssey*, 'in order to put the whole of humanity between myself and my too-private pain'. The remedy wasn't very successful. Where did I stand with Jacques? Two years earlier, disappointed by the chilly welcome he had given me, I had walked the boulevards planning 'a life of my own' in which he would have no place; now I had a life of my own. But was I to forget the hero of my youth, the fabulous brother of Meaulnes, he who was going to do 'fantastic things' and was perhaps branded by the cross of genius? No. The past still had me in its toils: I had longed so much, and so long, to carry it with me, all of it, into the future!

So I started to grope around again among my memories, my disappointments, and regrets, and one evening I pushed open the door of the Stryx. Riquet invited me to his table. At the bar, Olga, Riaucourt's friend, was talking to a dark girl swathed in silvery furs who I thought was very beautiful; her black hair was parted down the middle, and in her thin, pale face her lips were scarlet; she had long, slim, silk-stockinged legs. I knew at once that this was Magda. 'Any news from Jacques?' she asked Riquet. 'Didn't he ask after me? The bastard ups and leaves me – over a year ago now – and he doesn't even ask after me. Hah! I never have any luck! The bastard!' I took in her words, but at the time they hardly made any impression upon me. I talked quietly with Riquet and his friends until one o'clock in the morning.

But as soon as I got to bed, I broke down. It was a frightful night. I spent the whole of the next day on the terrace in the

Luxembourg Gardens, trying to sort out my feelings. It was hardly jealousy I felt. The affair with Magda was over; it hadn't lasted long: Jacques had soon got tired of her and he had broken it off in good time. *Our* love had nothing in common with that sordid little liaison. I remembered something; in a book by Pierre Jean-Jouve that he had lent me, Jacques had underlined a phrase: 'This is the friend I open my heart to; but the friend I embrace is someone else.' And I had thought. 'All right, Jacques. It's the other one I'm sorry for.' He encouraged this fatuous self-importance by telling me that women meant nothing to him, and that to him I was something more than just a woman. Then why should I feel this desolation in my heart? Why was I saying over and over to myself, with tears in my eyes, the words of Othello: 'But yet the pity of it, Iago: oh Iago, the pity of it Iago.' I had just made a very painful discovery: the fine story of my life was gradually going wrong as I went on making it up.

How blind I had been, and how mortified I felt now! Jacques' fits of depression, his self-accusations – I had been attributing them to some unspecified yearning for the impossible. How stupid the abstraction of my replies must have seemed to him! How far away I had really been from him, at those very moments when I had thought we were closest! Yet there had been hints I might have taken: those conversations with his friends, when they had talked about mysterious – but they had been real! – troubles. I remembered something else: I had caught a glimpse of a woman sitting beside Jacques in his car – a dark, thin-faced woman who was too elegant, and too pretty. But I had persisted in my acts of faith; with what ingenuity, and with what blind obstinacy I had deceived myself! It was I alone who had built up the image of our friendship over the last three years; I still clung to it today because of the past, and now the past was nothing but a lie. Everything was falling to pieces. I felt I wanted to burn all my boats behind me; to love someone else, or set off for the ends of the earth.

And then I chided myself. It was my own dream that was at fault, not Jacques. What had I to reproach him with? He had never set himself up as a hero or a saint and he had even told me himself that he was no good. The quotation in the Jouve had been a warning; he had tried to talk to me about Magda, but I had not made it easy for him to be frank. Besides, I had long suspected, and even known the truth. What was it within me that could be so shocked by it? My old Roman Catholic prejudices? I felt my equanimity had been restored. It was I who had been wrong in wanting life to conform to a preconceived ideal; it was for me to show myself equal to everything life might bring. I had always preferred reality to the mirage; I brought my meditation to a pious close by priding myself on having stumbled on a solid problem, and on having successfully solved it.

The next morning, there was a letter from Meyrignac; grandpapa was seriously ill and was not expected to live; I was very fond of him, but he was very old, his death seemed natural now, and I could feel no sadness about it. My cousin Madeleine was in Paris; I took her to eat ices outside a café in the Champs-Élysées; she nattered on about her affairs and I hardly heard what she was saying; I was thinking of Jacques with disgust. His liaison with Magda had been all too faithful a copy of the classic set-up which had always sickened me: the rich elder son who loses his virginity to a low-born mistress; then when he decides it's time to lead a respectable life, he drops her flat. It was banal; it was beastly. I went to bed, and woke up still full of bitterness and scorn. 'One's integrity is no greater than the number of compromises one makes with oneself': I repeated to myself this phrase of Jean Sarment's during my lectures at the École Normale and during a lunch I had with Pradelle in a sort of dairy called the Yvelines on the boulevard Saint-Michel. He was talking away about himself. He was protesting that he was not as calculating and ponderous as his friends declared; only he detested showing-off; he would not allow himself to express sentiments or ideas which he felt were not well-grounded. I approved of his conscientious attitude. Though sometimes I thought he was too indulgent to the faults of others, he always judged himself with the utmost severity: which is better than the opposite, I thought bitterly. We discussed the merits of all the people we admired and at one fell stroke he dismissed as 'nobodies' all the 'bar-corner aesthetes'. I agreed with him. I went back to Passy with him in the bus and then took a stroll in the Bois de Boulogne.

I smelt the fragrance of freshly cut grass as I wandered there in the Bagatelle, dazzled by the profusion of daisies and jonquils and flowering fruit trees; there were whole beds of red tulips, heavy-headed, high lilac hedges, and enormous trees. I read Homer beside a stream; little ripples of water and great blasts of sun were playing on the rustling leaves. What sorrow so great, I wondered, that it could remain impervious to the beauty of the earth? Jacques, after all, was no more important than one of the trees in this park.

I was talkative; I liked to make public everything that happened to me; and besides, I was hoping that someone would be able to take a more impartial view of my dilemma. I knew that Herbaud would find it faintly comical; I thought too highly of Zaza and Pradelle to expose Jacques to the judgement they would pass on him. On the other hand, I was no longer intimidated by Clairaut, and he would weigh the facts in the light of that Christian morality to which, despite myself, I still bent the knee: I opened my sorry case to him. He listened greedily, and heaved a sigh: girls – how intransigent they can be! He, for example, had admitted to his fiancée that he had had several lapses – they were, he hinted to me, solitary pleasures – and instead of admiring his frankness she had seemed to be disgusted. I supposed that she would have preferred to listen to some more glamorous kind of confession; failing that, he should have held his tongue; but that was not the point in question. As far as my own case was concerned, Clairaut thought I had been too severe on Jacques, who therefore was justified in his conduct. I decided to fall in with Clairaut's opinion of the case. Forgetting that I had been immediately shocked by the middle-class banality of Jacques' liaison, I blamed myself for having condemned him in the light of purely abstract principles. In fact, I was lost in a dark tunnel, battling against shadows, brandishing the useless sword of an ideal I no longer believed in against the dead past, against Jacques' own phantasmal shade. But if I abjured this ideal, what other yardstick could I use? In order to protect my love, I swallowed my pride: why should I insist on Jacques being different from other men? The only thing was, if he was the same as all the others – and I knew that in many respects he was inferior to a great number of his sex – what point was there in putting him above the rest? My indulgence was finally turning to indifference.

A dinner at his parents' house only served to increase my confusion. In that gallery where I had spent so many sad, so many precious moments, my aunt informed me that he had written: 'Do remember me very kindly to Simone when you see her. I've not been very nice to her, but then I'm never very nice to anyone; not that she'll be at all surprised.' So he looked upon me simply as one among many! The thing that disturbed me even more was the fact that he had asked his mother to let him look after his young half-brother when he, Jacques, returned to Paris: so he was going to continue his bachelor existence? Really, I was incorrigible. I could have kicked myself for dreaming-up a past in which he had no part; and here I had been making plans for our future life together. I gave up all my make-believe. I don't care what happens, I told myself. I went as far as to think that it would be better for me to write the whole thing off and get started on a new tack. I still didn't really want to make this clean break, but it was a tempting prospect. In any case, I decided that if I wanted to live my own life, write, and be happy, I could perfectly well do without Jacques.

*

On the Sunday, a wire brought the news of grandfather's death; my past was certainly on the way out. I wandered alone through Paris, heart-free, or in the Bois de Boulogne with Zaza. On the Monday afternoon, sitting on the sunny terrace in the Luxembourg Gardens, I read *My Life* by Isadora Duncan and day-dreamed about my own existence. It wouldn't be a stormy life, nor even a startling one. All I wanted was to be in love, to write good books, to have children and 'friends to whom I can dedicate my books and who will show my children by personal example what poetry and philosophy can be'. My husband was to play a very small part; that was because while still investing him with the characteristics of Jacques I was eager to treat with friendly indulgence those failings which I no longer closed my eyes to. In this future life, which I began to feel was imminent, the essential thing would still be writing. I felt I had been right not to bring out anything too despairing while I was still so young: at present I wanted to express both the tragic sense of life, and its beauty. Meditating thus upon my destiny, I caught sight of Herbaud walking round the lake with Sartre: he saw me, and did not acknowledge me. How mysteriously misleading private diaries can be! I made no mention of this incident which nevertheless had made me sick at heart. I was hurt that Herbaud should have made this denial of our friendship, and felt that sense of exile which I hated above everything else.

The whole family had gathered at Meyrignac; it was perhaps

because of this great upheaval that I remained unmoved by the sight of grandpapa's dead body, the house, and the garden. When I was thirteen, I had wept at the thought that one day I would no longer feel at home at Meyrignac; that day had come; the property belonged to my aunt and cousins; this summer I would visit them as a guest, and very soon, no doubt, I would never return there: but I didn't heave a single sigh of regret. My childhood and adolescence and the sound of the cows' hooves kicking the stable door as I leaned out into the starlit night – all that was far, very far behind me. Now I was ready for something else; I was all expectancy, and in the violence of this feeling all regrets were swept away.

I returned to Paris, dressed in heavy mourning, wearing a hat swathed in black crêpe georgette; but all the chestnuts were in flower, the tarmac was soft underfoot, and I could feel through my dress the gentle force of the sun. The fair was on in the Esplanade des Invalides: I strolled about there with my sister and Gégé, eating nougat that made our fingers sticky. They met a fellow art-student who took us off to her studio to listen to her records and drink port. What a lot of pleasure for one afternoon! Every day brought me something new: the smell of oil-paint in the Salon des Tuileries; at the Européen, there was Damia, whom I went to hear with Mallet; there were walks with Zaza and Lisa; the blue air of summer, and the sun. I was still filling the pages of my diary: they spoke unendingly of my new-found happiness.

*

I met Clairaut at the Nationale. He offered me his condolences and inquired, with gleaming eyes, after the state of my heart; it was my own fault for having talked too much, but all the same I felt exasperated by his inquisitive concern. He made me read the typescript of a short novel in which he expatiated upon the differences he had had with his fiancée: how, I wondered, could a cultivated person, said to be intelligent, waste his time recounting in such colourless phrases such tasteless anecdotes? I made no secret of the fact that I thought he hadn't any talent for writing. He appeared not to mind. As he was very friendly with Pradelle whom my parents thoroughly approved of, he came to dinner one evening at our house and made a great impression on my father. He seemed very conscious of my sister's charms and in order to prove to her that he was no pedantic stick-in-the-mud he delivered himself of a number of witticisms whose ponderousness filled my sister and me with consternation.

I saw Herbaud a week after my return from Meyrignac, in one of the corridors of the Sorbonne. Clad in a light beige suit, he was sitting beside Sartre on a windowsill. He gave his hand to me and held it in a long, affectionate clasp, casting a curious look at my black dress. In the lecture-room I sat next to Lisa and they took their places a few rows behind us. The next day he appeared at the Nationale and told me that he had been worried about my absence: 'I assumed that you were in the country, and then yesterday I saw you were in mourning.' I was pleased that he had thought of me; he set the seal on my pleasure by referring to the occasion on which I had seen him with Sartre in the Luxembourg Gardens; he would have liked to introduce Sartre to me then, 'but though I don't respect Clairaut's philosophical ruminations,' he added, 'I would not allow myself to disturb you when you are meditating.' He gave me a present from Sartre – a drawing which the latter had dedicated to me and which represented 'Leibniz bathing with the Monads.'

During the three weeks before the competitive examination, he came to the Nationale every day; even if he wasn't working there himself he would come to meet me before it closed and we would go and have a drink somewhere. He was a bit worried about the examination; nevertheless we kept Kant and the Stoics out of our conversations. He was teaching me the 'Eugenic cosmology' which derived from Cocteau's *Potomac*, and in which he had managed to interest Sartre and Nizan; all three of them belonged to the highest caste, that of the Eugenes, as exemplified by Socrates and Descartes; they relegated all their other fellow-students to inferior categories: among the Marrhanes who loll about in the infinite or among the Mortimers who slop about in the blue of the heavens: certain of them were very peeved by their classifications. I was ranked among the 'earthy' women, the ones with a future. He showed me also the portraits of the principal metaphysical animals: the Catobelpas, that eats its own feet; the Catoboryx, that expresses itself in borborygmic rumbles: to this latter species belonged Charles du Bos, Gabriel Marcel, and the majority of the contributors to the *NRF*. 'Let me tell you that all thoughts of order are unbearably sad': this was the Eugene's first lesson. He disdained science and industry and made a mock of all universal moral systems; he spat on Monsieur Lalande's logic and on Goblot's *Traité*. The Eugene tries to make his life an original work of art, and, as Herbaud explained to me, to reach a certain 'comprehension' of the singular. I wasn't against this, and even used the idea to construct a pluralist morality which would allow me to justify attitudes as radically different as those of Zaza, Jacques, and Herbaud himself; every individual, I decided, possesses his own law, which is as exacting as a categorical imperative, although not universal: one only had the right to approve or disapprove of his actions in so far as they were a reflection of this personal norm. Herbaud didn't think much of this effort at systematization: 'It's the sort of thinking I detest,' he told me in an angry voice; but the eagerness with which I had entered into his mythological fantasies secured me a free pardon. I liked the Eugene very much; he played a great part in our conversations: of course, he was one of Cocteau's creations, but Herbaud had invented some very charming adventures for him and he made ingenious use of the Eugene's authority against the Sorbonne philosophers, against order, reason, self-importance, stupidity, and every kind of vulgarity.

Herbaud admired three or four people this side of idolatry and despised the rest. His severity delighted me; I was enchanted to hear him pulling Blanchette Weiss to pieces, and I left him free to do what he liked with Clairaut. He didn't attack Pradelle, although he didn't like him; whenever he saw me at the Sorbonne or the Normale talking to some fellow-student, he would hold disdainfully aloof. He reproached me for being so indulgent. One afternoon, in the Nationale, the Hungarian student came over to me twice to ask, among other things, if one could use the word 'gigolo' in the preface to a thesis. 'All these people who come pestering you!' Herbaud said. 'It's ridiculous! That Hungarian has done it twice! The same with Clairaut, and all your friends! You're wasting your time on people who aren't worth a second look. You must be a pathological case, otherwise there's no excuse for you!' He didn't mind Zaza, although he thought she looked too serious, but when I talked to him about Stépha he turned on me: 'She made eyes at me!' He disliked provocative women: they were stepping outside their womanly role. Another day he told me rather angrily: 'You're at the mercy of a whole troop of people. I keep wondering

if there's any room left for me in your universe.' I assured him –
and he already knew this perfectly well – that there was very considerable room for him in my life.

I liked him more and more, and the pleasant thing about it all was
that he made me like myself more; others had taken me seriously,
but *he* found me amusing. When we came out of the Library he
would say gaily: 'How fast you walk! I love that: I feel as if we
were going somewhere!' 'Your funny husky voice!' he remarked
another day. 'It's very much your own voice, but it's husky.
Sartre and I are much amused by it.' I discovered that I had a way
of walking and a voice: it was something new. I began to take
more care with my appearance; he would reward my efforts with a
compliment: 'That new hair-style, that collar suit you very well.'
One afternoon, in the gardens of the Palais Royal, he told me, with
an air of perplexity: 'Ours is a strange relationship. At least it is for
me: I've never before had a feminine friendship.' 'Perhaps that's
because I'm not very feminine.' 'What! You?' He laughed in a way
that I found very flattering. 'No. It's more that you are so open-
minded, you accept things so easily, and at once we are on an
equal footing.' At the beginning, he used to call me, affectionately,
'Mademoiselle'. One day he wrote on my exercise-book, in large
capital letters: BEAUVOIR= BEAVER. 'You are a beaver,' he said.
'Beavers like company and they have a constructive bent.'

We shared all kinds of secrets; we understood each other almost
instinctively; yet things did not always have the same effect on us.
Herbaud knew Uzerche, where he had spent a few days with his
wife, and he was very fond of the Limousin: but I was astonished
when he discoursed eloquently upon dolmens, menhirs, and forests
where the druids cut their mistletoe. He loved to lose himself in
historical day-dreams; for him, the gardens of the Palais Royal
were peopled with shadows of the great; but the past left *me* stone-
cold. On the other hand, judging by his dry tone of voice and his
take-it-or-leave-it manner, I thought that Herbaud was fairly
devoid of sentiment; I was touched when he told me that he liked
The Constant Nymph, *The Mill on the Floss*, and *Le Grand
Meaulnes*. As we were talking about Alain Fournier, he murmured,
in a voice that shook slightly: 'There are some people you would
have liked to be yourself'; for a moment he was silent, then went
on: 'Fundamentally I am much more intellectual than you; yet at
heart, I find within myself the same sensibility as yours, though I

wouldn't accept it.' I told him that I sometimes found it intoxicating simply to be alive: 'I have wonderful moments!' I added. He nodded: 'I should hope so indeed, Mademoiselle; you deserve them. I never have any wonderful moments; I'm a poor sap: but I *do* wonderful things!' A smile took the bumptiousness out of this statement: but how far did he really believe in it himself? 'You mustn't sit in judgement on me,' he sometimes told me, without my being able to tell if he was asking me a favour or giving me an order. I was quite willing to look upon him in a favourable light; he would talk to me about the books he would write: perhaps they would indeed be 'wonderful'. Only one thing distressed me about him: the fulfilment of his individualism depended on social success. I was completely lacking in this kind of ambition. I wanted neither money nor public recognition nor notoriety. I was afraid I might sound like a 'Catoboryx' if I used the terms 'salvation' or 'inner fulfilment' which often appeared in my journal. But the fact is that I still had a quasi-religious concept of what I called 'my destiny'. Herbaud was interested in the figure he would cut in society; he envisaged his future books solely as elements of his personality. But this was a point on which I would never give way: I couldn't understand how one could make compromises with one's life in order to enjoy the dubious applause of a dubious public.

We hardly ever talked about our personal problems. But one day Herbaud unintentionally revealed that the Eugene is not happy because the ideal of insensibility is one which he never attains. I admitted to him that I understood the Eugenes of this world very well because there was one in my own life. The relationships between Eugenes and 'earthy' women are usually difficult, he declared, because they want to swallow everything up and the Eugene sets up a resistance. 'Do you think I haven't found that out already?' I asked. He laughed loudly. There and then I told him about my relationship with Jacques and he urged me to marry him; or if not him, then somebody else, he added; a woman ought to get married. I was surprised to see that on this point his attitude hardly differed at all from that of my father. In his view, a man who remained a virgin after the age of eighteen was a neurotic; but he claimed that a woman should only 'give her all' after marriage. But I would not admit that there should be a law for one sex and a different one for the other. I wasn't blaming Jacques; but suddenly I found myself admitting that women should be as free to dispose of their virginity as men were. I was very fond of one of Michael Arlen's novels, *The Green Hat*. A misunderstanding had separated the heroine, Iris Storm, from Napier, the great love of her youth; she would never forget him, even though she now popped in and out of bed with scores of men; in the end, rather than take Napier away from a lovable and loving wife, she killed herself by running her car into a tree. I admired Iris: her loneliness, her free-and-easy life, and her proud integrity. I lent the book to Herbaud. 'I have no liking for women of easy virtue,' he told me as he handed it back. He smiled at me. 'Although I like a woman to please me, I find it impossible to respect any woman I've had.' I was indignant: 'But one doesn't "have" an Iris Storm.' 'No woman surrenders herself with impunity to a man's most intimate embraces.' He insisted that our society only respects married women. I didn't care twopence about being respected. Living with Jacques and marrying him were all one to me. But in those cases where love could be disassociated from marriage, it seemed to me better to stake everything on love, and to hell with domesticity. One day in the Luxembourg Gardens I caught sight of Nizan and his wife who was pushing a perambulator; it was my ardent hope that my own future would have no place for that sort of thing. I thought it was terribly awkward that married couples should be inseparably bound by material cares: the only link between two people who loved one another should be love.

So I didn't see entirely eye to eye with Herbaud. I was dismayed by the triviality of his ambitions, by his respect for certain conventions and sometimes by his aestheticism; I would tell myself that if we had both been free, I should never have wanted to link my life with his; I saw love as a total engagement: therefore I was not in love with him. All the same, the feelings he inspired in me resembled strangely those I had for Jacques. Immediately I left him, I would begin to look forward to our next meeting; I used to store up for him everything that happened to me, everything that passed through my head. When we had finished talking and started working side by side, my heart would sink because already the best part of our meeting was over, and our parting was beginning to come in sight: I was never quite sure when I would see him again and this uncertainty saddened me; at times, the frailty of our relationship distressed me. 'You're very sad today!' Herbaud would say gently, and he would do everything he could to restore my good humour. I called upon myself to live this thing out from day to day, without either hope or fear; this thing that from day to day brought me only joy.

And it was mainly joy I felt. As I was revising for the examination in my room one warm afternoon, I recalled very similar hours when I had been preparing for my school-leaving certificate: this was the same peace I had known then, the same fervour: but how much richer I had become since then – three long years ago! I sent a note to Pradelle fixing the time of a meeting, and ended with the words: 'Be happy!' Two years ago, he reminded me, I had asked him to make sure that I was always on my guard against happiness; I was touched by his vigilance. But the word had another meaning now: happiness was no longer abdication from responsibilities or a sluggish torpor, for it no longer depended on Jacques. I made a decision. Next year, even if I was ploughed, I would leave home; and if I passed, I wouldn't take a teaching post, but would stay in Paris: in either case, I would take a place of my own and earn my living by giving private lessons. My grandmother had been letting rooms since her husband's death. I would rent a room from her; this would give me complete independence without alarming my parents. They were in agreement. I would earn my own living, and be free to come and go, to have people in and to write: life was really beginning to open out.

*

I made my sister a part of this future. At nightfall, on the banks of the Seine, we would talk and talk about our triumphant tomorrows: my books, her pictures, our travels, the world. . . . In the flowing river waters trembled reflected columns and shadows went gliding over the inverted bridges; we would pull down our crêpe veils in order to make the sight even more fantastic. We often brought Jacques into our plans; we would talk about him, not as the great love of my life, but as the brilliant elder cousin who had been the hero of our youth.

'*I* shan't be here next year,' said Lisa, who was with great difficulty struggling through her final exams; she had applied for a post in Saigon. Pradelle had probably guessed her secret: he was keeping out of her way. 'Oh! how unhappy I am!' she would murmur, with a wry smile. We would meet at the Nationale and at the Sorbonne, and drink lemonade in the Luxembourg Gardens. Or we would eat mandarines in the dusk of her room fragrant with pink and white hawthorn blossom. One day, as we were talking to Clairaut in the courtyard of the Sorbonne, he asked us in that intense tone of voice he affected: 'What do you like best in yourselves?' Lying like mad, I declared: 'Someone else.' Lisa answered: '*I* like a door left open.' On another occasion she had told me: 'The really good thing about you, Simone, is that you never refuse anything, you leave all your doors wide open. Now *I'm* always out, and I take everything with me. Whatever possessed me to knock on your door, and enter? Or was it you who came to me, and had the good sense to wait for me while I was out? Of course, when the tenant is away, one may think that he'll be back in a moment; but people don't think that way ... not about me.' She sometimes looked almost pretty, in the twilight, in her white lawn négligé; but her face was withering with despair and weariness.

Pradelle never uttered her name; on the other hand, he often talked about Zaza: 'Why don't you bring your friend!' he urged when he invited me to a discussion between Garric and Guéhenno. She dined at our house, and then went with me to the rue Dufour. Maxence was chairman of the meeting, at which Jean Daniélou, Clairaut, and other high-minded thinkers from the Normale were present. I recalled Garric's lecture of three years ago, when he had seemed to me like a demi-god and Jacques had shaken hands with all kinds of inaccessible people: today, I was shaking hands with all and sundry. I still enjoyed listening to Garric's warm, eager voice: unfortunately, I thought he talked a lot of nonsense; how remote I now felt from all these 'Holy Willies', with whom the whole of my past was bound up! When Guéhenno got up to speak, a lot of *Action Française* louts started kicking up a row, and nothing would make them shut up. Garric and Guéhenno went to have a drink in a neighbouring bar, and the audience dispersed. Despite the rain, Pradelle, Zaza, and I walked back along the boulevard Saint-Germain and the Champs-Élysées. My two friends were much more light-hearted than usual and joined forces in teasing me affectionately. Zaza called me 'the amoral woman' – Iris Storm's nickname in *The Green Hat*. Pradelle improved the shining hour by telling me: 'You have the mind of a hermit.' Their complicity amused me.

Although the meeting had been a pitiable flop, Zaza thanked me a few days later for a happy evening; in a voice touched with emotion she told me that she had suddenly understood, once and for all, that she could never accept that atrophy of the heart and mind which her environment imposed upon her. Pradelle and I took our orals, and she came to listen; we celebrated our success by having tea at the Yvelines. I organized what Herbaud called 'the great Bois de Boulogne do'. One fine, warm evening, Zaza, Lisa, my sister, Gégé, Pradelle, Clairaut, Zaza's second-eldest brother, and I all went boating on the lake. There were races; we laughed and sang songs. Zaza was wearing a dress of pink silk, a little straw hat, and her dark eyes were sparkling – never had I seen her looking so pretty; in Pradelle I found again all the youth and gaiety which had rejoiced my heart at the beginning of our friendship. Together with them both in a rowing-boat, I was again struck by their conspiratorial air, and felt rather surprised that their affection for me on that particular evening should be so demonstrative: they kept giving *me* the fond looks and smiles which they didn't yet dare to give one another. The next day, I went with Zaza in the car to do some shopping, and she talked to me about Pradelle in ecstatic terms. A few moments later, she told me that the thought of getting married upset her more and more; she would not be forced to marry someone mediocre, but she didn't think she was worthy to be loved by a really fine man. Once again I failed to put my finger on the exact cause of her melancholy. To tell the truth, despite my affection for her, I was only giving her half my attention. The competitive examination was to take place the day after next. I had said good-bye to Herbaud; for how long? I would catch glimpses of him during the exams; then he was expecting to leave Paris, and on his return was going to prepare for his oral with Sartre and Nizan. Our daily meetings at the Nationale were over: how I would miss them! Nevertheless I was in good spirits the next day when 'the Bois de Boulogne gang' met for a picnic in the forest of Fontainebleau. Pradelle and Zaza were radiant with happiness. Only Clairaut seemed to be rather cast down; he was paying marked attention to my sister but without making the least impression upon her. He went about it in the queerest manner; he invited my sister and me to have a drink in a baker's back-shop, and without consulting us ordered, in a masterful voice: 'Three teas!' 'No, I'll have a lemonade,' said Poupette. 'Tea is more refreshing,' he stated. 'I prefer lemonade.' 'Oh, very well, then, three lemonades!' he called out angrily. 'But *you* have tea if you want it!' 'I have no wish to make myself conspicuous,' he retorted, in a huff. He tirelessly collected injustices which filled him with rage and resentment. From time to time he would send my sister an express letter in which he would beg her forgiveness for having been in a bad mood. He would promise to be merry and bright in the future; he would cultivate a gay spontaneity, and so on: but at our next meeting his forced exuberance would give us the shudders and again his face would be contorted with hatred.

'Good luck, Beaver,' Herbaud said in his most affectionate voice when we took our places in the library at the Sorbonne. I put a thermos flask full of coffee and a box of biscuits within reach: Monsieur Lalande's voice announced the subject: 'Liberty and Contingency': faces stared at the ceiling, and pens started to scratch; I covered page after page and had the feeling that I hadn't done too badly. At two o'clock in the afternoon Zaza and Pradelle came to fetch me; after drinking a lemonade in the Café de Flore, which was then only a small local bar, we walked for a long time in the Luxembourg Gardens which were flagged with giant mauve and yellow irises. I had a sharp but friendly discussion with Pradelle: we had always thought differently on certain points. He held that it was a very short step from happiness to sadness, from faith to unbelief, from any feeling I cared to mention and its absence. I argued the contrary with fanatical intensity. Although Herbaud reproached me for associating with any Tom, Dick, and Harry, I placed people in two categories: the few for whom I felt a lively affection, and the common herd, for whom I had a disdainful indifference. But Pradelle wanted everybody to be in the same boat. During the last two years we had become more set in our attitudes. The day before, he had written me a letter in which he brought me to book: 'We are separated by so many things, many more, probably, than you or I are aware of . . . I cannot bear to think that your attitude towards people should be so narrowly exclusive. How can one live without gathering all mankind into the same wide net of love? But you are so intolerant when it's a question of doing just that.' He ended on a cordial note: 'Despite your fanaticism, which upsets me as much as if it were a lack of consideration for others and which is so contrary to my own way of thinking, I have the greatest and most inexplicable affection for you.' Once more that afternoon he gave me a sermon on loving my fellow-men; Zaza gave him cautious support, because she believed in the New Testament precept: 'Judge not . . .' In my opinion, one cannot love without hating: I loved Zaza, but I hated her mother. Pradelle and I took leave of one another without either of us having budged an inch. I stayed with Zaza until dinner time: for the first time, she told me, she had not felt like an intruder with Pradelle and me, and she was deeply grateful. 'I don't think there can be any man as fine as Pradelle,' she added enthusiastically.

They were waiting for me in the courtyard of the Sorbonne, deep in an animated conversation, when I came out of my final examination a couple of days later. What a relief it was to have it all over and done with! That evening my father took me to the Lune Rousse, and we had fried eggs at Lipp's. The next day I slept till noon. After lunch, I went to see Zaza in the rue de Berri. She was wearing a new dress in blue voile with a black and white all-over pattern and a huge straw sun-bonnet: how she had blossomed out since the beginning of the summer! As we sauntered down the Champs-Élysées, she expressed her astonishment at this self-renewal. Two years ago, when she had broken with André, she had thought that from then on her life would be a living death; and here she was now as calm and happy as she had been in the best years of her childhood; she had begun to take an interest in books, ideas, and her own thoughts again. Moreover, she was facing the future with a self-confidence which she found hard to explain.

The same day, as we were leaving the Cinéma des Agriculteurs round about midnight, Pradelle told me how highly he thought of my friend; she never laid down the law about things on which she was an authority or about which she felt very deeply, and that was why she was so often silent: but when she *did* speak, every word was charged with meaning. He also admired the way in which she kept a firm hand on her feelings in the very difficult circumstances in which she found herself. He asked me to invite her to come for another walk with us, and I went home highly delighted. I recalled how attentively Pradelle had listened, that winter, whenever I had had news of Zaza, and how she had often spoken affectionately of him in her letters. They were made for one another; they loved one another. One of my dearest dreams was about to be realized: Zaza's life would be a happy one!

The next morning, my mother told me that while I had been to the cinema Herbaud had called at the house: I was sorry to have missed him, all the more so because as we had left the examination room he had felt he hadn't done himself justice, and had not arranged when we were to meet again. Sadly disappointed, I went out about noon to buy a cream tart and met him at the bottom of the stairs; he invited me to lunch. I got my shopping done in double-quick time. For old time's sake, we went to the Fleur-de-Lys. He had been enchanted by the welcome my parents had given him; my father had propounded anti-militarist sentiments, and Herbaud had heartily agreed with him. He laughed long and loud when I told him how mistaken he had been. He was leaving the next day to join his wife at Bagnoles-de-l'Orne; on his return, in ten days' time, he would be preparing for his oral with Sartre and Nizan who had issued a cordial invitation to me to join their group. Sartre wanted to make my acquaintance; he had suggested meeting me one evening in the near future. But Herbaud asked me not to go: Sartre would take advantage of his absence in order to monopolize the conversation. 'I don't want the bloom knocked off my most cherished opinions,' Herbaud told me in a conspiratorial manner. We decided that my sister would go to meet Sartre at the time and place that had been arranged; she was to tell him that I had had to leave suddenly for the country and that she had come to take my place.

So I would soon be seeing Herbaud again, and I was accepted by his group: I was over the moon. I made half-hearted attempts to revise for the oral. I did some light and amusing reading, I strolled around Paris, I enjoyed myself. During the evening Poupette was spending with Sartre, I went over in my mind the year which was now coming to a close, and the whole of my youth; I was moved by thoughts of the future, and wrote in my journal: 'Curious certainty that this reserve of riches that I feel within me will make its mark, that I shall utter words that will be listened to, that this life of mine will be a well-spring from which others will drink: the certainty of a vocation. . . .' I felt as intensely elated as in the days when I had been borne aloft on mystical flights of fancy; but now I had my feet still on the ground. My kingdom was definitely of this world. When my sister returned, she said I had done well to stay at home. Sartre had courteously accepted our little white lie; he had taken her to the cinema and had been very kind; but conversation had dried up. 'Everything Herbaud says about Sartre is pure invention,' my sister told me; she knew Herbaud fairly well, and found him amusing.

I took advantage of my free time to go and see people I had more or less neglected. I visited Mademoiselle Lambert, who took fright at my serenity of mind, and Suzanne Boigue, whose conjugal felicity was making her run to seed; I spent a boring time with Riesmann, who was becoming more and more esoteric. Stépha had vanished from the scene during the last two months; she had set up house in Montrouge with Fernando, who had rented a studio there; I assumed that they were 'living in sin' and that she had stopped seeing me in order to cover up her misconduct. Then she showed up again with a wedding ring on her finger. She called on me at eight o'clock in the morning; we lunched at Dominique's, a Russian restaurant which had opened in Montparnasse a few weeks earlier, and we spent the whole day walking and talking; that evening, I had dinner in her studio, its walls were hung with pale Ukrainian carpets; Fernando was painting from morning to night, and had made great progress. A few days later, they gave a party to celebrate their marriage; there were Russians, Ukrainians, Spaniards, all of them connected vaguely with painting, sculpture, or music; there was drinking, dancing, singing, and dressing-up. But Stépha would soon be leaving for Madrid with Fernando, and they intended to stay there permanently; she was wholly taken up with preparations for this journey and with domestic worries. Our friendship – which later was to find a new lease of life – survived mainly on memories.

I still went out frequently with Pradelle and Zaza, and now it was I who began to feel I was an intruder: they got along so well together! Zaza still hardly dared give free expression to her hopes, but they gave her courage to stand up to renewed maternal on-slaughts. Madame Mabille was busy gerrymandering a marriage for her and kept on at her with merciless persistence. 'But what have you got against this young man?' she would cry. 'Nothing, Mama,' Zaza would reply. 'I just don't love him, that's all.' 'My dear, it's the man who loves, not the woman,' Madame Mabille explained. She got exasperated: 'As you've got nothing against the young man, why won't you marry him? Your sister made do with a boy much less intelligent than herself!' Zaza would tell me of these set-to's with her mother more in sorrow than in anger, for she could not take a light-hearted view of her mother's dissatisfaction with her. 'I'm so tired of fighting her that two or three months ago I might have given in,' she told me. She thought her suitor was quite nice, but she couldn't see him becoming a friend of Pradelle or myself; he would have seemed out of place among us; she didn't want to take as a husband a man whom she could not look up to as she did to others.

Madame Mabille must have suspected the real reasons for her daughter's obstinacy; when I rang at her front door in the rue de Berri, she received me with an extremely frosty expression on her face; and she was soon objecting to meetings between Zaza and Pradelle. We had made plans for another boating party; the day before it was to take place, I received an express letter from Zaza:

I've just had a talk with Mama which makes it absolutely impossible for me to come boating with you on Thursday. Mama is leaving Paris tomorrow; as long as she is here, I can argue with her and refuse to do what she wants; but I just cannot take advantage of her absence to do something which would cause her grave displeasure. It's very hard for me to give up Thursday evening, for I had hoped then that I might enjoy as wonderful moments as those I spent with you and Pradelle in the Bois de Boulogne. The things Mama told me have upset me so frightfully that I very nearly made up my mind to run away to some convent where I would be left in peace for a while. I'm still considering it; I'm in a state of acute mental distress....

Pradelle was deeply disappointed. 'Remember me very kindly to Mademoiselle Mabille,' he wrote to me. 'Surely it would be possible for us to meet, as it were, by accident, so that she would not be breaking her promise?' They met at the Nationale where I had started working again. I had lunch with them and they went off together for a walk afterwards. They were able to see each other alone two or three times after that, and towards the end of July Zaza, dumbfounded, announced that they were in love: they would get married when Pradelle had passed his exams and done his military service. But Zaza dreaded her mother's opposition. I told her not to be so pessimistic. She was no longer a child and Madame Mabille, after all, only wanted her happiness: she would respect the choice she had made. What could she find to object to? Pradelle came from an excellent family, and was a practising Catholic; he would obviously have a brilliant career, and in any

[333]

case his university studies would make him sure of getting a decent situation: Lili's husband wasn't exactly rolling in money either. Zaza shook her head. 'That's not the point. In our kind of society, marriages aren't made like that!' Pradelle had got to know Zaza through me: that was a black mark against him from the start. And then the prospect of a long engagement would worry Madame Mabille. But the main thing that Zaza insisted upon was that 'it wasn't done'. She had decided to wait until the autumn term before speaking to her mother about it; however, she was counting on hearing from Pradelle during the holidays: Madame Mabille would notice the letters arriving, and then what would happen? Despite her uneasiness, when she arrived at Laubardon Zaza felt full of hope. 'I am convinced of one thing, which enables me to bide my time hopefully, and to go on living, even though it may involve me in many awkward contrarieties,' she wrote to me. 'Life is marvellous.'

*

When he returned to Paris at the beginning of July, Herbaud sent me a note inviting me to spend the evening with him. My parents disapproved of my going out with a married man, but by now I had so very nearly escaped from their sphere of influence that they had practically given up interfering in my life. So I went to see *Le Pèlerin* with Herbaud, and afterwards we had supper at Lipp's. He brought me up to date with the Eugene's latest adventures, and taught me 'Brazilian écarte', a game he had invented which would enable him to win all the time. He told me that his 'comrades' were expecting me on Monday morning at the Cité Universitaire; they were counting on me to help them work on Leibniz.

I was feeling a bit scared when I entered Sartre's room; there were books all over the place, cigarette ends in all the corners and the air was thick with tobacco smoke. Sartre greeted me in a worldly manner; he was smoking a pipe. Nizan, who said nothing, had a cigarette stuck in the corner of his one-sided smile and was quizzing me through his pebble lenses, with an air of thinking more than he cared to say. All day long, petrified with fear, I annotated the 'metaphysical treatise' and in the evening Herbaud took me back home.

I went back each day, and soon I began to thaw out. Leibniz was boring, so we decided that we knew enough about him. Sartre took it upon himself to expound Rousseau's *The Social Contract* upon which he had very decided opinions. To tell the truth, it was always he who knew most about all the authors and all the aspects of our syllabus: we merely listened to him talking. I sometimes attempted to argue with him; I would rack my brains to find objections to his views. 'She's a sly puss!' Herbaud would laugh, while Nizan would scrutinize his finger-nails with an air of great concentration; but Sartre always succeeded in turning the tables on me. It was impossible to feel put-out by him: he used to do his utmost to help us to benefit from his knowledge. 'He's a marvellous trainer of intellects,' I noted. I was staggered by his generosity, for these sessions didn't teach him anything, and he would give of himself for hours without counting the cost.

We did most of our work in the mornings. In the afternoons, after lunching at the restaurant in the Cité, or at Chabin's near the Parc Montsouris, we would take lots of time off. Nizan's wife, a beautiful, exuberant brunette, would often join us. There was the fun-fair at the Porte d'Orléans. We would play at the pin-table machines, at miniature football; or we would try the shooting-gallery, and I won a huge pink vase on the Wheel of Fortune. We would all cram into Nizan's little car and go for a spin round Paris, stopping here and there for a glass of beer at a pavement café. I explored the dormitories and the students' dens at the École Normale, and made the traditional climb over the roofs. During these escapades, Sartre and Herbaud would sing at the tops of their voices; they usually made up the songs themselves; they composed a motet on one of Descartes' chapter headings: 'Concerning God: wherein is given further proof of his existence.'* Sartre had a fine voice and an extensive repertoire, including *Old Man River* and all the current jazz hits; at the École Normale, he was famed for his comic gifts: it was always he who took the part of Monsieur Lanson, the principal, in the annual Students' Revue, and he scored great successes in *La Belle Hélène* and romantic operettas of the 1900s. When he had done the donkey's share of the work for the day, he would put on a record, and we would listen to Sophie

* Here the author has confused the chapter headings to the third and the fifth of the *Méditations métaphysiques*: 'De Dieu, qu'il existe', and 'De l'essence des choses matérielles, et, derechef de Dieu, qu'il existe' (Translator's note).

Tucker, Layton and Johnstone, Jack Hylton, the Revellers, and to Negro Spirituals. Every day the walls of his room were adorned by fresh drawings: metaphysical animals; the latest exploits of the Eugene. Nizan specialized in portraits of Leibniz, whom he preferred to depict as a priest, or wearing a Tyrolean hat, and bearing on his backside the imprint of Spinoza's hoof.

Sometimes we would abandon the Cité for Nizan's study. He lived with his wife's parents in a house in the rue Vavin whose façade was covered with glazed earthenware tiles. On the walls of his study there was a large portrait of Lenin, a Cassandre poster and the Venus of Botticelli; I admired his ultra-modern furniture and his very carefully chosen books. Nizan was the most go-ahead member of the trio; he had already had a book published, belonged to various literary circles and had joined the Communist Party; he introduced us to Irish literature and the new American novelists. He was abreast of all the latest fashions in the arts, and even ahead of them. He took us to the dreary Café de Flore 'to do the old Deux Magots in the eye', he said, gnawing at his fingernails like a mischievous rat. He was working on a pamphlet attacking 'official' philosophies, and was also engaged in writing a book on 'Marxist Wisdom'. He rarely laughed, but often treated us to his ferocious lop-sided smile. His conversation delighted me, but I found him difficult to talk to because of his air of disdainful abstraction.

How was it that I managed to fit in with them so quickly? Herbaud had taken care not to shock me, but when they were all together the three 'comrades' didn't pull their punches. Their language was aggressive, their thought categorical, their judgements merciless. They made fun of bourgeois law and order; they had refused to sit the examination in religious knowledge: I had no difficulty in agreeing with them on that score. But I was still, in many respects, the dupe of bourgeois humbug; *they* jabbed a pin in every inflated idealism, laughed high-minded souls to scorn – in fact, every kind of soulfulness, the 'inner life', the marvellous, the mysterious, and the precious all fell under their lashing contempt; on every possible occasion – in their speech, their attitudes, their gestures, their jokes – they set out to prove that men were not rarefied spirits but bodies of flesh and bone, racked by physical needs and crudely engaged in a brutal adventure that was life. A year before, they would have scared me; but I had made much progress since the beginning of the academic year and I very often felt the need of stronger meat than that to which I was accustomed. I soon understood that if the world these new friends opened up to me seemed crude, it was because they didn't try to disguise its realities; in the end, all they asked of me was that I should dare to do what I had always longed to do: look reality in the face. It did not take me long to make up my mind to do so.

*

'I'm delighted that you should be getting on so well with the comrades,' Herbaud said. 'But all the same. . . .' 'I know what you mean,' I answered. '*You* are different.' He smiled. '*You* will never be one of them,' he added. 'You're not a comrade, you're the Beaver.' He told me he was as jealous in friendship as he was in love and demanded preferential treatment. He insisted on having the first place in my friendship with the 'comrades'. When the question of our all going out together came up one evening, he shook his head: 'No. This evening I am taking Mademoiselle de Beauvoir to the cinema.' 'Oh, very well,' said Nizan with a sardonic smile, and Sartre graciously gave his consent. Herbaud was feeling depressed that day because he was afraid he had failed in the competitive examination, and because of obscure reasons connected with his wife. After seeing a Buster Keaton film, we went to a small café, but conversation flagged. 'I hope you're not bored?' he inquired with a touch of anxiety and more than a touch of studied charm. No; but his preoccupations made him seem rather remote. We were drawn together again during the day I spent with him ostensibly helping him to translate *The Ethics of Nicomachus*. He had rented a room in a small hotel in the rue Vanneau and that was where we worked, though not for long, because Aristotle bored us to tears. He made me read him some fragments of Saint-John Perse's *Anabase* which I had never heard of before, and showed me reproductions of Michelangelo's *Sibyls*. Then he talked to me about the differences between him and Sartre and Nizan. He openly enjoyed the good things of life: works of art, nature, travel, love-affairs, sensual pleasures. '*They* always want to find a reason for everything, especially Sartre,' he told me. He added, on a note of apprehensive admiration: 'Except when he's asleep, Sartre *thinks* all the time!' He agreed that Sartre should spend the evening of the

Fourteenth of July with us. After dinner in an Alsatian restaurant we sat on the lawn in the Cité Universitaire and watched the fireworks. Then Sartre, whose munificence was legendary, took us in a taxi to the Falstaff in the rue Montparnasse, where we were lushed up with cocktails until two o'clock in the morning. They put themselves out to see who could be nicer to me and regaled me with a host of stories. I was in a seventh heaven of delight. My sister had been mistaken: I thought Sartre was even more amusing than Herbaud; nevertheless we all agreed that Herbaud should have first place in my affections, and out in the street he very ostentatiously took my arm. Never did he give such obvious proofs of his affection as in the days that followed. 'I really do like you very much, Beaver,' he would tell me. Once when I was to dine with Sartre and Nizan when he was not free to join us he asked me, with a possessive tenderness: 'You'll think about me this evening, won't you?' I was sensitive to the smallest inflexions in his voice, and also to his frowns of displeasure. One afternoon as I was talking to him in the entrance hall of the Nationale, Pradelle came up to us and I was delighted to see him. Herbaud said good-bye very angrily and stormed away. All that afternoon I ate my heart out over him. That evening I met him again: he was very pleased with the effect his conduct had had on me. 'Poor little Beaver! Was I not nice to her?' he gaily inquired. I took him off to the Stryx which he thought 'madly gay', and I told him about my escapades there. 'You're out of this world!' he laughed. He talked about himself, about his country childhood, his coming to Paris, his marriage. We had never talked so intimately before. But we were feeling worried, because the next day we were to get the results of the written papers. If Herbaud had failed, he would leave at once for Bagnoles-de-l'Orne. Whatever happened, next year he would take a post in the provinces or abroad. He promised to come and see me during the holidays, in the Limousin. But something had come to an end.

The next day, I walked to the Sorbonne, my heart thumping with anxiety; at the door, I met Sartre; I had passed, as well as Nizan and himself. Herbaud had been ploughed. He left Paris that very evening, without saying good-bye to me. 'Give the Beaver my best wishes for her happiness,' he told Sartre in an express letter which he sent telling him of his departure. He reappeared a week later, for one day only. He took me to the Balzac. 'What will you have?' he asked me, and added: 'In the good old days, it was always lemonade.' 'It will always be the good old days with us,' I answered. He smiled, and said: 'That's what I was hoping you would say.' But we both knew that it wasn't true.

*

'From now on, I'm going to take you under my wing,' Sartre told me when he had brought me the news that I had passed. He had a liking for feminine friendships. The first time I had ever seen him, at the Sorbonne, he was wearing a hat and talking animatedly to a great gawk of a woman student who I thought was excessively ugly; he had soon tired of her, and he had taken up with another, rather prettier, but who turned out to be rather a menace, and with whom he had very soon quarrelled. When Herbaud had told him about me, he had wanted to make my acquaintance at once, and now he was very pleased to have me all to himself; for my part, I was beginning to feel that time which was not spent in his company was time wasted. During the fortnight of the oral examinations we hardly ever left one another except to sleep. We went to the Sorbonne together to sit the examinations and to listen to our fellow-students. We went out with the Nizans. We would have drinks at the Balzac with Aron who was doing his military service in the Meteorological Corps and with Politzer who by now had joined the Communist Party. But usually we went about alone together. At the second-hand bookstalls by the Seine Sartre bought me copies of *Pardaillan* and *Fantomas* which he far and away preferred to the *Correspondence* of Rivière and Fournier; in the evenings he would take me to see cowboy films, to which I brought all the enthusiasm of a neophyte, for until then I had been mainly interested in abstract cinema and art films. We would talk for hours sitting in pavement cafés or drinking cocktails at the Falstaff.

'He never stops thinking,' Herbaud had told me. This didn't mean that he cogitated over formulas and theories all the time: he had a horror of pedantry. But his mind was always alert. Torpor, somnolence, escapism, intellectual dodges and truces, prudence, and respect were all unknown to him. He was interested in everything and never took anything for granted. Confronted with an object, he would look it straight in the face instead of trying to explain it away with a myth, a word, an impression, or a preconceived idea: he wouldn't let it go until he had grasped all its ins and outs and all its multiple significations. He didn't ask himself what he ought to think about it, or what it would have been amusing or intelligent to think about it: he simply thought about it. Thus he was always the despair of the aesthetes who were all yearning for elegant elaboration. A couple of years ago, having heard him give an analysis of a philosophical work, Riesmann, who was dazzled by Baruzi's verbal quibbling, had told me sadly: 'He has no soul!' That same year, giving a talk on 'classification' his scrupulous honesty had put our patience to the test: but in the end he had compelled our interest in his subject. He always intrigued people who were not afraid of something new, for though he never tried to be original, he never fell into the trap of conformity. The freshness and dogged tenacity of his perceptions grasped the very essence of things in all their lively profusion. How cramped my little world seemed beside this exuberantly abundant universe! Later, it was only certain madmen who could inspire in me a similar sense of humility when they discovered in a rose-petal a tangle of murky intrigues.

We used to talk about all kinds of things, but especially about a subject which interested me above all others: myself. Whenever other people made attempts to analyse me, they did so from the standpoint of their own little worlds, and this used to exasperate me. But Sartre always tried to see me as part of my own scheme of things, to understand me in the light of my own set of values and attitudes. He listened without enthusiasm to what I told him about Jacques; for a woman who had been brought up as I had been, it would perhaps be difficult to avoid marriage: but he hadn't a good word to say for it. Whatever happened, I would have to try to preserve what was best in me: my love of personal freedom, my passion for life, my curiosity, my determination to be a writer. Not only did he give me encouragement but he also intended to give me active help in achieving this ambition. Two years older than myself – two years which he had turned to good account – and having got off to a better start much earlier than I had, he had a deeper and wider knowledge of everything. But what he himself recognized as a true superiority over me, and one which was immediately obvious to myself, was the calm and yet almost frenzied passion with which he was preparing for the books he was going to write. In the past I had always despised children who played croquet or worked with less intensity than I did: here was someone in whose eyes my frantic determination seemed weak and timid. And indeed when I compared myself with him, how lukewarm my feverish obsessions appeared! I had thought I was an exceptional person because I couldn't imagine living and not writing: but he only lived in order to write.

He certainly had no intention of leading the life of a professional literary man; he detested formalities and literary hierarchies, literary 'movements', careers, the rights and duties of the man of letters, and all the stuffy pompousness of life. He couldn't reconcile himself to the idea of having a profession, colleagues, superiors, of having to observe and impose rules; he would never be a family man, and would never even marry. With all the romanticism of the age, and of his twenty-three years, he dreamed of making tremendous journeys: in Constantinople, he would fraternize with the dock-workers; he would get blind drunk with pimps and white-slavers in sinks of iniquity; he would go right round the world, and neither the pariahs of India nor the monks of Mount Athos nor the fishermen of Newfoundland would have any secrets from him. He would never settle down anywhere, and would never encumber himself with possessions: not merely in order to keep his freedom of movement, but in order to prove how unnecessary possessions are. All his experiments were to benefit his writing, and he would sweep aside all experiences which would in any way detract from it. We were arguing on firm ground here. I admired, in theory at any rate, the systematic derangement of the senses, dangerous living, lost souls, all excesses – drink, drugs, and sex. Sartre held that when one has something important to tell the world, it is criminal to waste one's energies on other occupations. The work of art or literature was, in his view, an absolute end in itself; and it was even – though he never said so, I was sure he believed this – the be-all and end-all of the entire universe. He shrugged disdainful shoulders at all metaphysical disputes. He was interested in social and political questions; he sympathized with Nizan's position; but as far as *he* was concerned, the main thing was to write and the rest would come later. Besides, at that period he was much more of an anarchist than a revolutionary; he thought society as it was then was detestable, but he didn't detest detesting it; what he called his 'opposition aesthetics' admitted quite openly the existence of imbeciles and knaves, and even required their presence in the world: if there was nothing to attack and destroy, the writing of books wouldn't amount to much.

Apart from a few minor differences, I found a great resemblance between his attitude and my own. There was nothing worldly in his ambitions. He reproved me for making use of religious vocabulary, but he, too, was really seeking 'salvation' in literature; books brought into this deplorably non-essential world a necessity which redounded to the credit of the author; certain things had to be said by him, and were therefore an entire justification for the means he used to express them. He was still young enough to feel emotional about his future whenever he heard a saxophone playing after his third martini; but if it had been necessary, he would have been willing to remain anonymous: the important thing was that his ideas should prevail, and not that he should enjoy any personal success. He never told himself – as I had sometimes done – that he was 'somebody', that he had a certain 'value' or place in the world; but he believed that important truths – perhaps the Truth itself – had been revealed to him, and that he had a mission to teach those truths to society. In the notebooks he showed me, in his conversations and even in his University writings he persistently put forward a system of ideas whose originality and coherence astounded his friends. He had given a detailed outline of them on the occasion of an 'Investigation' carried out among University students by *Les Nouvelles Littéraires*. 'We have received some remarkable observations from J.-P. Sartre,' wrote Roland Alix in an introduction to Sartre's reply, of which long extracts were printed; indeed, a whole philosophy was brought to light in it, a philosophy which had hardly any connexion with what we were being taught by the 'official' philosophers at the Sorbonne:

It is a paradox of the human mind that Man, whose business it is to create the necessary conditions, cannot raise himself above a certain level of existence, like those fortune-tellers who can tell other people's future, but not their own. This is why, as the root of humanity, as at the root of nature, I can see only sadness and boredom. It's not that Man does not think of himself as a *being*. On the contrary, he devotes all his energies to becoming one. Whence derive our ideas of Good and Evil, ideas of men working to improve Man. But these concepts are useless. Useless, too, is the determinism which oddly enough attempts

[342]

to create a synthesis of existence and being. We are as free as you like, but helpless. . . . For the rest, the will to power, action and life are only useless ideologies. There is no such thing as the will to power. Everything is too weak: all things carry the seeds of their own death. Above all, adventure – by which I mean that blind belief in adventitious and yet inevitable concatenations of circumstances and events – is a delusion. In this sense, the 'adventurer' is an inconsequential determinist who imagines he is enjoying complete freedom of action.

Comparing his own generation with the preceding one, Sartre concluded: 'We are more unhappy, but nicer to know.'

This last phrase had made me laugh; but as I talked to Sartre I came to realize the wealth of meaning in what he called his 'theory of contingency', and in which were to be found already the seeds of all his ideas on being, existence, necessity, and liberty. It was positive proof that he would one day write a philosophical work of the first importance. But he wasn't making things easy for himself, for he had no intention of composing a theoretical treatise on conventional lines. He loved Stendhal as much as Spinoza and refused to separate philosophy from literature. In his view, Contingency was no abstract notion, but an actual dimension of real life: it would be necessary to make use of all the resources of art to make the human heart aware of that secret 'failing' which he perceived in Man and in the world around him. At the time, such an attempt was regarded as very daring: it was impossible to take as his starting point any existing mode of thought or any model system; and because Sartre's thought had impressed me by its maturity, I was all the more disconcerted by the clumsiness of the essays in which he expressed it; in order to present its truths in all their singularity, he had recourse to myth-making: *Er the Armenian*, made use of gods and Titans: the effect of this antiquated machinery was to make his theories lose a great deal of their bite. He realized its shortcomings, but didn't worry too much about it; in any case, no amount of immediate success would have given him an excuse for rash confidence in the future. He knew what he wanted to do and he had all his life ahead of him: he would do it in the end, all right. I didn't for one moment doubt this: his vitality and good humour would see him through every ordeal. His self-confidence obviously stemmed from so unshakeable a determination that one day, in one way or another, it would bear fruit.

It was the first time in my life that I had felt intellectually inferior to anyone else. Garric and Nodier, who were much older than me, had impressed me in their time: but their dominance had been remote and vague, and I had had no chance of measuring up to them in person. Day after day, and all day long I set myself up against Sartre, and in our discussions I was simply not in his class. One morning in the Luxembourg Gardens, near the Medici fountain, I outlined for him that pluralist morality which I had cooked up to accommodate the people I liked but whom I didn't want to resemble: he soon demolished it. I clung to my system, because it authorized me to look upon my heart as the arbiter of good and evil; I argued with him about it for three hours. In the end I had to admit I was beaten: besides, I had realized, in the course of our discussion, that many of my opinions were based only on prejudice, dishonesty, or hastily formed concepts, that my reasoning was at fault and that my ideas were in a muddle. 'I'm no longer sure *what* I think, nor whether I can be said to think at all,' I noted, with a sense of anti-climax. I took no credit for that. My curiosity was greater than my pride; I preferred learning to showing-off. But all the same, after so many years of arrogant solitude, it was something serious to discover that I wasn't the One and Only, but one among many, by no means first, and suddenly uncertain of my true capacity. For Sartre wasn't the only one who forced me to take a more modest view of myself: Nizan, Aron, and Politzer were all much further advanced than I was. I had prepared for the competitive examination at the double: their culture had a much more solid grounding than mine, they were familiar with hosts of new things of which I was ignorant and they were used to discussion; above all, I was lacking in method and direction; to me the intellectual universe was a great jumble of ideas in which I groped my way blindly; but *their* search was, for the most part, well-directed. Already there were important divergencies of opinion between them; Aron was accused of being too much in favour of Brunschvig's idealism; but they had all explored much more fundamentally than I had the consequences of the inexistence of God and brought their philosophy right down to earth. Another thing that impressed me about them was that they had a fairly precise idea of the sort of books they wanted to write. I had gone on fatuously declaring that I 'would tell all'; it was at once too much and too little. I was alarmed to discover that the novel sets countless problems whose existence I had not even suspected.

But I didn't let myself be discouraged; the future suddenly seemed as if it would be much more difficult than I had reckoned but it had also become more real and more certain; instead of undefined possibilities I saw opening out before me a clearly-marked field of activity, with all its problems, its hard work, its materials, its instruments, and its inflexibility. I no longer asked myself: what shall I do? There was everything to be done, everything I had formerly longed to do: to combat error, to find the truth, to tell it and expound it to the world, perhaps to help to change the world. I should need time and it would need hard work to keep to my purpose, if it meant keeping only a small part of the promises I had made myself: but that didn't frighten me. Nothing had been done: but everything was possible.

And then, I had been given a great chance: I suddenly didn't have to face this future all on my own. Until then, the men I had been fond of – Jacques, and to a lesser extent Herbaud – were of a different order from my own: they were detached, changeable, rather incoherent, stamped with a sort of fatal charm; it was impossible to communicate with them without reserves. Sartre corresponded exactly to the dream-companion I had longed for since I was fifteen: he was the double in whom I found all my burning aspiration raised to the pitch of incandescence. I should always be able to share everything with him. When I left him at the beginning of August, I knew that he would never go out of my life again.

But before my future took definite shape, I had first of all to clarify my relationship with Jacques.

*

What would I feel when I found myself face to face with my past? I was anxiously asking myself this question when, on my return from Meyrignac in the middle of September I rang at the door of the Laiguillon house. Jacques came out of the offices downstairs, shook my hand, smiled at me, and took me upstairs to the apartment. Sitting on the red velvet sofa, I listened to him talking about his military service, Africa, his boredom; I was happy, but my heart was unmoved. 'It's as if we'd just said good-bye a day or two ago,' I remarked. 'It's so easy, meeting again like this.' He ran his fingers through his curly locks. 'I should think so, too!' he answered. Here I was back in the semi-darkness of the gallery; I felt I knew him only too well – those gestures, and that voice. That evening I wrote in my journal: 'I shall never marry him. I don't love him any more.' On the whole, this brutal liquidation of our relationship did not surprise me: 'It's only too obvious that in those moments when I loved him most there was always a deep division between us which I could only overcome by denying myself; and so I had to take up arms against my love.' I had been lying to myself by pretending to wait for his return before risking my future: for many a long week now the die had been cast.

Paris was still half-empty and I often met Jacques. He told me about his affair with Magda, giving it a romantic slant. In return, I told him about my new friends: he didn't seem to think much of them. Had I offended him? What was I to him? What did he expect of me? It was all the more difficult for me to guess the answers to these questions because almost always, at his house, or at the Stryx there would be a third party with us; we used to go out with Riquet, or with Olga. I felt rather upset. From a distance, I had given Jacques all my love, and if he was going to ask me to give it to him now, my hands were empty. He didn't ask me for anything, but he would talk about his future sometimes in a vaguely doomed tone of voice.

I invited him one evening to come with Riquet, Olga, and my sister to celebrate my removal to my new quarters. My father had paid for the furniture, and I was very pleased with the room. My sister helped me to set out bottles of cognac and vermouth, glasses and plates and little cakes on the table. Olga arrived, rather late and alone, which made us feel very disappointed. Nevertheless after a few drinks the conversation picked up; we were wondering what Jacques' future would be. 'It will all depend on his wife,' said Olga; she heaved a sigh: 'Unfortunately, I think she's the wrong one for him.' 'Who do you mean?' I asked. 'Odile Riaucourt. Didn't you know he's going to marry Lucien's sister?' 'No,' I replied, dumbfounded. She took great pleasure in giving me all the details. On his return from Algeria, Jacques had spent three weeks at the Riaucourt's country home; Lucien's sister had fallen for him at once and had told her parents then and there that she wanted him for her husband. Jacques, forewarned by Lucien, had accepted. He hardly knew her, and, apart from a very considerable dowry, she had, according to Olga, nothing else to recommend her. I understood now why I had never seen Jacques alone: he neither dared keep silent, nor speak to me about it; and this evening he had let me down in order to give Olga a chance to bring me up to date. I feigned indifference as best I could. But as soon as we were alone together, my sister and I gave vent to our consternation. We wandered for hours in the streets of Paris, heart-broken at the thought of seeing the hero of our youth transformed into a calculating bourgeois.

When I next saw Jacques he talked with some embarrassment about his fiancée and with much self-importance about his new responsibilities. One evening, I received a mysterious letter from him: it was he who had opened up the way for me, he said, and now he was being left behind, with the wind taken out of his sails, unable to follow me: 'Wind and weariness make the eyes water – with tears of a kind.' I was touched; but I didn't reply, for there was nothing I could say. In any case, it was all over now.

What had our relationship meant to Jacques? And what sort of person was he really? I was mistaken when I thought that his marriage showed him in his true colours and that after a period of youthful romanticism he was going to settle down calmly and become the bourgeois he had always been at heart. I occasionally saw him with his wife: their relationship was one of only moderate rapture. All connexions were broken off between our families, but later on I used to see him fairly frequently in the bars of Montparnasse, lonely, puffy-faced, with watering eyes, obviously the worse for drink. He produced five or six children and made reckless speculations. He moved his plant to the factory of a man in the same line of business, and had the old Laiguillon factory pulled down, intending to replace it with a large block of flats; unfortunately, after he had had the old house pulled down, he couldn't manage to raise enough capital to build the block of flats; he quarrelled with his wife's father and with his own mother who had both refused to be associated with him in this venture; Jacques spent his last penny on it, then had to mortgage, and finally sell his plant. For a few months he worked in his associate's business but was soon given the sack.

Even if he had proceeded with circumspection and the gamble had come off, why had Jacques wound up the family business? It is certainly not without significance that he was concerned in the manufacture not of ironmongery but of stained glass. During the years that followed the 1925 Exhibition, the decorative arts took a great forward leap; Jacques was enthusiastic about modern art styles and he thought that there were immense possibilities in stained glass. In theory this was true, but in practice he had to draw in his horns. In furniture, glass-work, textiles, wallpapers, it was possible and in fact essential to experiment because bourgeois customers were agog for novelty; but Jacques had to cater for little country priests with very undeveloped tastes; either he had to ruin himself, or go on making the traditional and hideous Laiguillon stained glass in his workshops; ugliness made him sick. He preferred to put everything he had into a business that had nothing to do with art.

Without either money or work, Jacques lived for a while on his wife, whose father made her an allowance; but things were going from bad to worse between the two; idler, spendthrift, womanizer, drunkard, liar – to mention the least of his failings – Jacques was without any doubt the most detestable of husbands. In the end Odile asked for a judicial separation and turned him out of the house. I hadn't seen him for twenty years when I met him one day by accident in the boulevard Saint-Germain. At forty-five, he looked more than sixty. His hair had gone completely white; his eyes were bloodshot; excessive drinking had turned him nearly blind; his face was blank, unsmiling; the flesh had wasted away and his head, reduced to its bone-structure, resembled feature for feature that of his grandfather Flandin. He was earning 25,000 francs a month doing some sort of vague clerical work in a toll-house on the Seine: on the papers he showed me, he had the rank of a road-mender. He was dressed like a tramp, slept in doss-houses, ate next to nothing, and drank as much as he could get. Shortly after that, he lost his job and was left entirely without means of support. When he went to ask his mother and brother for food, they accused him of having no pride; only his sister and a few friends came to his assistance. But it wasn't easy to help him; he wouldn't lift a finger to help himself, and he was a physical wreck. He died at the age of forty-six of malnutrition.

'Oh! Why didn't I marry *you*!' he had cried, shaking my hands effusively the day we met. 'What a pity! But my mother kept telling me that marriages between cousins always turn out badly!' So he must have been thinking of marrying me; when had he changed his mind? And what had been the real reason? Why, instead of staying single, had he rushed so young into such an absurdly calculated match? I couldn't get to the bottom of it all, and perhaps he, too, no longer knew why he had done it, his brain was now so clouded by drink; nor did I attempt to ask him about his downfall, for he did his best to make me forget about it; on the days when he was wearing a clean shirt and had eaten his fill he liked to recall the past glories of the Laiguillon family and then he would talk like some great bourgeois gentleman: he sometimes told me that if he had succeeded it would have been no more than what other men had done, but this self-deprecation was beside the point: it was no accident that his ruin had been so spectacular. He hadn't been satisfied with an ordinary failure; he might be blamed for many things, but he never did anything by halves; he had fallen so low that he must have been possessed by the self-destructive folly which I had had an inkling of in his youth. He had obviously married in order to relieve himself of responsibility. He believed that by sacrificing his pleasures and his liberty he would make a new man of himself, a man firmly convinced of where his duty lay and of what was his due, a man who could adapt himself to business life and cosy domesticity; but wishing cannot make us what we would like to be. He still remained the same, unable either to put himself inside the skin of a bourgeois family man, or to shake it off completely. He sought escape in the bars from his role of husband and father of a family; at the same time he tried to rise in the bourgeois social scale, but not through patient hard work. He wanted to get to the top in a single leap, and he staked everything with utter recklessness, as if he secretly wanted to come a cropper. Without any doubt, this destiny was bound up with the heart of the lonely, frightened little boy who at the age of seven strolled around among the dusty glories of the Laiguillon workshops as if he were already the master of its fate; and if in his youth he so often urged us to 'live like everybody else', it was because he suspected that he would never be able to do so himself.

*

While my own future was being decided, Zaza was fighting for her happiness. Her first letter was radiant with hope. The second one was less optimistic. After congratulating me on my success in the examinations, she wrote: 'It is especially hard for me to be away from you at this moment. I should like so much to talk to you – just a few words here and there, and without trying to say anything definite or precise – of what my life has been like during the past three weeks. Apart from a few moments of pure happiness, I encountered many difficulties and felt a terrible anxiety until last Friday. On that day I received from Pradelle a rather long letter in which nothing is said, in which there is not one word that would give me the irrefutable proof I need in order to combat the doubt that, despite all my efforts, continues to haunt me. The hardest things of all to bear are these doubts, these failures of self-confidence, these utterly blank despairs, which are so totally devoid of hope that I sometimes wonder if everything that's happened hasn't been a dream. But then when I am filled with happiness again I am terribly ashamed that I had the cowardice to write him a letter which he has since referred to, and without exaggeration, as "rather fierce". Your own arrived just in time to restore me to life. . . . I have been with you ever since it came, silently in touch with you, and it was with you beside me that I read the letter I received from Pradelle on Saturday and which has set the seal on my happiness, made it so light, so youthful, that for the last three days my gaiety has had the quality of an eight-year-old child's. I feared that my unjust reply to his first letter might have caused fresh difficulties to arise between us; but he answered it so intelligently that on the contrary everything has become easy and wonderful again. I don't think it can be possible for anyone else to scold people in such a delicious way, to tell them off so delightfully, and then to forgive them so absolutely, and to persuade them with even greater gaiety and gentleness that everything is going to be quite simple, that everything is lovely if only we will believe that all will be well.'

But very soon other difficulties, more serious ones, arose. At the end of August I received a letter which filled me with dismay: 'You must forgive me for this long silence. . . . You know what life is like at Laubardon. There have been hosts of visitors and we've spent five days in Lourdes. We got back on Sunday, and tomorrow Bébelle and I will again be taking the train, this time to go and stay with the Brévilles in the Ariège. As you may well imagine, I'd gladly go without all these distractions; it's so tiresome to have to be amused when one hasn't the least desire to be entertained. And I have all the more need of quietness just now because life, without ceasing to be "marvellous", seems likely to be difficult for some time to come. Scruples which were finally poisoning my happiness made me decide to speak to Mama, whose inquisitive, worried, and even mistrustful attitude, I found unbearable. But as I could only tell her a half-truth the result of my confession is that I may not write to Pradelle any more, and Mama insists that until further notice I must not see Pradelle again. It's very hard; in fact it's frightful. When I think of what those letters meant to me, and that now I have to give them up; when I try to foresee the long year ahead, of which I had such high hopes, and which will now be bereft of those meetings that would have made it so wonderful, a suffocating sadness rises in my breast, and my heart seems to shrink with anguish. We shall have to live entirely apart from one another – how terrible! As far as I'm concerned, I'm ready to submit, but it's much more difficult for me when I think of him. It sickens me to think that he may suffer on account of me; I have long since become accustomed to suffering, so much so that I have come to look upon it almost as my natural condition. But to accept *his* suffering would be as bad as if I no longer believed in it. Besides, I find it difficult to reconcile the present Pradelle with the one I knew three weeks ago, to link his letters with those fairly recent meetings when we were still so far from one another, and still so mysterious to one another; I feel sometimes that it is all just a game, that everything will suddenly return to the reality and silence of three weeks ago. How could I see him again without wanting to run away from this boy to whom I have written all kinds of things – all so easily – and in front of whom I shouldn't dare to open my mouth? For I feel so strongly that his presence would intimidate me now. Oh, Simone, what on earth am I saying – how badly I express these things! There is however one thing you ought to know. It is that there are marvellous moments when all these doubts and difficulties fall away from me like things devoid of meaning, and in which I only know the profound and unalterable joy that still abides in me and informs my whole being, over and above all my miseries. Then the mere thought that he exists is enough to move me to tears, and when I think that it is partly for me and through me that he goes on existing, I feel a blissful pain in my heart, and it almost seems to stop beating under its load of unbearable happiness. So you see, Simone, what is become of me. This evening I haven't the heart to tell you about the sort of life I'm living. The great joy that comes from deep down inside me these days seems to irradiate the meanest things. But I am so weary of being obliged to go on joining in walks, games of tennis, tea-parties, and other amusements when I'm living such an intense inner life and have such a vast longing for solitude. The one important moment in the day is when the post arrives . . . I have never loved you as much as I do now, my dear Simone, and I am with you always, with all my heart.'

I sent her a long letter in reply, in which I tried to give her some comfort, and the following week she wrote back: 'Blissfully happy – I'm only just beginning to know what that means, my dear, dear Simone, and oh, how good it feels! I'm now quite certain that nothing can upset me any more, a wonderfully sweet conviction that has triumphed over all my ups and downs and over all my rebellious feelings. When I received your letter . . . I was still in a very unsettled state. I hadn't enough self-confidence to be able to read properly the very sweet but also very inscrutable letters which Pradelle was writing me, and, giving way to an unreasonable attack of pessimism, I had just sent him one which he didn't at all deserve – and when I remember how I love to see him radiating happiness as he did that day with you and me on the lake in the Bois de Boulogne, oh! how bitter it all is! Yet I would be ashamed to complain. When one has received this great thing which I feel inside me, unalterable, then one can bear anything. The root of my joy is not at the mercy of external circumstances; it could only be attacked by some fresh difficulty stemming directly from one or other of us. But there's nothing more to fear on that score; our profound understanding is so complete that he is still the one who is speaking when he is listening to me, and I am still the one who is speaking when I am listening to him, and now, despite physical separation, we can no longer be really disunited. And my great joy, dominating my most cruel thoughts, goes on rising and illuminating everything. . . . Yesterday, after having written Pradelle the letter I found so hard to write, I received from him a note overflowing with that beautiful love of life which until now was less apparent in him than in you. Only it wasn't quite the pagan love-song of the dear, amoral woman. Speaking of his sister's engagement, he told me of all the enthusiasm that the phrase *Coeli enarrant gloriam Dei** can arouse for "the pure glorification of the universe" and for "a life reconciled to all the sweetness of earthly things". Oh! Simone!

* The heavens are telling the glory of God.

how hard it is to have to give up letters like yesterday's! One must really believe in the value of suffering and want to bear Christ's cross for Him in order to accept such pain without complaining, and of course I am not able to do so. But let us leave that subject. Despite everything, life is splendid, and I should be terribly hard-hearted if I didn't at this very moment feel my heart overflowing with gratitude. Can there be many people in the world who have what you and I have, and who will ever know anything else remotely like it? And would it be too much to suffer anything, everything if need be, for this precious gift, and to suffer any length of time? Lili and her husband are here just now; I really think that during the three weeks they have been here the sole topic of their conversations has been the price they will pay for their apartment and how much it will cost to furnish. They are very sweet; I'm not blaming them for anything. But what a relief to know now for sure that there will be nothing in common between their life and mine, to feel that though I have no outward possessions I am a thousand times richer than they are, and that finally, when I am confronted by all those people who are as foreign to me, at least in certain respects, as the wayside stones, I shall never be alone again!'

I suggested what seemed to me an obvious solution: Madame Mabille was worried by the vague nature of the relationship between Zaza and Pradelle. All he had to do was to make a formal request for her daughter's hand in marriage. In reply I received the following letter:

I found your long-awaited letter here yesterday on my return from the Ariège, where I spent ten utterly exhausting days. Since reading it, I've been ceaselessly drafting a reply in my head, speaking quietly to you all the time, despite all the preoccupations, the weariness and the outward circumstances of my life. The circumstances are awful. During the ten days at the Brévilles, with Bébelle in my room, I didn't have a moment to myself. I was so unable to bear someone watching me while I wrote certain letters that I had to wait until she was asleep and write them from two to five o'clock in the morning. During the day, we were taken on long excursions, and I had to keep up a flow of conversation all the time without ever daring to allow my attention to wander, and to respond to the kindnesses and pleasantries of the people we were visiting. The last letter he received from me must have been terribly revealing; he must have sensed how weary I was; I had read his last letter in a state of such complete exhaustion that I now realize I must have misunderstood certain passages in it. Perhaps the reply I sent him made him suffer; I wasn't able to tell him all I wanted to, all I should have told him. All this makes me feel rather desolate; and though until now I wouldn't acknowledge the slightest merit in my behaviour, I feel that in these last few days I have acquired some, because I have had to use such will-power to resist the desire to write and tell him all I am thinking, all the eloquent and persuasive things through which I would protest from the depths of my being against the accusations that he persists in making against himself, and against the pleas for forgiveness that he in his ignorance of the circumstances addresses to me. Simone, I shouldn't want to write to Pradelle through you; it would seem to me a worse hypocrisy than a flouting of the decisions which I have accepted. But I keep remembering passages in his later letters which I didn't give adequate replies to and which keep tearing at my heart: 'You must have been disappointed by certain of my letters. . . . The sincerity with which I spoke to you must have caused you a certain sadness and distress,' and other phrases like that which made me wild. Simone, you know what happiness I owe to P., that every word he has written to me and spoken to me, far from disappointing me, only increased and confirmed the admiration and the love I have for him. You know what I was like, and what I am now; you know what I felt was lacking, and what he has now given me in such marvellous profusion. Oh, Simone! try to make him understand a little that it is to him I owe all the beauty with which my life at this moment is overflowing, that there is nothing concerning him which is not precious to me, that it is madness on his part to excuse himself for what he has said, or for the letters whose beauty and profound sweetness I understand better every time I read them. Simone, you who know me better than anyone and have followed this year every beat of my heart, tell him that there is no one else in the world who has given me or could ever give me the total joy, the unalloyed happiness which I have had from him and which I shall always, even if I never tell him so, feel myself unworthy of.

Simone, if what you suggest were possible, everything would be much easier this winter. But Pradelle has reasons for not doing so which to me are as valid as they are to him. Under these conditions, Mama, without asking me to break completely with him, has put so many difficulties and restrictions in the way of our meeting that, in the end, dreading another unrelenting struggle with her, I prefer to face the worst. His reply to what must have been a sad letter made me realize only too well what such a sacrifice would mean to him. Now I no longer have the courage to make it. I am going to try to arrange things better, to be patient and submissive in the hope that Mama may look a little more favourably upon me, and upon us both, and that she may give up her idea of sending me abroad again. It won't be easy, Simone; it will be very hard, and I feel heart-broken on his account. He spoke twice about fatalism to me. I understand what he's trying to tell me in that roundabout way of his, and for his sake I am going to try to do all in my power to improve our position. Whatever happens, I shall bear it eagerly, finding a kind of ardent joy in suffering for his sake, and above all finding that whatever the price I have to pay I shall never pay too dearly for the happiness I have been privileged to know, for the joy that no accident of chance can kill. . . . I came here, dying to be alone. I found, besides my brother-in-law, five of his brothers and sisters in the house; I share the room in which I was so happy with you and Stépha with his eldest sister and the twins. I've written all this in less than three-quarters of an hour before going to the market in the neighbouring town with the rest of the family; tomorrow all the du Moulins will be spending the whole day here; the day after tomorrow Geneviève de Bréville arrives, and we shall have to go to a dance at the Mulots. But though no one knows it I remain disengaged. To me it is as if all these things didn't exist. My real life is spent secretly smiling at the sound of the voice I hear within me all the time, and hoping to find refuge in him, for ever. . . .

I was annoyed with Pradelle: why should he not accept the solution I had suggested? I wrote to him. He replied that his sister had just become engaged; his elder brother – who had married some time ago, and of whom he never spoke – was about to leave for Togoland; if he were to tell his mother that he, too, was thinking of leaving her, he would deal her a mortal blow. And what about Zaza? I asked him when he returned to Paris at the end of September. Didn't he realize that she was wearing herself out in these deadly struggles? He replied that she approved of the attitude he had taken and however much I inveighed against it he refused to adopt any other.

Zaza I thought was in a very low state; she had grown thin and pale; she had frequent headaches. Madame Mabille had given her permission, provisionally, to see Pradelle again, but in December she was to leave for Berlin once more and would spend a year there; she was terrified at the thought of this exile. I made another suggestion: that Pradelle, without consulting his mother first, should put his case to Madame Mabille. Zaza shook her head. Madame Mabille would not listen to his explanations; she knew all about that already, and in such a meeting with Pradelle would only see an attempt to evade the issue. She was of the opinion that Pradelle had not definitely made up his mind to marry Zaza; if he had, he would have gone through the usual formalities; no mother breaks her heart because her son gets engaged — a likely tale, indeed! I agreed with her on this point; in any case, the marriage would not take place until two years later, and I didn't see where the tragedy lay for Madame Pradelle: 'I don't want her to suffer because of me,' Zaza told me. Her high-mindedness exasperated me. She understood the reasons for my anger. She understood Pradelle's scruples and Madame Mabille's prudence; she understood all these people who were failing to understand each other and she had to bear the brunt of their misapprehensions.

'There's only a year to wait: there's nothing to it!' Pradelle kept saying irritably. This kind of sage remark, instead of comforting Zaza, put her confidence to a bitter test; in order to be able to accept a long separation without too much pain, she would have had to have that reassurance which she had often longed for in his letters and which in fact was so cruelly withheld from her. My guess had been right: Pradelle wasn't an easy person to love, especially for someone with Zaza's violent emotions. With a sincerity that resembled narcissism, he complained to her that she was lacking in passion, and she couldn't help drawing the conclusion that his love for her was rather lukewarm. His conduct did nothing to reassure her; he had a rather excessive squeamishness about meeting her family and didn't appear to care when she suffered for it.

They had so far only had a short meeting, and she was impatiently awaiting the afternoon they were to spend together when that very morning she received an express letter from him; one of his uncles had just died, and he felt that his sorrow was not compatible with the happiness he had been hoping for from their meeting that afternoon: he begged to be excused. The next day, she came to my room for a drink with my sister and Stépha, and was unable to raise a single smile. In the evening, she sent me a note:

I'm not going to ask your forgiveness for being so depressing today, despite the vermouth and your warm welcome, because you surely understand that I was still feeling shattered by the express letter I had received the evening before. It came at a very bad time. If Pradelle had known with what expectancy I had been looking forward to our meeting, I believe he wouldn't have put it off. But it's just as well he didn't know; I'm very glad he has acted as he did, and it was good for me to see just how deep my despair could be when I am absolutely all on my own in my attempts to resist the sharp comments and lugubrious admonitions which Mama sees fit to give me. The saddest thing is that I am unable to get in touch with him: I haven't dared send a letter to his home. If I had seen you alone, I would have written him a short note and you could have addressed the envelope for me in your illegible handwriting. It would be very kind of you if you would send him an express letter telling him what I hope he knows already, that I am with him in his sorrow as in his joy, and that he may write to me at home as much as he likes. It would be as well if he didn't put this off too long, as it seems hardly likely I shall be seeing him for some time now, and I shall want terribly to have at least a word from him. He needn't be afraid of finding me too gay: even if I were to speak about ourselves, it would be on a serious note. Even supposing that he could, by his presence, deliver me from care, there are any number of sad things in life which are suitable subjects for conversation when one is in mourning. *Dusty Answer*, by Rosamund Lehmann, for one thing. I started reading this book again yesterday evening, and found it moved me no less than it did at the beginning of the holidays. Yes, Judy is a magnificent character, very attractive; all the same, she remains somehow incomplete and oh! how sad! I can accept that her love of life and of all created things might be able to save her from the harshness of existence. But such superficial happiness would be no good in the face of death and it's not enough to live as if death didn't exist. When I put the book down I felt ashamed of being cast down at times when always I feel, beyond all the difficulties and sadnesses which keep it from me, a real joy – hard to accept and too often denied me through my own weak-mindedness – but which at least depends on no other person in the world, not even on myself. This joy does not alter anything: those whom I love need not feel anxious, I'm not trying to run away from them. And at this moment I feel one with the earth and with my own life as never before.

Despite the optimistic note of this conclusion, despite the determined approval she gave to Pradelle's decision, Zaza couldn't keep the bitterness out of her letter; in order to set against 'all created things' the supernatural joy 'which at least depends on no other person in the world' it was obvious that she no longer hoped to be able to depend on anyone again. I sent an express letter to Pradelle, who wrote to her at once; she thanked me: 'Since Saturday, thanks to you, I have been delivered from the phantoms that were tormenting me.' But the phantoms didn't leave her in peace for long, and she felt very much alone in the face of them. The very concern I felt for her happiness kept us apart, for I was furious with Pradelle, and she accused me of misjudging him; she had chosen the path of renunciation and turned a deaf ear whenever I urged her to make a fight for her happiness. Moreover, her mother had given orders that I was not to be admitted to the house in the rue de Berri, and used all kinds of dodges to keep Zaza at home. Nevertheless we managed to have a long talk in my room, and I talked to her about my own life; the next day she sent me a note to tell me, in the warmest terms, how happy it had made her. But she added: 'For family reasons which it would take too long to explain, I shan't be able to see you for some time. Wait a while.'

Pradelle had warned her that his brother had just left for Togoland and that for the next week he would be fully occupied in consoling his mother. Again she seemed to find it quite natural that he should sacrifice her for his mother; but I was sure that she was obsessed by fresh doubts and I felt dismayed that during the next week there would be no word from him to counteract the 'lugubrious admonitions' doled out by Madame Mabille.

Ten days later I met her by accident in the Poccardi bar; I had been working in the Nationale, and she was doing some shopping in the neighbourhood: I accompanied her. To my great astonishment, she was bubbling over with gaiety. She had been thinking things over very carefully during the past week, and gradually everything had fallen into place in her mind and heart; she was no longer terrified even at the thought of her departure for Berlin. She would have lots of free time there, and would try to write the novel she had so long been contemplating; she would read and study: never had she felt such a longing for books. She had just rediscovered Stendhal, and admired him immensely. Her family detested him so completely that until now she had never quite succeeded in surmounting their objections to him: but while reading him again during the last few days she had finally come to understand him and love him without reserve. She felt a need to revise many of her former judgements: she had the impression that an important change had taken place inside her. She talked to me with an almost incredible warmth and exuberance; there was something frenzied in her optimism. All the same, I felt glad for her sake that she had drawn fresh reserves of strength from somewhere and I felt that she was going to be even closer to me than before. I said good-bye to her, and my hopes were high.

Four days later, I received a note from Madame Mabille: Zaza was gravely ill; she had a high temperature and frightful pains in the head. The doctor had had her moved to a clinic at Saint-Cloud; she needed absolute quiet and solitude; she was not allowed to receive any visits: if her temperature did not come down, there was no hope for her.

I went to see Pradelle. He told me all he knew. The day after my meeting with Zaza, Madame Pradelle had been alone in the flat when there came a ring at the bell; she opened the door, and found a well-dressed young lady standing there, but who wasn't wearing a hat: in those days, this was 'not done'. 'Are you Jean Pradelle's mother?' the young woman asked. 'May I speak to you?' She introduced herself and Madame Pradelle asked her to come in. Zaza stared all round her; her face was white as chalk, except for the cheeks which had patches of bright red on them. 'Isn't Jean here?' she asked. 'Why isn't he here? Has he gone to heaven already?' Madame Pradelle, who was frightened out of her wits, told her that he would be back soon. 'Do you hate me, Madame?' Zaza had asked. The old lady said of course not. 'Then why do you not want us to get married?' Madame Pradelle did her best to calm her down; she was in a less confused state when Pradelle came in a little later, but her forehead and hands were burning. 'I'm going to take you home,' he told her. They took a taxi and while they were on the way to the rue de Berri, she asked him reproachfully: 'Won't you give me a kiss? Why have you never kissed me?' He kissed her.

Madame Mabille put her to bed and called the doctor; she had a long talk with Pradelle: she didn't want to be the cause of her daughter's unhappiness, and she was not opposed to their marriage. Madame Pradelle wasn't against it either; she too didn't want to cause anyone unhappiness. It would all be arranged. But Zaza had a temperature of 104° and was delirious.

During the next four days in the clinic at Saint-Cloud she kept calling out for 'my violin, Pradelle, Simone, champagne'. The fever did not abate. Her mother had the right to spend the final night with her. Zaza recognized her and knew then that she was going to die. 'Don't cry for me, Mama darling,' she said. 'There are outcasts in all families; I'm the outcast in ours.'

When next I saw her, in the chapel at the clinic, she was laid on a bier surrounded by candles and flowers. She was wearing a long nightdress of rough cloth. Her hair had grown, and now hung stiffly round a yellow face that was so thin, I hardly recognized her.

The hands with their long, pale fingernails were folded on the crucifix, and seemed as fragile as an ancient mummy's. Madame Mabille was sobbing. 'We have only been instruments in God's hands,' Monsieur Mabille told her.

The doctors called it meningitis, encephalitis; no one was quite sure. Had it been a contagious disease, or an accident? Or had Zaza succumbed to exhaustion and anxiety? She has often appeared to me at night, her face all yellow under a pink sun-bonnet, and seeming to gaze reproachfully at me. We had fought together against the revolting fate that had lain ahead of us, and for a long time I believed that I had paid for my own freedom with her death.

INDEX